Nigel MacNeill

The literature of the Highlanders : a history of Gaelic literature from the earliest times to the present day

Nigel MacNeill

The literature of the Highlanders : a history of Gaelic literature from the earliest times to the present day

ISBN/EAN: 9783337157210

Printed in Europe, USA, Canada, Australia, Japan

Cover: Foto ©Thomas Meinert / pixelio.de

More available books at **www.hansebooks.com**

THE

LITERATURE OF THE HIGHLANDERS.

THE

LITERATURE OF THE HIGHLANDERS:

A HISTORY OF GAELIC LITERATURE-FROM THE EARLIEST TIMES TO THE PRESENT DAY.

BY

NIGEL MACNEILL,

AUTHOR OF "NENLÆ: WITH OTHER POEMS;" "THE HIGHLAND HYMNAL," ETC.

& MINISTER OF BEDFORD CHURCH, LONDON.

" *Móra ic senaib bar senscéla.*"—TOGAIL TROI.

INVERNESS :

JOHN NOBLE, CASTLE STREET.

1892.

PREFACE.

—o—

It is hoped that the readers óf the following chapters will bear in mind the fact that this is the first complete account of Gaelic literature that has yet been offered to the public, and that it must inevitably exhibit traces of the natural imperfections of all pioneer works. To other workers in the same field I am of course greatly indebted ; and if any of them had published a fairly full history of our Highland literature it is quite unlikely that the present volume would ever see the light.

The names of about one hundred and eighty composers of Gaelic poetry alone occur in this volume, while not more than a third of that number will be found in any previous work on the subject. Still I am aware that some mistakes and omissions will be met with, but these, I trust, will not elicit so much reprehension as material for correction hereafter.

On the subject of the science of language and race movements glanced at in the Introduction, the student will find the latest views in the works of Penka, Schrader, Sayce. Hyde Clarke, and others. The " Ultonian Hero-Ballads " of Mr Hector MacLean and the *Reliquæ Celticæ* of the late Dr Alexander Cameron will be prized by those interested in the fields on which the great Cuchulin fought and Ossian sang.

My studies in the Celtic field have been carried on in the midst of duties of a sacred and exacting character ; and I have often been hindered by the thought that the attraction in this direction ought to be resisted. Still I have felt like many others the need of making a speciality of some helpful study ; and what for me could be more natural as a mental exercise than to be found searching out in those obscure fields of an ancient literature for the intellectual products of my forefathers ?

I am much indebted to several friends who encouraged me from time to time. It gives me great pleasure to mention among these the name of Dr Stoddart, late editor of *The Glasgow Herald* whose kindness and generosity to myself personally I will always cherish with gratitude, and whose sympathies with all that is good and noble in any people were the natural outcome of the cultured heart of a gentleman and a Christian. To him I owe the title of this book as well as the privilege, through the columns of his influential journal, of showing some of the treasures of our Gaelic literature to the great English world beyond our Highland Israel. With his name ought to be associated in this matter that of the able manager of the paper, Mr Alexander Sinclair, an Argyleshire Highlander. The articles then published in 1881 were the first of the kind to appear in a newspaper of such high standing. The names of other gentlemen from whom I have received kindness occur to me also as I write : Mr D. H. Macfarlane, ex-M.P. ; Mr Fraser - Mackintosh, M.P. ; Dr R. Macdonald, M.P. ; Mr Duncan Macneill ; and Mr John Mackay, C.E. I have also much pleasure in acknowledging the readiness with which the Messrs Nisbet, publishers, London, have granted me permission to use in the following chapters some articles I contributed to *The Catholic Presbyterian.*

This book may be described as the child of the peaceful Highland revolution on which the political and Christian genius of the Right Hon. W. E. Gladstone stamped imperial sanction and approval in the Crofters Act of 1886. Its growth and delivery in various lectures, magazine articles and otherwise, during seventeen years, have been coincident with the workings of the spirit of racial fusion and union which recent political struggles after a

Brito-Irish brotherhood have well-nigh perfected. On the following pages, therefore, I am occasionally an advocate of the just rights and claims of a noble race and an obscure literature ; but at the same time I remain a lover of the great English people. I have learned during a residence of upwards of ten years to appreciate and love the generous qualities of my English fellow-citizens.

N. MACNEILL.

67 Lady Margaret Road, London, N.W.

CONTENTS.

INTRODUCTION.

"Forchubus caichduini imbia arrath inlebrán colli aratardda bendacht
forammain intrnagáin rodscribai."

Gaelic (Scot.) MS. of 9th Cent.

THE Celts and the Teuton started westward from the cradle of
the human race, spreading themselves over Europe ; while other
members of the same stock went eastward, extending themselves
over wide tracts of Asia.   From the Celts, the Greeks, the Romans,
and the Teutons have sprung the chief nations in whose possession
Europe still remains.   It is interesting to think that the brothers
who parted thousands of years ago, somewhere in teeming Asia, the
one going east and the other west, are now meeting again on the
plains of Hindostan.   Their movements during those thousands of
years have encircled the whole earth.   Fiercely have they fought
and disputed over every inch of the ground which one or other of
their tribes at one time or other occupied.   Theirs has always
been the chief ruling power in the world.   They begin to know
one another again.   From the extreme west of Europe, across the
New World, the Anglo-Celt arrives in India and recognises the
Hindoo as his brother.

The Aryans migrated into Europe in a somewhat advanced
state of civilisation.   According to Sayce their advent was from
the north, a theory which subverts nearly all previously accepted
opinions on the subject.   Some of them, however, such as the
Greeks first and the Romans afterwards, favoured by the maritime countries in which they settled, made more rapid progress

than the others. It was largely their self-conceit that led the Greeks and Romans to describe all the nations beyond their bounds as "barbarian." Our ancestors in these islands, whether Celtic or Teutonic, were never mere savages. They had a religion, if not radically the same, fully as enobling in its tendency as that of Greece and Rome. They evidently made some progress in the useful arts, while in the days of Rome's greatest splendour they were in possession of military weapons which were not much inferior to her own. The form of government among the Celts was patriarchal, and this continued for a long time among the Gaels of Scotland. There was the king or chief, who was regarded as the father of the clan, tribe, or nation. With him was associated a council of chieftains or elders, and in important matters the *mot* of the whole people. But with all this political organisation they could not make such progress in civilisation as the Greeks and Romans, who mostly dwelt in cities. The Gaels who along with the Germans acted the part of pioneers on the plains of Europe, and living a rural life, could not compete successfully in the race for higher civilisation with the brother races who inhabited the maritime cities of Greece and Italy, and who, besides, obtained much of an earlier civilisation from Phœnicia and Egypt.

The early migrations of the Gael are involved in much obscurity. By the study of topography, however, we can follow many of his footsteps westward. This study, however, is rendered very difficult, and at times very uncertain, because the discoverable traces of the presence of the Celt lie embedded in the soil of the life of the powerful pre-Celtic races. The Celt and the Teuton have always been close neighbours. The progress of the two westward appears to have been somewhat simultaneous, at least on the Continent. The geographical positions of France and Germany at the present day represent not inaccurately the attitude of the Gaelic and Teutonic races towards one another in their earlier movements from the east. It has been said that the Celts came too soon into Europe, just as the Slaves came too late. It would be difficult to verify this remark in the light of history and in the face of existing facts. While admitting that the remark may have an element of truth in it, we must remember, with regard to the Slaves, that it is premature to anticipate what they may become. We see them a mighty threatening wave on a westward course. The Chinese hordes, who are already a trouble, press behind the Russians ; and the growing power of the latter in Europe is a matter of serious concern to our statesmen. The struggle between

Celt and Teuton again cannot be said to be at an end as long as France and Germany maintain their present watchful and hostile attitude. As to their racial composition respectively the former may be said to be as much Celtic as the latter is Teutonic. But on the other hand, in the United Kingdom, Celt and Teuton may be said virtually to agree. They have so blended for centuries that, notwithstanding boasts on both sides, which science cannot sustain, it is impossible almost to produce a pure Saxon or a pure Gael. It cannot certainly be done in Scotland. This intermingling of races in the British Islands has produced a national character very unlike our Continental neighbours. The Anglo-Celtic power of the British Empire is not so immobile or sluggish as the German, nor so light and airy as the French ; and its rule appears almost to have arrived at the incipient stage of universal dominion.

Great Britain was peopled in the north and in the south simultaneously from the Continent, and Ireland was similarly peopled from the north and south of Britain The Gaels of Ireland and of Scotland were the same people, having the same language and music ; and all the elements of civilisation about them were the common property of both. At the same time there are evidences that the Gaels of the North of Ireland stood in closer relationship to those of Scotland than those in the South of Ireland. And this holds true even to this very day. It should always be borne in mind that there have been different tribes of pre-Celts, Celts and Teutons in Ireland, which has hitherto prevented that national cohesion in the time of danger which alone could secure the independence of the country. Ireland being peopled at a later period, has taken a longer time in developing a full-orbed nationality. On the other hand there has been an earlier homogeneity among the Scottish Celts ; whether called Picts, Gaels, Scots, or Albanaich, they were always one against the common foe, whatever might be the feuds among themselves. In more recent days the reformation of religion in the 16th century helped to produce in the Scottish Gael a distinctively different character from that of the Gael of Ireland ; it also destroyed in Scotland many of the old Gaelic things which were associated with a religion that was regarded as superstitious. Thus much of the history and the literature of the Scottish Gael was lost. In Ireland, where no violent changes took place in the condition and religious beliefs of the people, we find very extensive manuscript literature—rich with interesting spoils of the past—as well as more relics even of earlier Gaelic life in Scotland.

Chiefly through the great labours of Zeuss, the distinguished Bavarian, the Gael is now, as already remarked, universally admitted to belong to the Aryan family. No student of the science of language will now contend that he has any special affinity to the Semitic race. The *Keltae* of the Greek, the *Galli* of the Roman, and the *Gàidheil* of Scotland and Ireland, are the same people. In the east and in the west *Galatia*, or in Gaelic [*Gaidheallachd*, contracted] and pronounced *Gaellachd*, is the *Celtica*, or land of the Celts or Gaels. *Gaellachd* or *Galatia* is literally Gael*dom*, or the country of the *Gaels*. The term "Gael" is the same as "Celt," the only difference being that the original *Gaidel* comes to us through Latin in the former and through Greek in the latter. So the two may be used indiscriminately, although some writers have endeavoured to preserve a distinction, using "Gaelic" for the language spoken in Scotland and Ireland, and "Celtic" as a more generic term, embracing all the Gaelic Brythonic dialects. "Gael" —the Roman "Gaul"—and the original "Gaidel," aspirated into "Gaidhel," which in its aspirated form at last drops the *dh*, and becomes "Gael" or Gaul, is just the same word. The Gael stands in the same relation to the Welsh, the Cornishman, and the Armorican, that the Englishman and German, the Roman and Greek, stand to one another. The Gael, the Manx, and the Irish constitute one branch of the stock, while the Welsh, the Cornish, and the Breton constitute the other.

The Celtic element enters largely into the population of the United Kingdom. Just as Celtic dialects were spoken at one time throughout the whole of the British Islands, so to the present day a powerful Celtic element pervades the people of Great Britain and Ireland from the lowest to the highest classes. John Knox and Robert Burns, two representative Scotchmen, were more Celtic than Teutonic. The national perfervid spirit and genius are so still. The name of the great Reformer is from the Gaelic *Cnoc*. Ireland can produce many Anglo-Celtic names, among which we find that of the Duke of Wellington. The mothers of the greatest epic poet and the greatest general that England ever produced were Celts. Sarah Caston, the mother of Milton, was the daughter of a Welsh gentleman ; and Elizabeth Steward, the mother of Cromwell, was the daughter of William Steward, in Ely, a descendant of the Celtic Stewards of Scotland. Professor H. Morley says :—"The main current of English literature cannot be disconnected from the lively Celtic wit in which it has one of its sources. The Celts do not form an utterly distinct part of our mixed population. But for early, frequent, and various contact with the race that, in its half-barbarous days, invented Ossian's dialogues with St. Patrick, and that quickened afterwards the Northerner's blood in France, Germanic England would not have produced a Shakespeare." It is only the other year that a Cambrian Celt disappeared from our midst—one of the greatest names in English literature—Mary A. Evans, better known by her assumed name of George Eliot. This other quotation from Professor Morley's " Library of English Literature " is as true as it is suggestive :—" The Celts are by nature artists. Mr Ferguson has felt this in his own art, and said in his ' History of Architecture :'—' The true glory of the Celt in Europe is his artistic eminence. It is, perhaps, not too much to assert that without his intervention we should not have possessed in modern times a Church worthy of admiration or a picture or a statue we could look at without shame.' It would be far too much to assert this of books ; but certainly Teutonic England could not have risen to the full grandeur and beauty of that expression of all her life in all her literature . . . without a wholesome blending of Teutonic with Celtic blood. The Celts are a vital part of our country, and theirs were the first songs in the land,"

Before parting with this subject let me note three remarkable facts which the history of Gaelic Scotland presents. They have not always been fully recognised. The first is that the Caledonians were never fully conquered by the Roman Power which brought almost all other nations of the world into subjection. The second is that a Gaelic people gave its present name to the country. The third is that a Gaelic King has given us the line of monarchs which we have still represented in the present sovereign of the British Empire. To these another fact might be a.lded— that the earliest modern literature is to be found among the Scoto-Irish Gael. After the decadence of Greece and Rome the Celts were the first of the European tribes to cultivate letters. While the Germans and the Northmen were yet roving heathen tribes the Gael in Ireland and in Scotland had their seminaries of learning, where literature was loved and cherished. And from the Colleges of Durrow and Iona missionaries, whose well-trained minds and zealous hearts fitted them for their great undertaking, went forth to Christianise the people of England and the Teutonic tribes on the Continent. The extant manuscripts in Gaelic and Latin which came from their pens are monuments of their learning and piety, as well as of the reverence in which they were held by the people to whom they brought the light of the Christian truth. Some ol these manuscripts, now studied with such rich results by Continental Celtic scholars, are to be found in some of the great libraries on the Continent; in St. Gall, Milan, Wurtzburg, and Carlsruhe, Zeuss found those Gaelic ones on which he based his great work the "Grammatica Celtica," pnblished in 1853. These facts ought to make the study of Gaelic interesting—the oldest living language in Europe that can boast of such early relics of culture.

It is now necessary that some remarks should be made on the language in which the literature we are to examine is to be found. The Celtic forms a branch of the Indo-European group of languages. It is divided into two nearly distinct languages, which are thus classified :—

$$
\text{CELTIC ..}
\begin{cases}
\text{THE GAIDELIC,} \begin{cases} \text{Gaelic.} \\ \text{Irish.} \\ \text{Manx.} \end{cases} \\[1em]
\text{THE BRYTHONIC,} \begin{cases} \text{Welsh.} \\ \text{Cornish } (extinct). \\ \text{Breton.} \\ \text{Gaulish } (extinct). \end{cases}
\end{cases}
$$

The differences between Gaelic, Irish, and Manx are merely dialectic. The Cornish became extinct last century. The Gaulish is also extinct; and what remains of it is found only in the names of places.

To Zeuss is due the credit of having assigned its proper place to Celtic in the family of languages. The problem before his great publication in 1853 was the relationship in which the Gaels, the Welsh, and the old Gaulish people stood to one another and to the other nations of the world. Numerous publications on this question appeared during the last two centuries. But from a scientific point of view they are of very little value. . Errors and unscientific theories abound in every work. At that time the scholars of France and Germany never mastered the Celtic languages ; indeed, there were few reliable grammars by which they could be acquired. The native scholars were deficient in linguistic training, in common sense, and frequently in common honesty. No Gaelic scholar was conscientious enough to learn Welsh, no Welsh scholar to learn Gaelic ; but each and all were ready enough to compare their languages with Phœnician, Persian, Etruscan, Egyptian, Hebrew, Arabic, &c., of which, again. they knew in reality next to nothing ; though a few of them might know a little Hebrew. There was one remarkable exception, however, to this

—the great Welsh scholar Edward Llhuyd, of whom it may be said that he lived a century and a half before his time ; but, incapable of following him, the native school of philologists sank into chaotic and puerile etymological dreams. The Celtic problem became more hopeless than ever, and Gaelic philology became distasteful to sober minds.

At the same time many Celts insisted " on the lofty claim they used to advance of speaking the primeval language." It is only recently that they have learned " to submit to the logic of facts and listen to the voice of science." A Gaelic poet, in an elaborate poem on his native language, thus declares his conviction on the much-debated subject, what language was spoken in Paradise—

> " By Adam it was spoken
> In Eden, I believe,
> And sweetly flowed the Gaelic
> From the lovely lips of Eve."

Some fifty years ago the science of comparative philology began to make itself felt, and Celtic scholars tried to apply its principles to Celtic. Pritchard, Bopp, Diefenbach, Pictet, and others worked in the right direction, but they failed fully to solve the Celtic problem. J. Caspar Zeuss, a Bavarian Highlander, at last succeeded, by combining with a mind of unusual power a devotion to the subject which amounted well-nigh to a sacrifice of his life. This devotion might not even have been sufficient if he had not possessed what no one before him possessed—the really oldest manuscripts of both the Irish and Welsh dialects. The labours of Zeuss have shown :—That the Gaelic and Welsh languages were originally one ; that dialectic differences in Cæsar's time were so small that an old Gael would be at once understood in Wales ; and that the Gaels and Cambrians were identical with the Celts of the Continent—with those of Spain, Gaul, Lombardy, and the Alpine countries ; that this Celtic tongue is one of the branches of the Aryan stock of languages.

The consequence of these estab'ished facts is to put an end to all attempts at connecting the Celtic with the Semitic class of tongues.

We know the Gaelic language now in three stages :—

1. Old Gaelic up to 1000 A.D. The most ancient relics of this period are the glosses of St. Gall in Switzerland, the Ambrosian Library of Millan, &c., discovered by Zeuss.

2. Middle Gaelic, from 1000-1500 A.D., is represented by an extensive mass of manuscript literature.

3. Modern Gaelic from the sixteenth century, when books began to be printed, to the present day.

The softening caused by excessive aspiration is the greatest change which the language has undergone.

As spoken in Scotland at the present day the chief dialectic differences are : —

1. The *ia* of the North for the *eu* of the South and West Highlands, illustrated by BIAL BEUL, *mouth ;* FIAR, FEUR, *grass.*

2. The vowel-tone difference, illustrated in such words as ORAN, song. The *e* is pronounced in three different ways ; in Islay and other parts of Argyll like *o* in *old ;* in Mull and other place like *ou* in *foul :* in the North generally like *aw* in *law.*

3. The consonantal difference illustrated in the pronounciation of *c* and *chd.*

4. The accentual or rhythmic tone difference, observed in the conversation of natives of different places.

In Arran and Perthshire, and to some extent in Caithness and Sutherland, the people in speaking cut off the terminal syllables of many words. In the North Highlands they speak with a slow, sometimes swinging emphasis ; in the South Highlands they are more hurried in their utterance. Any Highlander, speaking distinctly, will be readily understood, North and South.

Gaelic appears to possess wonderful vitality. While English has stamped out Gaelic among the Celts of Galloway and Ayrshire, Gaelic has stamped out the Norse language in the Western Isles, where the people are largely of pre-Celtic and Norse origin. It is remarkable that although of the same family of languages, Gaelic and English, like oil and water, cannot readily commingle.

Other subjects associated with early Gaelic literature are the Druids and the Féinne. That dim, indefinite, prehistoric period of our annals which terminated in the contact of heathenism with the living forces of Christianity may be termed pre-Celtic. In the dawn of the historical period a mysterious class of men called Druids, and a mysterious body of heroes called the Féinne or Fianna, emerge into view, just as we mark the vanishing or absorption of the pre-Celtic peoples. Whatever they were, a certain class of *Magi* existed once in these islands. But their sudden disappearance in history, like that of the Féinne, has induced many to question whether such an order of men ever lived. But it is historically certain that a class of men, answering to the description, met and tried to oppose Columba from Iona when he visited King Brudeus at Inverness. They have been called Druids, but that term should be regarded in a general or conventional sense. They were without doubt the priests of learning and religion among the ancient Scots. In possession of some knowledge, meagre as it probably was, they were invested with mystic importance by the ignorant and superstitious. With the introduction and enlightenment of Christianity it would be seen that this exclusive order and priestly caste found their supremacy undermined. Their teaching, whatever it was, appears to have had a beneficial influence on the formation of the national character. They do not seem to have indulged in any enervating services or gross idolatry in the kind of worship which was maintained among the people. We see the moral significance of their influence more fully when we contrast the ancient Gaels with the ancient Greeks. With all their fine ethical and æsthetic perceptions, we find that the latter throughout their whole history were never a very moral people. Just as their bodily senses were enslaved by their keen sense of the beautiful in form, colour, &c., so were their moral energies by many vices. The sensual and luxurious life of the Romans also soon sapped the foundations of the empire, and made it a prey to the less civilised nations around. But from the earliest times down to the present we find among the people once influenced by the Druids a very high moral tone. Guilty as they might be of plundering other races with whom they openly waged warfare, strict honesty among themselves as neighbours was inculcated and observed. The internecine quarrels and the mutual plundering of the later periods arose from the dissensions purposely sown by the Scottish kings. To weaken the clans and the bond of union existing between them unrighteous charters were granted to certain lands in favour of pretenders that could present no valid claim. Hence the majority of the clan feuds which frequently drenched the Highland hills and glens with blood.

One particular result of the early teaching has been the national respect for woman. It is one of the finest moral traits in the character of the Gael. At this day it is among the Gael of the Outer Hebrides and of the more recognised Celtic districts of Ireland, such as Munster and Connaught, that the Registrar General finds the smallest percentage of illegitimacy. The high-toned morality which the poems of Ossian exhibit in this respect has been used as an argument against their authenticity. And yet it should be no argument at all for one who can trace out and analyse the early sources whence developed the moral elements of the national character.

The Celt has been generally very religious. The religion of the Gael of Scotland, like that of the Kymry of Wales, whether in ancient or in modern Christian times, has always flourished in an atmosphere of deep severity. The rigid ethics of the early religion, combined with a hard life at a distance from enervating centres of civilisation, help to explain this. This sternness of doctrine also, no doubt, prepared the modern Gael to accept with such absolute entirety, and with such earnest heartiness, the Calvinistic system of Christian truth which many regard as severe and harsh. The higher results of the literary and moral culture of the Druidic religion we have embodied in the relics of Ossianic poetry. The order of Druids, with their ideals of philosophy and religion, have vanished ; but their power for good remains embedded in the foundation of the national name, with its educating influences and its inspiring associations. In this power lay the moral strength of our early ancestors. Christianity, in its early Celtic and Reformed stages, developed into higher and purer issues this national virtue ; and the character of the people is exponent of the results of the process. Other tribes and communities have had Christianity among them too, but with different results. This line of thought suggests an explanation of why, as has been already remarked, the Irish Gael appears to be somewhat unlike the Scottish Gael.

A glance may now be appropriately bestowed upon that other somewhat mysterious body—those heroes called the Féinne.

Chief among the early Gaelic inhabitants was the renowned order of heroes known as the Féinne, the Fianna, or the followers of Fingal, or Finn, the leader. They are supposed to have lived in the second and third centuries of our era, and to have been the Caledonians who checked the progress of the legions of Rome. Very little reliable help can be found regarding this question in the extant annals of the Gael. In general it may be held that this race of Finn came from the shores of the Baltic to North Britain, and that they were not unrelated to the ancient Norse. Recently a new theory has been adopted by some, like Mr Campbell of Islay, whose views are entitled to much respect. They argue that the existence of the Féinne is only a myth—part and parcel of an old world system, not unconnected with the classical and oriental—a system of which we have the same with variations in the Militia of Ireland, and in the Knights of the Round Table of the ancient British. It is held that Fingal and King Arthur are the same personages ; that Graine, the faithless wife of Fingal is the same as the faithless Guinevere, the spouse of Arthur ; and that the unhallowed love of Diarmad and Graine has a suggestive similitude in that of Sir Launcelot and Guinevere. On the other hand, it is argued that the similarity of these relations, however systematic in appearance, may still be adequately explained by the fact that human nature is much the same in all lands and amongst all races ; that this symbolic theory does not seem to be supported by the well-grounded conviction of the people in whose traditions the memory of the heroes of the Féinne has been handed down to us ; that it is not at all probable that the names of merely fictitious heroes would live in the topography of a hundred hills, like the name of Finn ; that it does not find support in the more philosophic theory regarding the heroes of ancient peoples—that all the mythological characters are only exaggerations of real ones ; that human nature is never satisfied with the barely mythic and unreal, and that the patriotic and other affections never derive sustenance from false and unbelievable characters.

Can a vague statement of this character not .satisfy the inquiring student? To the patriotic Celtic inquirer, next in importance to the evangelisation of the Highlands by Columba, stands the great question of the Féinne, who have so indelibly impressed their individualities on the Gaelic imagination of Scotland. To the more inquiring spirits of recent times these brilliant heroes have appeared very strange and mysterious indeed. They have had a Melchisedec kind of existence in our traditional history ; no one has been able to suggest whence they came, or whither they have gone. The names of their leaders have become woven with fable, song, and story ; with the hills and glens of Albin and Erin ; with the warlike struggles which the various conflicting races have fought on our Ero-Albinic shores. So vague and romantic however, has their history been, that a few clear-sighted writers, conversant with comparative mythology, have come almost to the conclusion that the Féinne were, as we have already seen, a mere Gaelic expression of a world-wide mythus, whose various component elements can be found from Japan to the Hebrides. The popular tales and the bardic ballads have been regarded as the *debris* that may be still collected on the shores of the ages.

The plain Highlander living in the mere tents of history and literature, has been reluctant to accept so vague an account of a very heroic ancestry. Has not he the poems of Ossian still in his hands ? Are not the names of Finn and fellow-heroes stamped on a thousand hills in Albin and Erin ? So the invariable conclusion has been that in some mysterious way and during some mysterious

period " Fingal lived and Ossian sang." The disappointing question all along has been, however, where can any account be found
of these people in our accredited national histories ? The inquiring spirits among our patriotic youth examine recent histories
in vain. Our antiquaries write of names and places, but they have
failed to assign a local habitation and a name to the Finian people.
The only approach to a definite representation of the race we have
in the famous mystifications of James Macpherson in his dissertations, notes, and poems. But the geography of Macpherson
appears to have been as mistily convenient for himself as it has
been perplexing to his commentators. Not even the genius of Dr
Waddell in his goodly volume has been able to identify the localities of Macpherson, or remove the veil of ghostlike existence in
which the Ossianic heroes are enshrouded.

Our ordinary historians appear to have avoided treating of so
perplexing a period or class of men. Browne is satisfied with a
statement on the Ossianic question. He does not touch on the
history of the Finnic period. Keltie ignores the whole question.
MacLauchlan in his " Early History of the Scottish Church,"
which embraces the Ossianic age, has nothing to say of the Finnic
environment. In his introduction to his edition of Ossian, Clerk
is equally silent as to the accurate identification of the people of
whom Ossian became the laureate bard. Nor is anything very
definite to be found even in the learned works of Skene. When
such admirable authorities are almost universally silent, it becomes
a very hazardous matter to attempt any statement on the question.

It must be admitted that hitherto the sources of much of our
definite accounts have been Irish compilations. Notwithstanding
Macpherson's comparative contempt for the character of the Irish
Finian heroes, and for the Irish Ossianic compositions, yet much
of the ground work of his own historic ideals was furnished by
Irish productions. But any historic truth the Irish compositions
may have had perished in the using in the hands of Macpherson.
The result has been a system of chronology that neither he nor
his friends have ever been able to explain.

The question still remains, Who were the Féinne ? The answer
in general has been that they were Gaelic heroes of the second
and third centuries of the Christian era ; who fought with Romans,
with Danes, and with one another ; and finally struggled with the
converting powers of Christianity. In Ireland they have appeared
under the guise of a Milesian militia, a conception which is
thoroughly in harmony with the chivalrous ideals of that interest-

ing island. The following sentences contain the gist of all the information that is now available :—" It is quite a mistake to suppose *Finn Mac Cumhaill* to have been merely imaginary or mythical character. Much that has been narrated of his exploits is, no doubt, apocryphal enough ; but Finn himself is an undoubtedly historical personage ; and that he existed about the time at which his appearance is recorded in the annals, is as certain as that Julius Cæsar lived and ruled at the time stated on the authority of the Roman historians. I may add here that the pedigree of Finn is fully recorded on the unquestionable authority of the Book of Leinster, in which he is set down as the son of *Cumhall*, who was the son of *Trenmor*, son of *Snaelt*, son of *Eltan*, son of *Baiscni*, son of *Nuada Necht*, who was of the Heremonian race, and monarch of Erinn about A.M. 5090, according to the chronology of the Four Masters, that is, 110 years before Christ. Finn himself was slain, according to the Annals of the Four Masters, in Anno Domini 283, in the reign of *Cairbre Lifeachair*." Little can be added to this statement by O'Curry. The great battle of *Gabhra*—Garristown in Meath—took place in 284 ; and the ballads represent the brave Oscar, and *Cairbre Lifeachair* as falling by each others' hands in the deadly struggle. Oscar was the beloved son of Ossian, and his grandfather Finn, who died a year before the battle of *Gabhra*, is brought back to life by the Romancists to pronounce a eulogy on the fallen Oscar.

Irish annalists are satisfied that the fatherland of Finn and his heroes was Ireland ; but no one appears to be able to point out the territories over which Finn reigned. It is an undoubted fact that *Cairbre Lifeachair* was the monarch of Erin when Finn died, and when the battle of *Gabhra* was fought. What can be more natural then than to suppose with Macpherson that Finn was monarch of Albin ? In Macpherson's works Finn is represented always as going from Albin to Erin, a rendering of history which the Irish authorities refuse to accept. When we look for the Kingdom of Finn in Scotland where Macpherson has located it, we certainly fail to ascertain its boundaries by means of his mistifying phrases. That his Morven is not the Morvern of Argyllshire has been pointed out long ago ; nor is much satisfaction to be found in Dr Clerk's interpretation of *Mor Bheanna*, the Great Hills, as a general characteristic of Scotland. It is another illustration of Macpherson's prudent indefiniteness behind which the secret of his works has been preserved.

Now it appears to me that I am led aright in my studies of this

period of Albin's history, when I regard the Féinne as the last
leaders of the great race in Albin and Erin who disappeared in
history before the extension of the Gaelic conquest and supremacy.
The spirit of their struggle is truly recorded in the ballads when it
is repeatedly declared that they went forth to the battle, but that
they always fell. This is the melancholy key-note of the Ossianic
poetry. This is the passionate patriotism—a brave, resolute and
chivalrous race, ever ready for the fight, ever ready to go forth to
battle--and has always appealed to the popular heart. The brave
Finians, however, seemed to go forth to die. The fate of possible
extinction appears to have pressed heavily on the heart of the
people. And when the leaders were all dead and gone, Ossian
the immortal singer of their exploits and enterprises mourned in
his blindness and solitude the departure of his brother heroes and
hunters,—dwelling with pathetic tenderness on the oft-recurring
refrain : " The last of my race !"

The Albinian monarchy, whose head-quarters were situated
near Loch Ness, exercised rule over various tribes. Early in our
era its sway appears to have extended, to use the proverbial sayings, from the Ord of Caithness to the Rhinns of Islay, from the
Hen of Lewis to the Cock of Arran : *O'n Ord Ghallach gus an
Roinn Ilich, 's o'n Chirc Leoghaisich gus a' Choileach Arrannich.*
This Albinian kingdom was, no doubt, the scene of the Finian
exploits which have formed the subjects of poetic romance. It
was frequently assailed by the Norse on the north-west and east ;
and by Celts on the south-east. The latter finally prevailed, be-
stowing their Celtic tongue on the conquered Albinians. The
Féinne appear to have been the last leaders of the national cause.
They were probably bilingual, as the more educated classes were
in the days of Columba. Many of them may have been fully
Gaelicised, while resisting the encroachments of an alien civilisation. Ossian and his fellow-leaders would be of this class. And
just as many patriot bards in our own time in Ireland and Britain,
lament the decay of Celtic nationalities in the language of the
Teutonic conqneror, so the laureate bard of the Albinian people
has sung of " the last of his race " in the tongue of the conquering
Gael.

The kindred of these remarkable heroes appeared in those early
ages in various lands. They were the immediate predecessors,
not only of the Celtic, but in some cases also of other races. They
were the most ancient Lochlins that ploughed the German Ocean
with their trembling barks. They were the earliest Vikings that

sailed round the Orkneyan skerries ; that visited their kindred and fought with them on the shores of Albin, of Erin, and of Breatun. And clearly it is their connections we have in the north-east of Europe, where they survive in a trying climate with shrunk proportions and exhausted national energies. The famous ballad on the *Battle of Gabhra* represents four companies of Finians as engaged in the terrible fight—the Féinne of Albin, the Féinne of Erin, the Féinne of Breatun, and the Féinne of Lochlin. The names of these heroes are still to be found in Lochlin, Erin, and Albin, the lands in which their celebrated deeds were chiefly performed. We find them in the pages of Adamnan like the shadows of a departing people. Finn or Fionn, appears in various forms, as in *Findchanus, Fintenus*, &c. Here we have also the first, or most ancient, written form of the name of the great bard himself, in Latin disguise, " Oisseneo nomine." ·

The territory of the Caledonians lay from Loch Long eastward to the Firth of Tay and the German Ocean, and northward in later times to the Moray Firth. The Caledonian Forest is represented as extending in a north-eastern direction from Loch Lomond to the river Isla. The Caledonian territories, however, were always shifting. Like the *Celtia* of the Continent of Europe, the *Gaeltachd* of the British Islands was alway under a process of change, but at the same time it was ever the region or the land of the Gael. Lands were won from the tribes whom the Gaels conquered, while territories were surrendered to those who pressed on behind them. At first the *Gaeltachd* was in South Britain ; but as the Gaels moved northward, Albin contracted, and the land of the Gael extended. Finally, the Caledonians became the general term for all the Gaelic clans who opposed the legions of Rome.

The etymology of *Caledonia* has not been satisfactorily explained. The celebrated James Macpherson explains it as follows :— " When South Britain yielded to the power of the Romans, the unconquered nations to the north of the province were distinguished by the name of *Caledonians*. From their very name, it appears that they were of those Gauls, who possessed themselves originally of Britain. It is compounded of two Celtic words, *Gael*, signifying *Celts* or *Gauls*, and *Dun* or *Don, a hill* ; so that *Gael·don*, or Caledonians, is as much as to say *Celts of the hill country*." In the very next sentence Macpherson unconsciously suggests quite a different and better etymology : " The Highlanders to this day call themselves *Gael*, their language *Gaelic* or *Galic*, and their country *Gaeldoch*, which the Romans softened into

Caledonia." Consideration for Latin Inflections would readily transform *Caeldachd* into *Caledonia.* A rival explanation has found place in many school books—Coille-daoine, rendered *Men of the Wood.* This, however, is not the accurate translation. The compound is absurd and unnatural. It reads to a Gael like *Men-Wood* in English. Another explanation has been *Gaedhil dhonna,* brown-haired Gaels ; but physiological facts and the laws of phonology do not support this derivation. The Welsh have given us its meaning from a Cymric standpoint ; and as the word is unknown in Gaelic in its historic form the Welsh suggestions appear very reasonable. The Caledonian Forest in Welsh has always been Calydin or Celydin, a term which means *Wood.* Its Gaelic cognate would be *Coilltean,* which also supplies the representative consonants of Caledonia. The great forest of the Central Highlands would be very naturally spoken of as the *Woods,* Coiltean ; *Caledonii* being only a Latin derivative.

With the spread of Christianity the Caledonians became the great people in Albin. In the later ages they consisted of Gael-icised Albinians, Gaels, and Brythonised Gaels. Among them appeared those who stand first on the roll of literary Scots : the poetry and tales of the Féinne developed into their present shape in the hands of the ancient Christian Gaels of our land. The poetic compositions which relate to this period furnish us with gleams of life from the borderland of decadent heathenism and Christianity.

From the first proclamation of the latter onwards the outlines of Scottish story become continually clearer, shining more and more until the day of national freedom and independence shone on a brave and struggling people. In glancing very briefly at the history of the Gael of Albin we find that it naturally suggests the following periods, described by terms which indicate the fresh elements introduced or fresh changes taking place :—

I. The Pre-Celtic Period embraces the unrecorded ages which partially terminated in the third century, when the influence of Christianity began to be felt. The Roman province in Scotland became nominally Christian by the Imperial adoption of Christianity by Constantine in the year 313.

II. The Celtic Period extends from the third century to the year 1068. During these dark and unsettled times there was much intercourse carried on between the old inhabitants of Albin and the people of Lochlin ; generally the intercourse took the form of a fierce struggle for supremacy. In 1068 Malcolm III. married an English princess, known afterwards as the saintly Queen Margaret ; Gaelic afterwards ceased to be the language of the Scottish Court. At that time Picts and Scots being united under one monarchy the sway of the Northmen in the north-west became much enfeebled. The power of the latter was completely broken by the disastrous defeat of Haco, at Large, in 1263.

III. The Norman or Feudal Period extends from 1068 to 1567. Few of the Gaelic preachers, or representatives of the early Scottish Church, survived the repressing influence of Queen Margaret, who was a zealous Roman Catholic. The Norman conquest of England caused many Saxons to seek refuge in Scotland, where they were welcomed by the Queen and her royal husband, *Ceann Mor*. Norman influences also began to be felt in Scotland. The lands of Celtic chiefs were chartered away by the King to Norman barons, of whom many became as Celtic and as identified with the Gaelic inhabitants as the Celtic mormaers whom they supplanted. The patriarchal system began to decay, and feudalism was gradually introduced.

IV. The Protestant and Jacobite Period extends from the middle of the sixteenth century to the year 1745, when Jacobitism on Culloden Moor received its death-blow. The nominal first, afterwards the actual, acceptance of the Reformation doctrines by the Scottish Celts in the sixteenth century has very vitally affected their literature, as well as completely changed their relations with the Irish Celts.

V. The Anglo-Gaelic Period begins in 1745. The influence of the English language and English thought has been extending in the Highlands since then ; while through the general intermingling of races, and a better mutual understanding, the prejudices of Celt and Saxon respectively have been everywhere dying away, especially among the classes by whom the force of the democratic tendencies of our age has been felt and acknowledged.

The dates assigned to the above periods are only approximately accurate, but they may serve to shadow forth some of the chief influences which have been at work in the history of Celtic Scotland, and of which we have traces in the literary annals of the Gael. Perhaps the surprising thing in connection with these meagre annals is the fact that there are any literary remains at all, when it is remembered how frequent and how violent have been the changes which have occurred in the course of the history of Albin.

The Anglo-Gaelic era of Highland history commences, as has been pointed out, with the decay of the Jacobite cause. The changes that have taken place since 1745 have deeply affected the destiny and character of the people. In some respects the contact with the fresh forces brought into play was beneficial, in other respects it was a moral loss; but it is to be hoped that on the whole there has been considerable gain, and that not altogether material.

Under the social and educational changes that have been taking place during the last century the Highlanders have shown wonderful adaptableness in the course of the process they have been undergoing. The revival of a more earnest spirit of Christianity in many districts has completely altered the social habits of the people, while the influence of educational agencies has reached the most secluded glen and remote headland.

The English language is everywhere taught, the people, knowing its use in the sphere of secular success, preferring to have their children educated in a purely English rather than in a Gaelic school. The present rising generation all understand and talk a little Saxon of some sort, but Gaelic will be the language of the mass of the population for some generations yet. English thought and culture also reach the people through the hundreds of University-bred ministers who preach Gaelic in Highland pulpits.

These important changes in the Celtic world are not effected without many venerable regrets being uttered by sentimentalists both in Ireland and Scotland. If we look across the channel we find that the Irish Gael indulges in the same unpractical wail over an irrevocable past, that we find so prevalent with his brother of Albin. The cry of the sentimentalist there is even more intense, more persistent. The unpromising present of the Gael there appears to attract like a magnet all the revolutionary sympathies of the usually stolid Teutonic heart, after a little contact of the races. Just as in their political difficulties the Irish have always looked for help from Spain, France, or America, so unless the gods somehow interfere to preserve their native tongue, all they can or will do, waiting for external or divine deliverance, is to take up the refrain—" It is dying." This is how an Irish poet, the Rev. M. Mullin, Clonfert, sings with incomparable sadness :—

" It is fading ! it is fading ! like the leaves upon the trees ;
It is dying ! it is dying ! like the Western Ocean breeze !
It is fastly disappearing, as footsteps on the shore,
Where the Barrow, and the Erne, and Lough Swilly's waters roar ;

Where the parting sunbeam kisses the Corrib in the West,
And the ocean, like a mother, clasps the Shannon to its breast ;
The language of old Erin, of her history and name—
Of her monarchs and her heroes, of her glory and her fame—
The sacred shrine where rested, through her sunshine and her gloom,
The Spirit of her martyrs, as their bodies in the tomb !
The time-wrought shell where murmured, through centuries of wrong,
The secret voice of Freedom in annal and in song
Is surely, fastly sinking into silent death at last,
To live but in the memories and relics of the Past !"

It must be very consoling to give one's grief utterance in this highly poetical fashion ; it is a question whether the poetry loses or gains in force, when it is remembered that the singer perhaps never put forth any effort to preserve the life of that ancient tongue which he is harping into her grave. Perhaps he does not know the language at all. He may be among those who first spurned and then starved her scholars ; of the sentimentalists who, after learned devotees gave to the world in books the results of a life's labour, on the publication of which they had expended more than all their own means, might borrow but would not buy a copy. The accomplished Archbishop MacHale of Tuam, found out to his cost the full meaning of this remark. Few were the copies of his excellent Græco Irish Homer that were sold ; and here we have an illustration of the extent of the encouragement that real Irish scholarship receives. At the same time it must be admitted that the writers of Celtic books are frequently much to blame. They bury their productions in expensive volumes which can never obtain general circulation, or they do not furnish the precise thing required ; or if they do, it is not always in a saleable popular fashion. Thus we have to regret the evil results of contemptuous neglect on the one hand, and extravagant claims and impracticable theories on the other, as well as an imaginary sense of loss and wrong, on the part of those who ought to give a more practical direction to the people's sentiments.

But the Celt is neither dead nor dying. He is still an important factor in the making of the world's history. Apart from the very large Celtic element that has been absorbed in the Anglo-Celtic intermingling of races under the supremacy of Teutonic rule in these islands we find some four or five millions of people talking one or other of the Celtic dialects. The number of Gaelic speaking Highlanders is not much under half a million. There will be about 300,000 of a Gaelic-speaking population within the geographical limits of the Highlands, the area of which is upwards of three-fifths of Scotland. There is a larger Gaelic population in Glasgow than the whole population of Greenock. The Gaelic bard of to-day has thus as large an audience to sing his lays to as the great Ossian himself had in ancient Albin.

Still it is constantly asserted that whether or not the Gaelic language is dead and ready for burial it has no literature ; and the assertion has been repeated for several generations with emphatic persistence. The following chapters are intended to show that there is a literature ; and that it does not altogether deserve the contempt with which it has been hitherto regarded. And the English-reading public have a right to know from the pens of Gaelic scholars what is the value of the literature still extant in the ancient language of a people with whom they are so closely united, and who form an important integral portion of their common empire. All have an interest in bringing the reign of ignorance, apathy, and prejudice to an end.

At last in the midst of neglect and apathy, of petty rivalries and discords which so readily breed within circumscribed spheres, when our Gaelic scholars, MacLauchlan and Clerk, Skene and J. F. Campbell, and others, were giving to the world the results of their laborious efforts to uphold the character and literary prestige of their countrymen, and were thus paving the way, one voice began to be heard on behalf of a despised language and literature. That voice crying in the Highland wilderness was that of Professor Blackie ! By inimitable eloquence and unwearied energies he interested high and low at once and for years in the establishment of a Celtic Chair in the University of Edinburgh. From the Queen, from lord and laird, and from peasant, he charmed, by his sweet and natural manner, the gold on which that Chair is now so successfully founded. Not only that, but he has also given us the fullest account hitherto published of the language and literature of the Scottish Highlands. It is needless to speak of the affection and gratitude which Highlanders cherish towards the learned and venerable Professor, who has been a most potent Celtic force in this generation. " *Saoghal fada 'n deagh bheatha dhuit !*"

Irish scholars have recently laboured hard and successfully in furthering the interests of their native literature. It is enough here to mention the names of O'Donovan, O'Currie, Whitley Stokes, Joyce, Standish O'Grady, and Bourke—men whose learning and talents would adorn the literary annals of any nation. While the Irish have accomplished more than the Scottish Gael, the Welsh have done more than either to preserve their language and culti-vate their literature. Under systematic efforts to suppress it entirely the Kymry have adhered to their ancient tongue with unwearying pertinacity. While the Gael of Ireland and Scotland have not yet been successful in supporting one purely Gaelic news-paper, the Celt of Wales has his Welsh newspaper in every town of importance in the Principality. It is to the Kymry that we owe the best work yet published on Celtic philology—the "Welsh Philology" of Professor Rhys of the Celtic Chair at Oxford. So now it may fairly be said that we are in the midst of a Celtic Renaissance. Books of a certain useful character do sell, notwith-standing the well-founded complaint referred to above. The first edition of Canon Bourke's "Aryan Origin of the Gaelic Race" was exhausted in a very short time. Campbell's "Tales" are out of print. These are signs of the times which, along with the estab-lishment of Celtic Chairs at the central seats of learning, decisively indicate a reviving interest in Celtic studies. In talking once of the emotional element of the Celtic nature, an enthusiastic Irish scholar jocularly remarked to the writer that the Gael was dying away in song. If this turns out to be true, it is evident that his remains will be examined with pious and scientific care.

It is interesting to find that, meagre as Gaelic literature is—and the great wonder is that what we have should have been produced in so unpromising a field—it extends over sixteen centuries. Its stream issued from that fount of Gaelic heroism which began to burst forth in the first centuries of our era, when the ground of the old European world was on every side shaken by the heavy tramp of the Roman legions and by the consequent disturbance of equili-brium among the clans and races everywhere. Epic products of genius, of course, there are not in Gaelic literature. Perhaps the pure Celtic genius, as Mathew Arnold held, is incapable of pro-ducing epic works—is too emotional, and is only rich in lyrical and ballad power. Great works requiring leisure, quietness, and per-severance there are not ; the life of our ancestors, active, earnest, and practical—its energies ceaselessly being called forth to combat the ruthless forces of nature—did not admit of the necessary cultivation and ease for such productions. Extensive fruits of Gaelic thought and letters we do still possess, however, although much has been lost, especially of what was produced in earlier days. But these should not for a moment be spoken of in comparison with the magnificent monuments of intellectual endeavour which Greece and Rome and Anglo-Celtic Britain have reared. But

Gaelic literature will compare favourably with that of many other countries, especially when united with its sister product, Irish literature. And Welsh literature, no doubt, should also be added. English literature, because of the basis it has in the soil of Christianity, is the grandest product of the human intellect, the master works of Greece and Rome not excepted. It is great ; it is partly Celtic ; and we, as Anglo-Celts, admire it. But we may with advantage look beyond the bounds of our English studies, and then see more clearly the foundation of our Anglo-Celtic empire when we have examined with tender and sympathetic care the interesting relics of Celtic thought enshrined in the ancient language of the British Islands.

It ought perhaps to be acknowledged that the English-speaking peoples of these islands are, at present peculiarly ready to accept any authentic information respecting Celtic history and literature. The same remark replies to Continental scholars. In our own islands the stirring of nationalities in Ireland, Scotland and Wales, and that simultaneously with the movements of the practical politics of the parties of the day and the advocacy of the reform of our land laws, has deepened the interest in all questions relating to Celtic life and thought.

It is a mere truism to remark that the language and literature of the Gael have been much neglected. All attempts to bring their claims before the English speaking world were, till recently, treated with systematic indifference if not with contempt. The national, historical, and scientific value of the study of both does not appear to have occurred even to many who ought to know better. Interesting and inviting as the field was, it lay long unoccupied. Highlanders conscious of some talent were attracted by the rich prizes and honour obtainable within the sphere of English letters. A few who dipped into Celtic studies found them either unprofitable or turned away with disgust from a path in which they were met on all sides with petty jealousies and ignorant pretence. The Rev. Dr John Smith, of Campbeltown, distinguished alike for his learning and general culture, sacrificed much of his time and means to Gaelic studies ; and, finding them unprofitable, turned in his leisure hours to farming on his glebe. He was also annoyed by a truthless, pedant schoolmaster, Duncan Kennedy, of Lochgilphead, who laid claim to the authorship of some ballads which Dr Smith had published. The English Republic of letters could not be blamed for disregarding the intellectual history of a people who ignored their own productions and all that they inherited from their ancestors. Yet is it a reproach to Irish and British scholars that Continental students should be the first to create interest in Celtic studies and place them on a scientific basis. The real parties, however, who ought to bear the blame are the Celts themselves— the Kymry of Wales, and the Gael of Ireland and Scotland. It is with much propriety that Professor Geddes of Aberdeen, thus addresses British Celts with regard to their languages :—" *Your* advantages are great. To you it is a mother-speech, whereas to others like myself it has to be laboriously learned, and after all imperfectly, so that it can hardly be said to be a speech at all in such mouths as mine. It is otherwise with you ; you are within the shrine, such as I are without, and just as the radiance of a cathedral window, rich with the spoils of time, looks blurred and poor to the eye that seeks to comprehend it from without, but streams in full glory on the eye that gazes from within. so your native speech rightly studied ought to be to you resplendent with linguistic treasures, such as no stranger can be expected to unveil." The Highlander alone can fully know and appreciate the language and literature of his race. But if he takes up the obsolete harp of his fathers, and rehearses in melancholy strains that his people are perishing and that his language is dying, it is quite natural, that his Teutonic neighbour should chime in with an emphatic and not always a sympathetic amen.

This sort of harping is the species of music with which many Highlanders, and Irish Gaels also, have been pleased to humour and feed their patriotic feelings over the general neglect of Celtic interests. Well may the disinterested spectator declare that they are not much in earnest—that the wail is partly hypocritical ; for they have done so little to preserve their language and nationality. And no doubt the cry is to a certain extent hypocritical with not a few self-constituted patriots, and the bulk of the people disregard it. The latter do not take up the wail, and they are mainly in the right. The enthusiast and the sentimentalist, who indulge in the dirge, run away with one small truth, or the phase of a truth—with a pathetic misconception of the true state of things. Sometimes they hire themselves to do the coronach, like the Irish professional mourners who do the wailing over the departed. But the people in general are not drawn by the charming of the sentimentalist ; they are more practical. They know and feel the power of circum-stances and destiny which they have to overcome and bear, and act accordingly. While they find their native hills barren, and their native glens inhospitable, they betake themselves to the rich woods of Canada and the prairies of the United States. Witness what a large body of the Glengarry Highlanders once did. Again, when they find the want of the English language a bar to their secular success in life, they protest, while cherishing dearly their native tongue, against pure Gaelic schools being thrust upon them, and demand English teaching first. This has been the case not so long ago in the Long Island. And the reason is quite patent. Before arriving at school age the children are in possession of their mother tongue ; and the parents consider, and very rightly, that the sooner their sons and daughters acquire good English the better for their own comfort, interest, and success in the great English-speaking world in which they have necessarily to perform a part. English ought to be taught from the first through, and simultaneously with, the Gaelic. In all this the people show that their utilitarianism is sensible, intelligent. They recognise the facts of their surroundings. They listen to the charming of the senti-mentalist, but they go on their own practical way rejoicing. Hundreds of Highlanders in our large towns never enter a Gaelic church. English-speaking mothers and children do not find the arrangement of services convenient. and, consulting the general good of all the members of the family, they take their seats else-where. In this they cannot be deeply blamed In Scotland we are quite familiar with the stereotyped arguments and phraseology which are applied to depopulation and other matters. But many of those who rehearse the one on public platforms and weave the other into elegiac verse do not always give us a practical illustra-tion of their theories and teaching by living in the Highlands and by having Gaelic taught in their own families.

This conviction and cry of the imaginative Celt that the world is slipping from his grasp—that his affairs are in a hopeless con-dition—has done much injury to his own interests. And it is not at all surprising although his neighbours and the rising generation of his own people have regarded his language and literature with persistent indifference. Ossian himself is proverbially known to us —" Oisein an déigh na Féinne "--as the " last of the race." It would almost seem that every generation of Gaels during the last millennium regarded itself as the last of the " race." Yet, strange to say, the Gaelic language is spoken to-day within pretty nearly the same limits as it was a thousand years ago, a fact encourag-ing to the sanguine and poetic natures of men like William Livingston. that very original Islay bard, who once sang as follows : .

" Cànain àigh nam buadhan òirdhearc,
  A b' fharsuing cliù air feadh na h-Eòrpa ;
  Bithidh i fathast mar a thòisich,
  Os ceann gach cainnt 'na h-iuchair eolais."

ENGLISH :—

Strange mystic pow'rs lie in that tongue,
Whose praise through Europe wide has rung ;
As 'twas of yore in school and college,
It shall be first—the key of knowledge.

CHAPTER I.

" Si labhair Padric 'nninse Fail na Riogh,
'S an faighe caomh sin Colum naomtha 'n I."—
Maclean in Lhuyd's Ar. Brit. (1707.)

ENGLISH : *'Twas it that Patrick spoke in Inis-Fayle,
And saintly Calum in Iona's Isle.*

THE present state of our knowledge does not enable us to assign
an exact date to the first beginnings of Gaelic literature. The most
ancient ballads have certainly come down to us through the hands
of Gaelic Churchmen ; and it may be taken as absolutely certain
that writing was unknown until it was introduced by Christian
missionaries. The monuments of Runes and Oghams, the study
of which may be pursued in the works of Stephens, Anderson,
and Ferguson, can scarcely be regarded as literature in the proper
sense of the term. At the threshold of the temple of Gaelic letters
we are confronted with one name which can not be ignored—that
of Ossian which we see inscribed on the portals.

In his days and those of his peculiar people, the Féinne, the
Pagan and pre-Celtic Period was coming to a close. Let us look
a little at the picture that has been handed down to us of this great
bard, with whom the heathen dispensation ended.

That a Fingal lived and an Ossian sang is a proposition that
cannot be successfully disputed. It was in the eighteenth century,
when James Macpherson published his fragments of ancient Gaelic
poetry, that the controversy which rages yet around the name of
Ossian arose. This controversy, as well as the poems, English and
Gaelic, published by Macpherson, will be afterwards considered.
In the meantime, the name of Ossian is used in a conventional

sense, just as the name Homer is frequently used. He lived, let us say, in the third or fourth century, when the heathen dispensation of the pre-Celts and of the Gaels was drawing to a close, when the Druidic period, with its mysteries, was coming to an end. It is neither affirmed nor denied here at this stage that Ossian was the author of the Gaelic poems at present in circulation, and from which Macpherson ostensibly translated. But what may be safely affirmed is, that there was in the days of Gaelic heathenism an eminent bard of the name of Ossian, who started the key-note of some poetry, which may be styled Ossianic. That fragments of his compositions have been handed down to us may with equal safety be affirmed. But of the early poems and ballads contained in Campbell's " Leabhar na Féinne " we are absolutely unable to say which was composed by Ossian or which by his imitators and others. In that vast and valuable collection there may be pieces of Ossian's ; and certainly the authorship of many poems is directly attributed to him, though evidently in many cases by loose tradition. His name is also attached to several productions which can easily be proved to belong to some unknown authors. " A hoodir Oiscin " would be readily prefixed by reciters and scribes to any anonymous piece of merit to gain currency for it.

But granting that Ossian is not a myth, but a veritable man who was a great bard among his people, a further question arises, Was the poet Irish or Scottish ? The Irish have all along declared that the true and original Ossian belonged to them, and lived in their country. Their indignation over Macpherson's productions knew no bounds. All Macpherson's heroes are represented as *going from* Alba *to* Erin, which harmonizes well with the recent deliverances of Sayce and Rhys. He described all the Irish Ossians as fictions and fables manufactured by monks in the Middle Ages, and as so far inferior to the genuine remains of Ossian as the most insipid heroics of the present day are to the immortal productions of Homer. He showed that their system of chronology could not be harmonised- -that it was, in fact, absurd. As represented in the everlasting dialogues between the poet and the saint, he asked how could Ossian, who was supposed to live in the third century, hold converse with St. Patrick, who did not arrive in Ireland till the fifth century ? No such objections could be brought against Macpherson's Ossian, whose chronology was, perhaps conveniently vague, fairly consistent with itself. The Irish *literati* then betook themselves to the manufacture of poems *a la* Macpherson, whom they denounced first as a thief and afterwards as a forger. When

they failed to produce any poems of such superior merit as those
of Macpherson, the theory of theft from the Irish was given up,
and that of forgery substituted. It was quite evident that the
Scottish "Ossian" published by Macpherson was very different
from the composer of Irish ballads and Finian tales. It was admitted by the Scottish patriots that there was a Scottish Ossian
very like the Irish one—that of the later or heroic ballads and of the
popular tales. But they held that this was a spurious, inferior,
and more recent bard or bards, who attached the name of the great
father of Gaelic poetry to their own productions; and that the
genuine, true, and original poems of Ossian, the immortal poet of
the ancient Caledonians, were translated and published by Macpherson. The claims of the two countries cannot be satisfactorily
adjusted or reconciled. History, however, conclusively shows that
the Gaels of the North of Ireland and those of Scotland were at
this period very closely related—were, indeed, but one people.
Just as Shakespeare is claimed by all sections of the English-speaking world as their common heritage, so Ossian would be regarded
by all the Gaelic-speaking tribes or clans as their common property.

Ossian occupies the same place in both the Irish and Scottish
genealogies of the great Finian family. He is the son of Finn or
Fingal, the father of the brave and peerless Oscar, the chief bard
of his people.

Fionn, whose name means *fair*, the leader, and king of the
Féinne, is the most remarkable figure in the annals of the Gael.
The popular conception of his prowess may be gathered from the
following grand passage of Highland poetry :—

" With loud-sounding strides he rush'd westward
    In the clank of his armour bright ;
And he looked like the Spirit of Loda, that scatters
    Dismay o'er the war-way and fight !

" Like a thousand waves on a crag that roll, yelling,
    When the ugly storm is at its height,
So awful the clash of mail and his weapons,
    While his face wore the winter of fight !

" His smooth claymore glittered aloft,
    In his champion hand it was light ;
And the snoring winds kept moving his locks
    Like spray in the whirlpool's might !

" The hills on each side they were shaken,
    And the path seemed to tremble with fright !
Gleamed his eyes, and his great heart kept swelling—
    Oh ! cheerless the terrible sight !"

This is a picture of Fingal going to battle, and a "terrible sight."
indeed, it must have been, especially to his foes. The leader of
the Féinne was surrounded by a worthy band of followers. The
bards and senachies, or oralists, agree in the character, outlines,
and abilities of these heroes. Ossian, the son of Fingal, was himself a hero ; but, being generally a supposed narrator, gives us
little insight into his own distinctive character. He was a great
bard, a brave warrior, but an unobtrusive man. His son Oscar
was the pride and hope of Selma, peerless as to strength and skill
in arms, generous to a fallen foe, and ever ready to meet the
fiercest champion that ever came from Lochlin. Gaul or Goll is
stout and valiant, and next to Oscar in prowess, but is at times
morose. He is never worsted, but he never courts danger for its ·
own sake. The beautiful and brown-haired Diarmad cannot be
seen by any woman without being loved. He is devoted to his
brothers in arms, and when necessary he can combine sleight of
hand with heroic daring. Cailte is a poet, and celebrated for his
swiftness of foot. Then there is the hardy Rayne, the majestic
Cochulin, and the faithful though rash Conan. Fingal himself has
been limned from more than one point of view by the oralists.
His greatness and courage in battle are indisputably pre-eminent.
He is a prudent, cautious general, and disapproves of unnecessary
bloodshed. In affairs of the heart he is relentless towards a rival,
generous though he is in other respects. The worst thing that
can be recorded of him is his unfeeling and revengeful conduct
towards his nephew, the gallant Diarmid, when the latter eloped
with Queen Gràine. These were the principal warriors of that
gallant band of Finian heroes whose names are indelibly engraven
on the hills and straths of their native land, while their deeds are
recorded in a thousand songs. They lived at a time when the
world was undergoing a mighty metamorphoses. Tribes were
beginning to assume a national cast, and as organised nations to
develope an individuality. They were preparing to run the race
sketched out to them by destiny, the path of each bounded by a
particular line or limit of sea, stream, mountain, or valley, and
were throwing aside all the encumbrances of superseded customs
and laws that might clog their progress. Fingal and his followers
appeared in immortal brilliance, crowned with the laurels of death-
less heroism on the stage of the world, and soon they disappeared
from the scene. They were seen but for a short time like the sun
in a wintry day. And the picture is beautifully brought before us
in the following verses translated by Pattison :—

" Like a sun-gleam in wild wintry weather
    That hastens o'er Lena's wide heath,
So the Feinne have faded together,
    They were the beam the showery clouds sheathe,
When down stoops the dark rain-frown of heaven,
    To snatch from the hunter the ray,   .
And wildly the moaning bare branches are driven,
    While the weak herbs all wither away.

" But the sun, in his strength yet returning,
    The fair-freshened woods will espy,
In the springtime that laugh for their mourning,
    As they look on the Son of the sky,
Kindly unveilling his lustre,
    Through the soft and the drizzling shower,
All their wan heads again will he muster,
    From their drear and their wintry bower.

" Then with joy will their small buds keep swelling ;
    Not so they who sleep in the tomb—
No sunbeam that darkness dispelling,
    Shall waken them up from their gloom."

Ossian, the blind warrior-poet, survives them all. And now, as he muses on the departure of his kindred heroes and hunters, and on the loneliness of his own state, led by the white-armed Malvina, the betrothed of his fallen son Oscar, he seeks their former haunts, and breathes as he rests in the well-known shades the pathetic lamentation, " the last of my race !"

" Chula tu bàrda nam fonn :
'S taitneach, ach trom do ghuth ;
'S taitneach a Mhalmhine nan sonn ;
Leaghaidh bròn am bochd an am tha dubh."

Croma.

From the picture of Ossian in his shadowy Pagan domain it is refreshing to turn to those names which have played a great part in connection with our earliest Christian civilization and literature. They are the names of Patrick of Strathclyde, Bridget of the South Gaels of Albin, and Columba of Donegal, subsequently of Iona.

The first glimpse we have of Albin on the canvas of written record is a very confusing one. The one outstanding fact is the Roman occupation. The next fact that strikes and enchains the eye is the presence of Christianity in the land. Among the Gaels of the south-west of Scotland we mark the person of Ninian, around whom we see across the ages the light of the gospel shining.

This preacher of the cross, of whose labours in Galloway very interesting traces were discovered quite recently, appears to have carried the gospel not only to the Gaels of the south-west, but also to the southern Picts north of the Forth and Clyde. His labours began as early as the year 397, and resulted in the first church organization known in Scotland. The evengelisation of Ninian extended over probably the whole of Romanised Scotland towards the end of the fourth century. The races embraced in his sphere of operations were Latin-speaking peoples of various nations, Brythons, and Gaels.

Among the last-mentioned, the Gaels of the Strathclyde kingdom, whose chief seat was Alcluaidh, now Dumbarton, there appeared the family of Patrick, whose name has shed holy lustre on the early annals of that period. This family had been Christians for two generations. The father of Patrick was a *decurio*, one of the council or magistracy of a Roman provincial town. His name was Calphurnius, which some have rendered by the familiar form of MacAlpine. Being recognised as a Roman magistrate he thus took his place among the local aristocracy of Banavem in Taberniæ, where villas of the Roman style could be seen, and the sonorous Latin could be heard mingling with the kindred accents of the ancient Gaelic. This place was probably not far from that attractive spot on the banks of the Clyde where a topographical monument has been reared to the celebrated Irish apostle in Kilpatrick. Calphurnius was not only a magistrate ; he was also a deacon in the Christian church. His own father, the grandfather of Patrick, was called Potitus, and filled the office of Presbyter in the Strathclyde church. It is also stated that this family cultivated a small farm.

As there is a great deal of literature extant on the nativity of Patrick which conflicts with the results of recent discussion, it may be satisfactory to many to have the latest authorative declarations on the subject before them. No one has ever attempted to deprive the north of Ireland of the honour of having supplied the Highlands with the great gospel preacher who evengelised the north-west ; who revived the Christianity of the Lowlands ; whose earnest disciples supplied the north of England with the teachers who converted its people to the power of Christ. But while Protestant Scotland has made no attempts to deprive Ireland of its Columban honours Catholic Ireland has persistently endeavoured to denude Scotland of its legitimate claims to the honour of being the fatherland of Patrick. Ireland's misrepresentations have been acquiesced in by Scotsmen, especially by timid historical writers, of a certain ecclesiastical type, who have made needless concessions to Romanist claims in connection with a question which is purely historical. It is with peculiar pleasure that we are now able to assign Patrick, the son of the Gaelic Church of Strathclyde, his true place on the roll of Gaelic Scots ; and to regard him as a link in the Gospel succession which Columba brought with him to the West Highlands.

In the *Catholic Dictionary*, issued a few years ago, and compiled by Addis and Arnold of the Royal University of Ireland, with the approving seal of his Eminence Cardinal Manning on its publication, the following satisfactory sentence occurs : " The general conversion of the Irish nation was reserved for St. Patrick, who was probably born at the place now called Kilpatrick on the Clyde whence he was carried as a slave into the north of Ireland while still a youth." To this there is appended a foot-note referring to the excellent article of an Irish bishop on St. Patrick in one of the Irish periodicals : " Dr Moran, Bishop of Ossory, who formerly leant to the opinion that the place was near Boulogne in France, has lately written convincingly in favour of the Scottish site." The Bishop's article has finally decided the question ; and has enabled the Gaels of Scotland, with the tacit consent of their Irish brethren, to add to the list of their heroic Christian missionaries, a name whose brilliant halo of holy effort is unsurpassed in the ancient annals of the Christian Church of these islands.

We are thus enabled to point out the first home of Christianity among the Gaels of Scotland. We find it on the banks of the Clyde, where many Christians of the same people, still talking the same tongue, may still be found, rejoicing in the same Gospel. The picture of this early Gaelic Church of Strathclyde from whose bosom the devoted Patrick came forth, is in itself a sufficient reason why the Early History of the Gaels should be re-written. It is a chapter added to the Celtic civilisation of the Highland people, which has been hitherto ignored or hidden through Roman, Teutonic, or Norman influences.

A good deal has been written about Patrick's visit to Rome, where it was necessary to take him by the Romanist writers of later times in order that he might receive consecration from an order of Ecclesiastical Fathers which had scarcely yet developed. The *Catholic Dictionary*, already quoted, is forced to confess, after reference to Patrick's autobiography in his *Confession* as follows :—" He does not mention the Pope or the Holy See." We thus find that in his own authentic writings Patrick makes no reference to, or acknowledgment of, the Roman Bishop of his day. The reason for this is not far to seek.

Patrick does not appear to have come in contact with any Christianity except that which he was taught on the banks of the Clyde in the Gaelic Church of his fathers. He had neither been to Rome nor known the Roman Bishop (Celestine) of his time, so he makes no reference to either in his genuine writings. On this question his own words in his *Epistle to Coroticus* deserve quotation- *Ego, Patricus, indoctus, scilicet, Hibernione, constitutum episcopum me esse reor*: *a Deo accepi, id quod sum.* " I, Patrick, an unlearned man, to wit, a bishop constituted to Ireland : what I am I have received from God." Thus in the establishment of his Church Patrick in no instance appeals to any foreign Church, Pope, or Bishop. On authority received from God he superin-tended the Irish Church for 34 years. These clear statements of his are utterly at variance with the fabricated ones which adorn the lives of him which appeared centuries afterwards, and which are now regarded as authorities by the fabulously inclined.

In his own writings Patrick gives us in a somewhat unconscious manner a beautiful picture of his devoted character :—" I was born free. I was the son of a father who was a decurio. I sold my nobility for the advantage of this nation. But I am not ashamed, neither do I repent ; I became a servant for Jesus Christ our Lord, so that I am not recognised in my former position." Elsewhere he says—" I was about 16 years old ; but I knew not the true God, and was led away into captivity to Hibernia, with a great many men, according to our deservings." His occupation for six years in Antrim was keeping cattle. But the spirit of the Eternal took possession of him. " My constant business was to keep the flocks ; I was frequent in prayers, and the love and fear of God more and more inflamed my heart. My faith and spirit were enlarged, so that I said a hundred prayers in a day and nearly as many at night, and in the woods and on the mountain I re-mained, and before the light I arose to my prayers, in the snow, in the frost, and in the rain ; and I experienced no evil at all. Nor was I affected with sloth, for the spirit of God was warm in me." This was the man that the Gaels of Strathclyde gave for the con-version of Ireland to Christianity.

There are several interesting questions suggested by the nativity and life of Patrick. The land of his birth is now clearly ascer-tained ; but there are subsidiary questions in connection with that fact which require further consideration. Was Patrick a Gael, a Brython or one of non-Aryan races which as recently as the fifth century were a powerful people? What language did he speak, or what language did he acquire in his Christian conquest of Ireland? Who were the Irish as a race, and how far they had been Christianised before his arrival? As to the question of race, the evidence appears to lean distinctly in favour of the conclusion that he was a Gaidel and not a Brython, notwithstanding the Brythonic suggestiveness of the letter **P** in his name. It ought not to be forgotten also in connection with this question that the radical differences between the Brythonic and Gaidelic dialects at this time were far less important than they are now ; and that the capital of the district of Patrick's birth-place had its earlier Gaidelic designation of Alcluaidh before it received its Brythonic name of Dunbretton. Philologists tell us of the loss of the letter **P** in the Gaidelic dialects ; but the phonologists on this question have not fully cleared up the difficulties which are suggested by the fact that in some of the most north-westerly districts of the Highlands at the present time many of the non-Anglicised natives are incapable of making a clear distinction between the letters **P** and **B**, and hard **C** and **G**. If we take the evidence afforded by literature, we can come to no other conclusion than that Patrick was of the Gaidelic or Gaelic race ; for if we have not actual compositions in the Gaelic language by him we have productions in that language ascribed to him by ancient countrymen who must have known what his native tongue had been.

The language which Patrick appears to have acquired in course of his missionary labours for Ireland's conversion could have been no other than that of the non-Aryan races, or *Cruthnic*—the prevailing *Erinic*—probably related closely to the *Albinic*, which at that time was spoken all over the north-west of Scotland. In the north-east of Ireland he no doubt found considerable numbers of the Gaidelic race, his kinsmen who had preceded him. But the language of those who had been already partly converted by Palladius, a semi-mythic saint, who is at least as much connected with Albin as with Erin, was certainly different from that of the large mass of the Irish people. To extend the conquests of Christianity over the fair fields of Erin south as well as north, it was necessary that Patrick should master the tongue of the non-Aryan races. There can be no doubt that his labours in this direction helped also to extend the area of the Gaelic speaking regions,— the more literary language of the incoming saint and his race

making natural acquisitions in every direction. Similar results
followed the Gospelising efforts of Columba in the Highlands in a
subsequent age.

The conclusions fairly deducible from a consideration of Patrick's
life point to many interesting matters in connection with the
History of the Highland People. We obtain first a clear conception of a living Christian church existing among the Romanised
Gaels of Strathclyde. We also learn that from the bosom of the
Gaelic Church of Ninian, decayed as it possibly may have been,
there came forth the great messenger of the Cross, who recalled
to life if he did not originate the forces of Christianity in Ireland.
Again we find the gospel succession of the spirit of truth, coming
back in a generation or two into the Highlands of Scotland in the
person of Columba. The lamp of heavenly wisdom, lighted on
the banks of the Clyde, which Patrick flashed over the fields of
Erin, became the holy beacon which the fervid fingers of Columba
planted on the shores of Iona.

The Scottish missionary that went to Ireland and became its
patron saint is often referred to in the early ballads, Irish and
Scottish.   His Creed-Prayer is given here.   It is a curious mixture of dogma and poetry ; but undevotional as it may seem to us
had the " green " and other coloured Finians of the day appropriated its earnest petitions and aspirations they would be saved
the troubles of many " Pursuits."   It begins thus in prose :
" Patraicc dorone innimmunsa." *Patrick made this hymn.* It
then states that it was made in the time of Leogaire, son of Neill.
The cause assigned to its composition was the need of " protection
with his monks against the mortal enemies who were in league
against the clerics."   It was to be a corslet of faith for soul and
body against demons, men, and vices.   Demons could not stand
before the face of him who sang it ; envy and poison could do
no harm ; in this life it would be a safeguard against sudden death ;
and it would be a covering of defence *(lurech* in Gaelic, from the
Latin *lorica)* after death.   When Patrick sang it as he went forth
to sow the faith the opposition of Leogaire gave way.

Then the hymn properly begins :' The singer declares his belief
in the Trinity—in Threeness—confession of Oneness in the Creator
of the world.

I bind myself to-day—

> To the power of the TRINITY ;
> To belief in the all-gracious Three ;
> To confession that the Three are one
> In the Maker of the world and sun.

I bind myself to-day—

To the power of the birth of CHRIST ;
To the truth that Jesus was baptised ,
To the fact that path of death He trod,
That three days He lay beneath the sod ;
To the pow'r of Resurrection morn,
That from the earth to heaven he was borne ;
To the power of His Judgment call,
When final state shall be assigned to all.

I bind myself to-day—

To the power of the CHERUBS high ;
In obedience of the angels nigh ;
In attendance of archangels' might ;
In the hope of resurrection's light ;
In the prayers of the sires of eld ;
In the visions that the seers beheld ;
In the precepts the apostles taught ;
In the faith by which confessors wrought ;
In the innocence of virgins pure ;
In the deeds of just men that endure.

I bind myself to-day—

To the power of HEAVEN,
To the lustre, sun-given ;
To the pureness, snow-driven ;
To fiery flames brightening ;
To the swiftness of lightning ;
To the speed of the breeze ;
To the depth of the seas ;
To the firmness of land,
And the rocks that there stand.

I bind myself to-day—

To God's pow'r to be controlled ;
To His might me to uphold ;
To His wisdom me to bow ;
To His eye the path to show ;
To His ear to hear my cry ;
To His word to speak my sigh ;
To His hand me to protect ;
To His way me to direct ;
To His shield as my defence ;
To His host till I go hence.

Against demons' dire devices ;
Against allurements of all vices ;
Against strong solicitations
Of our nature's inclinations ;
Against all the bad desires
With which sin men's hearts inspires,
Afar or near where'er I be
In solitude or company.

Thus I have sought protection from on high
Against the powers of ill and cruelty ;
Against deceitful prophets' incantations :
Against the black laws of the gentile nations ;
Against the false laws of all heretics ;
Against the craft of the idolator's tricks ;
Against the spells of druids, smiths, and women ;
Against all lore that taints the spirit human.

Let Christ protect me to-day against poison—
Against burning, drowning, against wound,
Until abundance of reward comes round.

Christ be with me, Christ before, behind,
Christ without me, Christ within my mind,
Christ above me, and in breadth, length, height,
Christ below me, at my left and right.

Let Christ in all who think of me reside,
And on all lips that speak to me abide ;
Christ be in every eye that sees my walk,
Christ be in every ear that hears my talk.

I bind myself to-day—

To the power of the Trinity,
To belief in the all-gracious Three,
To confession that the Three are One,
In the Maker of the earth and sun.

Dr Cameron, who has a learned article on " St. Patrick's Hymn"
in *The Scottish Celtic Review*, and to whose accurate prose translation as well as to Dr Stokes's in his Goidelica, I am so much
indebted in the above rendering, makes the following remark :—
"This hymn forms one of the Irish hymns in the 'Liber Hymnorum,'
a MS. belonging to Trinity College, Dublin, and written, as Dr
Stokes conjectures, about the end of the eleventh or the beginning
of the twelfth century. The hymn itself, however, belongs to a
much earlier date."

The chief dates in the life of Patrick, who was probably born
about 387, are his landing in Ireland in 432 when he is represented
as attending the assembly of the Irish Kings and Chieftains which
was held on the hill of Tara that year ; his celebrated letter against
Coroticus in 453 to regulate church discipline ; and his death
which occurred in 493.

A very remarkable incident, related in the " Book of Armagh "
and quoted in Todd's " Life of Patrick," which bears internal
evidence of high antiquity, and now evidently written at a time
when paganism was not yet extinct in the country, illustrates the
way in which Patrick set before the Celtic mind the faith which he

proclaimed. One morning he and his attendants repaired to a fountain called Clebach at Cruachan, now Rath-croghan, an ancient residence of the kings of Connaught. Thither came the two daughters of King Laogharie, and on seeing the strangers supposed them to be Duine Sidhe fairies, "men of the hills," and said to them, "Who are ye ?" And Patrick said unto them, " It were better for you to confess to our true God, than to inquire concerning our race."

' The first Virgin said,—

" Who is God ?

" And where is God ?

" And of what nature is God ?

" And where is his dwelling place ?

" Has your God sons and daughters, gold and silver ?

" Is He everliving ?

" Is He beautiful ?

" Is He in Heaven or in earth ?

" In the sea ?

" In rivers ?

" In mountainous places ?

" In valleys ?

" Declare unto us the knowledge of Him ?

" How shall He be seen ?

" How is He to be loved ?

" How is He to be found ?

" Is it in youth ?

" Is it in old age that He is to be found ?"

' But St. Patrick, full of the Holy Ghost, answered and said,—

" Our God is the God of all men.

" The God of heaven and earth of the sea and rivers.

" The God of the sun, the moon, and all stars.

" The God of the high mountains and of the lowly valleys.

"The God who is above heaven, and in heaven, and under heaven.

" He hath an habitation in the heaven, and the earth, and the sea, and all that are therein.

" He inspireth all things.

" He quickeneth all things.

" He is over all things.

" He sustaineth all things.

" He giveth light to the light of the sun.

" And he hath made springs in a dry ground.

" And dry islands in the sea.

" And hath appointed the stars to serve the greater lights.

" He hath a Son co-eternal and co-equal with Himself.

" The Son is not younger than the Father.

" Nor is the Father older than the Son.

" And the Holy Ghost breatheth in them.

" The Father, and the Son, and the Holy Ghost are not divided.

" But I desire to unite you to the Heavenly King, inasmuch as you are the daughters of an earthly king—to believe."

' And the Virgins said, as with one mouth and one heart,—

" Teach us most diligently how we may see Him face to face, and whatever thou shalt say unto us we will do."

' And Patrick said,—

" Believe ye that by baptism ye put off the sin of your father and your mother ?"

' They answered, " We believe.''

" Believe ye in repentance after sin ?" " We believe."

" Believe ye in life after death ? Believe ye in the resurrection at the Day of Judgment ?' " We believe."

" Believe ye the unity of the Church ?' " We believe"

' And they were baptized, and a white garment put upon their heads. And they asked to see the face of Christ, and the Saint said unto them, " Ye cannot see the face of Christ except ye receive the sacrifice." And they answered, " Give us the sacrifice, that we may behold the Son, our Spouse." And they received the Eucharist of God, and they slept in death.

" The articles of the Creed recited in this extract are those alone, it has been observed, which are to be found in symbols of the very highest antiquity, and the dialogue illustrates. what has been already noticed, the Celtic belief in genii or aerial beings, inhabiting mountains, plains, rivers, lakes, and fountains, and the existence of nature-worship in its simplest form."—See the works of SKENE, TODD, CUSACK, HENNESY, FOSTER, SHERMAN, and for special purposes WHITLEY STOKES, MISS STOKES, G. T. STOKES, along with MACLEAR'S " CELTS."

CHAPTER II.

IT has been usually taken too much for granted that the early Christian preachers of Britain and Ireland succeeded in fully Christianising the districts in which they laboured, and with which their names are associated. This is a very imperfect apprehension of the results of their efforts. No missionary of the cross could excel Patrick and Columba in their enthusiasm for work, in their devotion to the Gospel cause, and in their resolute attempt to conquer the whole land for Christ. Yet we find that their evangelisation of the races to which they were respectively sent was very incomplete. Patrick writes of the large numbers who were converted under his preaching, but there is no evidence that Christianity was universally adopted by the whole people. On the contrary it is clear that the Ardri, or chief king of Ireland, continued to be a Pagan during the whole period of the mission of Patrick. It was only in the year 513 that a Christian sovereign exercised rule for the first time from the throne of Tara. This was some time after the death of the apostle of Ireland, which occured in 493.

While Patrick was labouring to lay the foundations of the Irish Church, spiritual decay appears to have crept over the heart of of his own native church among the Gaels of Strathclyde. The poetic and literary flowering of this period we have in the person of the celebrated Brigit. In those who are familiar with the revivals and declensions of church life, as unfolded in history, such a decay can excite no surprise. In our own times, with all the rich aids of civilization and Christian literature, enkindling and preservative that we possess, we find that one generation of earnest believers in a district is frequently succeeded by an apathetic one. So the living church of Strathclyde from which Patrick went forth, was in a decadent condition when his name began to shine and burn brightly on the shores of Erin.

There were many causes that contributed to the weakening of this Gaelic Church of the Clyde valleys. The Roman arms had been withdrawn and all over the Romanised provinces political

disintegration set in.   Dependence on a foreign rule, and the
enervating luxuries of more southern lands had not only paralysed
the native manliness of the British races, but had also greatly
emasculated the primitive Christianity of these islands.   Indeed,
in southern Britain the early Christianity became so completely
extinguished that it had to be re-kindled from the north in the
sixth and seventh centuries.   The vigorous forces of the unconverted and unconquered tribes of the north were too powerful for a
Church which had been accustomed perhaps to lean too much on
the civil protection afforded by an alien power.   It must not also
be forgotten that those early Christians had literally no help to
feed the flame of their devotion.   The fragments even of the
Scriptures that may have been in circulation could only have been
in the hands of a very limited number ; while the languages in
which they were written were utterly unknown to the people, and
there were no translations.   When all this is remembered it becomes rather a matter of marvel that the sacred glow of Christian
truth survived so long in some places after the personal life that
kindled it ceased to be.   Those were truly ages when Christian
witnesses were, and had to be living epistles known and read of
all men ; for the personal life became practically the literature in
which the gospel was heralded.   So the strength of a Church
depended mainly on the character and personality of the teachers.

But notwithstanding the deadening influences around and in
the Gaelic Church of the Clyde districts subsequent to the period
of Patrick's mission, we still mark in the sixth century the rays of
Gospel truth struggling there with the thick inclosing darkness of
Paganism.   One heroic figure emerges from the surrounding
gloom.   It is that of Kentigern, or Mungo, forever associated
with the origin and rise of the powerful commercial metropolis of
Glasgow.   The traditions of his life abound with myths and
marvels ; while his name has been a rich and suggestive theme
for the etymological fancy.   From the romantic literature that has
gathered around his name, we glean what appears to be recognised
as generally accepted facts—that he was born at Culross, and that
he died at Glasgow about 601-3.   He had been the pupil of the
famous St. Serf in the east in the northern boundaries of the
Brythonic race with Gaels to the north of them.   So he may have
been a Highland or a Welsh Celt.   One or other of the forms of
his name has been resolved, apparently with equal ease, into
either a Gaelic or a Welsh etymon.   Perplexing or unsatisfactory
as this undoubtedly is it yet may suggest an explanation.   As

happens in our own and other times his name would assume
various forms according to the dialects or languages of the speakers
and writers. The forms of his name, therefore, furnish no key as
to the race of his fathers.

When Kentigern began his labours on the Clyde the church of
St. Patrick's people had lost much of its first love. Many of the
Gaels themselves had also been driven westward under Brythonic
pressure from the east and from the south. As Christian soldiers
or Milesians some had sailed to the north of Ireland to find a
home ; others had drifted into Perthshire and Argyll, which at
this period became the true " Gaidhealtachd," or the " land
of the Gael." Kentigern strove devotedly to revive the drooping
church. In his cold stone bed strewn with ashes on the classic
banks of the Molendinar stream he cultivated the spirit of prayer ;
rehearsed the sacred strains of the psalmist ; and warmed his spirit
by visions of divine fellowship. In the local sovereign of the
name of Morken he encountered much disagreeable opposition
and sarcastic interpretation of the saint's faith in a Providence.
Kentigern virtually made an application for an ecclesiastical
establishment and endowment of himself and his presbyter followers. King Morken received the application for temporalities in
a spirit that would do no discredit to a statesman of modern times.
He reminds the saint of his own popular saying : " Cast thy care
upon the Lord and he will care for thee." But argued the King
further : " Now here am I, who have no faith in such precepts, who
do not seek the kingdom of God and His righteousness ; yet for
all that, are not riches and honours heaped upon me ?" The
royal granaries were full, while the Christian saints were starving.
How could he expect to believe in a Providence that thus
arranged the possessions of men. The saint's replies and inter-
pretations proved unavailing with the royal sceptic, so broken in
heart the holy man retired to his oratory to pray. His emotions
were profoundly stirred ; he began to weep. Then as the tears
started in his eyes and coursed down his cheeks, so did the waters
of the Clyde begin to rise and swell into a mighty flood, which at
last overflowed around the royal granaries, carrying them down the
stream, and leaving them stranded at the very door of the saint on
the banks of the Molendinar. The sanctity of his youth and the
faith of his mature years have been in this fashion richly attested
by miraculous manifestations, according to his rather credulous
biographer, Jocelyn.

The earnest and heroic labours of Kentigern were not confined to Strathclyde. We obtain glimpses of him beyond the Mounth among the northern Picts of Aberdeenshire, while his Christian fellow-worker and friend, Columba, was beginning to proclaim the gospel in Perthshire. In his latter days we find him in Wales where he founded the church of St. Asaph, and where he finally died, leaving behind him a name whose holy influence has shed lustre across the course of thirteen centuries.

Kentigern is peculiarly associated with the origin of Glasgow. In the armorial bearings of this city we have perpetuated, according to very remarkable legends, three remarkable miracles which were wrought by the holy man, and which it would be probably unfair to pass by without reference, considering that the sons of Gaeldom ever since have helped and shared so very specially in the prosperity of Glasgow. A pet robin redbreast, which belonged to the college over which St. Serf presided, is represented on a shield argent by a bird proper. This bird either through accident or mischief was torn to pieces among the students. When the president appeared to punish, young Kentigern, the best boy among them, was made the scapegoat. The pieces of the bird were thrown in his lap ; but the hidden holiness of the boy was such that the creature gathered up his limbs, flapped his wings, and sang a joyous song on the approach of the holy master. On another occasion Kentigern found his fire extinguished by his enemies ; so he was compelled to bring a tree from the frozen forest and breathe into it the breath of fire. The remembrance of this feat is preserved in the tree or branch which forms the crest. The figure of a fish, with the ring in its mouth, recalls the scriptural reference to the finding of a fish with the needed coin in its body. The biographer of Kentigern, Jocelyn of Furness, knew well how to enrobe his hero, with the help of the mythic accounts already developed, with those miracles which had served sacred ends in the lives of other saints at that period. Fishes with rings in their bodies had always been found on critical occasions.

This brief sketch, in connection with the lives of Patrick and Kentigern, of the Gaelic Christianity of Scotland in the fifth and sixth centuries, will help to show forth in clearer outlines the work of Columba. The spiritual forces that waved forth from Iona were certainly not the first that brought religious light to the land of the Gael. Nor were they so exclusively of Irish origin as they are represented to be. In eastern Gaeldom in Scotland Christianity had been already known. But in the course of the century which elapsed from the time of Patrick it had greatly decayed.

Columba came to the west of Scotland to revive and to proclaim the faith afresh. He came back among his ancestral people from the midst of whom the gospel had been sent a century previously to Ireland. In Iona the religious centre of the land of the Gaels was simply removed further west and north. The Gaelic-speaking people themselves were drifting in the same direction towards the Atlantic. As they themselves were largely absorbed by the Brythons behind them, so they absorbed in their north-west progress those brave non-Aryan clans to whom they became the missionaries of the cross and the channels of letters. They extended the area of Gaeldom, and imposed their Christian and literary tongue on the conquered just as the Christian and more literary Latin had been previously imposed on many of their own ancestors. In the fourth century we mark gospel light in Strathclyde ; in the fifth we see it kindling on the shores of Ireland ; in the sixth it begins to burn from Iona.

It was among these South Albin Gaels at an early period that we mark the appearance of Brigit : the Mary of the Gael. There is no standard of Gaelic maintained in the orthography of this proper name. *Brigit* is used here as one of the most ancient forms ; as also to preserve a chronological harmony with the secondary significant title of " Mary of the Gael." As we all know the present form of the name is *Bridget* in English ; but it has been so little talked of in later ages by Gaelic Highlanders that it becomes almost a serious matter for the majority of them even to spell it in Gaelic. It is only in the compound " *La-Fheill-Brighde* "—[Bride] or *The Day of the Feast of Bridget*, and surname MacBride, that we are familiar with this female saintly name.

This by necessary phonological laws recalls *Brigid*, which in its turn reminds us of the more ancient orthography *Brigit*, which is adopted by Dr Stokes in his "Three Middle Irish Homilies." Other Irish scholars have spelt it *Brigid*, even when they are quoting from productions such as the poem ascribed to Brigit, found in the Burgundian Library, Brussels, headed thus : ·

> *Brighitt* (CCT.)
> [Brigid (Cecinet)].

The distinguished Stokes follows accurately the spelling of *Leabhar Breac*, *Brigit*. This is the form which we also find in "Cormac's Glossary " compiled originally nearly a thousand years ago. The definition or explanation appended in Cormac's work is suggestive and instructive. " Brigit i.e. a poetess, daughter of the Dagda

(doctus ?).   This is Brigit the female sage, or woman of wisdom,
i.e. Brigit the goddess whom poets adored, because very great and
very famous was her protecting care.   It is therefore they call her
goddess of poets by this name.   Whose sisters were Brigit the
female physician [woman of leechcraft] ; Brigit the female smith
[woman of smithwork] ; from whose names with all Irishmen a
goddess was called Brigit." To this Dr Stokes adds that the
" name is certainly connected with the Old Celtic goddess-name
Brigantia as possibly with the Skr. Brhaspati and O. Norse Bragi."
p. 23. This gives us a glimpse of a "female smith " : a " female
physician " ; and a " female saint " (sanct Brigit) rolled into one,
and that one a goddess of Indo-European connections.

With these lofty associations and suggestions clinging to the
name of Brigit we almost find it difficult to descend to the regions
of ordinary earthly womanhood ; and recognize in her a mere
Gaelic Christian maiden.   Her name has never been absolutely
dissociated from the realm of myth, or rather *mythus* ; but at the
same time we cannot help regarding her as a historical character.
Her name became celebrated very early wherever the Gaelic folks
did congregate.   We find her name associated with King
Nectan of Albin, and with a church founded in her honour at
Abernethy.   So her fame was not confined to the Gaelic regions
of Erin.   That illustrious Scot, Patrick, a native of the district of
Strathclyde, is supposed to refer to her in his confession, where he
says, " There was one blessed Scottic maiden, very fair, of noble
birth, and of adult age, whom I baptized ; and after a few days she
came to me, because, as she declared, she had received a response
from a messenger of God desiring her to become a virgin of Christ,
and to draw near to God.   Thanks be to God, on the sixth day
from that, she with praiseworthy eagerness seized on that state of
life which all the virgins of God likewise now adopt."   These
notices help to bring us nearer what Carlyle calls the " actual Air-
Maiden, incorporated tangibility and reality," whose electric glance
has fascinated the Gaelic world.   It could not be expected that the
date of the birth of Brigit would be preserved ; but when she became a woman of consequence in the Gaelic or Scottic world her   •
movements began to be marked.   The accounts of the fabulous
lives are very circumstantial ; but sober-minded critics like O'Curry
are fairly satisfied with two principal dates, and most reasonable
folks will be the same.   These two dates are Brigit's advent at
Downpatrick on the 17th of March, 493, A.D. ; and her death in
525 A.D.

The historical and fabulous lives of Brigit suggest a few interesting questions which can only be hinted at in these remarks :—
1. Her conversion by the British Patrick to Christianity.
2. The probability that she belonged to a good British family who, in the days of the Roman occupation, crossed to the nearest Irish districts : (She is described as " of Kildare," a county close to the eastern shore).
3. And that she was a woman of exceptional character or culture, which was possible in that century, under the perpetuated influences of the Roman occupation.

That she and her people, like Patrick himself, were recent immigrants to Ireland from Roman and Christian Britain, there cannot be any serious doubt

These may be the possible or probable facts ascertainable relating to the life of the Mary of the Gael.   But around them has been woven a very interesting body of Gaelic literature which was loved and cherished and cultivated for upwards of a thousand years.

We have two ancient lives of Brigit, written on vellum ; and these are regarded as the oldest ; and are attributed to St. Ultán, whose death took place in the year 656.   The *Liber Hymnorum*, a production of the eleventh century is our authority for the information that the " Life and Acts of St. Brigid of Kildare, were collected and written by St. Ultán," who was her successor in her church, as Adamnan was that of Columba in Iona.

The two lives referred to are found in the *Lebar Breac* and in the Book of Lismore.   A life written within the last two hundred years on paper is also to be found in the Royal Irish Academy.   Her life is generally associated with the lives of Patrick and Columba, as they also very appropriately are in " The Three Middle-Irish Homilies," edited by Dr Whitely Stokes, (Calcutta ; 1877).   In one of the so-called prophetic poems, a Norse Chief Mandar, with a fleet, is represented as exhuming the body of Columba which was afterwards buried " in Downpatrick, in the same tomb with St. Patrick and St. Brigid."

In the celebrated *Domhnach Airgid*, one of the most ancient relics of the old Gaelic civilization, we are presented with the *figure* of Brigid.

Dr Petrie in his account of the relic says :—" The smaller figures in relief are, in the first compartment, the Irish saints Columba, Brigid, and Patrick."   Perhaps the most interesting relic associated with Brigit is " a very ancient crozier, said to have

belonged to *St. Finnbarr* (of Tormonbarry, in Connacht),- and
-believed to have been made by *Conlaedh*, the artificer of *St. Brigid*
of Kildare, early in the sixth century," which is "now in the
Museum of the Royal Irish Academy.".—*See O'Curry's M.S.
Materials.*

In early ecclesiastical annals Brigit is thus on the same platform
with Patrick and Columba in Gaelic Hagiology. True ; her name
is not found, for instance, in the Benchor Antiphonary ; but her
name is not unknown even in Latin Hymnology. The earliest
Latin poem that recognizes her is a fragment of three stanzas,
beginning with the letters X, Y, Z, respectively. It appears to
have belonged to an A B C Darian hymn of a somewhat biographical nature.—[See *Anecdota* etc., 1713 : Leabhar Imuinn : Dublin,
1855-1869.] The following Latin lines give us the earliest conceptions of this " Mary of the Gael." :—

> Ymnus iste angelicae
> Summeque sanctae Brigidae
> Fari non valet omnia
> Virtutum miribillia
> Quae nostris nunquam auribus
> Si sint facta audivimus
> Nisi per istam virginem
> Mariae sanctae similem.

Of this the following English rendering may be given :—
" This hymn, of the most angel like and most saintly, Brigit is
unable to speak of all the marvellous works of power, such as we
have never heard of as been wrought, except through this virgin,
like unto the Holy Mary."

The prevalence of Brigit's name in Gaelic Hagiology is not
surprising, when we take into account her reputation for superior
powers of knowledge and wisdom. And this exceptional distinction naturally suggests the question—Where could her superior
learning have been obtained ? The writer thinks that it can be
clearly established that Brigit, like Patrick of Strathclyde, was a
fruit of Ninian's celebrated monastery of Rosnat. Indeed,
there can be little doubt about this statement, although the
question has not been either put or answered hitherto. Philology
and history combine to make Brigit a native of that district known
first as that of the Brigantes, afterwards Bernicia, and later as the
Saxon Lowlands of Scotland. Professor Rhys thinks the folks
of this district in Brigit's time were Celtic and largely Cymric :—
" Thus the term Bernicii would seem to have meant the people of
the Brigantian land, which, in this case, was mostly that of the

ancient Otadini, or Gododin of Welsh literature, together with a
part probably of that of a kindred people, the Dumnonii." According to the same learned authority *brigant* is phonologically
" the Gallo-Brythonic form of a common Celtic *brigant*, which,
with the nasal suppressed, we have in the Irish name Brigit (for
Brigentis of the I declension), St. Bridget or Bride. On the whole
then, Brigantes would seem to have meant the free men or privil-
eged race as contrasted with the Goidelic inhabitants, *some of
whom* they may have reduced under them."

The Gaelic entries in the Book of Deer give us the name of
Brigit in compound forms, with which we are familiar. "Domnal
mac giric 7 mal *brigte*," *(Domnal* son of Girec, *and Maelbrigte).*
In the old Gaelic genitive this term is " moilbrigtae." The Latin
rendering has been "calvus Brigittae ;" similar to this is again
·· Servus Brigittae,'' or " Gillabrighde," as found in the Four
Masters, A.D. 1146. And it ought not to be forgotten that as
Columba's name has been perpetuated in that of the Clan Calum
so has that of Brigit in Gaelic Scotland been preserved in the
name of MacBride.

We have thus traced all that is actually known of Brigit in
philology and authentic history. But it is in poetry and fabulous
biography that her figure becomes haloed over with the interest of
romance and the veneration of ages.

Brigit herself was regarded as a poetess, and as we have already
seen, a MS. in the Burgundian Library has preserved a poem attributed to her. This poem was probably the production of a
Gaelic bard of "the time of Aengus" *Ceile De* ; but the ascription
of it to Brigit recalls her poetic reputation ; while its sentiments
reveal some of the inward life of the old Gaelic Church of Ireland
and Scotland. The first stanza runs thus in the original :—

> " Ropadh maith lem corm-lind mór.
> Do righ na righ,
> Ropadh maith lem muinnter nimhe
> Acca hòl tre bithe sir."

English :

> I should like a great lake of ale
> For the King of the Kings ;
> I should like the family of heaven
> To be drinking if through time eternal.

> I should like the viands
> Of belief and pure piety ;
> I should like flails
> Of penance at my house.

4

I should like the men of Heaven
In my own house ;
I should like kieves
Of peace to be at their disposal.

I should like vessels
Of charity for distribution ;
I should like caves
Of mercy for their company.

I should like cheerfulness
To be in their drinking ;
I should like Jesus
Too, to be here (among them).

I should like the three
Marys of illustrious renown ;
I should like the people
Of heaven there from all parts.

I should like that I should be
A rent-payer to the Lord :
That should I suffer distress,
He would bestow upon me a good blessing.

This production is peculiarly Celtic ; and is remarkable in its freedom from the growth of superstition which characterised the Latin Church of the time. But it must not be supposed that the old Gaelic Church was free from an external growth of a super-stition of its own. Indeed it set up rather a hagiology of its own in oppositiion to that of Rome, so keen, like all the true Scots that its members were, was its love of spiritual independence. Patrick, Columba, and Columbanus, became its *Papae*, or Papes, and Brigit herself its Virgin,—celebrated as the " Mary of the Gael."

Brigit was a very great and saintly personage to several of the authors of the Gaelic Hymns in the *Liber Hymnorum.* Ultán of Ard Breccain, who is said to have died in A.D. 656, composed a special " Hymn in praise of Brigit," whose extravagant sentiments and poetic power are but inadequately manifest in the following translation :—

Brigit, excellent woman,
A flame golden, delightful,
May (she), the sun dazzling splendid
Bear us to the eternal kingdom !
May Brigit save us
Beyond throngs of demons !
May she overthrow before us
Battles of every disease !

> May she destroy within us
> Our flesh's taxes,
> The branch with blossoms,
> The mother of Jesus !
> The true virgin, dear,
> With vast dignity :
> May we be safe always,
> With my Saint of the Lagenians !
> One of the pillars of the Kingdom,
> With Patrick the pre-eminent,
> The garment over *liga*,
> The Queen of Queens !
> Let our bodies after old age
> Be in sackloth :
> With her grace may Brigit
> Rain on us, save us !

In Colman's Hymn she is as usual associated with '' Patron Patrick with Erin's saints around him." The blessing pronounced 'on the sacred person of Brigit runs thus :

> A blessing on Patron Brigit
> With Erin's virgins around her :
> Let all give—a fair story—
> A blessing on Brigit's dignity.

The chief poetic tribute to Brigit's name is ascribed to Broccán Cloen, who flourished about A.D. 500. The first verse in the original runs thus :

> Nicar brigit buadach bith
> ' Siasair suide eoin inailt
> Contuil cotlud cimmeda
> Indnòib arecnairc ammaicc.

English :

> Victorious Brigit loved not the world :
> She sat at a seat of a bird on a cliff :
> The holy one slept a captive's sleep
> Because of her Son's absence.

The bard then proceeds to describe her virtues in more than two hundred lines of rich and glowing language.

> She was not a carper, she was not vile,
> She loved not vehement woman's ear :
> She was not a serpent violent, speckled :
> She sold not God's Son for gain.

We are told that it was in a "good hour MacCaille set the veil on Saint Brigit's head." The poet concludes his hymn of praise with the consolatory reflection :—

There are two nuns in heaven,
Whom I rely on for my protection,
Mary and Saint Brigit :
Under the protection of them both be we !

The life of Brigit printed by Dr Stokes from the Lebar Brecc, a manuscript of the fifteenth century, occupies about eighteen printed pages. Like Adamnan's life of Columba it is largely taken up with legends and traditional memories of miracles. Here is a specimen of this standard Gaelic of the 15th century :

Fecht and dorothlaig araile bannscal íressach codubthach condigsead brigit lea amuig life. arbói comthinól senaid laigen and.

The passage beginning with this sentence is translated thus :

Once upon a time a certain faithful woman asked Dubthach that Brigit might go in with her into the plain of the Liffey, for a congregation of the Synod of Leinster was held there. And it was revealed in a vision to a certain holy man who was in the assembly, that Mary the Virgin was coming thereto, and it was told him that she would not be (accompanied) by a man in the assembly. On the morrow came the woman to the assembly, and Brigit along with her. And he that had seen the vision said " This is the Mary that I beheld !" saith he to Brigit. The holy Brigit blessed all the hosts under the name and honour of Mary. Wherefore Brigit was (called) " the Mary of the Gael " thenceforward.

The last sentence in the original is as follows :—

Conidhi brigit muire nangædel ósin ille.

Dr Stokes points out how this life of Brigit furnishes a good " example of the way in which heathen mythological legends became annexed to historical Christian saints." He shows how the story of Brigit, in many of its recorded incidents, belonged originally to the myth or ritual of some goddess of fire. In proof of this the following incidents in the life are referred to : Brigit was born at sunrise ; and her name, in cognate Sanskrit *Bhargas* is associated, it is thought, with fire. Her birth takes place neither within nor without a house. She is bathed in milk. Her breath revives the dead. A house in which she is staying flames up to heaven. Cowdung blazes in her presence. Oil is poured on her head. The milk she is fed with comes from a white, red-eared cow. A fiery pillar is seen rising from her head. Her wet cloak is supported by sun-rays. And while she remains a virgin, she is yet

described as one of the two mothers of Christ the Anointed One.
Other authorities have described her as having perpetual ashless
fire, which was watched by twenty nuns, of whom she herself was
one, blown by fans or bellows only, and surrounded by a hedge,
within which no male could enter.

Various other interesting allusions, illustrative of the ancient
institutions of Gaeldom, are made in this life, such as the purchase
and sale of slaves, mulcts, *(eric)*, witchcraft, dowry. We are also
reminded that leprosy once existed in Ireland ; that Gaels practised
ale-brewing ; that jewellery was in use ; and that wattling was
employed for buildings.

But further discussion of these matters must be left to a future
volume. In the meantime, the writer's best wishes for all who
hear of the name of Brigit, are that they may all be endowed with
the moral beauty, goodness, and dignity, which have been assigned
to the godly *Mary of the Gael.*

CHAPTER III.

THE presence of the Romans in Scotland produced very little effect in the Highlands. Fringes of the eastern counties had been occupied for brief periods of time ; but the influence of Latin civilisation was slight and transient. The Christian churches that had begun to flourish in the Gaelic lowlands under Roman rule showed signs of decay upon the withdrawal of the Imperial legions which at first were a sort of protection to the somewhat feeble Christianity of the earlier ages. The chief source of weakness to this Christianity was the fact that it had not yet struck its roots deeply into the independent soil of the native races. A more virile gospel of natural native growth was needed. And this was now about to be proclaimed by a man whose name is associated with the most brilliant period and best aspirations of the history of the Highland people.

This man was Calum, the son of Feidlimidh, son of Fergus, son of Niall, of the " Nine Hostages," monarch of Erin, who was slain in the year 405. He was thus of blood-royal on the father's side ; while his mother Ethne was also of a princely house. He was born about the year 52ø at Gartan, in the county of Donegal. His people in these northern Highlands of Ireland, belonged to the same race that prevailed at this period in the southern Highlands of Scotland ; so in crossing the sea to the islands of Argyllshire Columba merely sailed from one Gaelic country to another. He was a man highly regarded in both countries on account of his family connections among the powerful ruling races on both sides of the sea. Before proceeding to detail the better authenticated and the more suggestive events of his life, it may help to remove some historical misconceptions and show more vividly the field of Columba's operations, if we glance at the condition of the various races with whom he came in contact, and at their relations to one another.

When the Highland people first emerge on the canvas of written records within their present limits, it is in connection with the proclamation of Christianity among them. We previously get a glance of their valiant clans in the great national struggle with the aggressive legions of Rome. The brave soldiers of these legions with which the Caledonians strove, were in the main of the same race as those to whom they were opposed. They belonged to the powerful clan Chatti of ancient Batavia, the modern Netherlands, where the Romans fixed their base for operations in Britain. It was these Batavian Celts with their better weapons, and not Latin soldiers, that fought the ancient Highlanders of the eastern counties. Centuries passed after this great battle between the Celts of Albin and those of Batavia who were in Roman pay. Then again the clans of the north came distinctly into view when the star of Christianity arose in the west. The sources of our information at this point, are the uncertain references of classical writers on the one hand—references which require careful sifting—and the vague glimpses of native Christian writers on the other.

It·is not to be expected that these sources would supply us with anything like a correct ethnological account. We may feel certain that race theories in the sixth century were at least as confusing and mistaken as they are in the present day even among fairly educated people. So it is only by a careful induction and much critical attention, that an approximation to the truth can be arrived at out of those classical passages and sentences which have been so severely tortured and twisted by Gaels and Goths, Brythons, and Teutons. Much choleric temper has extended itself over those ancient fields. In recent times sorely debated questions, however, have changed faces, and historians have become more humane. The Christ breath of the sentiment of human brother-hood has very largely soothed the racial asperities with which the wars of the Picts and the Scots have been fought again and again.

There is one phase of the history of those early centuries, which he who runs may read now, and in which the Highland people are naturally very much interested. It has come distinctly into view as the result of able discussions during the last ten years. The Celtic period of our national history used to receive very scant attention indeed at the hands of the recognised writers on such subjects. Our latest historians have shown a spirit of greater fairness. The first volume of Burton's " History of Scotland " may be said to be devoted to the Celtic period ; and, with the exception of the writer's evident anxiety to find the paternity of the higher influences of civilisation in Teutonic fields, may be re-garded as a fair representation of the events of the centuries described. Even the publication of such a work as Skene's "Celtic Scotland," bearing so suggestive a title, is a fact of much significance. A learned if not always discriminating volume, " Celtic Ireland," by Dr Sophie Bryant, has also just been published.

In the fifth and sixth centuries we are confronted with a group of races in north Britain which have formed the subject of bitter and exhaustive controversies. The terms " Pict " and " Scot " are the chief monuments of this fierce warfare. No one can pretend to say now who the races are of whom these terms are the exponents. They were bestowed on the people by outsiders, and are quite unknown in the native literature of the country. It is highly probable that they indicate personal characteristics such as dress rather than race. The clans or tribes to whom they were applied have been found all over north Britain and the north of Ireland at different times. To translate them into native terms will only make the confusion already existing more hopeless. To render *Pict* by " Cruthnec " would be as inaccurate as to render *Scot* by " Gàidheal." The most helpful way in which we can arrive at a fairly satisfactory conclusion at present is to take a brief survey of the various races from a Gaelic standpoint ; keeping the main results of ethnological inquiry before our minds. From this position the use of the terms " Pict " and " Scot " must be altogether discarded. Let us examine the terms which the Gaelic language supplies :—

1. *Albannaich.*—Who were or are the *Albannaich ?* The word has come from Albainn or Albin, and is now generally used to distinguish a Scotsman, whether Highland or Lowland, from the *Eirionnach* of Ireland and the *Sasunnach* of England. The application of Albion to the largest of these islands retreated in the course of centuries to the north-west, where it still indicated the presence of the pre-Celtic settlers who gave the name to the island. The occasional application of it by Celtic writers to southern districts, even as far south-west as the Isle of Wight, or the sea of Ictis, prevailed as late as the eleventh and twelfth centuries. *Albannaich*, or people of a distinctively pre-Celtic character still survived in the west, particularly in south Wales and Cornwall. In the time of Columba the *Albannaich* proper possessed and ruled the country from Drum-Albin northwards. The language they spoke is unknown.

2. *Gaidheil.*—" Gaidheil Alba " is an expression which indicates, what we otherwise know, that the *Gaidheil* were immigrants to the country of the Albinians. The precise term for the land inhabited

by themselves is "Gàidhealtachd," the application of which suggests that it is a part or district of Albin. A similar expression is "Gàidheil Eirin," which shows that Ireland is not more peculiarly the land of the Gael than Scotland ; indeed like "Scots" it is only in the latter that *the* "Gaels," emphatically "na Gàidheil," can be found. When we first know them in north Britain we see them in possession of the south-west Highlands and the Strathclyde valleys. Their Gaelic tongue prevailed south of Drum-Albin, and particularly in the fourth and fifth centuries, in that district or county to which they have given its name, Argyll. They were driven to Ireland in earlier times as well as into the Argyllshire Highlands under the pressure of the Brythons on the south-east, mixed up with, and supported by, the Romans and Roman rule.

3. *Bretunnaich.*—At the time of Columba men of this race pushed as far west as the Clyde. They have left a memorial of their presence in that ancient capital of their rule, Dunbreton, or Dumbarton. There were, no doubt, many Gaels still in the district, although the Brythons asserted for some time a supremacy ; and the former reasserted their presence before the valleys of the Clyde became finally Saxon in language.

4. *Sasunnaich.*—In the land of the Gael very little was known of the *Sasunnaich* when Columba landed in Argyllshire. They were well known to the *Bretunnaich* on the eastern shores, where they had for some time established themselves. But to the Gaels in the west they were as yet a mere shadowy name.

Columba's missionary enterprises were carried on among the Gaels of the southern Highlands and the Albinians of the north-west. The two languages in which he could freely and eloquently preach were Gaelic and Latin, so among the Gaels he found himself at once at home among a kindred people, many of whom had already heard of Christianity. Among the Albinians of the north-west neither his Gaelic nor his Latin could serve him ; and he had to engage an interpreter, who must have been familiar with Gaelic and Albinic. With the Christianising of the north-west the area of Gaelic speech extended, and Albinic gradually became extinct.

The advent of Columba on the shores of the Highlands constitutes a new era in the national history. In the centuries which elapsed from his time 553-97 to that of Queen Margaret 1c57-93, some 500 years, we have the truly Celtic period of Scottish national life. In the course of the preceding 500 years the Romans occupied large tracts of Scottish territory ; and after the withdrawal of their legions the Albinians maintained a powerful rule in the north-west ; so the Gaels had not as yet played so visible a part on the national canvas. Now, however, with the evangelisation of the country by Columba the Gaels, whose language became the organ of sacred eloquence, appeared as the prevailing people.

The conclusions established by the following facts deserve dis- tinct attention in our conceptions of our national history : —

1. That the Gaels were the prevailing race in north Britain for 500 years previous to the reign of Malcolm Canmore.

2. That during these centuries the Gaelic language was used in Court and church, and was the national speech of the people, even when an English dialect began to develop on the east coast and a Norse one temporarily prevailed in the western islands.

3. That a native Gaelic church flourished during this half millennium.

4. That it was during these centuries that the permanent founda- tions of our Scottish independence and nationality were laid, in the midst of many fierce struggles and bitter sorrows, and by means of many battles and much bloodshed. It was the Gaelic conquests of this period that paved the way for the national throne which Kenneth MacAlpine ascended, and which exercised sway in the north until its power merged in that of the British Empire upwards of a thousand years after the gospel was proclaimed by Columba in the Hebrides.

The missionary advent of Columba, or in his own native langu- age, *Calum*, on the south western shores of the Highlands consti- tutes one of the earliest and chief dates of our national history The evangelical succession of his Christianity has been traced in two directions. One source has been already touched upon, the Church of Ninian from which Patrick went forth to evangelize the north of Ireland. The mother home of this branch of Celtic Christianity was undoubtedly Ninian's celebrated monastery of Rosnat, which is mentioned under several designations, of which " Candida Casa " is the best known. Other names are the " Mag- num Monasterium," " Alba " and " Futerna," the latter being the Gaelic equivalent for the Anglic " Whithern." Abbots and bis- hops trained in this renowned monastery laboured in Ulster ; and founded monasteries there. The last of this family of ecclesiastics was Finian of the race of Dal Fiatach. This is acknowledged to be the first channel through which Monachism was introduced into Ireland, the personal links in the communication being Martin of Tours and Ninian. The second channel, as well shown by Dr Skene, was through Bretagne and Wales, the personal links in this case being "David, Gillas, and Docus, the Britons," otherwise David, the patron saint of the Welsh, Gildas, the historian, and Cadoc, the founder of Llancarvan in South Wales. Finian, an Irish Pict, repaired to the monastery of Kilmuine, or Manavia, in Wales, and became the pupil of these three distinguished men ; and on his return to Ireland founded in course of time the well-known monastery of Clonard in Meath, the Gaelic *Cluainerard*, where no less than three thousand monks are supposed to have been at one time under training. This became the source of living Christianity in the south-west of Ireland after the time of Patrick. Finian had twelve followers of celebrated name, who have been designated the twelve Apostles of Ireland. Their names run as follow :—

1. *Ciaran*, the founder of the Saighir monastery in Munster.

2. *Ciaran*, called "Mac-an-t-Saoir," the "Artificer's son," founder of Clonmacnois, in King's County, in 548.

3. *Columba*, son of Crimthan of Leinster, founder of Tirrdaglas in 548.

4 *Mobhi Clairenach*, founder of Glasnevin, in Fingall.

5. *Ninnidh*, of Loch Erne.

6. *Brendan*, of Birr.

7. *Brendan*, of the seven years' voyage, founder of Clonfert.

8. *Luisren* or *Molaisse*, of Devenish.

9. *Ruadhan*, of Lothra.

10. *Senell*, of Cluain-innis.

11. *Cainnech*, of Achabo.

12. *Columba*, of Iona.

With the exception of Brendan of Birr, Cainnech of Achabo, and the great Finian himself, who were of the Erinic race, all these were of the Gaelic race.

Highlanders cannot help feeling much interested in the main facts of Columba's life. The exact date of his birth, ascertained is fixed on the 7th of December, 521. He was baptised by the Presbyter Cruithnechan, and the church of his youth was *Tulach-dubh-glaise*, now Temple Douglas, where his frequent attendance procured him the title "Calum-cille" or "Calum of the Church." In due time he became the pupil of Finnbarr, or Finian of Magh-bile, where he was ordained a deacon. He acquired taste for general literature under the instruction of the bard Gemman. He completed his academic training under Finian of Clonard, when he became one of the twelve apostles of Ireland. In his religious course of instruction the influences of the two British monasteries of Candida Casa and Menavia met in the persons of the two Finians, respectfully of Maghbile and Clonard. About the year 545 he founded the monastery of Derry, or of Daire, and afterwards that of Raphoe in Donegal. Ten years after the date of the foundation of the church of Derry he started the celebrated religious centre of Durrow or *Daire-May*, distinguished by the profusion of oaks with which it was surrounded. Cennanus, or Kells, in Meath, is also associated with his name, as well as a large number of less famous churches scattered over many other counties.

This is the man who was about to Christianise the north-west of Scotland, as well as give a fresh impulse to the great missionary enterprises of the Celtic Church. Christianity was not altogether unknown in the Western Isles before his arrival. The saintly voyager, Brendan, one of his contemporaries, had been heard of in these regions upwards of twenty years before the arrival of Columba ; and left traces of his presence in Bute and the Garvelloch Isles, where his name has come down to us in that designation of Rothesay folks, *Brandanes*, as well as in Kil*brandan* Sound. He is also reported to have visited the island of Heth or Tyree.

The departure of Columba from Ireland for the Scottish coast was probably the result of mixed motives. He appears to have been implicated in some sanguinary struggle, particularly the battle of Culdremhne ; how far it is impossible now satisfactorily to ascertain. We are informed by Adamnan that the excommunication pronounced by the Synod of Taillte in Meath was for pardonable and trifling reasons. The silly story about the transcription of the Psalter, and the judgment about the cow and its calf are unworthy of the persons concerned and of the Christianity of the period. The so-called sentence of exile does not bear the criticism of common sense ; and is the product of very credulous times. That the heart of Columba yearned for the conversion of his kindred across the sea is highly credible and natural. Political motives may have entered into his thought ; but we may generally accept the impression of one of his biographers,—" his native country was left by the illustrious saint and illustrious sage, and son chosen of God for the love and favour of Christ."

In the year 563 Columba, in the forty-second year of his age, left Ireland for Scotland. The island of Colonsay was the first soil on which he landed ; but finding that he was still within eight miles of Ireland he sailed further north to Ia or the *Iouan* island, where he fixed his abode. He was accompanied by " twelve disciples, his fellow soldiers," in the fashion of the missionaries of the Celtic Church who went forth in their twelves, sometimes in their twenty-fours. At first on arrival at Colonsay these devoted brethren thought they had sailed far enough from Ireland and raised *Carn cul ri Kirin* ; but a clearer horizon soon revealed to them their mistake. On the nearest elevation in Iona they raised a similar *Carn* bearing the same title, and they were now satisfied that they had sailed far enough north from their native place, the vision of which could not tempt them to return. Had they been able to anticipate the power of modern glasses they would find that Ireland was still within their sight. The date of their arrival in Iona was Whitsuneve, which that year fell on the 12th of May.

The name of Iona is a source of everlasting charm all over the Christian world. Let us form to ourselves some conception of its position, size, and character. In his voyage to this islet Columba sailed by the fertile and lowlying shores of Islay, whence the high lands of the north of Ireland can be easily seen in the hazy distance. He landed on the lonely Colonsay, but stayed not there. Further north he found his future home. This was that isle of fame and beauty, situated at the south-west corner of the island of Mull.

Iona is separated from the Ross of Mull by a channel about a mile wide, in which the heavy swell of the ocean sometimes rolls unkindly for tiny barks. This channel is deep enough for the passage of the largest ships, but is not free from danger on account of sunken rocks. The island itself lies north-east and south-west ; and is about three and one-half miles in length, and a mile and a half in breadth. Its area is about two thousand acres, of which some six hundred are generally under cultivation, the rest being either pasture or barren. To see its northern end, as the writer first saw it, gleaming under the morning sun,—-its brows of sand flashing their radiance afar,—produces an impression that does not readily vanish. The diapason of the Atlantic and the responsive chorus of the seashores help to charm and soothe while they solemnize the human spirit. There truly you can find the spirit of nature's religion chanting lightly her morning hymns and rehearsing sweetly her evening psalms. A plain extends from side to side, at the narrowest part, in the centre of the island, with a small green hillock in its centre. In this part of it the soil is fairly fertile ; but towards the north the ground becomes rougher with grassy hollows and rocky rising-knolls which end in the highest point in the island, Dun-I, 327 feet in height. From that eminence north a strip of low land extends to the shore, terminating in a stretch of white sand, which is composed chiefly of broken shells which the swell of the ocean has rolled and wasted and worn together until it heaped them there. Along the east side of the island the ground is low-lying and fertile. South of the central plain the surface of the soil is irregular, showing stony heights and grassy dells, which afford good pasture. The shore abounds with little bays and headlands. The underlying rocks are Laurentian, with an almost vertical dip, and a strike from north-east to south-west. There are beds of slate, quartz, marble, with serpentine, and a mixture of felspar, quartz, and hornblende passing sometimes into a sort of granite. This is the island of which the proverbial saying has made Columba so tenderly sing :

"I mo chridhe, I mo ghràidh."
(Isle of my heart, Isle of my love.)

The name of Iona has appeared under a large variety of forms. The single capital letter I has stood for it, which pronounced like double *ee* as Gaelic requires, represents the universal Gaelic pronunciation for the island. Here are some of the other forms : Ia, Ie, Ii, Ieoa ; Hi, Hii ; Y, Hy ; Iona, Yona, Hyona, and Yensis ; I Chalumchille and Icolmkill. In Adamnan it appears as the *Iouan* island. This is an adjectival form in which the radix is Iou, equivalent to the Gaelic I. Adamnan's Iouan was corrupted by the mistake of transcribers into the more euphonious Iona, an explanation which shows, the untenableness of such fanciful etymologies as I-thonna, "the island of waves," and *I shona*, "the island of the blest."

These were some of the peculiar developments of the Brito-Irish Church from whose bosom Columba came. The monasteries were usually located on grants of land, often very extensively made by the provincial kings or other chiefs who had been converted to Christianity, and desired to have the worship of God set up among their people, and thus became identified with the clan or tribe in which they were settled. It is in connection with these temporalities that the remarkable functionary called Co-arb comes into view. He appears to have been a person of greater consequence than the bishop, and to have exercised ecclesiastical as well as temporal power. Dr Todd defines his position and functions thus :--" On the whole it appears that the endowment in land, which were granted to the ancient church by the chieftains who were first converted into Christianity, carried with them the temporal rights and principalities originally belonging to the owners of the soil, and that these rights and principalities were vested, not in bishops as such, but in the co-arbs or ecclesiastical successors of those saints to whom the grants of land were originally made. In other words, the Co-arbs became the trustees of the temporalities of the monasteries and of the missionary enterprises of the church. They were the predecessors of those who in our own times hold property in trust for our training schools, colleges, churches, and missionary societies. There were no mines, docks, or railways in which shares could be held ; but the chieftain and his clan had real property at their disposal which in their piety and generosity they set apart, as occasion required, for the support of the gospel. The property the earnest-souled monks soon transformed into a centre of holy activity and Christian civilization."

Columba with his family of Christian brethren in Iona, labouring with hand and head ; studying, writing, and praying ; and sending forth to neighbouring lands and islands Christian workers whose hearts God had touched, formed a beautiful picture of pious effort which deeply impressed the imagination of succeeding ages. This band of ancient Gaelic Christians became known in course of time under the endearing designation of " The Family of Iona." The goodly number of twelve disciples accompanied Columba to Iona, the number being that usually sent forth together to labour in a district in imitation of the accidental features of the apostolic system. The names of the twelve brethren were Baithen, and Cobthach, brothers ; Ernaan, the uncle, and Diarmit the attendant of Columba; Rus and Fechno, brothers; Scandal, Luguid, Eachaid, Tochann, Cairnaan, and Grillaan.

Iona as a religious centre for the evangelising efforts of these brethren was admirably situated. It was on the confines of the Albinic and Gaelic jurisdiction. It was granted to Columba first by Conall, King of the Gaels, who were largely Christians. The great missionary also secured the grant by getting the approval of King Brude of the Albinians, whom he visited soon after his settlement at Iona. This visit to the king was paid at his fortress at the mouth of the Ness, and was afterwards repeated several times, which evinces the unchanging character of the friendship which existed between the king and the saint.

The interesting story of Columba's missionary labours in converting the Albinians and in reviving the drooping Christianity of the Gaels belongs to the province of Church history and can only be glanced at here as a fresh transforming factor which entered deeply into the civil life of the people. It was no doubt the determining influence in the historic process which ended in Kenneth's accession to the united throne in 843. Combined with the superior knowledge of letters, this factor of Christianity facilitated the Gaelic conquest of Albin. The struggle described in the popular ballads of the Finians was a real one—in which the heathen and decadent Féinne, the brave and chivalrous people of Ossian went forth against the psalm-singing forces of Christian clerics, but they always went forth to fall and die. The Gaelic and Christian conquest of the Albinians or Féinne was complete with the union of the two races in the ninth century. All through the struggle the members of "The Family of Iona" played a prominent part.

They had travelled north and east, earnestly labouring among the various clans and tribes, and founding churches and colleges which became not only Christianising but nationalising centres, and so preparing the way for the extension of Gaelic rule. When the proper opportunity came the nations were evidently well prepared for a fusion which appears to have been very thorough.

Judging by the number of churches which they founded, and the wide tracts of country over which their labours extended, the Family of Iona must have had a very earnest and successful brotherhood. The northern half of England was Christianised by men who went forth from Iona, a fact which, it is pleasant to notice, is specially acknowledged in the Dictionary of English History recently published.

It is to the Family of Iona we are also indebted for the first literary products to which we can refer. They were the first to love and cultivate the literature which we now so highly prize. If there were any such pre-Christian bards as Ossian, it is to the ancient clerics that we are indebted for the preservation of their compositions. Indeed it is a question whether the knowledge of the forms of poetry existed at all in pre-Christian times. There is no evidence that we posess a scrap of ancient poetry which belongs to ages before Christian pens began to cultivate letters. The brethren in Iona were much engaged in writing, which as an accomplishment was considered as an adornment even for the highest Church dignitaries. And great value was attached evidently to the products of their pens. The transcription of sacred

literature, particularly of the Psalter, occupied much of their time.
Columba himself was engaged in this work when death took him.
To be a ready *scribhnidh*, or scribe, was an object of worthy ambition. The position of *ferleighin*, or praelector, was one of
honour in the sacred brotherhood. Many of the terms used by
them in connection with letters have come down to us ; others
have been lost, or have since their time received different meanings
and applications. Columba's Stylus, or pen, was called in Gaelic
graib, from the Greek *graphium* ; but the *graib* of modern times
is an agricultural implement. A very poetic legend tells how this
stylus of Columba became the property of Gregory of Rome.
The leather cases in which the service books were kept for travelling were called *polire* and *tiagha*. The alphabet they styled
abgiter a form which has considerable philologic value ; according
to one authority Columba's *abgiter* was written on a cake. These
waxed tablets for writing introduced *ceir* from the Latin cera. The
library was *teach screaptra* ; and its keeper *leabhor coimhedach*.
These and many other terms once current in Gaelic literature, introduced by the Gaelic clerics in the British Isles and on the
Continent, ceased to be used in the centuries of greater ignorance
which succeeded their times.

In their ancient 'writings and lives occur many other terms
which have their value in shedding light on the social habits and
condition of the people. The family of Iona had their kitchen,
cuicin, or *coitchenn* ; in which the coquina, *coic*, or cook prepared
the meals of the brethren. Their chief season in the day time was
nona, or *noin*, still occasionally heard in *tra-noin*. Their cows
were sheltered in an outhouse, the Bocetum, or *bathaich* ; and in
the neighbourhood was the pasture-ground, or *buaile*. The grain
was stored in the barn, or, *sabhall*, the Gaelic term still in use.
They had also their Molendinum or *Muileann*, in which the grain
was ground by the *bra*, or quern. A caballus, a *capull*, or *gerran*,
was kept on the *faithche*, or green enclosure near at hand to be in
readiness for general purposes. When they wanted to move
along the shores they had their curucae, or *curraich*, whose light
frames covered with skins could so easily glide through the water.
For distant voyages and other purposes they had the scaphae, or
scadhan, still applied to a certain class of boats. Visitors and
guests from far-off lands arrived in their barcae, or, *barcan*, a term
still current in Gaelic. The Scologs, or lower order of the clergy
did not refuse to help the *Economus*, or *fertighis*, the butler, or
pincerna, or the baker, or *pistor*. It is curious to find that on one

occasion the baker was a stray Saxon. There were also among the brethren in Iona a smith, or *gobha*, and a brazier, or *cerd*, which in recent Gaelic has become a term of reproach. The term for one article of their dress at least, *cochall*, the Latin cuculla, had survived in familiar Gaelic. It is represented that the hardy brethren slept on the bare stones, and in their ordinary day clothes. They were truly a *Milesian* or soldier race, who by their persistent labours and self-sacrifices thoroughly deserved the name and fame which after ages accorded them.

While the name of Columba is that which shines above all the rest there were other labourers in the Highlands before, and contemporaneously with him who have left behind them illustrious memories, fragrant names which have entered very largely into the nomenclature of the soil. Brendan has been already referred to. Others like him made missionary journeys through the country, such as the two Fillans, Flannan, and Ronan, whose names are commemorated in the Highlands and Isles. Moluoc became the founder and celebrated patron of Lismore; and Kilmaluac in Tiree has preserved his memory. His death took place in 592. Maelrubha's labours are chiefly associated with Wester Ross, but he was honoured all over the Highlands. In 673 he founded a church and college at Applecross where he laboured zealously till he "rested," as the chronicles say, in 722 in the eightieth year of his age. He and Columba were the chief patron saints of Skye. The north-eastern part of the island was peculiar to Columba, the south-eastern to Maelrubha whose name survives in Kilmaree in Strath, and in Kilmolruy in Bracadale. As far south as Islay we find him venerated in the central parish of that Island, in Killarrow, where he may have laboured on his way from Ireland before he settled at Applecross Another heroic character in the same age was Donnan whose brave spirit and individuality have evoked admiration throughout the whole of Scotland. He was younger than Columba whom he regarded with ardent feelings of friendship, and among whose Christian family at Iona he desired to be enrolled. "This Donnan went to Columcille to make him his soul's friend; upon which Columcille said to him, I shall not be soul's-friend to a company (heirs) of red martyrdom, and thy people with thee. And it was so fulfilled." In the far north his figure emerges in *cric Chat*, or "regions of Catt," which included Sutherland and Caithness. The parish bearing his name, Kildonan, was the chief scene of his enterprise in the north. He closed his life truly in "red martyrdom" in the island of Eigg.

" To glorious martyrdom ascended,
With his clerics of pure lives,
Donnan of cold Eig."

An account already quoted says—" Donnan then went with his
people to the Hebrides ; and they took up their abode there, in a
place where the sheep of the queen of the country were kept.
This was told to the queen. Let them all be killed said she.
That would not be a religious act, said her people. But they were
murderously assailed. At this time the cleric was at mass. Let
us have respite till mass is ended, said Donnan. Thou shalt have
it, said they. And when it was over, they were slain every one of
them." Another version runs thus : " Donnan the great with his
monks. Fifty-two were his congregation. There came pirates of
the sea to the island in which they were, and slew them all. Eig
is the name of that island." In these west Highlands his memory
was preserved in Little Bernera, off Lewis, in South Uist, Loch
Broom, and Snizort, Skye, in each of which Kildonnans are found.
In the southern Highlands in Arran and Kintyre as well as in
Wigtonshire and Ayrshire we come across Kildonnans, or churches
dedicated to his memory. At Auchterloss in Aberdeenshire his
pastoral staff was preserved until it was broken by the Reformers.
His martyrdom took place on Sunday the 17th of April, 617 ; and
must have, along with that of the fifty-two brethren who were with
him, cast deep gloom on the prospects of Christian enterprise in
the West Highlands.

The journeys, the holy labours with their great results, of
Columba himself, and of his brethren from Iona, have been minutely and eloquently described by various writers. The name of
the founder of Iona is associated with upwards of 60 religious establishments or places in Scotland, and with as many in Ireland.
He died on the 9th of June, 597, seventy-six years of age. And
as we think of the memory which he left behind him for the veneration of his countrymen we are reminded of the bright pillar that
was seen to glow upon his head on one occasion after reading the
Gospel in common with brethren from a distance, who visited him
in Eilein-na-Naoimh : " Brenden Mocu Alti saw, as he told
Congell and Cainnech afterwards, a ball of fire like a comet burning very brightly on the head of Columba, while he was standing
before the altar, and consecrating the holy oblation, and thus it
continued burning and rising upwards like a column so long as he
continued to be engaged in the same most sacred mysteries." So
has the name of the saint burned and risen upwards like a monu-

mental column upon the brow of Scotland. He has had a devoted, if an increduluos biographer in Adamnan, his eighth
successor in the abbacy of Iona. To this writer we are indebted
for the most ancient piece of writing produced in the Highlands
that has been preserved. His name, which has undergone several
curious transformations, has been embalmed in the designations
of eight or ten places under the modifications of Teunan, Eunan,
Arnold, Avonia, and many. It has passed into personal names
of modern times in Gill-Adhamnain, or Gilleonan, borne by a
MacNeill of Barra in 1495. Adamnan was born in 624 ; succeeded Columba in Iona in 679 ; and died on the 23d of Sept.,
704. His veneration and estimate of his great predecessor may
be gathered from the following eloquent sentences taken from the
preface of his interesting work : " From his boyhood he (Columba)
had been brought up in Christian training in the study of wisdom,
and by the grace of God had so preserved the integrity of his body,
and the purity of his soul, that though dwelling on earth he
appeared to live like the saints in heaven. For he was angelic in
appearance, graceful in speech, holy in work, with talents of the
highest order, and consummate prudence ; he lived a soldier of
Christ during thirty-four years in an island. He never could spend
the space of even one hour without study, or prayer, or writing,
or some other holy occupation. So incessantly was he engaged
night and day in the unwearied exercise of fasting and watching,
that the burden of each of these austerities would seem beyond
the power of human endurance. And still in all these he was
beloved by all, for a holy joy ever beaming on his face revealed
the joy and gladness with which the Holy Spirit filled his inmost
soul." Columba, notwithstanding the strong martial element of
his nature, was evidently capable of attaching disciples very
powerfully to his person. We find this illustrated also in the
legend preserved in the *Book of Deer* about his founding the
mission-station of Aberdour in Aberdeenshire : " *Drostan's tears
came on parting from Columcille.* Said Columcille ' Let Deur
(Deer) be its name henceforward.' "

Among the relics associated with the person of Columba is the
Cath-bhuaidh, or *Battle-Victory*, a celebrated crosier. The following passage from a legend of the ninth century reminds us of the
great veneration with which the relic was regarded, as well as of
the spirit in which his followers, three or four centuries after his
death, went forth to meet the enemies of their country. " About
the same time the Fortreens and Lochlanns fought a battle.

Bravely indeed the men of Alba fought this battle, for Columkille was aiding them ; for they had prayed to him most fervently, because he was their apostle, and it was through him that they received the faith. One time when Imhar Conung was a young man, he came to Alba, with three great battalions to plunder it. The men of Alba, both lay and clerics, fasted and prayed to morning to God and Columkille ; they made earnest entreaty to the Lord ; they gave great alms of food and raiment to the churches and the poor, received the body of the Lord at the hands of the priests, and promised to do all kinds of good works, as their clergy would order them, and that their standard in going forth to any battle should be the crosier of Columkille. Wherefore it is called the *Cath bhuaidh* from that day to this. And this is a befitting name for it ; for they have often gained victory in battle by it, as they did at that time, when they placed their hope in Columkille. They did the same on this occasion. The battle was bravely fought at once. The Albinians gained victory and triumph, killed many of the Lochlanns after their defeat ; and their king was slain on the occasion, namely, Ottir, son of Iargna. It was long after until either the Danes or Lochlanns attacked them ; but they were at peace and harmony with them."

Writers in after ages have attributed poems and prophecies to Columba which such a good authority as O'Curry declares not to be the productions of the Saint, whose chief literary functions are associated with the transcription of the sacred writings.

In his Life of the Apostle of the Highlands, Dr John Smith of Campbeltown, has given translations of some of the Latin poems attributed to Columba ; the following abstract exhibits their manner :—

" The God omnipotent, who made the world,
Is subject to no change. He was, He is,
And He shall be : th' Eternal is his name.
Equal in Godhead and eternal power,
Is Christ the Son ; so is the Holy Ghost.
These sacred glories three are but the same,
In persons different, but one God and Lord.
This God created all the heavenly hosts :
Archangels, angels, potentates, and powers ;
That so the emanations of His love
Might flow to myriads diffusing good.
But from this eminence of glory fell
Th' apostate Lucifer, elate with pride,
Of his high station and his glorious form.
Fill'd with like pride, and envying God himself,
His glory, other angels shared his fate,

> While the remainder kept their happy state.
> Thus fell a third of the bright heavenly stars,
> Involv'd in the old serpent's guilt and fate ;
> And with him suffer, in th' infernal gulf,
> The loss of heaven, in chains of darkness bound."

Further remarks on the poetry attributed to Columba will be found in the next chapter.

CHAPTER IV.

THE following entry among the Irish Charters in the famous Book of Kells, illustrates the fate of much of our ancient Celtic literature, especially in Scotland ; " Anno Domini m⁰ ui⁰ *(alius* 1c07). Soiscela mor coluim cille do dubguit is ind aidci as ind iardom iartarach in daimliacc moir cenannsa," &c. A.D. 1006 *(alius* 1007)—The great Gospel of Calum-cille was sacrilegiously stolen at night out of the western portions of the great church of Kells. This was the chief relic of the west of the world on account of the singular cover. This Gospel was found in twenty nights and two months, with its gold stolen off, and a sod over it." Thus the " great gospel " of Columba was preserved from destruction by the merest accident. But cupidity has not been the only foe that the Celt's ancient manuscript literature has had to contend with. The ignorance and indifference of many into whose hands it fell have also played their part ;—a tailor was seen last century in the Hebrides cutting down Gaelic manuscripts for patterns. More fatal than ignorance has been the active depreciation of a hostile church operating on the animosity of a rival race. It is only now—a thousand years after the era of the ancient Celtic Church —that scholars and unprejudiced historians have succeeded in showing us a little of it. The " sod over it " has been partly removed ; and the " find " has not been altogether uninteresting, although the " gold " has been " stolen off." Zeuss has furnished us with materials for the reconstruction of the ancient Celtic language ; Skene and others have given us some account of the early Iro-British Church ; but Church history has not fully examined the available existing material that would show us the character of the Christian life and devotion of our early Christian ancestors in these islands. It is proposed in the following chapter to glance at the Latin Hymns of the ancient Celtic Church in order to realise to ourselves a little of the inner life of those early evangelists to whose extraordinary labours and unwearied zeal we are indebted for the conversion of our forefathers from heathenism. In these hymns we have relics of that early religious literature which helped to give Christian comfort to generations of lonely labourers on isle and mainland.   Here we have transmitted to us something of the loving heavenly motives, the Gospel inspiration, by whose persuasive force the strongholds of pagan darkness were pulled down throughout the British islands, as well as in many districts on the Continent.

These devotional compositions were the common property of the whole Celtic Church at home and abroad   It is intended to look at them here as remains of the use and wont which prevailed during the "golden age" of this early Free Church, as it existed in Scotland.   In doing so, it may deepen our interest in them if we briefly recall the historical setting and political surroundings in which the great work of this Church was accomplished.

In order to reach the heart of this Church, we must pierce through that belt of ecclesiastical and religious darkness which Papal Rome wove round the body of our national life during the four centuries which preceeded the Reformation.   Beyond these centuries we are enabled at once to grasp that one outstanding fact in our early annals, that from the days of Ninyas, in the beginning of the fifth century, to the accession of the "Sair Saint," King David, in 1124 a Free Church, comparatively evangelical and aggressive, existed in Scotland for a period of 700 years.   No definite attempt has been made to show the full national significance of this fact.   If we contrast that period of 700 years with the following period of similar length, we find that during the first half of the latter, decay and death prevailed ; and that even during the second half, with all the advantages attendant on post-Reformation times, large tracts of our country, once aglow with gospel life, remained practically heathen until the lost ground began to be reconquered and reclaimed by the modern Free Church of Scotland.⁘ In all this there is much to humble, instruct and encourage us.   We learn that the essential power of the gospel is the same in all ages, and that similar results follow the earnest proclamation of truth in ancient and modern times.   The Christian men that in early days made the gospel a living converting power throughout our whole land, even in every village of the Highlands, and every islet of the Hebrides, could not have been very unlike their countrymen of the present day, among whom evangelical truth is preserved and preached.

A glance at the early history of Ireland reveals the fact that a similar course of things took place there.   Pope Adrian IV.,

known to England as Nicolas Breakspere, the only Englishman
who ever sat in the chair of St. Peter, issued a bill in 1155, giving
the kingdom of Ireland to Henry II. of England. This is a remarkable fact, and deeply suggestive in connection with the
reasons assigned for its accomplishment. The Irish had all along
been Protestants against Rome and her rule. The Pope, who
like all the bishops of that holy ilk, claimed the right to dispose
of all Christian lands, finding that the Irish, according to Roman
estimate, were "Schismatics" and "bad Christians," like their
brethren of the same period in Scotland, made a present of the
island to Henry, in order to make good Catholics of the inhabitants. Here were two Englishmen engaged in perverting, or rather
completing the perversion of the Free Independent Church of
Ireland to Rome. Hence all the tears of Ireland, England's great
responsibility, much bloodguiltiness on all sides, the almost utter
futility of all attempts to restore to that much-enduring isle, the
comparatively pure faith of its ancient days. O'Driscol, an honest
Roman Catholic writer, describes the change as follows :—"There
is something very singular in the ecclesiastical history of Ireland.
The Christian Church of that country, as founded by St. Patrick
and his predecessors, existed for many ages free and unshackled.
'For above 700 years this Church maintained its independence.'
It had no connection with England, and differed upon points of
importance with Rome. The work of Henry II. was to reduce
the Church of Ireland into obedience to the Roman Pontiff.
Accordingly, he procured a Council of the Irish clergy, to be held
at Cashel in 1172, and the combined influence and intrigues of
Henry and the Pope prevailed. This Council put an end to the
ancient Church of Ireland, and submitted it to the yoke of Rome.
' That apostacy has been followed by a series of calamities, hardly
to be equalled in the world.' From the days of St. Patrick to the
Council of Cashel was a bright and glorious era for Ireland. From
the sitting of this Council to our time, the lot of Ireland has been
unmixed evil, and all her history a tale of woe."

The influence of Rome on the heart of the Scottish nation, began
with the marriage of Malcolm with the English Roman Catholic
Princess Margaret. This Saxon queen completed the outward
perversion of Scotland to Rome. She pretended to reform, but
only managed to enthral the native Church, whose clergy she
summoned to a Council in 1074. The Gaelic language was the
only language the clergy could speak--they had a professional
knowledge of Latin—so King Malcolm, her husband, acted as her

interpreter. They refused to recognise the absolute supremacy of the great Roman father ; they were unable to speak English ; and the queen set herself piously to rectify these abuses and shortcomings. The Roman Catholic influence of the Norman went on increasing until the Court, as the Celtic Professor at Oxford says, " in the time of David. who began to reign in 1124, after being educated in England in all the ways of the Normans, was filled with his Anglican and Norman vassals. He is accordingly, regarded as the first wholly feudal King of Scotland, and the growth of feudalism went on at the expense of the power and influence of the Celtic princes, who saw themselves snubbed and crowded out to make room for the king's barons, who had grants made to them of land here and there, wherever it was worth having. The outcome was a deep seated discontent, which every now and then burst into a flame of open revolt on the part of the rightful owners of the soil." The Celtic Church died away with the decay of the power of the Celtic princes. At the same time the Roman religion was warmly supported in the persons of Englishmen, Flemings and Normans, who received every encouragement to settle in Scotland. The predominance of the Celtic element seems to have passed away in the eleventh century. " At the time, however, of the War of Independence, Gaelic appears to have still reached down to Stirling and Perth, to the Ochil and Sidlaw Hill, while north of the Tay it had as yet yielded to English or Broad Scotch, only a very narrow strip along the coast." The bulk of Bruce's army at Bannockburn was composed of the Ivernian and Celtic descendants of the ancient Free Church of Scotland. The true Christian devotion of the Fathers had not altogether disappeared : like the Puritan soldiers of Cromwell these grand old Scots began the grim work of battle for national freedom, with a fervent prayer to the God of battles,---a species of homage which surprised the more Catholic English.

The Latin hymns of this ancient Church will be found in the " Leabhar imuin " (Book of Hymns) and the Bangor Antiphonary, both miscellanies of odes, canticles, blessings, prayers, &c. Altogether the number is upwards of thirty. The " Leabhar imuin " is a MS. of the ninth or tenth century in Trinity College Library, Dublin. of which two thirds have been printed. The first part, edited by the late Dr Todd, appeared in 1855, and contained the following four hymns, with extensive annotations from the " Leabhar Breac," &c. :— 1, The Hymn of St. Sechnall in praise of St. Patrick ; 2, The Hymn of St. Ultán in praise of St.

Brigit ; 3, The Hymn of Cummain Fota in praise of the Apostles ; 4, The Hymn of St. Mugint. These are specimens of the terminology of the hymn titles.

The Bangor Antiphonary is a MS. in the Ambrosian Library, Milan. It was written between 680 and 691 ; and was printed by Muratori in 1713. Some of the pieces in this MS. have a historical, as well as a devotional value, such as "The Versicles of the Family of Benchor," and "The Commemoration of our Abbots," in which the names of fifteen abbots of the Bangor (County Down) monastery are given in the same order in which their obits occur in the annals. Dr Reeves speaks well of its accuracy, considering that the MS. has been some 1200 years absent from Ireland. These are the sources in which this Latin hymnology of the ancient Gaels will be found. They are not very accessible. As already remarked, versions of them will be also found in the "Leabhar Breac ;" some of them were printed by Sir James Ware, in the appendix to his " Opuscula S. Patricii ;" while the Isidore Codex of the " Leabhar imuin " recently brought from Rome to Dublin, has never yet been printed. These MSS., written in a peculiar ornate style, have become known to archæologists under the description " libri Scottice Scripti," (books written in Scotch).

Some of these devotional compositions are as old as the fourth century, such as the " Hymnum dicat " ascribed to Hilary, and the " Mediæ noctis," ascribed to the famous Ambrose of Milan. The " Audite Omnes " was composed by Sechnall, the nephew of Patrick, towards the close of the fifth century, in praise of the Irish apostle. This piece, rather a poem than a hymn, bears to have been written " in Domhnach Sechnaill," (now Dunshaughlin in Meath), by the St. Sechnall, or Secundinus, who was a son of Patrick's sister, " by her husband *Restitutus*" of the " Longobards of Leatha." The superscription reminds us of the fact that the Scots and the Gaidels were the same people, whether found in Ireland or parts of Britain. It runs thus : " Incipit Ymnus sancti Patricii episcopi Scotorum." (" The hymn beginning, St. Patrick, Bishop of the Scots ") The following note on it occurs in the " Leabhar Breac " : "Tempus autem." (" But the time ") ;— viz : " when Leogaire, son of Niall, was King of Eirinn came to praise Patrick. Sechnall said to Patrick, ' When shall I make a hymn of praise for thee ?' Patrick said, ' I desire not to be so praised during my life.' Sechnall answered, ' Non interrogavi utrum faciam, sed quando faciam.' ('I did not ask whether I should do it, but when'). Patrick said, 'Si facias venit tempus.'

(' If you do it, the time has come ')—i.e. because Patrick knew
that the time of his (Sechnall's) death was at hand." In the third
verse we have the old Scottic interpretation of the famous passage
in Matthew on which St. Peter's chair is founded : —

> " Constans in Dei timore
> Et fide immobilis
> Super quem aedificatur
> Ut Petrum Ecclesia."

" Constant in the fear of God, and inmovable in faith, upon him
as upon a Peter is built a Church."

The student of these ancient writings is surprised to find the
modern Irish persist in making Patrick a Frenchman.   In the
" Leabhar Breac" the following note, as decisive of his nationality,
occurs in connection with this hymn.   " Patraic umorro do
bretnaibh h ercluaide a bunadus."   " Now Patrick in his origin
was of the Britons of Er-Cluaide "—i.e. of the Strathclyde Britons,
among whom his name has found its topographical monument in
Kilpatrick, as already pointed out.

The ancient Christian Scots had their own saints, to whom they
were naturally attached as the fathers of their Church.   The names
of Patrick, Columba, and others, as well as of Brigit constantly
occur in these Latin Hymns.   Brigit comes next in importance to Patrick in Hibernian hagiology.   Ultan's hymn
in praise of her begins with these words, " Christus in nostra insola
que uscatur hibernia ;" and towards the end, the " angelic and
most holy Brigit " in all her wondrous works of power, is spoken
of as " like unto the holy Mary."   We have only fragments of this
poem.   It appears to have been originally composed, like Sechnall's and several others in these MSS., in the A B C style, with
a stanza for each letter of the alphabet.   There is another found
in the beginning of an old Celtic copy of the Greek Psalter, in
praise of Brigit, whose feast day is also celebrated in another,
" Phœbi diem."   The feast day of Patrick has also its celebration
hymn, beginning thus : " Lo, the solemn feast day of Patrick is
shining most brightly."

The hymn " In Te Christe " is one of the three attributed to
Columba, and bears in some places the stamp of his majestic spirit.
The " Ignis Creator igneus " starts with the conception of the
Paschal candle, and proceeds to describe the columns of smoke
and flame which guided Israel out of Egypt.   A few of the metrical compositions in the Bangor Antiphonary have a more local
and historical than a devotional interest, such as the " Good Rule

of Bangor," and the commemoration of the abbots of that place, already referred to. The name of Comgall, the head of the monastery, who died in 602, occurs, as also Molaisran, or Molio of the Holy Isle, Arran, who died in 639. There is an evening hymn beginning with "Christe qui Lux es" and a Pentecostal one about the Apostles, with the initial words "Christi, Patris in dextera." There is one hymn, and only one, in the group in praise of the Blessed Virgin Mary, "Cantemus in omni die."

Metrical translations of seven, in whole or in part, of these hymns are given here, to indicate the general character of the devotional portions of the group. The one beginning with the words: "Precamur Patrem" has not had any date assigned it, but judging by internal evidence, it appears to belong to the era of Patrick. It contains one hundred and sixty-eight lines; starting with an address to the Lord's Day, it proceeds to give an abstract of the life of Christ. A comparison made between the beginning of the physical and that of the spiritual creation, is worked out in somewhat original fashion. In the following verses the Lord and His Own Day are contrasted as the first-born children of light:

PRECAMUR PATREM.   ✠

We worship Thee, Almighty King:
To God the Father praise we bring ;
To Jesus, Saviour of the lost ;
And to the Blessed Holy Ghost.

Thou art, O God, our life and might ;
The source of all the worlds of light,
Which on the brows of heaven lie,
And make resplendent earth and sky.

Of old this day was earth's first-born ;
It shone from heaven a holy morn :
Even so the Word, Eternal Light,
The Father gave this world of night.

That day the chaos dark destroyed ;
Dispelling night into the void :
So Victor o'er the foe did He
This world from death's fierce fetters free.

Upon the deep thick darkness lay
Before the dawning of that day ;
So Ignorance the heart enwound
Till Jesus shed His light around.

A remarkable composition, probably belonging to the same
period, and intended to be used on the birthdays of the martyrs
has, like a few others, the refrain "Alleluia" introduced after every
verse.   The term "birthday" does not bear here its ordinary
meaning, but birth by temporal death into a higher life.   This
hymn is regarded as one of the best production of the Latino-
Celtic muse :

SACRATISSIMI MARTYRES.

Martyrs of the God Most High,
Who for Christ did bravely die ;
Leaders on the heavenly road ;
Victors, sing with saints to God,—
Alleluia !

Christ exalted ! Cherubim
Render homage unto Him,
On the Father's throne on high,
While the saints with martyrs cry,—
Alleluia !

Glorious One !   The first to bear
Shame upon the Cross, our share ;
In thy triumph blessings came ;
Now the martyr saints proclaim,—
Alleluia !

The Apostles, strong in faith,
Suffered on the Cross to death ;
Shielded now, and saved by grace,
Chant within Thy holy place,—
Alleluia !

Christ ! the Helper of the saints,
Heard their weary hearts' complaints ;
Now these martyrs praises bring
And rehearse before their King,—
Alleluia !

Praised, O Lord, Thy power be,
Which obtains the victory ;
Crushes Satan by the way
While the saints with martyrs say,—
Alleluia !

God's strong hand will be their shield ;
With His grace their hearts are steeled
To resist the enemy's ways,
While with saints they ever raise,—
Alleluia !

Heirs with Christ ! Their crowns behold !
Filled with fruit a hundred-fold ;
Pains are past ; they now rejoice,
Uttering in thankful voice,—
                    Alleluia !

Let us humbly pray for grace,
Till we see the Father's face
In Jerusalem on high
Where we raise with saints the cry,—
                    Alleluia !   ,

Another very ancient hymn is the " Spiritus Divinae," which is
one of the matins used for the Lord's Day :

SPIRITUS DIVINAE.

O glorious Spirit of the Light Divine ;
        Come, favour me ;
Thou, God of Truth, in Israel once didst shine ;
        Lord, look on me ;
Thou, Saviour, Son, and Light of Light, I know :
Shed forth Thy living lustre on my woe.

Thy Spirit is one substance with the Son,
        Lord, look on me ;
Thou, Christ, the only first-begotten One,
        Wilt look on me ;
I have redemption from my sin in Thee ;
I seek Thy pardoning aid—Lord, look on me.

Born of the Virgin that poor men might live ;
        Lord, look on me ;
The rights of sonship, Thou alone canst give ;
        Lord, look on me ;
Joint-heir with Thee, Creator of all things :
God-Jesus, everlasting King of Kings.

King of the everlasting ages, Light of God,
        Illumine me ;
Out of thy boundless fitness shed abroad
        Thy love in me ;
Father, and Son, and Spirit, One in Three,
In power and substance One, Lord look on me.

The hymn " Sancti Venite " was intended for communion
service. Dr Neale has rendered it into English. A legend relates how Patrick and his nephew Sechnall heard a company of
angels once rehearsing it ; and declares, " So that from that time

to the present, that hymn is chanted in Eirinn when the body of
Christ is received " :—

SANCTI VENITE.

Take the blessed Bread and Wine,
Emblems of that Life Divine,
That for sin has been out-poured,
By our sacrificing Lord :
Blessed Jesus crucified,
Life flows from Thy bleeding side.

He renews us by his grace :
Let us give to God the praise :
He has died the lost to save,
Risen Victor o'er the grave :
Giver of salvation He ;
Let His Cross our burden be.

He, the Father's suffering Son,
Priest and Victim all in one,
Has become the Lamb of God
To remove our guilty load :
Saviour, Giver of all light ;
He will lead by day and night.

With pure minds let us draw near,
And discern the Shepherd here ;
For the hungry, bread He brings,
Water from the living springs ;
In our hearts He lives enshrined
Lord and Judge of all mankind.

The Spirit of Gildas, the Welsh monk, who was born in 520, and
who pronounced bitter jeremiads on the princes of his own race
and time, is clearly traceable in the next hymn, of whose prologue
a translation is given.   He is one of the Romish corrupters of the
native Church.   His " Suffragare " is one of the " Loricae "
breast-plates, used to protect those who rehearsed them against
evil :--

SUFFRAGARE.

O Unity in Trinity !
  Help, for in Thee I live,
O Trinity in Unity !
  My sins forgive :
Exposed, I need Thy help and sympathy,
Like one in peril of the mighty sea !

Thou wilt preserve me by Thy power
From all my raging foes ;
Thy heavenly host in danger's hour,
Before me goes ;
Cherubic and seraphic ranks in might,
Far scattering the forces of my night.

I see the Patriarchs of eld,
The Prophets bold and strong ;
Apostles who the Lord beheld,
The Martyrs' throng ;
All faithful witnesses, who hence have gone ;
I gaze, and pause afresh to reach the throne.

O Unity in Trinity !
In mercy grant Thine aid ;
O Trinity in Unity !
I seek thy shade,
Where Christ has made a covenant sure with me ;
Oh, fearless, there let me abide with Thee !"

There is a hymn by another author of Welsh extraction, St.
Mugint, in the " Leabhar imuin," beginning with the words " Parce
dne." The " Altus " of Columba, who arrived in Scotland from
Ireland in 563, is a production of considerable length and much
merit, in the A B C Darian style. It takes cognisance of the
whole sphere of sacred and Scriptural truths, somewhat in the
fashion of the compositions of the Brytho-Saxon Caedmon, and has
been regarded as a highly effective " Lorica " :–

ALTUS PROSATOR.

Great Father of all, the Almighty, we praise,
The One-unbegotten, the Ancient of Days,
Eternally first, and eternally last !
With Thee there remains neither future nor past.

With Thee co-eternal in glory and might,
Reigns Christ on the throne in the regions of light,
Thine Only-begotten, the Son of Thy love,
And there, too, the Spirit, the heavenly Dove.

Bright myriads of angels a ministrant throng,
Ring praises unceasing, rejoicing in song,
Where crowns are cast down at Immanuel's feet,
And anthems eternal the elders repeat.

The judgements of heaven shall be scattered abroad
On all who deny that our Saviour is God ;
But we shall be raised up with Jesus on high,
To where the new mansions all glorious lie.

6

There is a Gaelic hymn attributed to Columba, which illustrates the manner and occasions of using these " Loricae "—in Gaelic *lureck*. Its superscription runs thus : " Colum cilli cecinit, while passing alone ; and it will be a protection to the person who will repeat it going on a journey." The author in the first verse represents himself as lonely on the hillside, and addressing the royal " Sun." M'oenuran dam is in sliabh, &c. : —

> " Alone am I in the mountain,
>   O Royal Sun of prosperous path ;
>   Nothing is to be feared by me,
>   Not if I were *attended by* sixty-hundred."

The *rig-grian*—Sun-king, is applied to the Creator.

The third Latin hymn ascribed to Columba, and beginning with the words " Noli Pater " is also a " Lorica." It is connected with the lighting of fires on St. John's Eve. In some prefatory remarks, its virtues are thus described :—" It is sung against every fire and every thunderstorm, and whosoever sings it at bedtime and at rising, it protects him against lightning."

NOLI PATER.

> Father, restrain Thy thunder,
> Thy lightning from our frame,
> Lest in our trembling wonder
> They smite us with their flame !
> Thou Awful One ! we fear Thee,
> For there is none like Thee ;
> In thy dread steps we hear Thee ;
> And to Thy shelter flee.

> To Thee awake loud praises,
> One universal song
> The great creation raises,
> Sung by the angel throng :
> Our Jesus, King most loving !
> The lofty heavens extol :
> We see Thee grandly moving
> Where flashing lightnings roll.

> O King of kings ! Thou reignest
> In righteousness and love ;
> And righteous rule maintainest
> From Thy pure throne above.
> God's love—a blessed fuel—
> Burns in my heart a flame ;
> Like to a golden jewel
> Preserved in silver flame.

Much is made of the elements in this composition. In the Gaelic one already referred to, Columba guards in the last verses against any tendency to Pantheism that might be connected with his expressions. He declares :—

> " I adore not the voice of birds,
> Nor the *sreod*, nor a destiny, or the earthly world,
> Nor a son, nor chance, nor woman ;
> My Druid is Christ, the Son of God,—
> Christ, the Son of Mary, the Great Abbot,
> The Father, the Son, and the Holy Ghost.
> My estates are with the King of kings ;
> My order is at Cenannus and Moen."

Cenannus is now Headfort in Meath, where Columba erected a monastery. *Moen* is now Moon, in Kildare.

The renderings of hymns given in the preceding paragraphs will convey some idea of the hymnology of the Gaelic Church. The singing of these Latin compositions awoke echoes for ages along the glens of Gaelic Scotland as well as in the forests of Germany ; among the Swiss and Italian Alps, as well as along the sweet hills of Devon and Cornwall. They indicate a practical literary activity which served well its generation ; and frequently helped to soothe the relentless spirit of revenge of the Pagan nations of the period.

The primitive Free Church of the Gaels of Britain was an important branch of this powerful missionary Church of the Celts. Its operations and results were largely obscured by successors on the same fields who departed from its methods of work ; but recent efforts of impartial investigators, have helped to assign it its proper place in the ancient Christianization of Western Europe. It does not lie within the scope of this work to discuss the character of the organization of this Church of the Gaels.   Indeed the question has been already so thoroughly investigated by competent pens that it would be perfectly superfluous to attempt it.   To the literary student this period of church history is chiefly interesting on account of the fact that it is through the hands of these devoted workers of those ages that the first fruits of written literature have been handed down to us.   These men being our earliest literary artists, we naturally turn with perennial interest to the Christian organizations which some had founded, and in which others were bred.

A small production, some three quarto pages in prose, gives us a picture of a holy brother who might be expected to cultivate the virtues of the Gospel in solitude rather than in the circle of the active community. It is called the " Rule of Calumcille ; " and has been found in the Burgundian Library of Brussells. The Rule recommends residence close to a church ; a fast place with one door ; the company of one attendant only, whose duties must be light ; and access to be granted only to those whose converse will be of God and His Testament. The time is to be spent in prayers for those taught and for those dying in the faith. The day is to be divided into three parts, one for prayers, for good works, and for reading respectfully. The work is to be divided into three parts ; the first for his own benefit in doing what is needed for his own habitation : the second for the good of the brethren ; and the third for that of the neighbours. The work of benefiting his neighbours to consist in giving precepts, writing manuscripts, sewing clothes, or any other profitable industry. The great end to be obtained is that there " be no idleness ;" " ut Deus ait : non apparebis ante me vacuus."

This sentiment of " no idleness " is highly creditable to the ancient Gaelic Christian communities ; and if we combine with it another found in one of the lives of Columba,—

> " He drank not ale ; he loved not satiety :
> He avoided flesh ;"

we make a clean discovery which absolutely refutes the unneighbourly charges of more southern brethren in our own time which associate Celts, whisky, and idleness too closely and unfairly together. Our early Highland teachers inculcated industry and sobriety ; the dangerous powers of whisky were unknown to them ; and even the lighter inspirations of ale they eschewed until their own primitive virtues were undermined by contact with the beer-drinking Pagan Norse on the one hand, and in later times with the fiercer spirits which were imported from Teutonic fens on the other. Such are the strange reversals of popular opinions which accurate study of the facts of history unfolds. The alleged idleness of the Gael of the present day, does not appear thus to have any essential connection with the original sin of the race ; the development of the quality appears to have taken place in contact with a more sluggish and a less lively people.

In his great work on " English Writers," Professor Henry Morley writes :—" When darkness gathered over all the rest of western Europe, the churches and monasteries of the British island, first among the Celts and afterwards among the English, supplied, says the Danish scholar [Professor Sophus Bugge], in and after the seventh century, the only shelter and home to the higher studies.

The British clergy travelled far in search of books, until in the time of Charlemagne it was from the Church in Britain that the clearest light shone through the western world." The devotional spirit by which these men were animated, will be fairly illustrated by the renderings of their Latin Hymns contained in this chapter.

It is freely acknowledged that the ancient Free Church of the Scots, even in its golden age, held and practised peculiar tenets which in course of time developed undesirable and even unscriptural fruit. On the other hand, it must be allowed that it adhered for a long period to the main doctrines of evangelical Christianity. From the hymns which we have been considering, and from Patrick's "Epistle of Coroticus," and his "Confession," in which we have something of the nature of a creed or a confession of faith, as well as from other sources, we gather a fair representation of the chief dogmas of its faith. It held and taught the chief doctrines of the Trinity, of the incarnation, death, resurrection, and ascension of Christ, and of His coming again at the last day to judge all men ; and likewise of the outpouring of the Holy Spirit to make us sons of God, and heirs of immortality. It held, moreover, the Holy Scriptures to be the Word of God, and used them freely and exclusively as the authority by which all statements of doctrine are to be proved and confirmed. At the same time the doctrine of human merit, purgatory, saint-worship, transubstantiation, papal infallibility, and other distinctive tenets of modern Romanism, find no recognition. While, as we are told by St. Bernard, its followers "rejected auricular confession as well as authoritative absolution, and confessed to God alone, believing God alone could forgive sins," they would neither give to the Church of Rome the tenths, nor the first-fruits, which of course rendered them "schismatics and heretics" at Rome. Marriage was regarded as a civil rite, and was performed by the magistracy.

The purity of doctrine and generally healthy influence cultivated and exercised by the ancient Celtic Church, are shown in a remarkable manner in the products of Celtic art, which attained to its highest development in the tenth, eleventh, and twelfth centuries. The remains of this school of ancient sculpture, if collected into one national museum, would form an exhibition of native art such as, according to Mr Joseph Anderson, the Rhind lecturer, no northern nation can boast of. Respecting these sculptured stones, memorials that are not unworthy of our valiant Christian ancestors, Burton, in an interesting chapter, remarks : " It deserves to be commemorated that in the hundreds of specimens of native sculpture of this class recently brought to light there is no single instance of indecency, while in the scanty remains of Roman art within the same area it would be easy to point out several."

The character of the two races that blended into one through the agency of this Church and outward political pressure is not unfairly represented by Professor Rhys, when he says, touching first on the Gael or ancient Scot: "One of the lessons of this chapter is that the Goidel, where he owned a fairly fertile country, as in the neighbourhood of the Tay, showed that he was not wanting in genius for political organisation ; and the history of the kingdom of Scotland, as modelled by Kenneth mac Alpin and his descendants, warns one not to give ear to the spirit of race-weighing and race-damning criticism that jauntily discovers, in what it fancies the character of a nation, the reasons why it has not achieved results not fairly placed within its reach by the accidents either of geography or history." The other ancient race of Albin was neither Celtic nor Aryan in its origin. It has been generally known as Pictish, and constitutes the backbone of the Scottish nation. Mr Rhys calls it *Ivernian*. The following sentences state a fact and describe a process : " The trouble the non-Celtic Picts were able to give the Romans and the Romanising Brythons has often been dilated upon by historians, who have seldom dwelt on the much more remarkable fact, that a power, with its headquarters in the neighbourhood of the Ness, had been so organised as to make itself obeyed from the Orkneys to the Mull of Cantyre, and from Skye to the mouth of the Tay, so early as the middle of the sixth century. It is important to bear this in mind in connection with the question as to how far the earlier Celtic invaders of this country may have mixed with the ancient inhabitants ; since it clearly shows that there was no such a gulf between them as would make it impossible or even difficult for them to amalgamate ; and it may readily be supposed that the Goidelic race has been greatly modified in its character by its absorption of this ancient people of the Atlantic seaboard." The Latin hymns considered here are the remains of the devotional literature of these two races, and bind the history and memories of modern Scotsmen to the history and memories of a people among whom the fervid national genius of Scotland was first fashioned.

CHAPTER V.

> " Thoir an eachdraidh Mhaighstir Dòmhnull
> A tha chòmhnaidh 'n cois na tuinne ;
> An ùrnuigh bha aig Oisein liath-ghlas
> Nach robh riamh ach 'na dhroch dhuine."

ENGLISH :

> *To Master Donald take the story ;*
> *There he dwells beside the billow ;*
> *The prayer said by Ossian hoary,*
> *Who was aye a worthless fellow.*

IT has been well remarked that each of the literatures of the
two branches of our Celtic population was chiefly the utterance of
feeling stirred by a great struggle for independence, and that each
has at the heart of it " a battle disastrous to the men whose wrestle
with an overmastering power is the chief theme of their bards."
The Gaelic struggle and literature began earlier, and its great
battle is that of *Gabhra*, said to have been fought in 284 A.D.   In
the later Celtic literature of the Cymri the memorable battle described is that of Cattraeth, said to have been fought in 570 A.D.

While *Cath-Gabhra* is the chief theme of the Gaelic bards, individual combats, adventures, and other battles are also rehearsed
in the early ballads.

Macpherson's "Ossian" and Smith's "Old Lays." whose authenticity has been so fiercely disputed, are excluded from consideration at present.   They will be afterwards examined under the
dates of their production.   The number of lines in these works
and other two poems respectively is :—

Macpherson's Poems of Ossian............ ...10,232 lines.
Smith's Old Lays..... ... . 5,335 ,,
Clark's Mordubh...................... .... 758 ,,
MacCallum's Collath...................... ...... 504 ,,

Total...........16,829   ,,

Laying aside these 16,829 lines of suspected poetry, there is still the 54,000 lines of ancient poems of unquestioned genuineness in Campbell's "Leabhar na Féinne," enough surely to sustain the literary character and genius of our early ancestors.

The ballads which we are now to consider are all genuine and old, and may be found in manuscripts written ages before Macpherson was born.

The Ossianic or Heroic Ballads will be found in the following publications :—The Dean of Lismore's Book (1512, published 1862); Hill's (1780); MacArthur's (1784); Young's (1784); Gillies's (1786); Stewart's (1804); Highland Society's Report (1805); Turner's (1813); Grant's (1814); MacCallum's (1816); Campbell's great work (1872). Some of the ballads contained in these books were printed from old manuscripts; others were taken down during the last two or three centuries from the oral recitation of old men, living in all parts of the Highlands.

These collections represent a good deal of industry and literary activity, which reflect. very creditably on men who had not the stimulus of a vast reading public to work upon their minds.

THE GENUINE GAELIC BALLADS.

The place in time occupied by these compositions is one of considerale length—it extends at least as far back as the third century of our era. It is very interesting to note that this body of oral popular literature has been loved, preserved, and rehearsed by the Gaelic clans of Albin for at least a thousand years ; for a much longer period, indeed, if we rely on fairly credible tradition.

The inter-tribal struggles described in these ballads—the patriotic resistance against the Norse attempts to obtain the supremacy, mixed up as they are with the encroachments of Christianity within the realms of heathenism—took place mainly within the Albinic area. The geographical limits of this area in those early times were very vague and shifting. In a general way they may be said to have embraced the Western Islands, the North-west. and part of the central Highlands, as well as the Isle of Man and Ireland. Over all these regions we watch in these ballads the shadowy movements of our brave ancestors   We hear the faint echoes of their names, and the fame of their deeds, the war-cries and voices of their almost semi-mythic heroes.

We regard the tribes whose deeds are celebrated in these productions under two classes—those of the Cruithne or Albinic race and those who have become known as the Scottish Iro-Gaelic race. At that period there were Cruithne or Picts in Erin as well as in Albin.

Previous to the arrival of Patrick in Ireland and to that of Columba in the Highlands, there is strictly speaking no chronological history of either country. Of the earlier movements of the clans and their battles we have no authentic account. But there are traditions with a highly probable basis of truth sufficient for the purposes of the present Ossianic discussion. Two or three of the central facts of the Finian period, as related in a preceding section, are as follows :—

Finn MacCumhaill lived in the reign of Cormac MacArt who ruled from A.D. 227 to 266, and whose daughter Gràinne he married. Goll MacMorni was a contemporary. Finn was slain in 283, but the bards bring him somehow alive next year to pronounce a eulogy on his grandson, Oscar, who fell in the battle of Gabhra. Ossian and Caoilte lived for a hundred and fifty years longer ; and the blind old heathen bard relates the heroic achievements of his departed fellow heroes to St. Patrick who arrives in Ireland about 432. Chronology did not trouble the old ballad-makers of Albin and Erin. Such an anachronism as brings Ossian of the third, into conjunction with Patrick of the fifth century, did not disturb their heroic muse.

Ireland claimed this Ossian as her own, and her learned doctors declared that Macpherson stole his poems from their country. Two or three words will be sufficient to dispose of all this : 1. Macpherson never was in Ireland ; and never kept up any correspondence with Irishmen. 2. The Ossianic poems published by the Dublin Gaelic Society and the Ossianic Society were all collected and made known subsequent to the publication of Macpherson's Ossian. 3. It it admitted by the late Eugene O'Curry, one of the highest authorities, that prior to the 15th century there existed in Ireland only *eleven* Ossianic poems, which are extremely short, and which will be found in the Book of Leinster, compiled in the 13th, and in the Book of Lecan in the 15th century. Of these, seven are ascribed to Finn himself, two to Ossian, one to Fergus, and one to Caoilte. This clearly disposes of Irelands claim to possess anything like Macpherson's work. Indeed it has been given up by some who advanced it, while at the same time these writers and others laboured to manufacture and publish poems *a la* Macpherson ; but to the great chagrin of these learned sons of Erin the public will not assign them the same distinction and appreciation, which have been accorded to Macpherson's productions.

Let us now glance at the genuine, and indisputably ancient Ossianic ballads preserved in Scotland : 1. We have the tragic tale of *Deirdri* in the Glenmasan MS., bearing the date of 1238, now in the Advocate's Library. 2. There is a MS. of the 15th century, containing a glossary and a poem of five quatrains, attributed to Ossian. A text the same as this poem is in the Book of Leinster of the 13th century. 3. There is the Book of the Dean of Lismore, compiled between 1512-20 A.D. This book contains 28 Ossianic poems, nine of which are directly attributed to Ossian, two to Fergus, one to Caoilte ; two to Allan MacRuairi, and one to GillieCallum Mac an Olla, —these two last bards being hitherto unknown ; and there are eleven anonymous ones, which in style and subject belong to the Féinne. These twenty-eight poems extend to 2500 lines, or one-fourth of all Macpherson's Gaelic poems. The rest of the extant heroic poetry has been collected in the Highlands and Islands, chiefly within the last 150 years ; and in the main consists of versions of the same productions that we have in the Book of the Dean of Lismore. They are genuine Highland compositions of an ancient character, and some of them are instructive as showing how far oral transmission during the last 400 years has affected their style and language.

We thus find that the work begun by Sir James Macgregor upwards of 400 years ago, has been taken up at intervals by others since his time. Towards the end of the last, and the beginning of the present century the principal collectors of these ballads appeared. Old men in all parts of the Highlands and Isles, famous for their mnemonic and reciting powers were sought out by educated natives and strangers, and their versions of the old ballads taken down. The last and the greatest of the ballad and tale-collectors was Mr Campbell, who in 1859-60 traversed the whole Gaelic area ; and assisted by intelligent Highlanders formed large collections, of which he has given a considerable quantity to the world, in his four volumes of tales. All these are genuine productions of the Gaelic popular mind. No stigma or suspicion attaches to them. Some of them are at least as ancient as the time of Dean Macgregor—400 years ago ; and they were regarded as ancient then. In character and spirit they resemble—are in many cases only Scottish versions of—the kindred literature of the Gael of Ireland ; and possess much definite value to the student of social life and the philologist.

Although many of those heroic compositions have been probably lost and others marred in their oral transmission, yet enough remains to interest the literary student and the historic antiquary. Upwards of 54,000 lines have been preserved, and are accessible in that truly excellent and scientifically arranged work *Leabhar na Feinne.* In this body of literature we have indubitable proof of the existence of a large mass of popular literature among the ancient Gaels, who it is evident must have developed considerable taste for ballad, song, and story.

It is hard to assign any date to the composition of these ballads. They may have been composed centuries before they were committed to writing. We have fragments such as the Glen-mason MS. which were written as early as the 12th century, scarcely anything earlier. These are written in the hand and language common to the learned in both Albin and Erin at the time. The book of the Dean of Lismore, however, is written phonetically to represent the spoken language of his day, and is mainly in the Perthshire dialect. The various collections of ballads made between 400 and 70 years ago exhibit different styles of writing, and the unsettled modes of orthography prevalent at the time

The poetic form of these productions is generally that of the quatrain. Some pieces do not exceed a few stanzas in length, others extend to 80 or 100 quatrains or to between 300 or 400 lines. Many archaic expressions are to be met with ; but on the whole when presented in modern orthography they are understood by an ordinary Highlander. Not a few of these phrases, though not generally understood, have been preserved and transmitted even in the oral versions taken down within the last 100 years.

Some of the most ancient ballads relate to Cuchulin and his deeds of deathly valour ; others tell the tragic tale of Deirdri ; others relate to the Norse wars ; and not the least romantic describe the fierce combats and heroic conflicts in which the brave heroes of the Féinne indulged on the shores and plains of Albin and Erin. On many a field of fame, east and west, had the banners of the Finian heroes gleamed and gained renown ; but with all their victories they always fell as they went forth to the battle, until they all faded and disappeared " like sungleam in wintry weather."

THE COCHULIN BALLADS.

Taken in chronological order, the Cochulin ballads come up

first for consideration. Much credit is due to Mr Campbell for
his attempt at a chronological classification of these productions, a
very difficult matter, considering the vagueness, historically, of
everything connected with the heroic period. As far as dates of
composition are concerned, all that can be safely affirmed is that
these ballads were composed between the Christian era and the
thirteenth century, some of them undoubtedly belonging to the
earlier, and some of them to the later centuries of that period.
Copies of many of them were made by Sir James Macgregor, Dean
of Lismore, between 1512-26. Then they were regarded as very
ancient. Those relating to Cochulin and to his son Conlach are:
—*Cochulin and Evir*; *Cochulin's Sword*; *Cochulin's Car*; *Garbh
Mac Stairn*; *Conlach's Death*; *The Heads.* According to ancient
annals Cochulin lived in the first century. *Connal Cearnach Mac
Edirskeol* is the author of the last-mentioned ballad, *The Heads*,
and the most ancient of all the Heroic poets. Cochulin was his
foster-son; and when he was slain Connal revenged himself on his
enemies by putting them all to death. In the ballad, Evir, the
wife or betrothed of Cochulin, is told the names of those put to
death, whose heads he carried on a withe. There is a heroine of
Dun sgathaich, Skye, called Aoife, who also is mixed up with
Cochulin's story. The length of the ballad is 96 lines. The
following is a literal translation of the first six stanzas :—

> Connal, these heads are little worth,
>   Though in their blood thine arms did'st soil ;
> These heads thou hast upon the withe
>   Tell me their owners, now thy spoil.
>
> Daughter of Orgill of the steeds,
>   Evir, whose words sweet feelings waken,
> 'Twas to avenge Cochulin's death
>   That I these many heads have taken.
>
> Whose is that nearest thy left arm,—
>   That mighty, hairy, dusky head,—
> That head whose colour has not changed,
>   With cheeks than any rose more red ?
>
> The king of fleet steeds owned that head,
>   Said Cairbar's son, keen lance in war ;
> 'Twas to avenge my foster-son
>   I took that head and bore it far.
>
> Whose is that head I see beyond
>   Inwrapt with soft and flowing hair,
> His eye like glass, his teeth like bloom,
>   With beauty that is peerless there ?

Manadh, the one that owned the steeds,
The son of Aoife—pirate true ;
I left his trunk without its head,
His people every one I slew.

THE DEIRDRI BALLADS.

The next class is that of the *Deirdri Ballads*. The story of
Deirdri and *Clan Uisneach*, or the three brothers, Naos, Ainle,
and Ardan,'sons of Uisneach, is very affecting and tragic. Mr
Campbell says :—"The story of Deirdre is related to Indian Epics,
and is an Aryan romance which pervades the whole world. A
beautiful girl, shut up to baulk a prophecy, is beloved by an old
King. She runs away with a family of brothers, and after adventures of many kinds, the story ends in a tragedy." Connachar,
King of Ireland, whose reign is placed about the middle of the
first century, was preparing to marry the beautiful princess, Deirdri,
when she ran away with the three sons of his sister, Noas, Ainle,
and Ardan. They went to Scotland, where they were well received.
The names of places in the ballads indicate that it was in Argyllshire they settled. While the brothers were away on some expedi-
tion, to Lochlin, it is supposed, Deirdri was left in charge of a
" black-haired lad," it is said, in an islet north of Jura till they
would return. The "lad" began to make love to Deirdri in their
absence, but they came back opportunely to save her. By this
time Connacher sent them a message of peace from Ireland ; and
believing that the once wrathful monarch was sincere they returned
to Ireland. But they were at once met with the hostile forces of
the King ; and after a fierce struggle the King slew his nephews.
When Deirdri saw her beloved Naos and his brothers fall, she
rushed forward, bewailing them, and died upon their bodies.
There are six or seven versions of this story, the oldest being in
the MS. dated 1208, in the Advocates' Library. It was written
at Glenmasan, in Cowal. The versions vary in length. The
longest contains upwards of 400 lines. The ballad is sometimes
divided into several parts, and some collectors give only one or
two parts. It is the part in which Deirdri laments her departure
from Scotland that is here translated. This and the Book of
Deer are the earliest specimens that we possess of written Gaelic
in Scotland.

The glens and other places mentioned in the following farewell
of Deirdri are readily identified. The large number of proper
names occurring in the piece renders it difficult to give anything

more than a very stiff translation, which is almost absolutely
literal :—

"Do dech Deardir ar a hèise aɪ crichibh Alban, agus rochan an Laoidh" :
—(*Deirdri looked back on the land of Albin, and sang this Lay.*)

> Beloved land, that eastern land !
> Alba with waters wide :
> With Naos in those happy glens
> I wish I could abide !
>
> Beloved Dunfigha and Dunfin ;
> The Dun above them seen ;
> Beloved is Inis-Draighnde ;
> Beloved is fair Dun Sween.
>
> Coille-Chuan ! O Coille-Chuan !
> Where Ainle comes no more !
> Too short, I ween, was there my stay
> With Naos on Albin's shore.
>
> Glen-Laye ! O Glen-Laye !
> Oft by its stream I lay ;
> Fish, flesh and fat of badger
> My repast in sweet Glen-Laye.
>
> Glen-Masan ! O Glen-Masan !
> Where fairest boughs are seen ;
> Lonely was my place of rest
> By Inver-Masan green.
>
> Glen-Eitive ! O Glen-Eitive !
> There my first home was raised ;
> Beautiful were its woods in morn
> When there the sun had blazed.
>
> Glen-Orchay ! O Glen-Orchay !
> Straight vale of ridges smooth,
> Full joyful there round Naos
> Were the Glen-Orchay youth.
>
> Glen-Daruadh ! O Glen-Daruadh !
> I love its men—I love it !
> Sweet are the cuckoos on the boughs
> On the grey hills above it.
>
> Beloved is Drayen—its sounding shore ;
> Beloved is Avich of pure sand ;
> Oh, that I might not leave the east,—
> Beloved and happy land.

On this tale, and on its connection with Scottish topography, Dr MacLauchlan says :—" This is one of the most touching in the catalogue of Celtic tales, and it is interesting to observe the influ- ence it exerted over the Celtic mind by its effect upon the topo- graphical nomenclature of the country. There are several Dun Deirdres to be found still. One is prominent on the vale of the Nevis, near Fort-William, and another occupies the summit of a magnificent rock overhanging Loch Ness, in Stratherrick." *Ness*, the name of the loch, is thought to be from Naos. Dr Skene re- marks—" Adomnan, in his life of St. Columba, written in the seventh century, appears to mention only three localities in con- nection with St. Columba's journey to the palace of the King of the Picts, near Lochness, and these are Cainle (Ainle), Arcardan (Ardan), and the flumen Nesae (Naise). Two vitrified forts in the neighbourhood of Lochness are called Dun-*Dearduil*." The same authority also observes that " the ancient legends of Cochulin and the sons of Uisneach connect them with those remarkable structures termed vitrified forts." Dun-Sgathaig and Dun-mhic- Uisneachan are vitrified like Dun-dhearduil. It is suggested that a mythic meaning underlies this topography and story.

THE FINIAN BALLADS.

A class of ballads which is wholly taken up with the Finian heroes proper—with their intercourse and doings among them- selves—may be described as *Finnic* ballads. Finn is the central hero ; and the other Finian characters are his attendant satellites.

There was more than one class of heroes known as Féinn, or Fianna :—

1. Féinn of Albin : Albin was north· of the firths of the Forth and Clyde.
2. Féinn of Erin : The same class of heroes in Ireland.
3. Féinn of Breatan : Breatan was the southern districts of Scotland, Dunbreatan, or Dumbarton, being the principal seat.
4. Féinn of Lochlin : These according to Tacitus, dwelt on the right shore of the Suevic Sea, or the Baltic, and were called the Aestii.

There are some evidences which indicate that the last also were a Celtic people, who spoke a Celtic language. The inhabitants of this district now form part of the Kingdom of Prussia.

It is the Féinn of Albin and of Erin that the heroic lays generally celebrate: Trenmor, the fifth from Baoisgne, from whom Finn and his followers were called Clanna Baoisgne, was general of the Féinn ; Cumhal, his son, was the father of Finn.   Oisein, Fergus, Raoidhne, or Rayne, and Cairol were the sons of Finn. Oscar, the son of Oisein, was his grandson ; and Diarmad was his nephew, who eloped with his queen, Gràine, daughter of Cormac Mac Art, King of Ireland, A.D. 227.   Caoilte, or Cailt, was a relative ; and Goll, or Gaul, Conan, and Garaidh were chiefs of the Clann Morna. But the heroes, one after another, soon disappeared. The theme of several of the principal ballads is the deaths of Oscar, Diarmad, Gaul, &c., and lastly, of Ossian himself, who was left alone of all that noble band of heathen heroes.   In his last days the blind old bard came in contact with some Christian Patrick, and dialogues of their discussions were for ages repeated in Highland ballads.   The following ballad, entitled the " Sweetest Sound,' is a specimen of the less martial kind : —

> Once when the kindly feast was spread
>   On Almhin's golden slope,
> The bards they sang of bliss and woe,
>   Despair, and love, and hope.
>
> And heroes, as they drained the bowl,
>   With joy or sadness heard ;
> For those good harpers as they pleased
>   Men's rising feelings stirred.
>
> Lord of the feast there Fingal sat—
>   His fair hair touched with grey—
> Near his first son, the warrior bard,
>   Strong as the noon of day.
>
> The good MacLuy there conversed
>   With Oscar, young and bright,
> And bald head Conan, rash and bold,
>   Who never shunned the fight.
>
> And Diarmad there sat, beautiful,
>   And rolled his eye of blue,
> When Fingal spoke, and all the board
>   His regal question knew.
>
> " Come, tell me now, my chieftains good,
>   At Fingal's feast who be,
> What sounds are they that form for each
>   The sweetest harmony ?

" What are the notes that charm you most,
And send your cares to flight—
What sound most charms your inmost core,
And thrills you with delight ?"

The Conan—the rash Conan spoke—
Of all that company
The first to speak, the first to fight—
The last to think was he.

" The rattling dice I love the most,
When the play is running high ;
And my coming chances strain my ear,
And almost blind my eye."

" When heroes rush together,
When battle wakes around,
With clash, and clang, and crushing blows,
I hear my sweetest sound."

So Oscar spoke.—Thus Diarmad said,
" When in my secret ear
Sweet woman whispers love for me,
My best loved sound I hear."

" When first I catch my good hounds' cry,
Where the proud stag stamps the ground,
And stands at bay," MacLuy said,
" I hear my sweetest sound."

Then Fingal said, " My music is
The banner's fluttering fold,
When•winds blow free, and the brave I see
Beneath its streaming gold."

Alas ! alas ! my sweetest sound
Was once in Fingall's hall ;
To hear bards sing and heroes speak,
And now they've perished all !

The above has been translated by Pattison, and I use his rendering. It gives us a good picture of a social gathering of the
Finian heroes. The bowl goes round, the harpers begin, and the
warriors deliver themselves successively on the objects which most
moved their hearts. Fingal sat there as lord of the feast, and
directed their intercourse. Conan, rash and thoughtless, but bold,
loves the rattling dice ; Oscar loves the waking of battle, Diarmad
the whispering of woman's love, MacLuy the hound in the chase.
Fingal himself delights in the banner fluttering over the brave in

7

battle, and Ossian, as usual, regretfully declares that his sweet sound was once in the hall of Fingal, who now with his heroic followers have all perished.

The titles of some of the other ballads are *Ossian's Lament, Cailte and the Giant*, &c. We have a special set in several dialogues between Ossian and Patrick on the Féinn and their exploits, and on the comparative merits of the Christian religion and the stories of the Féinne. One of them is called *Oisein agus an Cleireach*, or Ossian and the Cleric, in which we have a descrip- tion of a battle between the Finians and the Norse. The saint is very agreeable in this poem, very unlike what he is in *Ossian's Prayer*, and concedes much to the bard, so much, indeed, that he is willing to rear an altar, not to God, but to Finn! It is difficult to say whether the ballad refers to a Manus, or Magnus, of the third or of the twelfth century. Actually known historic facts favour the latter. The length of the ballad varies; some of the versions are upwards of two, some three hundred lines long.

I here translate the first few verses :—

> *Ossian.*—O Cleric, that singest the psalms !
> Rude are thy thoughts I ween ;
> Hearest thou a little my songs
> On the Féinn thou hast never seen ?

> *Cleric.*—'Tis thine to delight in the songs
> Of the Féinn whom thou didst see—
> Sounds of psalms on my lips are sweeter
> Than Finian rhymes to me.

> *O.*—If thou darest liken thy psalms
> To the Finian arms blood-red,
> Cleric ! I swear I would sever
> By blade from its trunk thy head.

> *C.*—Great Bard ! I compare them not ;
> The lay of thy lips is sweet ;
> Let us raise an altar to Finn,
> And render him praise complete.

> *O.*—Kind Cleric ! if thou wert south-west
> At the Fall of the soft-flowing stream
> Where it hastens to join the sea,
> The Féinn thou wouldest greatly esteem.

> *C.*—Blessed be the soul of that hero !
> Who fought in his violent might—
> Mac-Cuhail, the chief of the host,
> Renowned in the field of fight.

O.—One day we were hunting for red-deer,
And failing to meet with game,
Ten thousand barks were seen,
And towards the shore they came.

We all stood there on the plain ;
Fins gathered on every side ;
Round the son of the daughter of Teig,
Flocked full seven tribes in their pride.

Their galleys they rushed ashore,—
That host of the blades blood-red ;
They were many the tents of cloth
That they reared above their head.

They hastened along from the woods,
And put on their armour bright,—
The weapons on shoulders great
As they moved from the shore for fight.

To his heroes Mac-Cuhail spoke,—
" These foes you have known before ?
You know how this cruel race
Wakes warfare along our shore ?"

It was then that Conan replied,—
" Who are these that came o'er the sea ?
Knowest thou who is chief, Finn of battles?
The flower of Norse Kings is he !"

F.—" Who will go from the ranks of the Feinn
To get word from the hostile host ?
My favour he'll have if he brings
Tidings sincere from the coast."

Then Conan made answer again—
" Whom should'st thou send, O King,
But Fergus, thy prudent son ;
Wise word, I ween, he'll bring."

" Let my curse take thee, bald-headed Conan,"
Said Fergus of gentlest face ;
" I will go, but 'tis not at thy voice,
To get word from this Lochlin race."

Young Fergus, all armed, went off
Those heroes to meet on the way ;
He mildly inquired, " What people
Came over the sea that day ?"

Magnus, all bloody and fierce,
Son of the red-shielded Bede,
Was Chief King of Lochlin—well fitted
Proud armies of men to lead.

" What moved thee, thou cruel man,
From the kingdom of Lochlin's shore ?
Unless thou hast come our heroes
To multiply more and more."

" I vow by thy hand, mild Fergus,
Though brave be the Féinn of thy pride ;
We'll make no terms with Finn without Bran,
And his wife we will take from his side."

" Ere Bran thou shalt get our heroes
Will try all thy strength in the strife,
And Finn thou must meet in fierce combat
Ere thou canst take captive his wife."

Since the days of Eve and Helen women have been the cause
of much evil and strife : and many of the sore troubles of the
Féinn arose from the bewitching charms which their Gaelic maidens
and mothers possessed. The chief King of the Lochlins came to
the shore of Albin with "ten thousand barks"—the Northmen's
galleys must have been very numerous in those times, our British
navy of the present day would be small in comparison—determined
to possess himself of the dog and wife of Finn, the Caledonian
monarch. In these days this might seem a small *casus belli* indeed ; but it must be remembered that the dog Bran was a most
remarkable one ; the posthumous poetic honours that have been
paid to this canine worthy have far exceeded those that Byron has
given his favourite. As to the Caledonian Queen, the elopement
of Graine with Diarmad must not be forgotten ; indeed, it may
help to explain the formidable descent of Magnus on the shores of
Albin. To put chivalrous heroes under *geasan* was then a favourite pastime among Gaelic ladies. And, being the weaker sex, it
was well that they should be invested with enchanting or super-
natural power that would somehow afford them protection in the
midst of the turbulent, ruthless forces by which they were surrounded in those days. The battle and its results are described
in thirty verses more. The Norse invaders were worsted ; Finn and
Magnus met in single combat ; "stones and the heavy earth were
wakening under the soles of their feet." At last the unfortunate
Magnus was overcome. Though unbecoming a king, he was
bound hands and feet ; but ultimately he receives kind and
chivalrous treatment from Finn ; and he repents of his conduct
towards him, to whose mercy he said he would trust when he
heard the bald Conan—who was "ever drinking"—express a wish
to be allowed to sever his head from his body. The author—the

ballad is put into the mouth of Ossian of course—concludes with
the declaration that he and his father and Gaul performed the
greatest feats that day, though they are now "without strength,"
compelled to listen to psalm-singing clerics.

A particularly interesting poem—one of the many dialogues
between Ossian and Patrick—is called *Ossian's Prayer*. I translate a few verses of the beginning of Macnicol's version, which
will give an idea of the piece. It is about 150 lines in length.
The author makes Ossian a thorough heathen, who prefers the
glories of Finian deeds and fame to all the Christian prospects
that Patrick can unfold.

Ossian.

O Patrick of the reading
To me a story tell ;
Say do the Féinn of Erin
In Heaven high now dwell?

Patrick.

Let me tell thee truly, Ossian,
To whom fame is given ;
That thy father, Gaul and Oscar,
Can not be in Heaven.

O. Sorry be the tale, O Patrick,
Which thou art telling me ;
If Erin's Féinn are not in Heaven
Why should I Christian be ?

P. Grievous be thy story, Ossian,
Fierce thy words have grown ;
What are all the Féinn of Erin
To one hour with God alone ?

O. I would rather see one battle
Waged by valiant Finn
Than to see that Lord of heaven
And thou cleric chaunting sin.

P. Although the humming fly be small
A mote beneath its wing
Can not be hid unknown to Him
Who reigns as mighty King.

O. Think you that He was like Mac Cùil,
The brave and mighty Finn ?
Into whose presence all on earth
Could freely enter in ?

> *P.* Ossian, long art thou in slumber ;
>   The psalms make thy delight,
> Since thou hast lost thy strength and fame,
>   And ne'er again can fight.

> *O.* If I have lost my strength and fame,
>   And nought of Finian worth remains,
> Thy cleric rank I slightly prize
>   With all its gloomy strains.

Poor Ossian will not receive the new doctrine of the saint ; and his arguments with Patrick are not of a very edifying character. The saint, in order to convey to the bard some conception of the Creator's omniscience, says that it would not be possible for the smallest midge to enter heaven without His knowledge. But the bard exclaims in reply, that that was very different from Finn, son of Cuhal, in his hospitable hall. Thousands might enter, partake of his cheer, and depart without notice. At last Patrick gets somewhat impatient with his rather unsatisfactory pupil, and requests Ossian to give up his elegiac strains over the departed glory of the Clan Baoisgne, and relate the particulars of some hunt, battle, or adventure. The old warrior-bard is nothing loth, and is consoled for the moment by the recital of the deeds of his perished kinsmen, the Fianna. As usual he ends with a wild burst of sorrow for having survived them all.

" *Ossian and Evir-Alin* " has been a great favourite. In this ballad we have the great poet's wooing of the beautiful Evir described. He sets out with twelve youths to ask the daughter of Branno " of the silver beakers." Hitherto the maiden refused the sons of kings and nobles, and even the great gloomy chieftain Cormac, whom she particularly disliked. After necessary preliminary questions the ballad (in Pattison's translation) proceeds :—

> " High is the place, O Ossian !
>   Do men's tongues to thee assign ;
> If I twelve daughters had," said Branno,
>   " The best of them should be thine."

> Then they opened the choice and spare chamber,
>   That was shielded with down from the cold ;
> The posts of its door were of polished bone,
>   And the leaves were of good yellow gold.

> And as soon as the bright Evir-Alin
>   Saw Ossian, great Fingal's son,
> The love of her maiden youth
>   By me, proud hero, was won.

Then we left the dark lake of Lego
And homeward took our way ;
But Cormac, fierce Cormac, waylaid us,
Intent on the furious fray.

Eight heroes had followed their Chieftain,
And their men behind them stood ;
The hillside flamed with their armour,
Their spears were raised like a wood.

Eight came with Ossian the lofty,
All equal to shield him in war.

Then the heroes met face to face, and the strife was fierce and long. Ossian and Cormac at last met in personal combat with the following result :

Five times he dashed on my buckler ;
Five times I hurled him back,
Ere I struck him down on the greensward, —
Cormac in conflict not slack.

I swept the head from his shoulders,
And held it up in my hand ;
His troops they fled, and we came with joy
To Fingal's mountain land.

Oscar, the peerless son of Ossian, and the favourite grandson of Finn, is one of the bravest and finest characters among the Fingalians, and his early death greatly affected the hilarity of that happy band of heroes and hunters. The following verses from Gillies's collection record, instructions and precepts which were inculcated by his royal grandfather ; (my own translation) :—

" Son of my son," said the King,
Oscar, thou young prince of might,
When watching thy glittering blade, 'twas my pride
To see thee triumph in the fight.
Cleave thou fast to thy fathers' fame,
And keep unsoiled their honoured name.

When Treunmor the prosperous lived,
And Trahal, great warriors' sire,
They were victors on every field,
Winning fame in the conflict dire.
Their names shall flourish in story and verse,
Which the bards hereafter shall rehearse.

> Oh ! Oscar, spare not the armed hero,
> But the needy and feeble sustain ;
> Like the spring-tide stream rushing in winter
> Attacking the foes of the Féinn ;
> But gentle as summer's breathing wind—
> To all that seek thy succour kind.
>
> Such was the victor Treunmor,
> And after him Trahal the brave ;
> And Finn, too, befriended the weak
> From the power of the tyrant to save.
> I would meet him with welcome hand,
> And shield him beneath my brand.

These are indeed noble sentiments and precepts from a semi-barbarian monarch such as Finn is supposed to have been. It may fairly be questioned whether this is not one of the more recent productions. One line, "'na aobhar shininn mo lamh "— *in his cause*, &c , reminds us of Christian conceptions. Such a word as *aobhar*, cause, does not, so far as I am aware, occur in the purely heathen poems.

The ballads on the deaths of Diarmad and of Oscar are among the best, and have been great favourites with popular reciters. The *Lay of Diarmad* seems to have given names to many places in Scotland and Ireland. The names of the heroes of the Féinn in general we find embedded in the nomenclature of the soil, especially the name of Finn, their great leader. This is evidence of the early era in which they lived, as well as of the affection with which the people cherished their memories. The death of Oscar is a very long ballad. What follows is a free rendering of upwards of the first half :—

> The feast was over and the morn
> Shed round its brilliant blaze ;
> The halls of Cairber gleamed afar
> Beneath the sheen of rays ;
>
> The light within lit up the face
> Of heroes stout and tall,
> Who started early to their feet
> To leave that ancient hall.
>
> Brown Oscar from the Albin shore
> Was there among the rest—
> Of beauteous form and boldest eye
> He stood in might confessed.
>
> " But ere we part," red Cairber said,
> In accents rude and strange,
> " Brown Oscar, come from Albin land,
> Our spear-shafts we exchange."

" Why so exchange," young Oscar said,
With calmly moving lips,
" Thou red-haired Cairber, why exchange,
Chief of the port of ships ?"

" Not much for me—not much for me,"
The frowning Cairber said,
" Though every warrior in your isles
To me a tribute paid."

" Whatever, Cairber, thou shouldst ask
Of gold or precious thing,
All that without disgrace might be
Asked by a manly King,

" Were thine at once ; but this exchange
Of shafts without the heads,
With ruthless scorn tears all the garb
Of kindness into shreds.

" Hadst thou not known, thou coward prince,
That Fingal is not by,
Thou hadst not dared to speak such words,—
Less loud would be thy cry."

" Though Fingal and thy father both
Were here, with sword in hand,
I would have asked, and I should have,
All that I now demand."

" If Fingal and my father both
Were here, with sword in hand,
Thou wouldst not, if they chose, retain
One foot of Erin land."

" I make a vow," quoth Cairber Red,
" Away to drive the deer
From Albin's sea-girt hills, and bring
The spoil to Erin here."

" I make a vow—a vow 'gainst that,"
Quoth Oscar. " With this spear
I'll drive thee back from Albin's hills
To Erin mount and mere."

Then Cairber roared, " I make a vow ;
This spear of might possessed,
Ere that, fair Oscar, thou shalt see,
I'll plant beneath thy breast."

" A vow ! a vow !" cried Oscar fierce,
" Ere that shall happen me,
Red Cairber ! in thy forehead proud
This spear shall planted be !"

Cold fear and rage alternately
   The other warriors shook,
When they had heard the dreadful vows
   Both heroes undertook.

They saw fierce gloom was gathering
   On Cairber's knitted brows ;
They marked how like the breaking storm
   The wrath of Oscar rose.

'Twas then a bard upon his harp,
   Gentle as evening's breath,
Poured forth the numbers that presage
   A mighty hero's death.

Then Oscar seized with rage his arms,
   And cast a glance around,
To see where stood his Albin chiefs—
   The few that there were found.

Great was the host of Cairber there ;
   But Oscar's friends were few,
Still they were brave and undismayed,
   And well their arms they knew.

The strife began. We heard the shouts
   That came to us afar,
And all the din of deadly clash
   From the dread scene of war.

Then up we rose and hastened
   To join the widespread fight ;
Each joined the battle as he reached
   With furious delight.

The bitter struggle lasted long,
   And many fell in death ;
Our smaller force still smaller grew
   On that dark fatal heath.

Thongh Oscar's sword—his friends oppressed—
   Was failing in its might,
We saw him struggling fiercely on
   Amid the woful fight,
Like a hawk darting on the birds
   That scattered in their flight !

His course was like the rushing roll
   Of surges with their roar
When winter storms have poured their force
   Upon the suffering shore.

The Sunbeam of the battle rose—
Finn's standard we did know—
Then slowly backward, foot by foot,
Retired the treacherous foe—

Scattered like sheep, and fall'n like leaves :
The wild pursuit rolled on ;
And on that field of dread were we
In silence left alone.

And there lay Oscar bleeding much
Upon the mournful plain ;
And every living Finian there
Had friends among the slain.

The bard Fergus is asked to relate to Finn how the Féinn fared in the conflict. In this part I follow a literal rendering of MacLauchlan's, modified by Morley :—

" Say, Bard of the Féinn of Erin,
How fared the fight, Fergus, my son,
In Gabhra's fierce battle-day ? say !"

The fight fared not well, son of Cumhal,
From Gabhra come tidings of ruin,
For Oscar the fearless is slain.
The sons of Cailte were seven ;
They fell with the Féinn of Alvin.
The youth of the Féinn are fallen,
Are dead in their battle array.
And dead on the field lies MacLuy,
With six of the sons of thy sire.
The young men of Alvin are fallen ;
The Féinn of Britain are fallen.
And dead is the king's son of Lochlin,
Who hastened to war for our right—
The king's son with a heart ever open,
And arm ever strong in the fight."

" Now, O Bard—my son's son, my desire,
My Oscar of him, Fergus, tell
How he hewed at the helms ere he fell."

" Hard were it Finn to number,
Heavy for me were the labour,
To tell of the host that has fallen,
Slain by the valour of Oscar.
No rush of the waterfall swifter,
No pounce of the hawk on his prey,
No whirlpool more sweeping and deadly,
Than Oscar in battle that day.

And you who last saw him could see
How he throbbed in the roar of the fray,
As a storm-worried leaf on the tree
Whose fellows lie fallen below,
As an aspen will quiver and sway
While the axe deals it blow upon blow.
When he saw that MacArt, King of Erin,
Still lived in the midst of the roar,
Oscar gathered his force to roll on him
As waves roll to break on the shore.
The king's son, Cairber, saw the danger,
He shook his great hungering spear,
Grief of Griefs! drove its point through our Oscar,
Who braved the death-stroke without fear.
Rushing still on MacArt, King of Erin,
His weight on his weapon he threw,
And smote at MacArt, and again smote
Cairber, whom that second blow slew.
So died Oscar, a king in his glory.
I, Fergus the bard, grieve my way
Through all lands, saying how went the story
Of Gabhra's fierce battle-day."   " Say !"

I take the following lines of the close of this grand ballad from
Pattison's blank-verse translation.   Finn was beside his grandson
before he breathed his last.   Oscar heard the great king's wailing
cry, and looking round on all he sighed and said, " Farewell ! I
shall return no more."   Finn, who never wept before in sight of
man but once, when Bran died, strode a pace away and wept.
But—

Then Finn came back ; and, standing near my side,
He bent again o'er Oscar, while he said :—
" The mournful howlings of the dogs distress me—
The groanings of the heroes old and grey—
The people's wailing and their blank despair.

O son ! that I had fallen in thy stead,
In the dire battle with thy treacherous foes,
And thou hadst loved to be a chief and leader,
And bring the Finians east and west with joy !

O Oscar ! thou wilt never rise again !
O'er thee, my old heart, like an elk, is leaping !
Thou wilt return, thou wilt return no more !
'Twas rightly said, ' I shall return no more !' "

These are some of the scenes of the great battle of *Gabhra*, the
Temora of Macpherson, fought about the year 284 A.D.

Strong-minded ladies in these days clamour for women's rights ; but if men are wise they will, before conceding these, consider what use was made by women in the early days of Finian chivalry of the rights which they then enjoyed. In these Islands in ancient days the gentler sex appears to have possessed some extraordinary powers and to have exercised terrible privileges which were sometimes abused. If a lady put *Geasan* (obligation) on a knight or chief there was no escape from the execution of her wishes. He had to obey her, however unreasonable the request might be. Thus when the great Finn himself was in the earlier stages of his barbarian youth, before he became the celebrated General of the Féinn, and when he had no better raiment than the skins of the animals he slew for food, he came across one fine morning a grand assemblage of ladies resting on one bank of a great chasm, and a party of gentlemen on the other. One of the former, a proud Princess, insisted in her lover's case that he should clear that chasm before she gave him her hand ; but the poor fellow kept clapping his arms round his body till he could screw his courage to the springing point. Finn understood the conditions, and observed the unfortunate fellow's predicament, and modestly asked if she would take himself for her wedded lord on his accomplishing the task. She replied that he looked a personable enough man, though marvellously ill clad, and that if he succeeded she would give him the privilege. Finn did succeed, but she laid *Geasa* on him that he should accomplish the same task every year. This was not the only one that laid *Geasa* on Finn. Another fair tyrant insisted on his leaping over a dallan as high as his chin, with a similar pillar stone of the same dimensions borne upward on the palm of his hand. In after days he acknowleged in confidence to his father-in-law, that this was the most difficult feat he had ever performed, and few indeed would be disposed to doubt his assertion. On one occasion Finn nearly failed in one of these exploits ; the cause of his failure was thought to be his meeting a red-haired woman on the road, and that it was a Friday morning. It is evident that these Gaelic princesses were a little too exacting, and that it would not do for every one to undertake satisfying their somewhat unreasonable demands. That the laying on of *Geasa* was attended at times with much discomfort and danger is illustrated in the history of the beautiful but unfortunate Diarmad MacDoon.

Diarmad appears to have possessed one fatal gift—the *ball-seirce* —that of kindling love in all the women he met. It is said that

there was a spot of beauty on his forehead which captivated all
the ladies that saw him.   He was the nephew of the king ; and
full proud was Finn at times of the deeds of valour which his
sister's son had achieved.   He was generally described as the
young, the beautiful, the brown-haired Diarmad.   He was as
brave and gallant as he was handsome, and a universal favourite
among the Féinn.   But he was soon to come under the influence
of the inexorable *Geasa* which decided "the woful fate of Mac-
Doon."   At the wedding feast of Finn and Graine, the daughter
of King Cormac, the bride lays *Geasa* on Diarmad to carry her off ;
and though this was highly repugnant to his loyal feeling, and in
direct contravention to his military oath, as well as against his
personal interests, he was obliged to comply.   With what result
the well known ballad, called "The Lay of Diarmad," describes.
There are many versions of this ballad ; the one translated here
is that found in "The Book of the Dean of Lismore."   It is here
entitled "Bàs Dhiarmaid ;" or, *The Death of Diarmad.*   "A
houdir so Allane M'Royree," or "*The Author of this is Allan
M'Rorie*," is prefixed.   MacRorie was probably a mere reciter.
The ballad begins thus :—

> Here is Glen-Shee of the elk and deer,
>   Where we hear the sweetest sounds !
> Where oft on its strath the Féinn
>   Have hunted with eager hounds.
>
> On the fair brows of blue Ben-Gulbin
>   The sun its bright rays has shed,
> Where Finn oft pursued the chase,
>   And the streamlets ran down blood-red.
>
> Come, harken a little ; I sing
>   Of one of these heroes great—
> Of Ben-Gulbin and generous Finn ;
>   Of Diarmad's sorrowful fate.

In other versions the name of Graine and her elopement with
Diarmad are introduced here, as well as some sharp colloquy
between the latter and Finn.

> Mournful was Finn on that day
>   That the fair ruddy Diarmad died,
> When he followed the terrible boar
>   That yet had all spears defied.

'Twas left to bright-armed MacDoon
   To meet with the dreaded boar ;
It was Fingal's deceitful plan
   That the others should flee it before.

Few were beloved like him—
   MacDoon of that lovely band !
By beautiful women bewailed
   As he lay with his spear in hand.

Bravely he roused the boar
   On the hillside where it had lain—
The old boar of the sweet Glen-Shee,
   The fiercest that ever was slain.

There Finn of the ruddiest hue sat down
   'Neath Ben-Gulbin's grassy side ;
Whence issued the boar for the woodland ;
   Oh, the ill that did there betide !

'Twas the clank of the Finian arms,
   And the echoing shout of the men,
That wakened the slumbering monster :
   Before them he rushed down the glen.

He attempted to distance the heroes—
   The old boar of the bristling hide—
Which the spear and the shaft of the quiver
   Of the hunter so often defied.

In another version Finn is here represented as saying to Diarmad
—" Son of Doon, dost thou wish to win honour ?"—thus the king
spoke wrathfully ; and added—" Slay that boar by thyself, thou
gay victor, which the heroes so long has defied." Diarmad
attempts the task.

Then MacDoon of the keen-edged arms
   Comes up with the monster fierce,
With his strong poisoned spear he tried
   The side of the boar to pierce.

But his spear broke—shivered in three—
   On that tough and bristling hide ;
With his warm and blood-red hand
   That spear he vainly plied.

Then from its sheath he drew
   His blade of renown—thin-leaved ;
And with it MacDoon slew the monster
   While no hurt he himself received.

Finn is greatly disappointed at Diarmad's success. He evidently calculated that in his struggle with the boar alone his nephew would receive his death-hurt. This was not the case, and—

> Then Finn of the Féinn grew sad,
>   And sat on the side of the hill ;
> It grieved him that brave MacDoon
>   Escaped without wound or ill.

From the first Finn cannot be said to have adopted a very magnanimous plan for punishing his nephew ; but jealousy being cruel as the grave, he has formed now a cruel expedient for compassing his death :—

> After long silence he spoke—
>   These evil words spoke he—
> " Diarmad, measure the boar from the snout,
>   Tell how many feet long he be."

> Finn he had never refused—
>   Alas ! him no more we meet—
> He measures the back of the boar—
>   MacDoon of the lightsome feet.

In the other versions it is told that Diarmad's feet were bare, and that the length of the boar was sixteen feet. Finn denied that he was so long, and insisted on a second measuring.

> " Diarmad, measure with care again,
>   The boar *against the hair ;*"
> Mournful it was to see
>   That deed of the hero fair.

> He went on that errand sad,
>   And measured the boar again ;
> But he trod on a poisonous bristle,
>   And he felt in his heel a pain.

> The hero fell on the field—
>   MacDoon that had no deceit ;
> He lay there beside the boar :—
>   Now, there is the tale complete.

At this part of the relation another version adds that Diarmad, in asking several times for a drink at the hand of Finn, rehearsed how he served him "eastward and westward." But the king replied that the ill he had done him in one hour outweighed all the good exploits he could tell. " Thou shalt yet get no drink from my shell." Diarmad then addresses a melancholy farewell to Ben-Gulbin, the hill of his love, and to courtship. He keenly feels his sorrowful plight as his life-blood is ebbing away ; and true to his character his last thoughts are, as he dies, of " the maids of the Féinn." Finn then relents, and pronounces a regretful eulogy over the dead body of Diarmad. In the Dean's version it is the bard himself that pronounces the praise of the dead, in verses which describe his person and character :—

> Pierced to the heart he lies,
> MacDoon in the battle brave,
> The suffering son of the Féinn ;
> On this hillock I see his grave.
>
> The blue-eyed hawk of Essroy,
> The victor in every fight,
> Pierced by the poisonous bristle—
> There he lies on the height !
>
> By the jealous design of Finn
> Fell the bright-souled MacDoon
> Redder his lips than the cherry,
> Whiter his breast than the sun.
>
> His tresses flowed golden yellow ;
> Long eyelash 'neath brow so fair ;
> Blue and gray in his eye ;
> Pretty and curled his hair.
>
> Gentle and sweet in his speech
> Was that champion clothed with might ;
> With elegant hands and a faultless form,
> And a skin of purest white.
>
> Fair winner of women's love,
> MacDoon of the witching eyes ;
> In courtship he'll ne'er engage,
> For there 'neath the sod he lies.
>
> Nor with steed nor with hunter shall Diarmad
> Go forth for the chase again ;
> The loved son of beauty and valour
> Is left there, alas, in the Glen !

The *Death of Diarmad*, like the *Death of Oscar*, has been a great favourite with reciters. But believers in the authenticity of Mac-pherson's " Ossian" regard the former as inferior poetry. The author of the version translated above, Allan Macrorie, lived probably in the thirteenth or fourteenth century. Glen-Shee, mentioned in the poem, is a well-known locality in Perthshire, and Ben-Gulbin

is a hill in Glen-Shee. But this is not the only place that is said
to be the scene of the slaying of the boar and of Diarmad's death.
The district around West Loch Tarbert, Kintyre, also affords
topographical indications of the famous hunt having taken place
there. Nor can the claims of our friends, the Irish, be forgotten ;
they also have their *Sliabh Gulbin.*

When some of the ballads are described as *Ossianic* it is not to
be understood that they were composed at the time that Ossian is
supposed to have lived, but that the theme is Ossianic. Of this
class is a eulogistic poem on Finn in the Book of the Dean of
Lismore. Although written nearly 400 years ago it has yet a
modern ring about it as compared with many of the other ballads.
The earlier versions of these Ossianic ballads were composed probably in Pagan times, but as the Pagan reciters of them were dying
off, the minstrels nominally Christian would take their place, and
adapt the old ballads to the new state of things. The elder productions would be undergoing continual transformations in the
hands of every new class of reciters. While the theme is the same,
sometimes the versions are so different that no single verse in the
one can be found in the other. It is in this manner that their
chronology becomes a puzzle. Anachronisms abound. Ossian,
who flourished upwards of two hundred years before, is introduced
by the Christian and post-Ossianic reciters as holding converse
with St. Patrick.

"Actor hujus Ossane M'Finn ;" or *The Author of this is Ossian,
the Son of Finn,* is prefixed to the poem of which I am now to give
a translation. In the course of the ages, Ossian has had to accept
the paternity of many productions ; but people took this as a
matter of course until the appearance of the celebrated works of
James Macpherson, 250 years after Sir James Macgregor prefixed
Ossian's name to this poem. The poetry of this piece is not of a
very high order, but is interesting as giving the popular conceptions
regarding Finn 400 years ago. It was probably composed by an
ecclesiastic, the number of which class at the time in the Highlands
was considerable. It begins thus :—

> For twice three days and one great Finn I did not see ;
> And ne'er before a week such sorrow brought to me.
> The son of Teigi's daughter, king of deeds and might,
> My teacher and my strength, my guidance and my light.
> Both poet he and chief, a king my love commands ;
> Finn, monarch of the Féinn, the lord of many lands.
> Leviathan at sea, a lion on the shore,
> Keen as the air-borne hawk, and wise in art and lore ;

He's courteous and just, a ruler firm and true,
Full polished in his ways, deceit he never knew.
A lofty chief is he in song and in the fight,
Resistless to the foe, to friends their fame and might.
His skin is like the chalk, his cheek is like the rose,
His eye transparent blue, his hair like gold down flows.
The trust of all his men, with every charm of mind,
Prepared for worthy deed, to women meek and kind.
Great champion was he, loved son of field and flood,
The brightness of the blades, the tree above each wood.
Full generous was the king—good and rich wine he poured
From the large green-hued bottle on the festive board.

We never read in the older ballads of such non-primitive things as bottles. *Am botul mor glas*, which the liberal Finn would place on the table, must have belonged to the fifteenth century. The good qualities of Finn are not yet exhausted.

Of noble mind and form and of a winning mien—
His people's Head—he walked with step so firm, serene.
In Banva of the hills the fame of war he sought ;
There battles twice fifteen the royal Fingal fought.
Assistance for the weak MacCuhail ne'er withheld,
In heart and on his lips no falsehood ever dwelled.
Finn never grudged his aid, his people ne'er oppressed—
The King above all kings, the sun above the rest.
In Erin of the saints before his mighty hand
The monsters left the lakes, the serpents fled the land.
I never could declare, though mine were endless days,
I ne'er could tell one-third of his good deeds and praise.

It is rather curious to find the stereotyped " Erin of the Saints," in a composition of the fifteeenth century. While suggesting the ecclesiastical character of the author, it does not prove that he was a very zealous " saint " himself ; for we find that he quietly ascribes to Finn exploits which the Irish ecclesiastical world has all along attributed to St. Patrick. " He cleared the lakes of monsters and the land of serpents." As usual, Ossian himself is described as *an deigh na Feinne :—*

But sad am I, and Finn of the brave Fianna dead ;
With him, the princely chief, my pride and joy have fled.
Well may my tears outpour, for no delight survives
The princes and the chiefs and all their royal wives.
I lean on death's cold arm—I'm like the shaking reed ;
I'm like an empty nut—I seem a reinless steed.
A feeble kern am I, with sorrow sore within—
Ev'n Ossian I, the bard, the son of noble Finn.

In his forlorn state the bard now remembers the house and court of Finn, his royal father :—

> Since Finn now reigns no more, all that I owned is gone—
> His house had seven sides—the house of Cuhal's son ;
> And seven score of shields did hang on every side ;
> There fifty robes of wool had been the king beside—
> Fifty warriors filled the robes, who were the royal pride.
> There were ten bowls full bright for drink, where Finn did dine,
> Ten horns of gold, and ten blue flagons of good wine.
> How goodly was that house ! how grand the home of Finn !
> Mean grudging hands, false lustful hearts, there ne'er had been.
> Each man had equal rights among the mighty Féinn ;
> To emulate the King his followers were fain.
> He was our chief renowned so far, so nobly good,
> Who never to the meanest man was proud or rude.
> None empty left his house, good, generous was he ;
> No gifts were e'er like his—gifts scattered wide and free.

In *Cnoc-an-air*, an Irish poem, there is a description of the treasures of the Finians, which were said to have been hidden under Loch *Lene* (Killarney), that reminds us of the robes of wool in Finn's house. The Irishman and the Highlander got the conception probably from the same source :—

> This is the lake—the fiercest to be seen,
> That is under the sun truly ;
> Many treasures belonging to the Fians,
> Are in it doubtless secured this night.
>   There are in the northern side
>   Fifty blue-green coats of mail ;
>   There are in the western side
>   Fifty helmets in one pile !

And hundreds of swords, "broad" and "glittering," and shields, and gold and raiment in plenty. The scottish author, perhaps because his ideas were cast in a more ancient mould, was somewhat more modest in his description of Finian wealth.

THE NORSE BALLADS.

The Norse ballads constitute another class. The wars between the Féinn and the Lochlins are the theme of many of the ancient Ossianic ballads. It is impossible to say exactly to what age they severally belong. The Vikings, or sea-rovers, began their visits to the Western Isles and Ireland as early as the first century, and continued these visits for more than a thousand years. The name Viking has no connection with King being derived from vic, a bay —vicing, baysman—as Mr Robertson has clearly shown. The erroneous translation *sea-kings* has been used by several writers. It is the same word as the Gaelic *Uig*, the name of places on the west sides of Skye and Lewis. In English it assumes the form of *Wick*—Inner*wick*. It also means a bay or creek in Gaelic, as found in the words of a poet, "*uigean saile.*" In 794 the Western Isles were ravaged and Iona destroyed. The monastery of Iona was burnt in 802 by these Vikings; and in 806 the family of Iona, sixty-eight in number, were slain. The abbot of Iona then retired to Kells, Ireland, and Iona ceased to be the centre of Gaelic learning, while all relics of Gaelic culture were removed to Dunkeld and other places.

The Gaelic people of Albin and Erin call the Danes and the Vikings Lochlins. The Vikings were originally half Celtic, if not altogether a Celtic race. Indeed the substrata of many of the Germanic tribes were originally Celtic.

The following ballad probably relates to the wars of the eleventh century :—

THE FINIAN BANNERS.

The Norland King stood on the height
   And scanned the rolling sea ;
He proudly eyed his gallant ships
   That rode triumphantly.

And then he looked where lay his camp,
   Along the rocky coast,
And where were seen the heroes brave
   Of Lochlin's famous host.

Then to the land he turn'd, and there
   A fierce-like hero came ;
Above him was a flag of gold,
   That waved and shone like flame.

" Sweet Bard," thus spoke the Norland King,
   " What banner comes in sight ?
The valiant chief that leads the host,
   Who is that man of might ?"

" That," said the bard, " is young MacDoon
   His is that banner bright ;
When forth the Féinn to battle go,
   He's foremost in the fight."

"Sweet bard, another comes ; I see
  A blood-red banner toss'd
Above a mighty hero's head
  Who waves it o'er a host ?"

"That banner," quoth the bard, "belongs
  To good and valiant Rayne ;
Beneath it feet are bathed in blood
  And heads are cleft in twain."

"Sweet bard, what banner now I see
  A leader fierce and strong
Behind it moves with heroes brave
  Who furious round him throng ?"

"That is the banner of Great Gaul :
  That silken shred of gold,
Is first to march and last to turn,
  And flight ne'er stained its fold."

"Sweet bard, another now I see,
  High o'er a host it glows,
Tell whether it has ever shone
  O'er fields of slaughtered foes ?"

"That gory flag is Cailt's," quoth he,
  "It proudly peers in sight ;
It won its fame on many a field
  In fierce and bloody fight."

"Sweet bard, another still I see ;
  A host it flutters o'er ;
Like bird above the roaring surge
  That laves the storm-swept shore."

"The Broom of Peril," quoth the bard,
  "Young Oscar's banner, see :
Amidst the conflict of dread chiefs
  The proudest name has he."

The banner of great Finn we raised ;
  The Sunbeam gleaming far,
With golden spangles of renown
  From many a field of war.

The flag was fastened to its staff
  With nine strong chains of gold,
With nine times nine chiefs for each chain ;
  Before it foes oft rolled.

"Redeem your pledge to me," said Finn ;
  "And show your deeds of might
To Lochlin as you did before
  In many a gory fight."

Like torrents from the mountain heights
That roll resistless on ;
So down upon the foe we rushed,
And brillant victory won.

The above set of verses occur in several ballads with consider-able variations. It was a sort of national war-song among the Finian leaders in their frequent conflicts with the Norwegians. In the translation several verses are taken from different sources.

Heroic daring and deeds are ascribed by the bard to each of the warrior-chieftains. Brown Diarmad MacDoon is foremost in the fight ; the valiant Rayne leaves cloven heads behind him ; great Gaul is ever the first to fight, and never turns his back on the foe ; Cailte has won his fame on many a field : Oscar bears the proudest name of all the chiefs ; and, finally, Finn himself comes before us, his banner, Deo-greine (Sunbeam), gleaming with its spangles of fame over that heroic band, whom he now invites to sweep down on the Lochlins.

The specimens now given of the ancient ballad poetry of the Gael will be sufficient to indicate its character and style. It only remains now to mention in connection with the heroic ballads the names of a few more of the better known ones.

There is a very fine ballad on the death of *Dearg* or Dargo. Others are the Expeditions or *Imeachd* of Finn, of *Naoinear*, or Nine, &c., and the Great Distress of the Fingalians—*Teantachd Mor na Feinne.* A Norwegian *Hug* is the theme of a good deal of composition, while the *Invasion of Magnus* or *Manus* is a ballad of considerable length and interest. This was probably the celebrated Magnus Barefoot, so well-known in the Hebrides, and throughout the north-west. From the Orkneys to the Isle of Man and Ireland, along the west coast of Scotland, the Lochlins traversed the seas for centuries and held rule ; and well did they and the Highlanders know one another.

CHAPTER VI.

" Lying, worldly stories concerning the Tuatha de Danann, the sons of Milesius, and Finn Mac Cumhail with his Feine."—CARSUEL *(A.D. 1567.)*

IT may be thought by some that too much has been said concerning the ballads and the character of the Féinne. Others may be quite dissatisfied with the fragmentary notices which have been taken of those grand Gaelic ancestors. The former ought to bear in mind that the authors of these Celtic romances were the fathers and for centuries the cultivators of Gaelic song and story ; and that they were also "the cause" of much rhyme and romance in others. The student of Gaelic literature can no more give up his devotion to Ossian and to the bards who were his contemporaries and successors than the English student can forget his Chaucer and Spenser and the glorious poetic host of the Elizabethan age. The latter ought to remember that instead of a few paragraphs it would require many volumes to bring forward with fair adequacy the literature and history of the Finian period.

Let us now glance at the popular fictions of Irish romancists. To the Scottish student these are suggestive as presenting similar but varying conceptions regarding the same class of heroes.

As bearing on the Irish character of the present day, it is very remarkable that the Irish versions of the stories and ballads are, as compared with those of Scotland, characterised by more magnificent exaggerations and more gorgeous romance. The glow of richer eloquence and of a more splendid verbiage, combined at the same time with more of the sense of the ludicrous and incongruous, is felt as you tread the famous field of *Magh-lene*, or the more renowned scene of *Cathgarbh* [Gabhra], or listen to the cleverly invented dialogues between Ossian and Patrick, in the company and under the guidance of the Irish Gaelic literati. This is worth noting, for it indicates how early essential differences began to develop between the two tribes of the same race. At this very day the natural eloquence of Irishmen (proberbially all born orators) far transcends that of Highlanders, whose hardy native hills appear to have made them generally more men of brave deeds than of eloquent good words. The richer soil and the softer climate of Ireland have had a more emasculating influence on the Irish brother tribes ; but nature is not always unkind ; this possible disadvantage is more than counterbalanced by the rich flow, suavity, and sweetness of the Irish tongue. It is not only the eloquence but the peculiar character of Irish wit and humour that is traceable in Eire's versions of the Celtic romances. There is also a stationary element observable in the history of the nation. The pre-Celtic, Celtic or Finian Ireland is very much to-day what it was upwards of a thousand years ago. St. Patrick may have made the most of Ireland nominally Christian but the essential heathenism of many of the people has never been yet eradicated ; nor was it in the Highlands till this century, deeply and powerfully as the people were touched by drastic ecclesiastical and political changes. A Highland bard of great natural abilities and poetic endowments—William Livingston—has very well expressed in an interesting poem, " Eirin a' gul " (Erin weeping), his satisfied conviction that the people have never changed. Livingston sang as a Scottish Gael of the pre-Reformation days would. He had as little regard for his Holiness in Rome as he had for the late Rev. Principal Candlish, of Edinburgh, when the latter was preaching in Greenock, and Livingston assumed a threatening attitude as if he would dirk the preacher, who had the temerity to touch up the Highlanders—about the Sustentation Fund, I suppose. It is melancholy to observe—especially suggestive to those who make so much of our boasted advancement in civilisation—that the Gaelic peasantry of Munster to-day cannot show that they have risen higher on the steps of their ancestral dead selves than what they were when the Gaelic ballads were first rehearsed on the glens and bens of ancient *Muiman*. The same remark till recently was applicable to many parts of the Highlands.

Among the most famous of the old Celtic romances are the three tragical stories of the " Children of Tuirrean," the " Children of Lir," and the " Children of Uisneach," whom we have already come across in the Gaelic ballads ; also the " Pursuit of Diarmad," and the " Cattle Raid of Cuailgne." As it has been always so popular in both Scotland and Ireland, let us look at the " Pursuit of Diarmad." There is no space for even the briefest outlines of the large number of other celebrated fictions. The following

paragraphs from this nearly endless *Pursuit* may be compared
with the Scottish poetical version already given.

Finn is about to be married to the daughter of King Cormac,
and high festival is held in the banquetting hall of royal Tara.
The King of Erin sits down to enjoy drinking and pleasure, with
his wife at his shoulder, and Gràine at her shoulder. Finn Mac-
Cuhail is at the King's right hand. Cairbre Liffeachair, the son
of the king, is there, and so is Ossian, the son of Finn. The other
chief Finian heroes are also there. (In the quotations I follow the
Irish orthography of the proper names.)

" 'Tell me now,' said Grainne to Daire Mac Morna of the
songs, 'who is that warrior at the right shoulder of Oisin, the son
of Fionn ?' ' Yonder,' said the druid, ' is Goll Mac Morna, the
active, the warlike.' ' Who is that warrior at the shoulder of Goll ?'
said Grainne. ' Oscar, the son of Oisin,' said the druid. ' Who
is that graceful-legged-man at the shoulder of Oscar ?' said Grainne.
' Caoilte Mac Ronain,' said the druid. ' What haughty, impetuous
warrior is that, yonder, at the shoulder of Caoilte ?' said Grainne.
' The son of Lughaidh of the mighty hand, and that man is sister's
son to Fionn Mac Cumhaill,' said the druid. ' Who is that
freckled, sweet-worded man, upon whom is the curling dusky-black
hair, and [who has] the two red ruddy cheeks, upon the left hand
of Oisin, the son of Fionn ?' ' That man is Diarmad, the grandson of Duibhne. the white-toothed, of the lightsome countenance :
that is the best lover of women and of maidens that is in the whole
world.' ' Who is that at the shoulder of Diarmad ?' said Grainne.
' Diorruing, the son of Dobhar Damhadh O'Baoisgne, and that
man is a druid and a skilful man of science,' said Daireduanach.
' That is a goodly company,' said Grainne "

Miss Gràine Mac Cormac, or rather Princess Gràine, might well
make this remarkable admission regarding the character of those
heroes. She was emphatically a woman. The above series of
questions is thoroughly in harmony with the inquisitorial character
of ladies of fashion in general, as well as with ordinary feminine
curiosity. This curiosity was awakened by the vision of and contact with a band of conquering heroes whose names have mysteri-
ously touched the heart of the Celtic world for centuries. Let
handsome young Diarmads be careful. Gràinne " called her attendant handmaid to her, and told her to bring to her the jewelled-
golden-chased goblet which was in the *grianan* after her. The
handmaid brought the goblet, and Grainne filled the goblet forthwith, and there used to go into it the drink of nine times nine men.

Grainne said, 'Take the goblet to Fionn first, and bid him take a draught out of it, and disclose to him that it is I that sent it to him.'" This was done by the obsequious handmaid ; the same dose was sent to Cormac, his wife, and son, by the orders of Princess Gràine, with the result that "one after another they fell into a stupor of sleep and of deep slumber." The scheming Gràine might well be satisfied with the immediate fruits of the potations which she administered to her father, Fionn and the rest. She is now to administer a dose of a different sort to Finn's nephew, Diarmad. And while we cannot refuse our sympathies to the brave and betrothed Finn, severe as our ethics in the marital sphere may be, yet we cannot also help remembering that it was hard for a young princess to be wedded to even a sovereign person whose son and grandson were present. She must have intuitively felt it would be the union of June and December. Diarmad, "the white-toothed, of the lightsome countenance ;" and "the best lover of women and of maidens in the whole world," and Finn's nephew, would naturally be esteemed a more desirable admirer by this highly passionate and royal girl.

Gràine turns to Diarmad and says to him : " Wilt thou receive courtship from me, O son of Duibhne ?" " I will not," said Diarmad. " Then," said Gràine, " I put thee under bonds of danger and destruction, O Diarmuid, that is, under the bonds of Drom-draoidheachta, if thou take me not with thee out of this household to-night, ere Fionn and the King of Erin arise out of that sleep." Diarmad replies by speaking of the bonds as " evil," and indulges in expressions of self-depreciation. She reminds him of some brave deeds he performed once "on the plain of Teamhair [Tara]," when " Fionn and the seven battalions of the standing Fenians chanced to be there." She insinuates that this was the cause of her admiration, seeing Diarmad taking ' his caman from the next man to " him, and winning the goal three times upon Cairber and upon the warriors of Teamhair." She turned the light of her eyes upon him that day, and never gave her love to another, nor would she till she died. Diarmad wonders why it was not Finn that was the object of her love instead of himself, because ' there is not in Erin a man that is fonder of a woman than he." He now makes another excuse : Finn has the keys of Tara ; they cannot leave the town. But the willing lady finds means of exit for herself and the reluctantly gallant gentleman. " There is a wicket-gate to my *Grianan*, and we will pass out through it." Diarmad, after some more ungallant excuses, goes to " his people," and particularly to

Ossian, and says, "O, Oisin, son of Fionn, what shall I do with these bonds that have been laid on me?" "Thou are not guilty of the bonds which have been laid on thee," said Oisin, "and I tell thee to follow Grainne, and keep thyself well against the wiles of Fionn." The soft-hearted, but irresolute Diarmad, questions the rest of the Finian heroes in a similar fashion; and they all appear to be favourable to Gràine's proposition and bonds; one of them, Caoilte, says very gallantly and emphatically, "I say that I have a fitting wife, and yet I had rather than the wealth of the world that it had been to me that Grainne gave that love." This sounds very like the possible determination of a chivalrous Irish colonel of "the seven battalions of the standing Fenians." After a little further hesitation, Diarmad at last exclaims, "Then go forward, O Grainne." The hero now enters on a series of manly exploits Gràine and he flee into Clanrickard, in Galway, where he fortifies a little grove in which they shelter themselves. Those in pursuit discover this grove, but Diarmad's sagacious advisers before he left send the knowing dog, Bran, half-human, half-brute, to warn him. Bran has "knowledge and wisdom," and thrusts his head into Diarmad's bosom. That, and the friendly shouts of the dog's far-off masters are sufficient.

There now appears in the relation a character well known in many stories—*Aonghas*, or Angus, *vel* Innes, *vel* Æneas, of the Brough, a place on the Boyne. He was the son of Dagdae, a king of the Danaans in Ireland; and *mirabile dictu* reigned over the island for eighty years. He was a great friend of Diarmad, to whom he presented two remarkable swords and two javelins equally remarkable and *venomous* in their character, designated—the former *Moraltagh* and *Begaltagh*; and the latter, *Gathdearg* and *Gath-buidhe*. He now comes to the help of the eloping fugitives in their besieged "grove," where "Grainne awoke out of her sleep" in a rather disconcerted state of mind. *Aonghas* carries her off in a fold of his mantle, but Diarmad will not submit to be rescued in that rather inglorious fashion.

After that Aonghas and Gràine had departed. Diarmad "arose as a straight pillar and stood upright, and girded his arms and his armour and his various sharp weapons about him." He came to a door of the seven-wattled doors that there were to the enclosure, and asked who was at it. One or other of the chiefs of the Féinne was at the first five doors at which he successively interrogated; and each and all of them were ready to permit him tacitly to make his escape, but his chivalrous nature would not 'allow him to regain his freedom in any unknightly fashion. The sixth wicket is hostile ; but it is not Finn's. He comes to the seventh :—" He asked who was at it? ' Here are Fionn, the son of Cumhaill, the son of Art, the son of Treunmhor, O'Baoisgne, and four hundred hirelings with him ; and we bear thee no love, and if thou wouldst come out to us, we would cleave thy bones asunder.' ' I pledge my sword,' said Diarmuid, ' that the door at which thou art, O Fionn, is the first [i.e, the very] door by which I will pass of [all] the doors.' Having heard that Fionn charged his battalions on pain of their death, and of their instant destruction, not to let Diarmad pass them without their knowledge. Diarmuid having heard that, arose with an airy, high, exceeding light bound, by the shafts of his javelins and by the staves of his spears, and went a great way out beyond Fionn and beyond his people without their knowledge or perception. He looked back upon them, and proclaimed to them that he had passed them, and slung his shield upon the broad arched expanse of his back, and so went straight westward ; and he was not long in going out of sight of Fionn and of the Fenians."

At Ros-da-shoileach (now Limerick) the hero found Aonghas and Gràine in a warm and comfortable hut, with half a wild boar on spits. Aonghas departs, leaving with them his best counsel against " the wiles of Finn."

After availing themselves of various refuges, the fugitive pair approach the west coast of Kerry, where they see the allies of Fionn from the French coast drawing close to the shore. Nine times nine warriors step ashore, and Diarmad inquires what was their business, and what county they came from. The reply that they are " the three royal chiefs of Muir-n-iocht," and are now come at Fionn Mac Cumhaill's order to seek and to curb " a forest marauder " called Diarmuid O'Duibhne, whom he has outlawed. In a trial of skill Diarmuid kills fifty of these French Finians. These are styled " green " Finians, with three of whom Diarmad deals somewhat remorselessly in the course of a day or two. Their names will be interesting to the Gaelic reader—*Duch-chosach* (black-footed), *Fionn-chosach* (fair footed), *Treun chosach* (strong-footed). Before he finally encounters these and the " three enchanted hounds " Diarmad thus accoutres himself :—" He girt about him his suit of battle and of conflict, under which, through which, or over which, it was not possible to wound him ; and he took the Moralltach, that is the sword of Aonghas na Brogha, at his left side, which [sword] left no stroke nor blow unfinished at the first trial.   He took likewise his two thick shafted javelins of battle- -from which none recovered, either man or woman, that had ever been wounded by them.   After that, Diarmuid roused Grainne and bade her keep watch and ward for Muadhan, [saying] that he himself would go to view the four quarters around him. When Grainne beheld Diarmuid with bravery and daring [clothed] in his suit of anger and of battle, fear and great dread seized her." But an off-hand reply "soothed Grainne, and then Diarmuid went in that array to meet the green Finians." These are part of the troubles and feats of Diarmad MacDoon, the alleged ancestor of the great MacCailein line.   The romance will be found in the third volume of the Transactions of the Dublin Ossianic Society, well edited by Mr S. H. O'Grady.   Our own Highland versions on the subject are tolerably well known.

During the dreamy period of the Middle Ages the great literary source of amusement among the Gaels of Scotland were the "Ursgeuls," *noble* or romantic tales, which upwards of thirty years ago were collected and published (1859-62) by J. F. Campbell, Esq., of Islay.   They were not produced in the heroic ages, the period of the great mass of our ballad literature.   The ballads and the tales, no doubt, have been mixed together ; but the latter are distinctly of a later growth.   Some of the tales were manufac- tured as recently as the eighteenth century ; but the most of them belong to the pre-Reformation period.   Some of them are traceable to classical sources ; others indicate relationship with Oriental stories.   From Japan to the Hebrides, as shown by Mr Campbell in his introduction and notes to the four volumes of his " West Highland Tales," are found the relics of the same original " Sgeul- achd,'' with the modifications which country, clime, and circum- stance would naturally necessitate.   In their fundamental lines or conceptions these tales are the common property of the whole Aryan race—of the Hindoo in the east, and of the German and Celt of the west.   The study of talelogy, as well as philology, leads us to the common origin of all the members of the Indo-European family.   Many of the Highland tales must have been matured under the spirit that the crusades into the east invoked in the west. We find reference in them to Turks, Greeks, Romans, Spaniards, Franks, &c., and to conditions of life which show their close relations to mediæval times.   They became the popular literary sustenance of the people, supplying the want which is met by the popular works of fiction or novels of the present day.   We find every phase of character exhibited in their outlines, extravagant as many of them often are. They are still waiting classification. Mr Campbell was a very enthusiastic collector of these tales for years. He traversed more than once the whole of the Highlands to gather up these fragments of bygone Celtic life. His success far exceeded his sanguine anticipations. His volumes constitute the monument of his success, as well as of the industry, talent, and scientific spirit which he brought to bear upon the work. He had many hearty assistants in all parts of the Highlands, whom he inspired with much of his own enthusiasm. Mr Hector Mac-Lean, of Ballygrant, Islay, an able Gaelic scholar, and a man of real culture and literary talent, helped him in transcribing the Gaelic, while he himself transferred the tales into literal idiomatic English. It has been fortunate for our limited Gaelic literature that Mr Campbell has left us so much of our popular prose in these goodly four volumes, and so much of genuine ballad poetry in his " Leabhar na Féinne." I give a specimen of these tales in translation. Space will not admit of giving the *sgeulachd* complete; but enough is presented to illustrate the general style and character. The reader of these tales realises at once their kinship with the Danish tales of Andersen, the German stories of Grimm, and the Welsh Mabinogion translated by Lady Guest.

MAOL A' CHLIOBAIN.

There was a widow once of a time, and she had three daughters, and they said to her that they were going to seek their fortunes. She prepared three bannocks. She said to the big daughter, " Whether do you like best the little half with my blessing, or the big half with my curse ?" " I like best," said she, " the big half with your curse." She said to the middle one, " Whether do you like best the big half with my curse, or the little half with my blessing ?" " I like best," said she, "the big half with your curse." She said to the little one, " Whether do you like best the big half with my curse, or the little half with my blessing ?" " I like best the little half with your blessing." This pleased her mother, and she gave her the other half likewise.

They left, but the two elder ones did not wish to have the younger one with them, and they tied her to a stone. They held on, and when they looked behind them whom did they see coming but her with the rock on her back. They let her alone for a while until they reached a stack of peats, and they tied her to the peat-stack. They held on for a while, when whom did they see coming but her with the stack of peats on her back. They let her alone for a while until they reached a tree, and they tied her to the tree. They held on, and whom did they see coming but her with the tree on her back. They saw that there was no use meddling with her. They loosed her and they let her come with them. They were travelling till night overtook them. They saw a light far from them. and if it was far from them they were not long reaching it. 'They went in. What was this but the house of a giant. They asked to remain overnight. They got that, and they were set to bed with the three daughters of the giant.

There were turns of amber beads around the necks of the giant's daughters, and strings of hair around their necks. They all slept, but Maol a' Chliobain kept awake. During the night the giant got thirsty. He called to his bald rough-skinned lad to bring him water. The bald rough-skinned lad said that there was not a drop within. " Kill," said he, " one of the strange girls, and bring me her blood." " How will I know them ?" said the bald rough-skinned lad " There are turns of beads about the necks of my daughters, and turns of hair about the necks of the rest." Maol a' Chliobain heard the giant, and as quickly as she could she put the strings of hair that were about her own neck and the necks of her sisters about the necks of the giant's daughters, and the beads that were about the necks of the giant's daughters about her own neck and the necks of her sisters, and laid herself quietly down. The bald rough-skinned lad came and killed one of the daughters of the giant, and brought him her blood. He bade him bring him more. He killed the second one. He bade him bring him more, and he killed the third. Maol a' Chliobain wakened her sisters, and she took them on her back and went away. The giant observed her, and he followed her.

The sparks of fire which she was driving out of the stones with her heels were striking the giant in the chin, and the sparks of fire that the giant was taking out of the stones with the points of his feet, they were striking Maol a' Chliobain in the back of her head. It was thus with them until they reached a river. Maol a' Chliobain leaped the river, and the giant could not leap the river. " You are over, Maol a' Chliobain." " Yes, if it vex you." " You killed my three bald red-skinned daughters." " Yes, if it vex you." " And when will you come again ?" " I will come when my business brings me," &c., &c.

The tale is a good deal longer ; but the above portion will give an idea of the style and manner of the whole. Unlike many of the ballads, the language of these tales is thoroughly popular. Mr Campbell had in his possession, besides what he published, much material deposited after his recent death in the Advocates' Library.

A Popular Rhyme, frequently occurring in the tales, is a great favourite as a boat song. It fills the same place in the popular romances that the "Banners" does in the heroic ballads. The original will be found in the second volume of Campbell's " Tales," and is regarded as very old. "The vigorous and elastic spirit that pervades the following verses must have strung the heart of many a hardy mariner who loved to feel the fresh and briny breeze driving his snoring Birlinn, bounding like a living creature over the tumbling billows of the inland loch, or the huge swell of the majestic main." Pattison translates thus :—

We turned her prow unto the sea, her stern unto the shore,
And first we raised the tall, tough masts, and then the canvas hoar ;
Fast filled our towering, cloud-like sails, for the wind came from the land,
And such a wind as we might choose, were the winds at our command :
A breeze that rushing down the hill would strip the blooming heather,
Or rustling through the green-clad grove, would whirl its leaves together.
It heaped the ruins on the land, though sire and sire stood by,
They could no help afford, but gaze with wan and troubled eye !
A flap, a flash, the green roll dashed, and laughed against the red ;
Upon our boards, now here, now there, it knocked its foamy head.
The dun bowed whilk in the abyss, as on the galley bore,
Gave a tap upon her gunwale and a slap upon her floor.
She could have split a slender straw—so clean and so well she went—
As still obedient to the helm her stately course she bent.
We watched the big beast eat the small—the small beast nimbly fly,
And listen to the plunging eels—the sea-gulls' clang on high—
We had no other music to cheer us on our way
Till round those sheltering hills we passed, and anchored in this bay.

When the hero or heroes of the tale had to undertake a sea voyage this rhyme was invariably introduced by the reciter as a fit description of how it was accomplished. *Ghearradh i cuinnlein caol coirce le feabhas a stiuraidh* appears to have been the highest conception of skilful steering, and we may readily believe that it would be hard to surpass such a marvellous feat. Much complaint has been made against these same "lying, worldly stories," which the good bishop Carsuel found obstructing his reforming efforts. Several of his profession since have uttered the same complaint. But surely if the minds of the people were not filled with a better gospel, the wisest thing they could do was to extract any lessons of prudence and morality that they could find in these simple tales.

As to the preservation and age of these romances the question is excellently stated in the following sentences by Standish G'Grady: " Whatever it may be that has given vitality to the traditions of the mythic and elder historic period, they have survived to modern times ; when they have been formed into large manuscript collections, of which the commonest titles, ' Bolg an t-Salathair,' answering to a 'Comprehensive Miscellany.' These were for the most part written by professional scribes and schoolmasters, and being then lent to, or bought by those who could read, but had no leisure to write, used to be read aloud in farmer's houses on occasions when numbers were collected at some employment, such as wool-carding in the evenings ; but especially at wakes.   Thus the people became familiar with all these tales.   The writer has heard a man who never possessed a manuscript, nor heard of O'Flanagan's publication, relate at the fireside the death of the sons of Uisneach without omitting one adventure, and in great part retaining the very words of the written versions."   " It has been already said that some of these legends and poems are new versions of old ; but it is not to be supposed that they are so in at all the same degree or the same sense as, for instance, the modernised *Canterbury Tales* are of Chaucer's original work.   There is this great difference, that in the former, nothing has been changed but some inflections and constructions, and the orthography which has become more fixed ; the genius and idiom of the language, and in a very great measure the words, remaining the same ; while in the latter all these have been much altered.   Again the new versions of Chaucer are of the present day ; whereas our tales and poems, both the modifications of older ones, and those which in their very origin are recent, are one with the other, most probably three hundred years old."

It was the authors, writers, and preservers of these tales and romances that manufactured and handed down to us the fabulous chronicles in which the early migrations and history of the Gaelic clans lie embedded.   Let us cast a glance at these interesting chronicles, the historical value of which has not yet been decided by our Celtic literati.   ·

It has been a question much discussed, how the British islands were first peopled ; whether some other nameless tribes landed before the Celts ; and in what manner the Celts came into possession.   It is admitted by some Cymri in traditions that their brother Gaels were before them, whoever had been in possession before the Gaels.   Hu the Mighty, the great ancestor of the

Welsh, being a wise ruler, entered into federal relations with the Gaels on his arrival, the land being extensive enough for the two Celtic tribes. This Hu Gadarn, who is said to have come with his people direct from the regions round about " where Constantinople now is," is thus described in the poetry of his country :—

> " The mighty Hu with mead would pay
> The bard for his melodious lay ;
> The Emperor of land and sea
> And of all living things was he."

Irish annalists make a certain Milesius and others leaders of the Gaelic colonies by which Ireland was peopled. These colonies came from the East, and having rested in Spain, they sailed thence directly to Ireland. There are many historical romances extant regarding these colonies of Gaels and their wanderings and final settlement in Ireland. " The Chronicles of Eri " is among the most interesting. Dr Keating, in his legendary history of Ireland, gives the descent of the Gael from Gathelus, or *Gaidheal Glas*, as follows :—Gathelus, who started westward from Egypt, was the son of Niul, son of Fenius Farsa, son of Baath, son of Magog, son of Japhet, son of Noah ! The force of reason could no further go. Niul was a man of much learning and wisdom, and was married to a daughter of Pharaoh, called Scoto. She was the mother of Gathelus, who, it is said, was an intimate friend of Moses. When the great exodus of Israel from Egypt took place Gathelus was in his eightieth year. After various adventures his descendants arrived in Spain, where they remained for some time masters of the country. Milidh or Milesius was an eminent warrior ; greatly distinguished himself before leaving Egypt in a war with the Ethiopians ; fought in Scythia, and became one of the kings of the descendants of Gathelus in Spain. He also was married to a Scota, a daughter of Pharaoh. His sons, in the year 500 before Christ, sailed to Ireland with a fleet of thirty vessels. They soon conquered the Tuatha de Danaan, and divided Ireland into two parts. Ebir was made king of the southern part of the island, and Eremon of the northern part.

The descendants of Gathelus in all their wanderings are supposed to have carried with them Jacob's Stone, the famous *Lia Fail*, or stone of destiny, stolen from Scone by that royal robber of Scotch antiquities, Edward I., now in the coronation chair in Wesiminster Abbey. It is alleged that it was removed from Ireland to Scotland in ₋03 A.D. by Murtogh MacEarc that his brother Fergus Mor might be crowned on it. Science makes havoc at times with tradition. After examining the *Lia Fail*, Professor Geikie, according to Dr Skene. declares that it is merely a block of Perthshire sandstone. At the same time, it must be a stone of great antiquity, and lies at last in a safe and honourable resting-place, at whose shrine, and before the mightiest and most beloved Monarch that ever sat on an earthly throne, Celt and Saxon, Dane and Norman, bend the knee in loyal unity. There is an interesting prophecy of a very ancient origin connected with the *Lia Fail*. O'Hartigan, an Irish poet, who died in 975, speaks of it in the following couplet—

> An cloch a ta fam dha shail,
> Uaithe raidhtear Inis Fail.
> *The stone beneath my two heels,*
> *From it, is said, the Isle of Fail.*

Hector Boece, the Scottish historian, gives the following Latin couplet :—

> Ni fallat fatum, Scoti, qnocunque locatum,
> Invenient lapidem, regnare tenentur ibidem ;

Of which Keating gives the following Gaelic :—

> Cineadh Scuit saor an fine,
> Mun budh breag an fhaisdine,
> Mar a fuighid an liagh-fhail,
> Dlighid flaitheas do ghabhail.

Rendered thus in English—

> The Scots shall brook that realm as native ground,
> If weirds fail not, where'er this chair is found.

So much for the *Lia Fail*.

There is a reluctance on the part of Irish writers to accept any theory that implies the colonisation of Ireland from Britain. On the contrary, they rather attempt to prove that the Scottish Gael emigrated from Ireland—a theory which appears to have been invented in the fifteenth century. It was afterwards adopted unquestioningly by Scottish antiquarians, with few exceptions, of whom James Macpherson of Ossianic fame was one. For some time the Highlanders generally accepted the theory, and almost all the Highland clans were somehow or other traced to an Irish original. *MacMhaighstir Alastair* thus sings of the original country of the clans according to the belief of last century :—

> " There are thousands now in Alba
> As stout as are in any land ;
> *The grey Gaels from Scota,*
> Who cheerful round your colours stand."

By *Scota* Ireland is meant. All the elaborate and romantic chronicles by which Milesian and Spanish colonies are made to land on Irish soil were mostly manufactured by monks in the Middle Ages, and have no defensible historical foundation ; the same may be affirmed of the alleged colonisation of Argyllshire by Irish Gaels.

Some of the romances and the chronicles, however, suggest what appear to be reliable facts respecting the several races of Erin and Albin. Just as there were several tribes of Finians in ancient Eire, so there are different tribes of Celts in modern Ireland. A powerful pre-Celtic element, as in the north-west of Scotland, prevails in the south-west of Ireland. On the other hand a Norse element also prevails in the north-west of Scotland, which has largely entered into the population of the north of Ireland. The difference of character exhibited by the generic Irish and generic Scottish Celt is to be traced no doubt to the degrees of original difference in the blending of races.

The Norse element has always been recognised by the more intelligent of the Highlanders. We find Mary MacLeod, the Harris poetess, born in 1569, addressing the Dunvegan chief of the day in these words :—

> " In counsel or fight, thy kindred
> Know these should be thine—
> Branch of *Lochlin's* wide-ruling
> And king-bearing line !
> And in Erin they know it
> Far over the brine ;
> No Earl would in Albin
> Thy friendship decline."

The matter of religion is, no doubt, an important factor in the later difference ; but the sturdier Norse element in the Highlander's constitution may account for much. In reading the literature of the two countries, we are at once struck with the different keys to which the bards attune their harps. An Irish bard, in English, sings thus of his country :—

"She sits alone on the cold gravestone,
    And only the dead are nigh her ;
In the tongue of the Gael she makes her wail ;
    The night wind rushes by her :

"'Few, O few, are the leal and true,
    And fewer shall be, and fewer ;
The land is a corse ;—no life, no force—
    O wind with sere leaves strew her !

"'Men ask what scope is left for hope
    To one who has known her story ;
I trust her dead ! Their graves are red ;
    But their souls are with God in glory.'"

This note is not to be found in the whole range of Highland
poetry.   Perhaps it is because the retrospect of the past is not so
full of sadness for the Highlander, who, notwithstanding his rebellions and their frequent non-success, has fairly maintained his
ground in Scotland.   He has had his share in the struggles for
Scotland's independence ; and he now identifies himself with the
whole nation, proud of the name, and rejoicing in her glorious
history.   The Jacobite bard, Alexander Macdonald, addresses the
Scottish Lion thus : —

"Hail ! thou rending Lion,
    Of matchless force and rampant pride !
When up thy chieftains roused them
    Gay banners fluttered far and wide.
.   .   .   .
Strong rock and everlasting,
    Hard and old and undecayed,
High thy royal crest show,
    For thousands gather in thy shade,
With mirth in their armour bright—
    The dauntless race that never yield—
The spectres that stir panic flight,
    When quick striking swords they wield.
Many gallant youths beneath thee,
    With stout hands and shoulders great,
Go rushing on where's honour won—
    For wild fight they're never late.
With steady foot and agile hand
    To thrust or cut each weapon gleams ;
Red on the ground death gasps around,
    But gay o'erhead the Lion streams.

Thou roaring, frowning Lion !" &c.

This is the kind of poetry on which the Highland national spirit has been fed. Retrospects have less weight and prospects more with the Highlander. On the other hand the Irish Gael dwells intensely on the past, and thus grievously sins against his future. As appendix to this chapter on prose romances, I give some Irish *literary facts* and a Hibernian *picture of Ossian* in verse, as—

IRISH VERSIONS.

The early literature of the Scottish Gael cannot be well under-stood apart from early Irish literature. The ballads of the two countries describe the same struggles ; the characters engaging in the strife are the same, and bear the same names. So it ought to be interesting to compare some of the idealised characters of early Irish literature with those that we find in Scotland.

The early history of Ireland and its literature has not yet been written, and the same remark is applicable to the Highlands of Scotland. One able and scientific work has been recently pro-duced in the latter country—the learned three volumes of Dr W. F. Skene—" Celtic Scotland." The indefatigable labours of the late Professor Eugéne O'Curry have prepared the way for an authentic history of Ireland ; and it is to be hoped that such works as those of the Gradys. Stokeses, &c., will clear the ground of fables and reveal the genuine lines of early Irish annals. In his "Lectures on the Manuscript Materials of Ancient Irish History," O'Curry remarks – " It will be found that all the writers who have published books on the subject up to the time of deliv-ering these lectures—books some of them large and elaborate—*not one* ever wrote who had previously acquired the necessary qualifications, *or even applied himself at all to the necessary study,* without which, as I think I have established beyond a doubt, the history of Ireland could not possibly have been written. *All* were ignorant, almost totally ignorant, of the greater part of the records and remains of which I have here, for the first time, endeavoured to present a comprehensive, and, in some sort, a connected account." Irish scholars have an immense mass of valuable ancient manuscrips in which they find rich remains of their early literature, as well as materials for their early history. Let us mention some of the most important. Here is a list of some of the old and middle Irish periods :—

A copy of the Four Gospels, stained with the blood of the Irish St Killian, who was martyred in 678 A.D. ; taken from his tomb in 743. In the library of Trinity College, Dublin, are found —A Latin copy of the Four Gospels, written previous to 700 A.D. ; the

Four Gospels of Dimma, Latin, with a few Gaelic words, 620 A.D. ; the Book of Durrow, containing the Four Latin Gospels, about 700 A.D. ; the Book of Kells, same contents as last, about 800 A.D. ; the Gospel of St. Moling, about 800 A.D. ; the Book of Armagh, containing the Latin New Testament, notes on St Patrick's life, and the life of St Martin of Tours, 807 A.D. ; the Book of Leinster, containing the Cattle Raid of Cuailgne, and the Destruction of Troy, 1150 A.D. ; the Yellow Book of Lecain, 1391 A.D. ; and the Book of Brehon Laws—the last-named three books are in the Irish language. In the Royal Irish Academy are the Book of the Dun Cow, also containing the Cattle Raid, 1106 A.D. ; the Book of Ballymote, 1391 A.D. ; also a copy of the Book of Lecain, 1416 A.D. These are all in the Irish language. Earlier dates than those given have been assigned to some of these books. These and the Annals of Loch Cè, the Annals of the Four Masters, the Annals of Tighernac, &c., are all of great interest and value to Gaelic scholars in Scotland. The ancient Celtic literature extant in Scotland cannot be at all compared in extent with that preserved in Ireland.

As already remarked, the picture of Ossian that the Irish ballads and tales present resembles that of the ballads and tales of Scotland. In the fourth volume of the Transactions of the Ossianic Society of Dublin, we find a description of the journey and residence of Ossian in *Tir-nan-Og*, "The Land of Youth." In Scotland this place is known as *Eilein-na-h-Oige*, "The Isle of Youth." Ossian and the rest of the Fianna were "hunting on a misty morning nigh the bordering shores of Loch Léin," when a fleet rider was seen advancing towards them—

> " A young maiden of most beautiful appearance,
> On a slender white steed of swiftest power."

The name of this maiden is " Niamh," and she describes herself as the " fair daughter of the King of Youth."

> " A royal crown was on her head ;
> And a brown mantle of precious silk,
> Spangled with stars of red gold,
> Covering her shoes down to the grass.

> " A garment, wide, long, and smooth,
> Covered the white steed :
> There was a comely saddle of red gold
> And her light hand held a bridle with a golden bit."

In answer to Fingal's inquiry she says that, " as yet she has not been spoken of with any man," but that " her affection and love she has given to his son "—Ossian. In these ballads and tales " geasan," some bewitching obligations or bonds, are frequently spoken of. It was by the exercise of this power—these invisible bonds—that the faithless spouse of Fingal compelled the beautiful Diarmad to elope with her. This Princess, " the golden-headed Niamh," put her " geasan " on Ossian. She thus addresses him :—

> " Obligations unresisted by true heroes,
> O ! generous Oisin, I put upon thee,
> To come with myself now upon my steed
> Till we arrive at the ' Land of Youth.'

> " It is the most delightful country to be found,
> Of greatest repute under the sun,
> Trees dropping with fruit and blossom,
> And foiliage growing on the tops of boughs.

> " Abundant there are honey and wine,
> And everything that eye has beheld,
> There will not come decline on thee with lapse of time,
> Death or decay thou wilt not see."

He is to get there a " hundred swords," and a hundred of every article or possession that could be dear to the heart of a warrior or a bard. Ossian thus replies :—

> " No refusal will I give from me,
> O charming queen of the golden curls !
> Thou art my choice above the women of the world,
> And I will go with willingness to the ' Land of Youth.' "

The poet then describes in melancholy strains his parting with his own people—the Féinne :—

> " I kissed my father sweetly and gently,
> And the same affection I got from him ;
> I bade adieu to all the Fianna,
> And the tears flowed down my cheeks.

> " Many a delightful day had Fionn and I,
> And the Fianna with us in great power,
> Been *chess-playing* and drinking,
> And hearing music—the last that was powerful ?

> " A hunting in smooth valleys,
> And our sweet-mouthed dogs with us there ;
> At other times, in the rough conflict,
> Slaughtering heroes with great vigour."

Macpherson's Ossian is never caught at "chess-playing," or speaking of other things that might savour of more recent days. The course of Ossian and Niamh is thus described :—

> " We turned our backs to the land,
> And our faces directly due west ;
> The smooth sea ebbed before us,
> And filled in billows after us."

Before they arrive at the " Land of Youth," Ossian rescues a distressed Princess from the hated hands of a giant ; and

> " We buried the great man
> In a deep sod-grave, wide and clear ;
> I raised his flag and monument,
> And I wrote his name in Ogham Cráobh."

They are welcomed to the " Land of Youth " by a " multitude of glittering bright hosts," and conducted to a Royal fortress, by whose side are seen—

> " Radiant summer-houses and palaces,
> Made all of precious stones."

> " When all arrived in one spot,
> Then courteously spoke the ' King of Youth,'
> And said, ' This is Ossin,' the son of Fionn,
> The gentle consort of 'golden-headed Niamh !' "

He spent a long time in the " Land of Youth ;" but in the midst of its calm, waveless existence, he longs for his old life with the Féinne, and for a sight once more of his lost brothers-in-arms :—

> " I asked leave of the King,
> And of my kind spouse—golden-headed Niamh,
> To go to Erinn back again,
> To see Fionn and his great host."

She reluctantly consents to Ossian's return ; and the parting is bitterly sad to both :—

> " I looked up into her countenance with compassion,
> And streams of tears run from my eyes,
> O Patrick ! thou wouldest have pitied her
> Tearing the hair of the golden head."

She warns him on his return never to alight off the white steed, or—

> " Thou wilt be an old man, withered and blind."

On his arrival in Erin he sought, with a doubtful and trembling heart, for the Fianna. He soon met a great troop of men and women, who saluted him kindly, and were surprised at the bulk of his person, his form, and appearance. He asked them whether Fionn was alive, and whether any disaster had swept the Fianna away. He was told that a " young maiden " came for Fionn, and that he went away with her to the " Land of Youth :"—

> " When I mysel heard that report,
> That Fionn did not live, nor any of the Fianna,
> I was seized with weariness and great sorrow,
> And I was full of melancholy after them."

The poet immediately betakes himself to "Almhuin" of great exploits in broad Leinster ; but could not see the " Court of Fionn," and—

> " There was not in its place in truth,
> But weeds, chick-weeds, and nettles."

While passing through the Glen of the Thrushes he sees three hundred men before him : their leader cries for help to the bard, whose chivalrous instincts are roused, and who, forgetting the strict injunctions of Niamh not to touch the earth, alighted and relieved them from their difficulty, performing the most marvellous exploits. But alas !—

> " No sooner did I come down,
> Than the white steed took fright ;
> He went then on his way,
> And I, in sorrow, both weak and feeble."

He had been a long time in the "Land of Youth," and intended going back to that country, perpetually "under the full bloom ;" but now he could not. His stay in that land reminds us of the seven sleepers of Ephesus. He tells the everlastingly occurring Patrick—

> " I spent a time protracted in length,
> Three hundred years and more,
> Until I thought 'twould be my desire
> To see Fionn and the Fianna alive."

The great prince-poet, as everywhere represented, is in his last days poor and blind. After declaring to Patrick that—

> " There is many a book written down,
> By the melodious sweet sages of the Gaels,
> Which we in truth are unable to relate to thee,
> Of the deeds of Fionn and of the Fianna ;"

he concludes his lengthy relation in these two stanzas :—

> " I lost the sight of my eyes,
> My form, my countenance, and my vigour,
> I was an old man, poor and blind,
> Without strength, understanding, or esteem.

> " Patrick ! there is to thee my story,
> As it occurred to myself without a lie,
> My going and my adventures in certain,
> And my returning from the ' Land of Youth.' "

Such is the picture we have of Ossian and his life in some of the Irish ballads. There is no resemblance between this poetry and that which Macpherson has given us. *Oisin an Tirna-h-Oige* is the production of a writer who lived not many centuries ago. It is certainly much more modern than even the Oisian of the older ballads, in which dialogues between the saint and the poet occur.

A very fine specimen of the old heroic poem of the Gael is the Battle of *Cnoc-an-air.* Here we have terrible fighting among the " Seven battalions of the standing Fenians." The Irish versions of the dialogues between Patrick and Ossian are very much like those of Scotland.

CHAPTER VII.

MEDIEVAL BARDS.

" Gach fili 's bard, gach léigh, aosdan is draoi,
Gach seanachaidh fòs, gach eoladhain shaor is saoi ;
Na diadhairean mòr bu chliú, 's bu ghloir do'n Chléir
B' ann leath' gu tarbhach labhair iad briathra Dhé."—MacLean.

THE unwise utterance of Dr Samuel Johnson that no Scottish
Gaelic manuscript of an older date than last century existed is
amply refuted by the catalogues of British, Irish, and Continental
Libraries. Private individuals also are in possession of Gaelic
manuscripts, some of which come to light now and then. In 1873
Admiral Macdonald sent to Mr J. F. Campbell of Islay the famous
Leabhar Dearg, or Red Book of Clan-Ranald, which he had recovered. This was one of the manuscripts which Macpherson
was supposed to have used and destroyed ; but after having read
it in company with Mr Standish O'Grady, Mr Campbell/declares
that this paper manuscript " does not contain one line of Macpherson's Ossian." It is highly probable that many others may
have ancient manuscripts among their family archives like this one
of Admiral Macdonald, the supposed destruction of which by
Macpherson caused so much literary waste in connection with the
Ossianic controversy.

There have been in Scotland many influences- -changes dynast-
ic, political, and ecclesiastical—unfavourable to the preservation
of our manuscripts. In the midst of these turbulent changes and
the ravages of wars, the vandal hands of foes that demolished
churches and burned houses would not spare the native literary
remains they might come across. We have lost much by the
ravages of the Norse in Iona, of the English at Scone, and of the
Reformers. But fresh access of national life came in each case.

It is not the intention of these chapters to describe at length the
MSS. that we have left us, but a few of the older ones may be
mentioned. The earliest, as already remarked, are to be found in
Continental Libraries— those on which Zeuss founded his " Gram-

matica Celtica." Some of them are no doubt Irish, but some of
them must have been also written by the missionaries who went
forth at that time from the College of Iona. The language and
MSS. of that period in Ireland and Scotland were of the same
character and were common property, and continued to be so to
a great extent till the period of the Reformation, which, as above
remarked, along with more violent political changes in Scotland before then, helped to destroy relics of preceding ages.
The oldest Gaelic MS. extant in this country is a folio beautifully
written on parchment or vellum from the collection of the late
Major MacLauchlan of Kilbride. It is in the possession of the
Highland Society, and is marked Vo. A., No. 1. It is supposed
to belong to the eighth century. The following remark is found
on the margin of the fourth leaf :—" Oidche bealtne ann a
coimhtech mo Pupu Muirciusa agus as olc lium nach marunn diol
in linesi dem bub Misi Fithil acc furnuidhe na scoile." It has
been thus rendered by the late Dr. Donald Smith :—" The night of
the first of May, in Coenobium of my Pope Marchus, and I
regret that there is not left of my ink enough to fill up this line.
Jane Fithil, an attendant on the school." The MS. "consists of a
poem, moral or religious, some short historical anecdotes, a critical
exposition of the *Tain*, an Irish tale."

One of the next oldest is named " Emanuel," and is ascribed to
the ninth century. Thirty-five lines are quoted in the appendix of
the Highland Society's report.

There is a parchment book that is attributed to the tenth or
eleventh century. It contains Biblical legends, a life of St Columba,
&c. It admits of no doubt that many Gaelic productions perished
in the eighth century, when Iona was sacked by the Norse. And
it is only a wonder that so many relics should have survived the
ruthless changes of those days.

Bishop Moore, of Norwich, afterwards of Ely, presented his
library, more than a century ago, to the University of Cambridge.
Among his large collection of books was a vellum MS. of 86 folios,
about six inches long by three broad. It is said that this MS. is as
old as the ninth century. The principal part of it is written in
Latin, and contains John's Gospel and portions of the other three
Gospels, the Apostles' Creed, and part of an Office for the visita-
tion of the sick. It belonged to an establishment of the Culdee
Church, and is an interesting relic of the Celtic learning and culture of the time, particularly of the ecclesiastics of that Church,
who, while cultivating their native Gaelic, could also read and

write Latin. To the Gaelic scholar the chief interest lies in the Celtic portion of the MS. —the Gaelic entries made on the margin and on other spaces in the volume. The MS. was published some years ago by the Spalding Club, under the excellent editorship of the late Dr John Stuart, who has given us the Gaelic entries as well as the original in a scholarly and careful fashion. A Gaelic paragraph on the founding of the old monastery of Deer has attracted much attention, on account of its reference to Columba, and because it shows the intimate connection that existed between the parent establishment at Iona and branch establishments in distant parts of Scotland.

The *Legend of Deer* is as follows :—

Columcille acus drostán mac cósgreg adálta tangator áhí marroalseg día doíb gonic abbordobóir acus béde cruthnec robomormáer buchan araginn acus essé rothídnaig dóib ingathráig sáin insaere gobraíth ómormaer acus ótbóséc. tangator asáúthle sen incathraig ele acus doráten ricolumcille sí iarfallán dórath dé acus dorodloeg arinmormáer .i. bédé gondas tabrád dó acus níthúrat acus rogab mac dó galár iarnéré na gleréc acus robomaréb act mádbec iarsén dochuíd inmormáer dattúc na glerec góndendaes ernacde les inmac gondisád slánte dó acus dórat inedbairt doíb nácloic intiprat goníce chlóic pette mic garnáit dorousat inuernacde acus tanic slante dó ; Íarsén dorat collumcille dódrostán inchadráig sén acus rosbenact acus foracaib imbrether gebe tisad ris nabab blienec buadacc tangatar deara drostán arscarthúin fri collumcille rolaboir collumcille bedeár áním óhúnn ímácc.

TRANSLATION :

(Columcille and Drostán of Gosgrach his pupil came from I as God had shown to them unto Abbordoboir and Bede the Pict was mormaer of Buchan before them, and it was he that gave them that town in freedom for ever from mormaer and tosech. They came after that to the other town, and it was pleasing to Calumcille, because it was full of God's grace, and he asked of the mormaer to wit Bede that he should give it to him ; and he did not give it ; and a son of his took an illness after [or in consequence of] refusing the clerics, and he was nearly dead [lit. he was dead but if it were a little.] After this the mormaer went to entreat the clerics that they should pray for the son that health should come to him, and he gave in offering to them from Cloch in tiprat to Cloch pette mic Garnait. They made the prayer, and health came to him. After that Calumcille gave to Drostán that town and blessed it and left as (his) word, " Whosoever should come against it, let him not be prosperous." Drostán's tears (deara) came on parting with Calumcille. Said Calumcille, " Let Dear be its name henceforward.")

According to this legend it seems that King Brude's court at Inverness was not the only distant place visited by the Iona Apostle, but that he also went as far east as the district of Buchan. The other chief Gaelic entries are records of grants of land made by the Monastery. The majority of the names entered, though mere patronymics then, became some time after clan names as understood at the present day.   It was then or very soon after that the ancient inhabitants of Celtic Albin began to form themselves into clans in the state in which they were found two centuries ago. The systems of feudalism and clanship began to blend and develop. Towards the end of the MS. the following interesting Gaelic entry is found :—" Forchubus caichduini imbia arrath in lebran colli aratardda bendacht foranmain in truagan rodscribai." This has been translated by the distinguished Celtic scholar Dr Whitley Stokes thus—" Be it on the conscience of every one in whom shall be for grace the booklet with splendour ; that he give a blessing on the soul of the wretchock who wrote it." The same eminent authority says—" In point of language this is identical with the oldest Irish glosses in Zeuss's *Grammatica Celtica.*" This precisely proves what has been elsewhere already stated, that the Gaelic of Scotland and Ireland at that time was exactly the same, and that it was at a later period that dialectic differences appeared. It also suggests that many of old existing MSS. might have been written by Scotchmen as well as by Irishmen.

The most ancient and authentic record of the Scottish Kings is to be found in a poem called " The Albannic Duan," which was recited by the Gaelic bard laureate of the day at the coronation of Malcolm III. It was found originally in the MacFirbis Manu-' script in the Royal Irish Academy. The name of the author is not known. The Duan consists of one hundred and eight lines, and is composed in the ballad measure. Being mostly a catalogue of names, it does not bear a verse translation very well. The first four stanzas run thus :—

> Ye learned men of Albin all,
>   Ye yellow-haired and gentle band,
> Who first invaded, do you know,
>   The ancient shore of Albin land ?
>
> Albanus came with active men,
>   That son of Isacon of fame,
> Brother of blameless Briutus he ;
>   From him did Albin get its name.
>
> Briutus sent his brother bold
>   Across the stormy sea of Icht,
> The sea-swept point of Fotudan
>   In Albin fair he took with might.
>
> Long after Briutus, brave and good,
>   The Nevi-clans the land enjoyed ;
> And Erglan, who came from his ship
>   When he had Conning tower destroyed.

It was probably in this reign that the ancient language of Albin ceased to be used in the Royal Court of Scotland. It continued, however, to be the fashionable speech of the provincial princes of the Isles until the lordship of the Isles terminated, towards the end of the sixteenth century, with Angus MacDonald of Duneevaig, Islay, and the Glens in Antrim. Sir James Macdonald of Antrim, who had no English, came with a magnificent retinue to visit James IV. of Scotland at Holyrood previous to his ascending the throne of England, and stopped for sometime at Court. Could the King, with whom Sir James was a great favourite, and to whom he was closely related, converse with him in the Gaelic language?

There is a parchment manuscript in quarto that belonged to the Kilbride collection. It is prettily written, and contains a metrical account or list of holidays, festivals, and saints' days throughout the year ; an almanack ; and a treatise on anatomy, abridged from Galen, &c. ; the Schola Salernitana in Leonine verse, drawn up about 1100 A.D., for the use of Robert, Duke of Normandy, the son of William the Conqueror, by the well-known medical school of Salerno. The Latin text is accompanied by a faithful Gaelic explanation. A specimen follows :—

> " Sivis incolumem, sivis te reddere sanum ;
> Curas tolle graves, irasci crede prophanum."

Gaelic—

> " Madh ail bhidh fallann agus madh aill bhidh slan ;
> Cuirna himsnimha tromadhit, agus creid gurub diomhain duit fearg de dhenumh."

Having the words *Leabhar Giollacholaim Meigleathadh* on the last page of the MS., it is supposed that it belonged to Malcolm Bethune, a member of a family distinguished for their learning and medical skill, that supplied for many ages with physicians the Western Isles of Scotland. It was one of them, Fergus Mac Beth or Beaton, that signed the holograph, of the famous Islay Charter of 1408 for Donald, Lord of the Isles. A MS. dated 1238 on the cover is supposed to have been written at Glenmason, in Cowal. It contains tales in prose and verse—one about *Deardri, Dearduil,* or *Darthula.*

Another valuable and interesting MS., dated 1512-26, belonging to Sir James Macgregor, Dean of Lismore—" Jacobus M'Gregor decanus Lismorensis "—has been mostly published. The editors who have done their work admirably, have been Dr Thomas Mac-Lauchlan and Dr W. F. Skene. The work of the former was very

difficult and laborious—first to change the orthography of the
Dean, which was phonetic, into modern Gaelic, and then give a
literal English translation.

Among other known manuscripts of the period is that of
Dunstaffnage, October 12 1603, by Ewen Macphaill. It contains
prose tales concerning Lochlin and Finnic heroes.

A paper manuscript 1654-5, by Edmond MacLauchlan. contains
sonnets, odes, epistles, and an ogham alphabet at the end.

A quarto paper manuscript of 1690-91 contains ancient and
modern tales and poems. It was written at Ardchonnail, on Loch-
awe side, by Ewen Maclean for Colin Campbell—" *Caillain
Caimpbel leis an leis an leabharan.*" This Gaelic inscription appears
on the seventy-ninth leaf of the manuscript.

In the fourteenth and fifteenth centuries we have arrived at a
period in which Gaelic is very generally written. To the latter
century belong the most of the manuscript materials extant. The
subjects of these manuscripts are of the most various descriptions.
We have among them compendiums of theology, fables and
anecdotes about saints, &c. The most valuable, perhaps, are the
genealogical manuscripts. The historian of Scottish annals is not
sufficiently equipped without knowledge of these. Some of them
no doubt, being family records very frequently, are very partial ;
but when collated the one will correct the other. Other subjects
treated of in these manuscripts are medicine and astrology. The
substance of these is translated from Greek and Moorish works,
Galen, Averroes, and Avicenna being the general sources. The
largest number of the medical manuscripts were written by or
passed through the hands of the Beatons, the well-known physicians
of the western isles. Astrology appears to have been studied by
the aid of Arabian writers ; so many of the superstitions or popular
ideas in the Highlands regarding the stars had probably an Arabic,
and not a Druidic origin, as the present Highlanders generally
believe. The surprising thing is that this science of the period
should be known and cultivated in such inaccessible places as the
Highlands and Islands. Dr MacLauchlan very pertinently and
truly remarks as follows :—" The metaphysical discussions [of the
MSS.], if they may be so called, are very curious, being characterised by the features which distinguished the science of metaphsies
at the time. The most remarkable thing is there are Gaelic terms
to express the most abstract ideas in metaphysics—terms which
are now obsolete, and would not be understood by any ordinary
Gaelic speaker. A perusal of these ancient writings shows how

much the language has declined, and to what an extent it was cultivated at an early period. So with astrology, its terms are translated and the science is fully set forth. Tables are furnished of the position of the stars, by means of which to foretell the character of future events. Whatever literature existed in Europe in the 14th and 15th centuries extended its influence to the Scottish Highlands. The nation was by no means in such a state of barbarism as some writers would lead us to expect. They had legal forms, for we have a formal legal charter of lands written in Gaelic; they had medical men of skill and acquirement; they had writers on law and theology, and they had men skilled in architecture and sculpture." But then these manuscripts, these evidences of light and culture among the Gaels of the Middle Ages, were buried in private and public libraries till some years ago; and historians and others not suspecting their existence did not look for them; and so wrote what their fancy dictated concerning the barbaric Gael.

In examining the older MSS. and assigning them a nationality, the student of Celtic literature must bear in mind that the language spoken in the Highlands of Scotland and in Ireland in early times was exactly the same, and that the dialectic differences existing just now have mostly developed since the period of the Reformation. The literature that the two Gaelic peoples possessed till then was also to a great extent common property. As to their writing, what is called "Irish hand," or vulgarly *Erse*, or "Irish character," is nothing more than what was once common throughout the whole of Europe. It was in it Gaelic writers once wrote in Scotland; and thus is how some of our early MSS. have been assigned an Irish origin.

With the reign of Malcolm III., or *Ceann-Mor*, in the eleventh century, and his marriage with an English Princess, Scottish institutions and habits began to be radically affected. The Anglicising and Romanising processes at work were in their final stages in the Lowlands about the time of the last invasion of the Norse in the thirteenth century. Soon after the laws and customs of Scotland were found quite transformed. Feudalism was introduced, and began to extend even among the Highland chiefs and clans. The system of clanship, although having apparent points of resemblance to feudalism, was in principle essentially different. "In the former case the people followed their chief as the head of their race, and the representative of the common ancestor of the clan; in the latter they obeyed their leader as feudal proprietor of the lands to

which they were attached, and to whom they owed military service
for their respective portions of these lands. The Highland chief
was the hereditary lord of all who belonged to his clan wherever
they dwelt, or whatever lands they occupied ; the feudal baron was
entitled to the military service of all who held hands under him,
to whatever race they might individually belong. The one dignity
was personal, the other was territorial : the rights of the chief were
inherent, those of the baron were accessory ; the one might lose
or forfeit his possessions, but could not thereby be divested of his
hereditary character and privileges ; the other when divested of
his fee ceased to have any title or claim to the service of those who
occupied the lands. Yet these two systems, so different in principle, were in effect nearly identical. Both exhibited the spectacle
of a subject possessed of unlimited power within his own territories,
and exacting unqualified obedience from a numerous train of
followers, to whom he stood in the several relations of landlord,
military leader, and judge, with all the powers and prerogatives
belonging to each of those characters." The system of clanship
was for a time better adapted for the Highlands ; but the tendency
of both clanship and feudalism was to obstruct the adminstration
of justice and impede the progress of improvement.

Let us now glance at the general culture of this period. From
the poetry of Finlay MacNab, in *The Book of the Dean of Lismore*,
we learn that the ancient bards were in the habit of writing their
compositions. Indeed there was far more literary culture among
the Gaels for many centuries before the Reformation than existed
for some time subsequent to that period. As in earlier ages there
was close intercourse in literary matters carried on during the
period of the Kingdom of the Isles between the Highlands and
Ireland. There are many names, Irish and Scotch, well known
in literary annals, to be found in the Highlands at this time. The
Beatons, originally O'Neils or MacNeills, were a family of learned
physicians in Islay and Mull. Manuscripts, either written by them
or in their possession, are still in existence. The MacVurichs,
descendants of Muireadhach Albannach, who were hereditary
senachies or bards to Clanranald. preserved the literary torch
lighted for generations in the Western Isles. Some of them are
said " to have received their education in Irish Colleges of poetry
and writing." On the other hand it seems to have been a general
practice for Irish scholars to come to the Highlands, where they
and their writings were well received and well known. Irish
annals inform us of Irish scholars who were regarded as masters

in the Highlands. These are the names of four of them :—

In 1185 died Maclosa O'Daly, ollave or scholar, a poet of Erin and Albin. He was famed for his poetry, hospitality and nobility.

In 1328 died blind O'Carril, chief minstrel of Erin and Albin in his day.

In 1448 died Tadgog, son of Tadg, son of Giollacoluim O'Higgin, chief preceptor of the poets of Erin and Albin.

In 1554 died Tagd, son of Aodh O'Coffey, chief teacher of poetry in Erin and Albin.

From this we learn that literature existed, and that it was sedulously cultivated both in the Highlands and in Ireland at this time ; and we also learn how much influence the one country exercised on the language and literature of the other.

During this period Gaelic scholars and culture were encouraged and fostered by the Princes, afterwards the Lords of the Isles. These Princes were also very liberal in their benefactions to the Church ; it was one of them, the great Somerled, that endowed the Abbey of Paisley. Iona and other places over which their sway extended had always their constant help. And thus in their patronage of churchmen they afforded shelter and protection to literature. The MacVurichs and the Beatons, already mentioned, were at one time their secretaries and senachies or clan-historians. Having in course of time extensive possessions in Ireland as well as in Scotland, much intercourse was maintained between the two countries, bards and scholars of both countries going and coming in their train. The most distinguished of them after Somerled were Donald, from whom the clan, Donald Bulloch, with his brother John Mor, and James Macdonald the last of the Isles who thus signs his name in a missive to the Irish Privy Council, on January 24, 1546 :- " James M'Connail of Dunnewaik and ye Glinnis, and aperand aeyr of ye Yllis." The Macdonalds, at one time or another, as Princes or Lords of the Isles, ruled for upwards of five centuries of the historical period over nearly the half of Scotland and part of the north of Ireland. They occupy a prominent place in Norse, Irish, and Scottish history. The Macdonalds finally lost all their lands in the West, the most of which passed into the hands of their powerful rivals the Campbells :—

> The Halls of Finlaggan no longer sound
> To joyous feasts and dances as of yore :
> The bard is dumb, the harper plays no more
> Where the proud princes of the Isles were crowned :—

> Their palace waste ! while sadness sits around ;
> And weeds and nettles flourish on the floor ;
> Stark silence hovers round the islet's shore
> Where tread of warriors oft had shook the ground.
> The chiefs and chieftains of the isles and west
> Are seen no more at great Macdonald's court ;
> Their galleys traverse not the island seas :
> They with their furious feuds are now at rest :
> Razed is each castle, ruined is each fort,
> Within thy bounds, Queen of the Hebrides !

The name that stands first on the roll of the bards of the Middle and Modern Ages is that of MUIREADACH ALBANNACH. He is the author of several poems which have been preserved in *The Book of the Dean of Lismore.* Religious subjects are the theme of all his compositions. None of the old bards exhibits so much earnestness and intensity of feeling. There is also more subjectivity in his poems than in other productions of the period. His name signifies Murdoch of Albin, or Scotland, given probably to distinguish him from another Irish bard of the same name. Muireadhach became the ancestor of a family of senachies and bards who have been very distinguished in the literary annals of Gaelic Scotland. They were hereditary bards and senachies to the Clanranald family. One of them, Lachlan Mòr MacMhuireadhach or Vurich, accompanied Donald Balloch of the Isles in 1411 at the battle of Harlaw, reciting his grand war-incitement poem. The last of them, Lachlan MacVurich, gives evidence in the report of the Highland Society on Ossian, and traces his genealogy through eighteen generations to Muireadhach Albannach. Muireadhach appears to have lived between A.D. 1180 and 1220. I give here a metrical version of a short religious poem of his in the Dean of Lismore's book. He is supposed to have been an ecclesiastic, as many of those who wrote in early times were.

> I praise Thee, Christ, that on Thy breast
> A guilty one like me may rest ;
> And that Thy favour I can share ;
> And on my lips Thy cross may bear.
>
> O Jesus, sanctify my heart,
> My hands and feet and every part ;
> Me sanctify in Thy good grace,—
> Blood, flesh and bones, and all my ways.
>
> I never cease committing sin ;
> For still its love resides within :
> May God His holy fragrance shed
> Upon my heart and on my head.

> Great glorious One vouchsafe relief
> From all the ills that bring me grief ;
> Ere I am laid beneath the sod :
> Before me smooth my way to God.

Another poem of Muireadhach is a curious dialogue between himself and Cathal Cròdhearg. King of Connaught, who lived towards
the end of the 12th century. Both of them were then entering on
a monastic life. It has been inferred from the dialogue that
Murdoch was a man of high birth. Another poem of his in the
Dean of Lismore's book I have translated as follows :—

> 'Tis time to leave for Paradise
> Since it is hard this pain to bear,—
> To win unsoiled, the heavenly prize
> Which others cannot with us share.

> Now to thy priest thyself confess,
> And all thy sins recall to mind,
> Seek not His court with guilt-stained dress,
> For in that state none entrance find.

> None of thy many sins conceal,
> Though sore it be their ill to tell :
> Thy secret thoughts and deeds reveal,
> Lest thou incur His wrath in hell.

> And with the clergy make thy peace,
> Unworthy, helpless though thou be ;
> Repent aright, and sinning cease,
> Lest heavy guilt be found on thee.

> He who forsakes the Lord Most High
> For love of sin, sinks deep in woes ;
> The evils wrought in secresy
> Full well the Eye all-searching knows.

> Let these be thoughts for Adam's race ;
> To me they do not seem untrue ;
> Men for a time may know their place,
> But death at last they can't eschew.

Muireadhach Albannach occupies the same relation to a
number of succeeding generations of bards in Scotland that the
famous Dafydd ap Gwilym (born, 1293) does towards succeeding
Welsh bards.

We have a specimen of the written Gaelic of this period in the
famous Macdonald charter, the earliest Gaelic one extant. In

1408 Donald, Lord of the Isles, granted lands in Islay to Brian Vicar Mackay of Rhinns, in that Island. The Mackays were an old family in Islay; from them came the Magees of Ireland, and I believe the present Bishop of Peterborough. The lands were Baile-Vicar, Cornobus, Cracobus, Tocamol, &c., in the parish of Kildalton. The charter conveying these lands, still in existence, is written in Gaelic. It was published some time ago by the Record Commission. It is an interesting document, and is here given in a literal translation. It was written by one of the Beatons, already referred to, who signs himself "Fergus M'Beth." He was probably at the time physician to the Lord of the Isles. As Dr M'Lauchlan, who deciphered it, says—"The style of the charter is that of the usual feudal charters written in Latin, but the remarkable thing is to find a document of the kind written in Gaelic, at a time when such a thing was almost unknown in the Saxon dialects of either England or Scotland."

It is interesting to find that the Gaelic of the charter, written 470 years ago, is the same as that spoken in Islay at the present day. One word *brach*, "ever," is spelt phonetically, just as it is pronounced now in the dialect of the island. The only word which seems to have changed its signification is *bheatha*, or un-aspirated *beatha*, which was then used for "world." *Beatha* in modern Gaelic means life, but an older form was *bith*, which now means being or existence, but in ancient Gaelic was used for "world." See *Zeuss's Grammar*.

In the name of God. Amen.

I, Mac Donald, am granting and giving eleven marks and a-half of land from myself and from my heirs, to Brian Vicar Mackay and to his heirs, after him for ever and ever, for his services . . . to myself and to my father before me; and this on covenant and on condition that he himself and they shall give to me and to my heirs after me yearly, four cows fit for killing for my house. And in case that these cows shall not be found, the above Brian and his heirs shall give to me and to my heirs after me, two marks and forty for the same above cows. And for the same cause I am binding myself and binding my heirs after me, to the end of the world, these lands, together with their fruit of sea and land, to defend and maintain to the above Brian Vicar Mackay, and to his heirs for ever after him in like manner. And these are the lands I have given to him and to his heirs for ever—namely, Baile-Vicar, Machaire, Leargariabhoighe, Ciontragha, Graftol, Tocamol, Ugasgog, the two Gleannastol, Cracobus, Cornubus, and Baile-Neaghtoin. And in order that there may be meaning, force, and effect in this grant I give from me, I again bind myself and my heirs for ever under covenant this to uphold and fulfil to the aforesaid Brian and his heirs after him to the end of the world, by putting my hand and my seal down here, in presence of these witnesses here below, and the sixth day of the month of the Beltane, and this year of the birth of Christ, one thouand four hundred and eight.

McDonald.

John Mac Donald.
Pat : Mac aBrian.
Fergus Mac Beth.
Hugh McCei.

It is a suggestive commentary on the uncertainty of sublunary things that these lands which Donald was to "uphold" "to the end of the world " to Brian and his heirs have passed through the hands of more than one family since—they being now the property of John Ramsay, of Kildalton. Neither a Mackay nor a Macdonald owns any land in Islay now.

Lachlan Mor MacVurich.—This senachie and bard to the Clanranald is the author of one of the most extraordinary poems in Gaelic or in any language. He was of the family of the famous Muireadhach Albannach. He accompanied Donald, Lord of the Isles, at the battle of Harlaw, in 1411, and rehearsed his poem to animate the followers of the Islay chief. This war song or battle incitement (Stewart's Collection) consists of three hundred and thirty-eight lines. The theme of the production is " O, children of Conn of the Hundred Fights! remember hardihood in the time of battle." Round this subject Lachlan Mòr has gathered some six hundred and fifty adverbial adjectives, arranged alphabetically, and every one of them bearing specially and martially on the great theme of the song. There is nothing in the poem but these adjectives, which certainly in themselves are not very poetical ; but rehearsed unhesitatingly from a good memory " in all their astonishing alliterative array by a ready speaker gifted with a strong and sensitive voice, they could not but have offered a rare opportunity for impetuous, vehement, and effective declamation."

It may be remarked here, en passant, that there is no decisive evidence for the assertions of historians that Donald of Islay lost that battle. He claimed the victory ; but even although it were more decided it would be equally barren of important results. It is also a misconception of the character of the forces engaged when it is said that one side was Celtic and the other Saxon, and that it was a struggle for race supremacy. There were many Gaels on the other side also, just as there were in the last battle fought on British ground—that of Culloden.

The Four Wise Men.—One of the most interesting poems in the Book of the Dean of Lismore is a dialogue between four men

who are supposed to stand at the grave of Alexander the Great.
It appears to be somewhat older than the fifteenth or sixteenth
century. It illustrates the strong masculine character of those
earlier ballads, where sense is not buried under a heap of verbiage.
Whoever the author was, he was evidently a man of sound judgment and cultured common-sense. Being of more than average
merit in the original, the poem bears translation better than other
inferior productions in the Dean's Book. It has been excellently
done by the late Mr Thomas Pattison, and I avail myself of his
version. It is very interesting to read the moralisings of Highlanders some five hundred years ago.

> For wise men met beside the grave
>   Where the Prince of Greece was laid—
> The mightiest Alexander ;
>   And these true words they said :—
>
> " But yesterday, to serve his need,
>   The world's great host would rise ;
> And there, alas !" the first man said,
>   " To-day he lonely lies."
>
> " Proudly rode he on the earth
>   Not many days bygone ;
> And now the earth," the second cried,
>   " It rests on his breast bone."
>
> Then did the third wise speaker say,—
>   " Not many days ere this
> He own'd the whole round world ; and now
>   Not seven short feet are his !"
>
> " Alexander treasured gold
>   To serve his every whim ;
> And now," the fourth man sagely said,
>   " 'Tis gold that treasures him.
>
> " Like gold was Philip's son—the gold
>   That binds the jewels bright ;
> Like the palm among the trees ; the moon
>   Amid the stars of night ;
>
> " Like the great whale among small fish ;
>   The lion 'mid the slain ;
> The eagle when she drives the birds
>   From the rock of her lone reign.
>
> " Like Zion hill amid the hills—
>   The hill that holiest seems ;
> Like the great sea unto the floods ;
>   Like Jordan 'mid the streams.

" He was a man above all men,
   Save the High King of Heaven ;
To him were armies, towns, and lands,
   And herds and forests given."

Thus o'er the great man's tomb they spoke !
   Wise do I count their lore ;
Unlike to women's idle prate
   Were the sayings of these four.

In the Dean's Book we have poems by two ladies—·the first Gaelic poetesses of whom we have any record. The name of one of them is EFRIC MACCORQUDALE or MACNEILL. This poetess, whose name is written " Effric neyn corgitill," is the authoress of a very spirited poem. She appears to have been the wife of the last MacNeill of Castle Sween, an ancient strong-hold at the mouth of Loch Sween in Knapdale, Argyllshire. The last constable of this clan was Hector MacTorquil MacNeill, whose name is found on a Macdonald charter in 1472. He was of the Gigha MacNeills, who sprung from Torquil MacNeill, designated " filius Nigelli " in his charter of the lands of Gigha and Taynish with the constabulary of Castle Sween. " MacTorquil," half Gaelic, half Norse, reminds us of the mixture of Teutonic and Celtic blood in the veins of this clan. When the last MacNeill died, leaving no heir in the direct line, the office and lands connected with Castle Sween were given, in 1431, to the Earl of Argyll. Efric, his wife, here laments the fact.

Rosary, thou kindlest sorrow ;
   Thou art ever my delight ;
Telling of the noble bosom
   Where I lay until to-night.

Death has filled me with its sadness ;
   Where's the arm I clung to long ?
Ah ! I saw it not departing ;—
   His the valiant and the strong.

Joyful voice of softest music ;
   Known it everywhere remains ;
Lion of Mull of the white towers,
   Hawk of Islay of smooth plains.

.   .   .   .

There's no joy among our women ;
   At the sport men are not seen ;
Like the skies when winds are silent,
   So with music is Dun Sween.

> On Clan-Neill they've taken vengeance ;
> See the palace of the brave !
> Cause to us of sad lamenting
> Till they lay us in the grave.

The other poetess is—

ISABEL, COUNTESS OF ARGYLL. In the Dean's Book this lady is described as "Isabella Ni vic Cailein ;" elsewhere she is called "Contissa Ergadien." She was Isabel Stewart, eldest daughter of John, Lord of Lorn.- She was married to Lord Colin Campbell, who was created Earl of Argyll in 1457, and died in 1493. The poems of these two ladies are interesting as showing that Gaelic literature was cultivated in fashionable quarters at that period. I have attempted a literal rendering in verse of the Countess's poem :—

> Pity one that bears love's anguish,
> Yet the cause that must conceal ;
> Sore it be to lose a dear one,
> And a wretched state to feel.

> And the love I gave in secret
> I must ever keep unknown ;
> But unless relief comes quickly
> All my freshness will be gone.

> Ah ! the name of my beloved
> Ne'er to other can be told ;
> He put me in lasting fetters ;—
> Pity me a hundredfold.

In surveying the arena of history we observe places geographically small sending forth the most prevailing of the forces that have fashioned the course of civilisation. A glance at one or two countries will readily illustrate the significance of the great factors at work in the making of the world's annals. We discern in Judea, a small strip of land, the country whence the all-conquering religion and civilisation of the whole earth have come ; we find in Greece—a small concatenation of tribes and provinces—a philosophic and æsthetic power which has supplied the minds of men with profound wisdom for centuries ; for our laws and many of our customs and institutions we are indebted to Rome, Pagan and Christian—a city in a comparatively petty peninsula ; in our own isles of the Gentiles, not excluding Man, Ireland, and St. Kilda, there has been developed the greatest moral force of the present, and it may be said of any millennium hitherto. Our British islands look small indeed on the chart of the world ; and it is possible that our geographical insignificance may tempt everween- ing, inimical powers, and some of our own subject nationalities, to touch unkindly some day the mane of the British lion ; but very vainly indeed as long as Christian manliness resides in the hearts of never-enslaved Britons.

Along the coasts of Britain lie several islets where were nursed and whence have emanated national elements of moral power which have to some extent influenced our all-prevailing Anglo- Celtic empire. Lindisfarne, Inchcolm, and Iona we generally know. Iona in Loch Erizort, Lewis, the interesting islets that stud the west coast of the latter island, the far north tiny little Rona, were in early days centres of light and religion, if not of culture. To-day the tourist finds few or none to welcome him in many of those once heaven-favoured island-homes that repose in their attractive poetic solitude and antiquarian suggestiveness on the majestic bosom of the Atlantic Ocean. But in the far-west St Kilda there still resides as monarch, priest, and judge, that zealous Free Church ordained missionary, Mr Mackay, who, according to artist Sands's admission, bravely wrestles with all the elements, moral and physical, that conflict with the interests of man. But leaving St Kilda in its loneliness and sailing in among the inner Hebridean Isles, we find in the fertile Island of Lismore—the *great garden*—a man in the fifteenth century, often now referred to in Gaelic literature, the Rev. Sir James Macgregor. A native of Perthshire, belonging to a royal clan that was afterwards "nameless by day," with a heart filled with the enthusiasm and perfervid spirit of his countrymen, he and his brother got up a collection of the songs and ballads of their native land, which was among the first of the literary offorts of the kind. In Lismore also resided in later days another literary ecclesiastic, the sturdy Mac-Nicol, who produced an able volume of obstinate Scottish prejudice, a pretty hearty, intelligent growl over the great lexicographer's "Journey to the Hebrides."

To Macgregor's book we are indebted for some specimens of the poetry of his own and previous periods. Some of the votaries of the muse to whom he assigned niches of honour in his collection have been already referred to ; the names of a few more, with a few specimen verses of their compositions, are here given.

SIR DUNCAN CAMPBELL is described as "Duncan MacCailein, the good knight." He was Sir Duncan Campbell of Glenorchy, son of Sir Colin, who died in 1478. He must have been a knight of some courtly and literary importance in his day, for he not only wrote poetry in Gaelic, but he obtained from the powers that were charters to extensive lands in Perthshire, and became one of the Earls of Breadalbane. He is the author of several pieces of poetry which have been characterised as remarkable for caustic humour, indulged in sometimes at the expense of the female sex. A published poem of his is a satirical elegy on a miser, a species of beggar humanity that the world has not yet succeeded in extinguishing. I give a literal metrical translation of some of the verses :—

> Who is now the chief of beggars
> Since the best of them is gone ?
> Sorely down our tears are streaming
> Since his begging face has flown.
>
> Piteous is the orphan's case ;
> Death to begging ill has brought ;
> In each homestead there is sorrow,
> As the begging can't be taught.
>
> Ever since our God created
> Man at first, I have not heard
> Of a mendicant like Lachlan,
> Whose decease our grief has stirred.
>
> Without father, without mother,
> Beggary grows weak and poor ;
> For none e'er could beg like Lachlan :
> How can I my loss endure !

DUNCAN MACPHERSON is thought to have been an ecclesiastic, a class, notwithstanding Professor Blackie's genial sneer about the "solemn sepulchral piety of certain North-Western Gospellers," who have been the authors and *media* of the most of what the literary Highlander can refer to with national pride. The " sombre nationality " of the old Ossianic bards is discernible in the following lines :—

> Alastair, art still in sorrow ?
> Or canst cast it to the ground ?
> The old year is swiftly passing,
> And yet godless art thou found ?
>
> Now while thou art grey and aged,
> Hast thou not the grace of heaven ?
> If there be aught good in sorrow,
> God to thee rich gifts has given.

JOHN MACVURICH.—This writer was likely a member of the famous family who were so long hereditary bards to Clanranald. Their ancestor was the famous Muireach Albannach of the thirteenth century. I give a metrical rendering of some verses :—

O, sorry is the fate
    I find mine own to-day !
Have pity kindly heav'n ;
    Save from this pain, I pray.

The misery I feel
    Is threefold here alone ;
And my misfortune black
    Comes weighted with a stone.

My rage and wrath are great
    For how she's grieving me ;
I see her sweet soft skin
    Like white foam on the sea.

So rosy is her hand ;
    Her lips like berries red ;
My soul she holds while sleep
    At night flies from my bed.

I fancied she was nigh,
    And that she smiled on me ;
But since my grief began
    The maid I can not see.

Her raven curly locks
    Are prettily arrayed ;
Five lovers there are knit
    To th' name of the fair maid.

O that she were my own :
    Then I should be so blest ;
My love for evermore
    To press her to my breast !

Many of the authors whose compositions appear in the Dean's Book were evidently professional men, either clerical or medical. It was among these two classes that the lamp of literature was kept burning. Many of the names are indeed suggestive of professional connections, such as Mac-an-Olave, MacNab, Macpherson, Maol Domhnuich, &c.

It has been held that the Romish system of the celibacy of the clergy was not introduced or acted upon till a century or two before the Reformation. Whether or not this is true we have at all events quite a crop of clans whose progenitors must have been the sons of ecclesiastical persons. We have Mac-an-Aba, MacNab, from the son of the Abbot ; MacVicar, from the son of the Vicar ; MacPherson, from the son of the Parson, or Persona ; MacTaggart, from the son of the Priest ; MacMaster, from the son of the Maighstir or Minister. Other names come to us through those who devoted themselves to be the *servants* or *gillies* of God or of some saints. Mac-gille-Chriost is Gilchrist, or the son of Gilchrist, or the servant of Christ. Mac-gill'-Iosa, is Gillies, or the son of the servant of Jesus ; Mac gill'-Iain, or MacLean, is the son of the servant of Seathain, or John ; Mac-gill'-aindreais is the son of the servant of Andrew ; Mac-gill'-Eóra (Gill'-an-Leabhair) is the son of the servant of the Book, Macindeor ; Mac-gill'-Mhoire is Morrison, the servant of Mary, &c. The clerical element appears to have been a powerful interest at one time in the Highlands and Islands. Indeed, this may be said of Scotland as a whole, a characteristic which has not yet become invisible. The Dean's book shows us the Highlands under the old order of things. A vast change was impending. The Catholic ecclesiastical dispensation was drawing to a close. The Church of Rome never gained a powerful hold of the people ; so in general they contemplated its downfall with indifference. The intelligent of them who were interested in religion had more sympathy with the old native Church—the Celtic—which Rome supplanted or were ready to embrace the new faith of awakening Christendom.

GILLICALUM MAC-AN OLAVE.—This bard is the author of several pieces of fair merit in the Dean's Book. He appears to have been one of the famous Beatons, *Clann-an-Leigh*, of Islay, Mull, and Skye. Of him and of several others in the Dean's MS. we know little more than their names, some of which I now give :—John of Knoydart, who poetises on the murder of the young Lord of the Isles by the Irish harper, Dermid O'Cairbre, at Inverness in 1490 ; Duncan Mor, from Lennox ; Gilchrist Taylor, Andrew Macintosh, the Bard Macintyre, John MacEwen MacEachern, Duncan Mac-Cabe, Dougall MacGille Glas, Maol Domhnuich (Servus Domini), Baron Ewen MacOmie, MacEachag, and Duncan, brother of the Dean, Sir James Macgregor, who transcribed the most of the manuscript so famous under his brother's name.

There are a good few verses of a satiric character to be found in the Dean's collection. The reader is rather surprised to find the religious Dean admitting such an estimate as the following of monks and monasteries into his collection :—

> I, Robert, went yesterday
> A monastery for to see ;
> But to my wishing they said nay,
> Because my wife was not with me !

Among the Irish pieces there are several satirical productions by an Irish Earl Gerald, the fourth Earl of Desmond, directed against the fair sex.

The ruthless and vindictive spirit which at this time prevailed in Scotland may be gathered from the following verses of a battle-incitement on the eve of the invasion of the English, which ended on the fatal field of Flodden :—

> Burn their women, lean and ugly !
> Burn their children, great and small !
> In the hut and in the palace,
> Prince and peasant, burn them all !
> Plunge them in the swelling rivers,
> With their gear, and with their goods ;
> Spare, while breath remains, no Saxon ;
> Drown them in the roaring floods !

These lines have been translated by Professor Blackie, as well as the next piece of banter.

Black John Macgregor of Glenstrae, who was buried at Dysart, in Glenorchy, May 26, 1519, was a kind patron to the red-haired bard Finlay MacNab, who begins his praises as follows :—

> I've been a stranger long
> To pleasant-flowing matter ;
> I'm tired of lashing fools
> With unproductive satire.
> I've dwarfed my Muse for nought,
> But now she shall grow bigger
> By chant of lofty theme—
> The praise of the Macgregor.
> A prince indeed is he,
> Who knows the craft of ruling ;
> Well taught in each degree
> Of proper princely schooling.
> Men make boast of noble blood :
> Though money has its praises,
> I'd much liefer be well-born
> Than count the wealth of Crœsus.
> Hear me gentles and commons all,
> Cease your blame and banter ;
> When I my pedigree rehearse,
> You'll find I am no vaunter.
> From great Clan Dougall I descend ;

I I

No better blood is flowing,
But richer made in me from founts
That I will soon be showing.
From the MacCailein a good part
Of my life's blood I borrow,
MacCailein bountiful to bards,
Then how should I find sorrow?
In Earla I was born and bred,
I tell you true the story,
A very noble place it is,
'Twixt Aros and Tobermory.
Macdonald lies off to the west :
I dwell with good Clan Gillean,
Brave men who stood in battle's breast,
A hundred 'gainst a million.
MacNeill of Barra, too, most sure,
Gives gentle blood to me, sir ;
And Colonsay doth make her boast,
I'm kin to the MacFie, sir.
The mighty masterful MacSween,
Clan Ranald and Macleod, sir,
The stoutest chiefs e'er tramped on green,
Give substance to my blood, sir.
The Cattanachs and the Macintoshes
Both make a goodly figure
In my proud line ; and linked with them,
Clan Cameron and Macgregor :
And Stewart's seed, though sown on earth
More wide than any other,
The tale is true that one of them
Was my grandsire's grandmother ;
And if you will to do me harm
I rede you will consider
That I have cousins stout of arm
In Breadalbane and Balquhidder ;
Clan Lauchlan and Clan Lamond, too,
All numbered with my kin, sir ;
I really see no end in view
When once that I begin, sir ;
For in my veins of noble blood
Dame nature was so lavish,
She added some drops from the flood
Of thy pure fount Clan Tavish,
Lads that plenish our green hills
With virtue and with vigour,
Tight little men, but with more pith
Than many who are bigger.
I visit MacDougall of Craignish,
And from the good MacIvor
I get my dinner full and free,
And never pay a stiver.

And now my race and lineage rare,
When you have bravely mastered,
You'll find the best of all your blood
Flows in my veins—the bastard !

The following poem is by a Phelim Macdougall. ' The power of his muse cannot be said to be of so high an order as his moral suggestions. But poetry and severe ethics do not always go together. So we can afford some literary and religious sympathies to poor Phelim in his fifteenth century gropings after light :—

'Tis not good to travel on Sunday,
Whoever the Sabbath would keep ;
Not good to be of ill-famed race ;
Not good is a dirty woman ;
Not good to write without learning ;
Not good are grapes when sour ;
Not good is an Earl without English ;
Not good is a sailor, if old ;
Not good is a bishop without warrant ;
Not good is a blemish on an elder ;
Not good a priest with but one eye ;
Not good a parson if a beggar ;
Not good is a palace without pay ;
Not good is a handmaid if she's slow ;
Not good is a lord without a dwelling, &c.

The author of the following verses was neither the first nor the last that fathered their petty productions on poor Ossian.

THE AUTHOR OF THIS IS OSSIAN, THE SON OF FINN.

Long are the clouds this night above me ;
The last was a long night to me.
This day that drags its weary way
Came from a wearier yesterday.
Each day that comes is long to me :
Such was not my wont to be.
Now there is no fine delight
In battle-field, and fence of fight ;
No training now to feats of arms,
Nor song, nor harp, nor maiden's charms,
Nor blazing hearth, nor well-heaped board,
Nor banquet spread by liberal lord,
Nor stag pursuing, nor gentle wooing,
The dearest of dear trades to me.
Alas ! that I should live to see
Days without mirth in hut or hall
Without the hunter's wakeful call,
Or bay of hounds, or hounds at all,
Without light jest, or sportive whim

Or lads with mounting breast to swim
Across the long arms of the sea—
Long are the clouds this night above me.
In the big world there lives no wight
More sad than I this night.
A poor old man with no pith in my bones,
Fit for nothing but gathering stones. ·
The last of the Finn, the noble race,
Ossian, the son of Finn am I,
Standing beneath the cold grey sky,
Listening to the sound of bells.
Long are the clouds this night above me !

One of the chief characteristics of the poetry of this period is the clearness or distinctness of the ideas. The authors seize at once their subject and straightway sing what they have to utter. They also appear to have a definite object in view when they invoke the muse, and they carry it out in a clear, direct, and unhesitating fashion. The vagueness and mistiness of Macpherson's Ossianic poems have been much commented upon, and sometimes with good reason. Nothing like mistiness can be affirmed of the Ossianic poems which were composed or transcribed and were popular at this period. The ideas of the authors stand out in brilliant distinctness, like stars looking forth beneath the brows of a frosty night.

The Lismore collection of songs and poems is not the only manuscript of the sixteenth and seventeenth centuries that received but scant attention from our forefathers. Many ancient Gaelic manuscripts carried by Christian missionaries to the Continent have never returned. More than two hundred, once in the possession of Gaelic scribes, may still be met with in the various European libraries. Drs Laing and Skene, especially the latter, have done good service to Scotland in this field The admirable collection of Gaelic MSS. in Edinburgh, some of which, it is hoped will yet be published, is the result of the energetic efforts of Dr Skene. The Fernaig manuscript which he has put in the hands of Professor Mackinnon, contains according to the latter, some 4000 lines of Gaelic poetry of the seventeenth century. It is hoped that Mr Mackinnon will lend his ability and scholarship to the early publication of this work. Judging by a published article of the Professor of Celtic in Edinburgh, at the present date (November, 1889), he seems to be unaware that the " Red Book " of Clanranald is not lost. He will be glad to know that it is in the possession of Admiral Reginald Macdonald. Mr Campbell of Islay, informed the writer once that he and Mr ~~Hennesy~~ had read the " Red Book."

Standish O'Grady

CHAPTER VIII.

JACOBITE BARDS.

" A field of the dead rushes red on my sight,
And the clans of Culloden are scattered in fight."—CAMPBELL.

A RETROSPECT of the remains of ancient Gaelic Literature establishes the following among other facts :— 1. That the Scottish Gael of the first centuries of the Christian era was not a barbarian. 2. That a considerable body of oral or traditional literature was then extant among the people. 3. That there is no evidence that writing was known in the British Islands before the Christian era. 4. That relics of the writings of Churchmen from the fifth century downwards still exist in manuscript. 5. That the literature of the Irish and Scottish Gael, till the period of the Reformation in the sixteenth century, had much in common, the language used in the north-west of Ireland and in the north-west of Scotland being the same.

We have come now to the consideration of the poetry which may be regarded as the beginings of modern bardic literature. It shows a different spirit, while it is generally presented in a different form. After Mary MacLeod, the chief productions of the Gaelic muse from *Iain Lom* to *MacMhaighstir Alasdair* were Jacobite.

The persecutions and sufferings of the Clan-Gregor, " the clan that was nameless by day," form the theme of many interesting and stirring ballads. The terrible valour, the undying courage, and the heroic faithfulness of this much injured sept have been beautifully drawn by Sir Walter Scott.

The authoress of Macgregor's Lullaby was a daughter of Colin Campbell of Glenorchy, and the wife of Gregor Macgregor, whose death she laments in this Lullaby. Her husband, his brother, Malcolm Roy, along with their father, Duncan Macgregor, were beheaded in 1552 by Colin Campbell of Glenorchy, Campbell of Glenlyon, and Menzies of Rannoch. The Black Duncan mentioned in the song was her brother, the seventh laird of Glenorchy.

whose picture is still preserved at Taymouth Castle. The following is Pattison's rendering of the Lullaby, which, along with the
next two songs referred to (not in the Dean's book), have always
been very popular :—

> Early on a Lammas morning with my husband was I gay ;
> But my heart got sorely wounded ere the middle of the day.
>
> Chorus—Ochan, ochan, uiri,
>   Though I cry, my child, with thee—
>   Ochan, ochan, uiri,
>   Now he hears not thee nor me.
>
> Malison on judge and kindred, they have wrought me mickle woe ;
> With deceit they came about us, with deceit they laid him low.
>
> Had they met but twelve Macgregors with my Gregor at their head ;
> Now my child had not been orphaned, nor these bitter tears been shed.
>
> On an oaken block they laid him, and they spilt his blood around ;
> I'd have drunk it in a goblet largely, ere it reached the ground.
>
> .   .   .   .
>
> When the rest have all got lovers now a lover have I none ;
> My fair blossom, fresh and fragrant, withers on the ground alone.
>
> While all other wives the night-time pass in slumbers balmy bands,
> I upon my bedside weary, never cease to wring my hands.
>
> Far, far better be with Gregor where the heather's in its prime,
> Than with mean and Lowland barons in a house of stone and lime, &c.

Other Macgregor Songs of the same era are "*Macgregor O
Ruara*" and "*The Braes of the Ceathach.*" *Macgregor O Ruara*
begins thus :—

> There is sorrow, and sorrow, and sorrow now fills me—
> Poor pitiful sorrow no man can redress ;
> It is sorrow and sighing, and sadness that thrills me—
> Oh ! terrible sadness I cannot repress.
>
> Macgregor has perished—Macgregor, pine-bannered—
> Macgregor, beloved in Glenlyon the green ;
> Macgregor, the brave, by whose foes ever honoured
> The threatening roar of our pibroch has been.

" The Braes of the Mist " is one of the sweetest and most affecting songs in any language. The singer—a woman—concealed her
husband and two sons of the fiercely persecuted Macgregors in a
bed as the enemies were approaching the house. She sat at the

fire and began singing her song. She sang of herself as waiting
in solitude for her persecuted friends. The people outside listened
as the woman sang, and accepting as true what she said, they
passed on without troubling her. Her heart's dearest wishes depended on the effect produced by her extempore verses. It has
been well said that "seldom, indeed, has song or ballad. been
composed or chanted in circumstances of such intense excitement."
The first verse runs as follows :—

> I sit here alone, by the plain of the highway,
> For my poor hunted kin, watching mist, watching by way ;
> I've yet got no sign that they're near to my dwelling ;
> At Loch Fyne they were last seen—if true be that telling, &c.

Mo Valie Veg Og is a very popular song, somewhat like "Helen
of Kirkconnel Lea," and Tennyson's " Oriana." The occasion of
the composition was as follows :—One of the chiefs of the Clan
Chisholm having carried off a daughter of Lord Lovat, placed her
on an islet in Loch Bruiach, where she was soon discovered by
the Frasers, who had mustered for the rescue. (Other accounts
of the origin of the song have been given). A severe
conflict ensued, during which the young lady was accidentally
slain by a chance blow from her own lover, in defending her from
her furious brothers. The lover was condemned to be executed
next day. The night preceding his execution he composed Mo
Valie Veg Og, *Young little May*. The following is a rendering of
the spirit of the song :—

> I groan for thee in prison,
>   Mo Valie Veg Og
> O, dost thy spirit listen,
>   Mo Valie Veg Og ;
> From where the dew-drops glisten,
> From thy deep sleep uprisen,
> While these lone arms I miss in,
>   Mo Valie Veg Og ?

> We met when summer flowered,
>   Mo Valie Veg Og ;
> Where am'rous birds embowered
>   Mo Valie Veg Og ;
> The trees that near us towered,
> Sweet dew-drops on us showered ;
> But something near us lowered,
>   Mo Valie Veg Og.

Wrapt in each other dreaming,
  Mo Valie Veg Og ;
We saw the distance gleàming,
  Mo Valie Veg Og ;
Thy kinsmen vengeful seeming,
With fell intention teeming
We strove, and blood was streaming,
  Mo Valie Veg Og !

Encountering their lance,
  Mo Valie Veg Og ;
I struck by sore mischance
  Mo Valie Veg og ;
Cursed aye be their advance !
I bent in trembling trance
To drink thy dying glance,
  Mo Valie Veg Og.

Condemned thus I am grieving,
  Mo Valie Veg Og ;
Aye longing to be leaving,
  Mo Valie Veg Og ;
To-morrow sees them cleaving
This frame ; hope, undeceiving,
Lifts me with thee believing,
  Mo Valie Veg Og.

The Owlet.—It is said that this poem was composed by a Badenoch deer-stalker about 1550. It is two hundred and sixty-eight lines in length. The "Owl" is the form of a dialogue between the author and an owl, which, old and feeble, the unkind hunter's wife, who was much younger than he, brought in to be a fit companion for her husband. There is a good deal of cleverness and poetical ingenuity in the piece. It is the only composition of the kind in the language, and reminds us of "Listen Little Porker," by the Welsh poet Merddyn Wyllt.

The Aged Bard's Wish.—This poem appeared towards the end of last century, in the days of the Ossianic controversy, and has come under the suspicions of the sceptical.' It was then regarded as an old poem, perhaps belonging to pre-Christian times. It probably belongs to the first part of the seventeenth century. It begins thus—

Oh ! place me by the little brook,
  Of gentle wandering pace and slow,
And lay my head near some green nook
  That kindly shades the sunny glow.

At ease upon the grass I'll rest
Of the balm-breathing flowery brae ;
My foot by the warm wave caress'd
That winds throughout the plain away.

There the pale primrose let me see,
There the small daisy close at hand,
And every flower so dear to me,
For grateful hue or odour bland.

About thy lofty banks, my glen,
Be bending boughs and blooming sprays,
Where small birds sing from bush and fen
To aged cliffs their amorous lays.

There have been several translations of this much-admired poem, but on account of occasional vagueness of conception and obscurity of the style it has been found very difficult to convey with certainty and accuracy the sense of the original. In one hundred and forty-four lines the bard conjures up many scenes and images before his mental vision, and finally welcomes the " Hall of Ossian and Daol "—he cries, " Open, fly, the night comes, and the bard is gone !"

Among the poetesses whose names have not been forgotten in the story of Scottish letters is that of Mary Macleod, *Mairi ni'n Alastair Ruaidh*, or Mary, the daughter of red haired Alexander. Her name as a poetess has become quite proverbial among the people. Apart from the mantle of poetry which she wore she was a very remarkable person, who would be long remembered. Like some others, her own assertive personality accounts for much of the popularity of her productions.

MAIRI NI'N ALASTAIR RUAIDH, who has been regardd by some as the first in point of time of the modern Gaelic bards, was born in Harris, in the Long Island, in 1569, and died at Dunvegan, Isle of Skye, in 1674, at the extraordinary age of 105 years. She received no education, yet her poetry is characterised by boldness, freshness, and originality. The metres she uses are often complicated and unusual ; but the native melody of her song and the pathetic character of her conceptions render her poetry very enjoyable reading. She was a well-known visitor among her neighbours, who generally rallied her by references to a beverage stronger than water. Pattison translates a song she composed on her being banished from Dunvegan by the young chief of the MacLeods ; who, on hearing her laudatory verses, sent a boat to bring back the affectionate poetess.

Alone on the hill-top, sadly and silently
Downward on Islay and over the sea
I look, and I wonder how time hath deceived me—
A stranger in Scarba, who ne'er thought to be.

Ne'er thought it, my island, where rest the deep dark shade
The grand mossy mountains for ages have made ;
God bless thee ! and prosper thy chief of the sharp blade
All over these islands his fame never fade !

Never fade it, Sir Norman ! for well 'tis the right
Of thy name to win credit in counsel or fight—
By wisdom, by shrewdness, by spirit, by might,
By manliness, courage, by daring, by sleight.

In counsel or fight, thy kindred know these should be thine—
Branch of Lochlin's wide-ruling and king-bearing line !
And in Erin they know it, far over the brine ;
No Earl would in Albin thy friendship decline.

The name of *Mairi ni'n Alastair Ruaidh* has been affectionately remembered by many generations of Highlanders.

JOHN MACDONALD. —This well-known Lochaber bard, called *Iain Lom*, or *bare* John, was of the Keppoch family ; lived in the reigns of Charles I. and II. ; was a very old man about 1710.

The heir of Keppoch was sent abroad to be educated ; and in his absence his affairs were entrusted to his cousins, who planned a scheme to get rid of him so that they themselves would get possession. The bard perceived their wicked scheme beforehand ; and comes prominently before us in his endeavours to expose them ; and again in the active part he took in punishing the murderers. The massacre took place in 1663 ; and soon after the poet persuaded Sir Alexander Macdonald to concert measures for punishing the perpetrators of the deed. They were seized and beheaded, and the awful retribution is commemorated by the ugly monument, " Tobar nan Ceann," or " Well of the Heads," in Invergarry. Macdonald was politician as well as poet in his day. He was a keen Jacobite, and acted as the laureate of the party in the Highlands. He was the means of bringing the armies of Montrose and Argyll together at Inverlochy, where, on Sunday, February 2, 1645, a bloody battle was fought, in which the flower of the Campbell clan were slain. He is a poet of great fire, vigour, and satiric power. He was buried in Dunaingeal, in the braes of Lochaber.

BATTLE OF INVERLOCHY.

Did you hear from Cille-Cummin
  How the tide of war came pouring ?
Far and wide the summons travelled,
  How they drove the Whigs before them !

From the castle-tower I viewed it,
  High on Sunday morning early,
Looked and saw the ordered battle,
  Where Clan Donald triumphed rarely.

Up the green slope of Cail-Eachaidh
  Came Clan Donald marching stoutly ;
Churls who laid my home in ashes.
  Now shall pay the fine devoutly !

Many a bravely-mounted rider,
  With his back turned to the slaughter,
Where his boots won't keep him dry now,
  Learns to swim in Nevis water.

On the wings of eager rumour
  Far and wide the tale is flying,
How the slippery knaves, the Campbells,
  With their cloven skulls are lying.

I have availed myself here of the rendering of Blackie, whose
literary deftness in translation and poetic genius have successfully
transferred not only the sense of, but frequently improved on, the
more artless of the productions of the Gaelic muse.   If the versatile Professor is not always boldly and simply literal in his
versions of Gaelic poetry, he never fails to seize and attractively
exhibit the spirit of the bard.

ARCHIBALD MACDONALD.—This minor bard, called "An Ciaran
Mabach," was a natural son of Sir Alexander Macdonald, 16th
baron of Sleat.   He was contemporary with *Iain Lom.*   He was
a clever and highly practical man, and was entrusted in matters of
importance by his father, who allotted him a portion of land in
North Uist.

NEIL MACKELLAR.—Mackellar was a farmer in Jura in 1694.
He does not appear to have composed much—a poetical address
of his to *John Ruadh Mac Cailein,* the Earl of Argyll, which I
found among the papers of the poet Livingston, was published in
the fifth volume of the "GAEL."

DIORBHAIL NIC-A'-BHRIUTHAIN, or Dorothy Brown, was a native of Luing, an island in Argyllshire. She lived towards the close of the seventeenth century, and, like many of the bards of the period, was a keen Jacobite. Like *Iain Lom*, she used her bitter satire against the Clan Campbell with considerable effect. She is known by her *Oran do Alastair Mac Colla*, the famous Sir Alexander Mac-donnell of Antrim, and the gallant lieutenant of Montrose.

SILIS NI'N VIC RAONAILL, or Cicely Macdonald, was the daughter of Macdonald of Keppoch, and lived from the reign of Charles II. to that of George I. Like Iain Lom and Dorothy Brown, this poetess was a Roman Catholic, and her muse was employed against the house of Hanover. Her husband having died in a fit of intoxication while on a visit to Inverness, she com-posed *Marbhrann air bas a fir*, and afterwards some hymns.

NEIL MAC VURICH, who was born early in the seventeenth century, was bard and senachie to the family of Clanranald. He belonged to South Uist, where the land he had is still known as *Baile-bhaird*. He was a descendant of Muireadhach *Albannach*, and grandfather of Lachlan Mac Vurich, whose name appears in the Ossianic controversy. He wrote a Gaelic history of the Clan Ranald, whose records he kept. He was living and an old man in 1715.

JOHN MACDONALD, or *Iain Dubh Mac Iain 'ic Ailein*, a gentle-man of the Clan Ranald family, was born in 1665. He held the farm of Grulean in the island of Eigg. One of his best pieces is a fiery martial poem called "Oran nam Fineachan Gaelach."

The AOSDAN MATHESON, who flourished in the seventeenth century, belonged to Lochalsh, Ross-shire, where he had as his bard free lands from the Earl of Seaforth. Much of his poetry, like that of Neil Mac Vurich, has been lost. A poem, *Do'n Iarla Thuathach, Triath Chlann Choinnich*, has been freely rendered by Sir Walter Scott : "Farewell to Mackenzie, high Chief of Kintail."

HECTOR MACLEAN, who lived in the seventeenth century, was bard and senachie to Sir Lachlan MacLean of Duart. The Chief's *Elegy* is the subject of a *special* poem by the bard.

LACHLAN MACKINNON, who lived in the seventeenth century, was a native of Strath, Isle of Skye. He was a bard of real power, and a good many of his pieces have come down to us. Mackenzie, collector of "The Beauties of Gaelic Poetry," who delighted in unearthing and publishing all the moral dirt he could lay his hands on, relates a story about Mackinnon which does not represent the bard's character in a very attractive light.

RODERICK MORRISON.—This famous bard, commonly called *An Clarsair Dall*, or the Blind Harper, was born in the island of Lewis in 1646. He was a descendant of the *Brieve Leosach*, well known in the annals of the island. Roderick's father was a man of piety and culture, in Lewis, whose memory is still fragrant among the people. It seems he was a true gospel light amid the half-heathenism which then prevailed in the Western Isles. He sent Rory and his other two sons to be educated at Inverness, intending to educate the three sons for the church. In course of time Angus settled in the parish of Contin, and Malcolm in Poolewe, Ross-shire. Roderick lost his eyesight through the small-pox when receiving his education in Inverness, and then turned his attention to the study of music. He soon became famous not only in Scotland, but also in Ireland. When returning from the latter country it is said that he called at every baronial residence on his way. Before going home to the north he visited Edinburgh, where at the time the Scotch nobility and gentry were met in Holyrood House. There he came across the chief, John Breac MacLeod of Harris, by whom Roderick was at once engaged as his family harper. While with MacLeod he composed many tunes and songs which are yet popular. His patron MacLeod afterwards gave him a rent-free farm at Totamor, in Glenelg. After the death of John Breac he went back to his native Lewis, where he was much respected in his old age. He died in this island, and was buried in the churchyard of I or Hy, near Stornoway. Morrison is a poet of considerable power and culture, although his fame as a harper—he was almost the last of that class so celebrated among the Gaels—has obscured his name as a poet.

JOHN MACKAY.—This bard, known as *Am Piobaire Dall*, or the Blind Piper, whose father was of the Sutherlandshire Mackays, was born in the parish of Gairloch, Ross-shire, in the year 1666. Being born blind he was taught music, first by his father, afterwards he was sent to the College of Pipers, in Skye, which was then presided over by MacCruimein, of world-wide fame. In course of time he became family bard to the chief of Gairloch. While he stayed with this chief he is said to have composed twenty-four *piobrachds* and many strathspeys, reels, and jigs. He died in 1754 at the great age of ninety-eight, and was buried in Gairloch. The poems of this bard are thoughtful and well finished, but, like many of that period, are scarcely known now.

The learned Edward Lhuyd published his " Archæologia Britannica " in 1704; and the imaginative Celt of the day was de-

Corrected 1707. See title page of Lhuyd's book AR

lighted that so much of the dying language of his forefathers would
be preserved—that so handsome a monument should be reared to
its memory.   In 1707 a second edition was issued, in which complimentary poetical addresses from Highland ministers were given.
There is one from the Rev. James MacPherson, Kildalton, Islay,
and another from the Rev. John Maclean of Killninian, Mull.
The following stanzas from Maclean's verses, are of considerable
merit in the original Gaelic :—

> When the grey Gael—Milesian race from Spain—
> To green Ierne had crossed the mighty main,
> Great was the fame they carried to our shore,
> Of skill in arms, of poetry and lore.
> When that good seed had spread out far and near,
> The Gaelic then was honoured there and here ;
> That musically sweet, expressive tongue,
> To which our fathers have so fondly clung.
>
> In royal courts a thousand years and more
> It reigned in honour—spoke from shore to shore ;
> Then bard and lyrist, prophet, sage and leech
> Wrote all their records in the Gaelic speech ;
> Since first Gathelus came from Egypt's strand
> That ancient tongue was written in our land ;
> The great divines whose fame is shed abroad
> In Gaelic accents learned to praise their God.
>
> 'Twas Gaelic Patrick spoke in Innis-Fayl,
> And sainted Calum in Iona's Isle.
> Rich polished France, where highest taste appears,
> Received her learning from that Isle of Tears ;—
> Ie, alma mater, of each tribe and tongue,
> Once taught for France and Germany their young !
> Well may we now our swelling grief outpour,
> That seat in ruin, and our tongue no more !
>
> Great praise and thanks, O noble Lhuyd, be thine,
> True learned patriot of the Cambrian line !
> Thou hast awaked the Celtic from the tomb,
> That our past life her records might illume.
> Engraved in every heart in lettered gold
> Thy name remains : thy silent words unfold
> To future ages what our sires had seen,
> While others say, ' A Gaelic race hath been.'

The first of the Gaelic addresses comes from Andrew Maclean,
Tyree, who calls himself " the son of the Bishop of Argyll :—

Aindra M'Ghileoin Fear an Cnuic, an tiridhc mac Easbuig
Earraghaoidhil, C.C.

Ordheirc an gniomh saor bhur comhluinn
Cliu do fhoghlum beirid uainn :
Ti do chur do na thuit or sinnsreadh
Cus do sgeimh bhur linn a mfuaim.
Molsid *M'Liath* na Sheanchas,
Ochd mhacigh'achd do leanmhuinn oirinn,
Brathreachus *Gaoidhil Fear Shaxan,*
Thabhart nar ccuimhne ceart na loirg :

which may be freely rendered thus :—

Excellent is thy work completed ;
Thy deep lore is widely known ;
The sweet language of our fathers
Grandly to the world hast shown.
Praise shall be of Lhuyd's great labours
Which henceforth we emulate ;
Friendship for the Gael of England
In our hearts he does create.

Robert Campbell, of Cowal, begins with the following dedicat-
ory preface :—

"Den Uasal oirdherc Maighsdir *Edward Lhuid,* Fear coimhead tigh na
seud a Noiltigh *Ath-Ndamh* a *Nsagsan,* Ughdar a Nfoclair Ghaoidheilg,
Failtc.
"*Robert Caimpbel* Fear Faraiste mhic *Chailin* an *Comhal* C.C."

To-day in Eire there is joy ;
While harp and song wake gentle sounds ;
The strains of tuneful throats are heard
Within old Albin's gladdened bounds.

The pow'r that kindles this delight
Is that sweet tongue of those fair lands
Which lay so long in captive chains ;
It wakens now and breaks the bands.

In it have terms of peace been sealed,
In it Jehovah's praises sung ;
Small be the lore of learned men
Who know not this rich ancient tongue.

This moved to work the noble Lhuyd,
Whose words of eloquence proceed
From that deep fount beside which grew
The Oakling of the Celtic seed.

'Tis time to teach and woo the muse
Where fair Oxonia rears her towers,
Where classic learning finds her home,
And Isis shows her banks of flowers.

Tyree, Mull, and Cowal are not the only places where clergymen were wont to " woo the muse " in those days.   Poetic expressions of admiration and encouragement were also sent to Lhuyd from Ardchattan, and Islay. . Here is that of the Rev. James Mac-Pherson, of Kildalton :

> Thou art welcome, gentle scholar,
>   To the Highlands' wave-worn shore ;
> In all provinces of Eire
>   Thine is welcome evermore.
>
> Welcome through the Gaelic borders,
>   England will accord thee hail :
> Chiefs will make of thee companion,
>   Praise will come from Ireland's Gael.
>
> From the tomb thou hast awakened
>   Our neglected ancient tongue,
> Which, though long in bonds forgotten,
>   Into printed life has sprung.
>
> Rich and wise is thy instruction ;
>   Clear and learned is thy speech ;
> Ancient words gain force and meaning
>   On each page as thou dost teach.
>
> Bear to learned Lhuyd my blessing,
>   Who our language has restored ;
> Hence to him great praise and welcome
>   Gaels shall everywhere accord.

The Rev. Colin Campbell wrote his in Latin, which till that period was the medium of communication among Highland ecclesiastics.

JOHN WHYTE, called *Forsair Choir'an-t-Si*, belonged to the end of the seventeenth and beginning of the eighteenth century.   He lived near Kilmun, and composed a good many songs which are recognised as of a superior order.   He was the ancestor of some of the name who have been known for their strongly Celtic sympathies.

WILLIAM MACKENZIE, otherwise known as *An Ceisteir Crubach*, was born in Gairloch about 1670.   He was a bard of superior powers ; but the loose character and profanity of some of his compositions caused the Presbytery that engaged his services as a Catechist to dismiss him from his office.   Mackenzie, of " The Beauties of Gaelic Poetry." has published a lengthy song of his which is a blot on the whole work.

JOHN MACLEAN, who was a native of Mull, where he was for

long a popular poet, is the author of a few songs of superior merit. His compositions were general favourites at the time of Johnson and Boswell's journey to the Hebrides. They heard some of his songs sung by a lady. He composed an excellent piece on Sir Hector MacLean when he went to France in 1721. The bard died in 1760.

MALCOLM MACLEAN, otherwise known as *Calum a' Ghlinne*, was a native of Kinlochewe, in Ross-shire. He was a soldier, and served for some time abroad, where he deeply learned the worship of Bacchus. " Mo Chailin donn og " is yet popular. It was composed for his daughter. He died in 1764.

AM BARD MUCANACH, a Macdonald, originally from Glencoe, lived in the island of Muck, and is the author of a very good poem on the " Massacre of Glencoe."

ANGUS MACDONALD, a native of Glencoe, is the author of the popular song " *Bha Claidheamh air Iain 'san t-searmoin.*" It was intended to ridicule the cowardly conduct of a John Gibeach, who was at the battle of Sheriffmuir in 1715, but who took to flight instead of remaining to fight.

JOHN MACCODRUM.—This original and witty bard was a native of North Uist. He lived at the same time as his more famous contemporary, Alexander Macdonald. The accomplished Sir James Macdonald, who died at Rome in 1766, made MacCodrum his bard, and gave him free land in North Uist. He met James Macpherson when collecting Gaelic materials for the poems of Ossian ; and the Uist bard appears to have indulged in wit at the expense of Macpherson. MacCodrum is a poet of great ability and satiric power. His poems on " Old Age " and " Whisky " are of a first-class order. He was, like many of the bards of his day, a keen Jacobite.

The poet's attachment to his patron inspired a tender elegiac song of which the following translated verses are a specimen :—

> As I awake it is not sleep
> That strives with me in troubles deep ;
> My bed beneath the tears I weep
>   Is in disquiet :
>   My bed beneath, &c.

> Of him, my patron bright, bereft,
> I have no fair possession left ;
> While pain of loss my soul has cleft
>   In sight and hearing :
>   While pain of loss, &c.

12

Sore tears are ours ; joy is no more ;
No hope of smiles ; no cheer in store ;
We seem like the brave Fians of yore
    And Finn forsaken :
    We seem like the, &c.

Ah ! true it seems the tale to tell ;
Our cup is filled with doings fell ;
Provoking in a rage of hell
    Bless'd God the Highest :
    Provoking in a rage, &c.

Blest One from Thee let us not swerve ;
Above with Thee he goes to serve ;
O Christ ! do Thou for us preserve
    Our loving brothers :
    O Christ ! do Thou, &c.

The early death of the subject of this elegy,—of Sir James Macdonald,—wrought the bard into unwonted seriousness. As his name indicates, this poet is a representative of the commingled Norse and Celtic races of the Hebridean people.

HECTOR MACLEOD was a native of South Uist. Like Mac-Codrum, he was a zealous Jacobite, and after 1715 lived in the Roman Catholic districts of Arisaig and Morar. There is much originality and poetical ingenuity in MacLeod, who, finding it dangerous to sing his Jacobite leanings without disguise, had recourse to allegorical ways of expressing himself.

ARCHIBALD MACDONALD, known as *Gilleasbuig na Ciotaig*, or left-handed Archibald, also 'a native of Uist, is one of the few comic bards that the Highlands have produced. An " Elegy " on John Roy, a piper while living, and the " Resurrection " of the same, are really clever productions, as well as his song for Dr MacLeod, a St Kildian, who was for some time a surgeon in a Highland regiment.

ZACHARY MACAULAY, whose father was an accomplished Episcopalian clergyman, was born in the island of Lewis at the beginning of the eighteenth century. He is thought in his youth to have written some " wanton " songs ; his published pieces show true poetic instinct and power. The air of one of his songs was a favourite with Burns. Lord Macaulay was a descendant of Zachary's family, from whom the brilliant essayist and historian evidently inherited his genius.

Like that of all other peoples, the limited literature of the Scottish Clans has had its periods of revival and decadence. The bolder and more original poetry of the early centuries of our story was followed by the feeble and imitative strains of the verse writers of the medieval generations.

ALEXANDER MACDONALD.

In the seventeenth century we had the silver age, and about the middle of last century the golden age of modern Gaelic poetry. Singers of orignal power appeared in every part of the country. Of these Alexander Macdonald was the first and the greatest. From the wilds of the Ardnamurchan regions he poured forth his imperishable strains. After him Duncan Macintyre comes next, the poet-hunter of Glenorchay. From the heart of central Argyll and Breadalbane he sent forth unique and inimitable songs. In the grand wilds of Perthshire Dugald Buchanan, the sacred bard of Rannoch, was writing his sublime poems on such awful themes as the "Judgement" and the "Passion" of the God-man. In the far North Robert Mackay, the famous Sutherlandshire herd, was gladdening the firesides, of a happy peasantry—whose descendants are now in Canada—with his witty and satiric compositions. In the West the delicate and fine-fibred William Ross began to sing soon after these, his sweet lays of love and sorrow. Jacobite rebellions no doubt stirred up the Highland heart at this period ; and in the midst of the political ferment of the times the muse appears to have thrown her choicest mantle on receptive spirits among the people to give song-utterance to their emotional aspirations. In the poetry of Macdonald, Mackay, and Macintyre, we see the greatest bards of modern times. It is difficult to decide which of the first and last mentioned is the greater poet— Mackay is not regarded as equal to either. As far as the works of preceding bards could help their poetic culture their minds were moulded by the same influences.

But in regard to ordinary education it must be remembered that Macdonald was for some time at a University, while Macintyre was never able to write. In their descriptions of outward nature their poetry shows very much like equal power, while the note of the one is not always distinguishable from that of the other. But the passionate depth of the one has no echo in the sweeter and gentler nature of the other. Each in his own way is a mighty singer of whom any country might be proud. And it is remarkable that both should be Argyllshire singers.

Alexander Macdonald, also more frequently called *Mac-Mhaigh-*

stir Alastair, son of Master Alexander, was born early in the eighteenth century, the exact date and place of his birth being nowhere recorded. His father, Mr Alexander, as he was always styled by the Highlanders, was an Episcopalian clergyman. He resided at Dailea, in Moydart, and is said to have united farming with his ecclesiastical functions. He had several sons and daughers, and Alexander was his second son. Alexander received his education first under the superintendence of his father, and afterwards for a session or two in the University of Glasgow. His academic career was cut off early by an imprudent marriage. It is not known with certainty whether it was for the Church or for the Bar he was originally intended. It was feared that his general character and conduct would scarcely warrant entrance into the former; while his wild changeableness and irregularities would seriously bar his progress for the latter. He ultimately settled in Ardnamurchan, teaching, farming, and writing poetry. He then changed his ecclesiastical creed, became a Presbyterian and an elder in the Established Church, which he continued to be till the year 1745, when again he changed his creed, became a Roman Catholic, and forsook his all to join Prince Charles. He held a commission in the Highland Army, which he tried to animate by his fiery and warlike songs. For some time after the battle of Culloden he suffered much hardship. One night, while lurking outside somewhere, so intense was the cold that the side of Macdonald's head, which rested on the ground, was grey when he rose in the morning. Soon after friends in Edinburgh procured teaching for the bard among Jacobite families. But he did not stay long there. He returned to the Highlands, where he died when he had reached a good old age. His life was stormy and checkered, like the historic period which was then also coming to a close.

Macdonald's first literary work was a Gaelic and English Vocabulary, published in 1741. It was the first attempt of the kind. His poetry was first published in Edinburgh in 1761, and his volume was the first book of original poems ever published in Gaelic. He wrote extensively, but two thirds of his works in MSS. have been lost or destroyed. As we read the works of Macdonald and those of Macpherson's Ossian—the two highest names in Gaelic poetry—we feel at once that we breathe the air of different regions, or move in the atmosphere of different ages. Between them and the common herd of bards we discern a vast interval in the range of their poetical conceptions. Both breathe the spirit of " Tir nam beann, nan gleann, 's nan gaisgeach," but their deep

utterances of the soul from the mystic land of fancy and passion
are not alike. The inspiration of both is that of the great Bens,
the mysterious-seeming valleys, and of deep crying unto deep.
Macdonald is wild, picturesque, and gorgeous, ever presenting the
dread and sad realities of nature. He loves to picture her coarser
characteristics more than her qualities of tenderness. His poetry
glows with sensuous imagery, overflows with luxuriance of thought
and voluptuousness of feeling, and exhibits much of the animal
and material elements of creation. His music is wild, impetuous,
and fiery; his metres sometimes smooth, and ruggedly rushing.
In accomplishing his more elaborate efforts he shows signs of
spasmodic tendencies. He excels in intensity of thought and in
fiery vehemence of expression. The force of poetical ardour with
which he

> Hurls the Birlin through the cold glens,
> Loudly snoring,

is deeply absorbing. Natural scenes in the West Highlands he
describes with vigour and striking effect. Sometimes he becomes
quite majestic, as when he sings of, "rain-charged clouds on thick
squalls wandering loomed and towered." Some of the parts of
his principal poem, *The Birlin*, a boat voyage in the Hebrides,
are very powerful and sometimes sublime. The unrestrained
vehemence and gorgeousness of *The Birlin* give place to simpler
delineations in *The Sugar Brook*. There is much delicious por-
traiture in this last poem.

The Praise of the Lion is a fiery appeal to the Scottish nationality.
The Jacobite cause is the theme of many of his songs, Prince
Charles being sometimes personified under female names, such as
"Morag." In his love songs Macdonald is sweet, tender, and
musical, rough though his muse is at other times. His "Praise
of Morag," in a sort of *piobrachd* measure, is powerful; but composed under such conditions as Burns wrote "Mary in Heaven,"
Macdonald's lawful spouse became alarmed and jealous. At once
he turns to "Dispraising Morag," which he works out elaborately
with Mephistophelian ardour and spirit, regardless of all poetic
justice and decency. "The Resurrection of the Gaelic Tongue"
is a powerful poem, celebrating the antiquity and supreme excellence of the language of the Gael.

As specimens of the sweet and tender in Macdonald's poetry,
let us take a verse or two from his fine piece, *The Sugar Brook*.
He has done for this insignificent burn what Burns has done for
the Doon and Gray for the Luggie. He describes the different

birds tuning their little throats in the morning to take up the
several parts assigned to them in the great harmonic chorus of
nature.   He hears the rich treble of Robin, the deep bass of
Richard, the "goo-goo" of the cuckoo ; while on a stake apart
from the rest the thrush sings lustily, and the blythesome brown
wren and the vieing linnet tune up their choicest strings.   The
blackcock croaks, and the hen sings her hoarse response.   Then
come the fishes, the bees, and the frisking calves, the milkmaid
and the herdsman, to fill up a scene already sufficiently gorgeous.
There also—

> The wailing swans their murmurs blend
>   With birds that float and sing ;
> Where joins the Sugar Brook the sea
>   Their tuneful voices ring.
> Softly sweet they bend and breathe
>   Through their melodious throat,
> Like the crooked bagpipes' wailing strain,
>   A sad but pleasing note.

The following two stanzas are very fine in the original, and Pattison has very successfully rendered them into English :—

> O ! dainty is the graving work
>   By Nature near thee wrought !
> Whose fertile banks with shining flowers
>   And pallid buds are fraught.
> The shamrock and the daisy
>   Spread o'er thy borders fair,
> Like new-made spangles, or like stars,
>   From out the frosty air.

> Ah ! what a charming sight display
>   The ruddy rosy braes,
> When sunbeams dye their flowers as bright
>   As brilliants all ablaze :
> And what a civil suit they wear
>   Of ribgrass and of hay,
> And gay-topt herbs, o'er which the birds
>   Pour forth their pompous lay.

The *Birlin* has been translated by Sheriff Nicolson, and a part
by Professor Blackie.   The complete translation of Pattison was
the first and is still the best.   This poem is a master-piece of
Gaelic poetry, and presents peculiar difficulties to the translator.
After this "Blessing of the Ship," the "Blessing of the Arms," we
have in the third part an incitement for rowing to a sailing place.
The rowers are asked with a powerful sweep to

Wound the huge swell on the ocean meadow,
    Rolling and deep.
With your sharp narrow blades white and slender,
    Strike its big breast ;
Hirsute and brawny, and rippled and hilly,
    And never at rest.
O, stretch, and bend, and draw, young gallants !
    Forward going !
Let your fists' broad grasp be whitening
    In your rowing !
Ye lusty, heavy, stalwart youngsters !
    Stretch your full length ;
With shoulders knotty, nervy, hairy,
    Hard with strength ;
See you raise and drop together
    With one motion.
Your grey and beamy shafts well ordered,
    Sweeping ocean.

In this spirit the poem extends to more than 500 lines, divided into 16 parts, until finally the voyage of the Birlin ends somewhat like that of St Paul.

Till within recent years the practice of walking cloth in peasant homes was a general thing. The writer has often witnessed it in the north as well as in the south Highlands, in places where walking mills did not extinguish the ancient ways of Highland women. The "MORAG" of Macdonald was a "Walking Refrain," or song for a young woman of fair bewitching tresses. In history her *alias* is Prince Charlie whose adventures touched the hearts of women, bards and weak-minded statesmen. "Ho Morag" in other words is a treasonable prayer, adoration, or incitement for Jacobitically-minded Highlanders and others. The bard's heart was evidently in this wretched and ill-starred rebellion ; but it ought not to be forgotten that if the poet's heart tended to disloyalty he had thousands of titled traitors and sympathisers close to the Hanoverian throne. The Jacobite bard rushes with inexhaustible enthusiasm into the "walking" labours of the Highland women as their thoughts travel after the fair adventurer :

Bright Morag of my heart's emotion
I long to see thy yellow tresses.
    Yes ; and Ho Morag, child of love,
    Beloved of many.
If thou art gone across the ocean
Return to help in our distresses.
    Yes ; and Ho Morag, &c.

Bring back a set of winsome beauties
To walk the red cloth well and tightly.
    Yes ; and Ho Morag, &c.
O ! here at home amid thy duties
Thy linen would be clean and sprightly.
    Yes ; and Ho Morag, &c.

And thou wouldst never be o'er-laden
In menial office of the servant.
    Yes ; and Ho Morag, &c.
She, Morag, my own handsome maiden,
With the hair circlets fair and fervent.
    Yes ; and Ho Morag, &c.

Further on the bard is " enthused " over the deeds of Montrose
and *Alastair Mac Colla*, the brave Sir Alexander Macdonald of
Antrim, whose heroism has not yet received its due reward :

On Mainland, Canna, Eigg, they wander,
Brave troops. whom Allan led delighted.
    Yes ; and Ho Morag, &c.
When great Montrose and Alexander
Proud Lowland hosts had fought and frighted.
    Yes ; and Ho Morag, &c.

The close of this stirring lyric gives us the warrior-bard, after the
ancient manner :

Thick and close, and walked and plaited
Blood-coloured, reddened be the heather.
    Yes ; and Ho Morag, &c.
Haste with thy walking maidens mated
With our brave girls to march together.
    Yes ; and Ho Morag, &c.

CHAPTER IX.

"That is what I always maintained. He has found names, and stories, and phrases, nay passages in old songs, and with them has blended his own compositions, and so made what he gives to the world as the translation of an ancient poem."—SAMUEL JOHNSON.

FEW questions have more deeply disturbed the equanimity of the literary world than the age and authorship of the "Poems of Ossian." The national antagonism and prejudices of three kingdoms were roused over the name of the poor old bard, when his reputed works first appeared nearly one hundred and thirty years ago. A controversy of exceeding keenness ensued; it has not ended yet; and we may well question whether it will ever be satisfactorily settled. It is proposed here to give the history of the poems and annex the opinions of all those entitled to be heard on the question of authorship,

THE OSSIANIC QUESTION.

1. *Sketch of the "Poems of Ossian."*—In the year 1759 James Macpherson was tutor in the family of Graham of Balgowan, at Moffat. There he met John Home, the author of "Douglas." Home was told by Professor Adam Fergusson, a Gaelic-speaking Highlander, that some remains of ancient Gaelic poetry existed; and getting translations of specimens from Macpherson, a native of Badenoch, he showed them to Drs Blair, Fergusson, and Robertson, by whom they were highly appreciated. Importuned by them, he translated all he had, and published in 1760 "Fragments of Ancient Poetry Collected in the Highlands of Scotland."

The friends already mentioned wished to secure all other relics that could be found in the Highlands; and the tutor, then a divinity student, was provided with funds, and undertook his famous journey through the Highlands, where he received MSS., and took down poetry from the recitation of old people. He was first accompanied by Lachlan Macpherson of Strathmashie, a gentleman and a scholar, and also a bard himself, for some time on his tour; he was also joined latterly by Captain Alexander Morrison, who subsequently assisted him. He returned to Badenoch, and remained there till January, 1761, preparing his materials for the next publication, assisted by Macpherson and Morrison. Two Perthshire clergymen were also near him—the Revs. Mr Gallie and James MacLagan, the latter no mean poet himself. By these also he was assisted, and he kept correspondence with them.

In 1762 appeared in London, "Fingal," an epic in six books, along with other sixteen poems.

Next year appeared "Temora," in eight books, and five other poems. "A specimen of the original of 'Temora,'" the seventh book in Gaelic, was also published in this volume.

These *epics* kindled scepticism in many minds; and the "translator," smarting under imputations of forgery, as well as filled with vanity at being thought the author of the poems, indulged himself in sullen silence.

2. *Dr Johnson.*—The great king who reigned in literary matters in those days was Samuel Johnson, a very worthy man, but full of obstinate prejudices against everything Scotch and Highland. He undertook a journey to the Hebrides purposely to investigate into the Ossianic question; but he came with the absolute belief that Gaelic was never written, and no poems of any consequence existed in that language. Boswell's journal:—" Dr Johnson proceeded—' I look upon Macpherson's " Fingal " to be as gross an imposition as ever the world was troubled with. Had it been really an ancient work . . it would be a curiosity of the first rate.' . .

"When Dr Johnson came down, I told him . . that Mr MacQueen repeated a passage in the original Erse, which Mr Macpherson's translation was pretty like; and reminded him that he himself once said he did not require Mr Macpherson's 'Ossian ' to be more like the original than Pope's ' Homer.'

" Johnson—' Well, sir, that is just what I always maintained. He has found names, and stories, and phrases, nay, passages in old songs, and with them has blended his own compositions, and so made what he gives to the world as the translation of an ancient poem.' So also thought Laing in his famous and elaborate essay; as well as thousands of others who accepted the dicta of these writers.

3. *The Highland Society's Report*, got up with great candour,

and after much inquiry and research, and with the testimonies of noblemen, gentlemen, and clergymen, bearing on the question, from all parts of the Highlands, appeared in 1806. It was prepared by Henry Mackenzie, the author of " The Man of Feeling." The result arrived at was :—

1st, That the characters of Macpherson's poem were not invented, but were subjects of Highland tradition ; and that poems certainly existed which might be called Ossianic.

2d, That such poems had been handed down from an unknown period by oral recitation, and that many Highlanders could still repeat them.

3d, That such poems had been written, and some were to be found in MSS.

4th, That Macpherson used many such poems in his work by joining separated pieces together, and that, by adding connective narratives of his own, he had woven them into larger poems and the so-called epics. No materials were found, however, to show the extent of this process and the amount of genuine matter the poems as published by Macpherson contained.

4. *The Gaelic Ossian* was published in 1807, accompanied with Macfarlane's Latin version and MacArthur's dissertation, It came through the hands of Macphersons's executors, assisted by Dr Thomas Ross, of Lochbroom. Money was collected in the East Indies by military gentlemen to defray the expense of publication, and before Macpherson died in 1796 he had the copy ready for the press ; but no traces were to be found of any ancient MSS. which he might have used in preparing his copy, if he ever had any such MSS. that he used. There is nothing exceptionally ancient about the text of 1807.

5. *New State of the Question.*—Highlanders, with very few exceptions, if any, on its appearance accepted the Gaelic text of 1807 as the genuine originals from which Macpherson translated, and which they regarded as composed by Ossian in the third century. But the views of Johnson and Laing were still subscribed to by the great majority of English-speaking people.

6. *Macgregor's "Genuine Remains."*—Patrick Macgregor, M.A., barrister, published in 1841 the genuine remains of " Ossian " in an English rhythmical translation not much inferior to Dr Clerk's with a very well-written historical introduction maintaining the authenticity of the Gaelic Ossian.

7. *Irish Writers* were all along jealous of the attention which Macpherson's translations secured for Gaelic poetry in Scotland.

Societies and individuals determined not to be behind Scotland in supplying the public with ancient Ossianic poems. The *Ossianic Society* especially published five volumes of tales, and poems, and translations ; Macpherson was charged with stealing the substance of his poems from Ireland ; and at the same time the arguments of Johnson and Laing were reiterated ; while the most of what they themselves published as ancient was not more than a century or two old. The Irish could neither manufacture nor lay their hands on epics like those of James Macpherson, so Dr Drummond, Edward O'Reilly, &c., charged Macpherson with *fabricating* the poems, when they found they could not prove that he stole them from Ireland. Ireland has extensive Celtic literature ; much of it ancient too ; but it can show nothing like Macpherson's productions.

8. *Dr W. F. Skene.*—This Celtic scholar says :—" A review of all the circumstances which have been allowed to transpire regarding the proceedings of James Macpherson seems rather to lead to the conclusion that the Gaelic version, in the shape in which it was afterwards published, had been prepared in Badenoch, during the months Macpherson passed there, after his return from his Highland tour, with the assistance of Lachlan Macpherson of Strathmashie, and Captain Morrison, and that the English translation was made from it by Macpherson in the same manner in which he had translated the fragments." The following facts appear to favour Dr Skene's conclusion :—After Lachlan Macpherson's death, a paper was found in his repositories containing the Gaelic of the seventh book of Temora, in his handwriting, with many corrections and alterations, and thus described—" First rude draft of the seventh book of Temora."

Mr Gallie sent to the Highland Society a part of the Gaelic of Fingal, which afterwards appeared as part of the Gaelic version. He had taken it from a MS. he had recovered, written by a friend, " who was at that time with Mr Macpherson and me—a gentleman well known for an uncommon acquaintance with the Gaelic, and a happy facility in writing it in Roman characters." Pressed to tell who this friend was, he says :—" His name was Lachlan Macpherson, of Strathmashy. He died in 1767." Dr Skene says :— " This Gaelic version seems, therefore, to have been put together before 1767 ; and if before 1762, it will account for the original of the seventh book of Temora having been published in that year, and also for an advertisement which appeared soon after the publication of the second quarto, that the originals were lying at the

publisher's, and would be published if a sufficient number of subscribers came forward ; but as few subscribers appeared. and fewer
came to look at them, they were withdrawn."

The view of Dr Skene was scarcely maintained hitherto by any
Scottish Gaelic scholar.   Shaw in 1788 echoed Johnson's sentiments.   He began to read through Macpherson ; and was held
immediately to scorn by the Gaelic literati.

9. *The Late Rev. Thomas Pattison*, author of "The Gaelic
Bards" (1866), and a man highly capable of forming judgment on
the question, says, "When we consider that the finest parts of
Macpherson's Ossian are incontestably proved to have been
popular poetry long anterior to his appearing, I think we should
throw all prejudice aside, and affirm that whoever composed the
poems attributed to Ossian, James Macpherson was not the man ;
and that whatever merit may belong to him as a translator, or
whatever claim he may have to be considered their compiler in
their present form, he has no legitimate title to be called their
author.   They are substantially older than he, probably by many
centuries."   Pattison, like many others before him, dwells on
Macpherson's inferior Gaelic scholarship ; but the facts do not
warrant the conclusion drawn, that Macpherson was incapable of
writing the Gaelic Ossian.   Macpherson was a man of genius, and
quite able to deliver himself in Gaelic as good and classical as many
scholars that lived then or since.

10. *John F. Campbell, Esq.*—The most formidable opponent of
the authenticity of Macpherson's Ossian recently is Mr Campbell
of Islay.   His earlier views, as expressed in the Highland Tales,
were those of Gaelic-speaking Highlanders in general.   But the
longer he dwelt among the genuine old ballads found in manuscripts and in collections taken down from the oral recitation of
Highlanders who lived before Macpherson's time, the more confirmed he became in his growing conviction that Macpherson was
both translator and author, and that the English was first composed.
"My opinion now," he says, " is that Macpherson's translation
was first composed by a great genius, partly from a knowledge of
Scotch nature and folk-lore, partly from ideas gathered from books,
and that he and other translators afterwards worked at it, and
made a Gaelic equivalent whose merit varies according to the
translator's skill and knowledge of Gaelic.   It is said that an early
copy of the 7th book of Temora, with corrections in Strathmashie's
hand, was found after his death.   I suppose that he revised a
Gaelic translation by Macpherson, or by some other.   His own

Gaelic songs are idiomatic, whereas the 7th book of Temora is Saxon Gaelic in general, and nonsense in many passages. The English equivalent is like the rest of Macpherson's work. In either case, because of matter, manner, orthography, and language, Macpherson's English and Gaelic Ossian, must have been composed long after Dean MacGregor collected his book in Macpherson's country, near his district, and in Morven." This is the opinion of a Gaelic-speaking gentleman thoroughly conversant with the facts of the case, and eminently qualified to maintain his side of the question.

11. *Mr Hector MacLean*, Mr Campbell's clever co-adjutor in much of his work, takes a similar view. He says—" The so-called Gaelic Ossian of Macpherson exhibits all the symptoms of being a translation from English. Anglicisms abound everywhere ; the structure of the verse is fully as much akin to English as to Gaelic poetry. It is deficient in all the good qualities of style, strength, clearness, and propriety. The versification is exceedingly rugged and irregular ; alliteration, so characteristic of Celtic poetry, is generally deficient, and frequently entirely wanting ; the sentiment is usually morbid and vapid ; and in fact the so-called original Gaelic Ossian is almost in every respect inferior to the so-called English translation." MacLean at the same time speaks of the ballads in Campbell's *Leabhar na Feinne* as " characterised by purity of language, vigour of expression, and smoothness of versification." MacLean's thorough knowledge of Gaelic as well as his English culture and philological attainments entitle him to be heard.

12. *Rev. Dr Archibald Clerk.*—The dissertation prefixed to the magnificent edition of Ossian. Gaelic and English, published in 1871, at the expense of the Marquis of Bute, and edited with a new literal translation into English by Dr Clerk, of Kilmallie, should be read by all who wish to know the history of the Ossianic controversy. Dr Clerk was an accomplished Gaelic scholar— a man of culture and sound judgment. He ably and warmly maintains that Macpherson was only a translator. In him his opponents find a writer thoroughly qualified, by his literary, scholarly, and philological attainments, to deal with this vexed question. When he and Mr Campbell fail to agree, it is very difficult for others less conversant with the facts of the case to arrive at any satisfactory conclusion. While Dr Clerk was patriotically engaged on his splendid new edition of Ossian, Mr Hector MacLean was regretting " that those who know Gaelic as their vernacular should

be so far duped as to spend their time translating into English what is really nothing else than an inferior and incorrect translation from that language."

13. *The Rev. Dr Hately Waddell.*—"Ossian and the Clyde" is the title of a large, and elaborate, and ingenious work by Dr Waddell. He holds that "Ossian" is historical and authentic; and he supports this position by a three-fold argument—geological, geographical and etymological, and traditional. The work is learned and eloquent; and the author pursues his argument with much minuteness and research. He believes in Ossian by instinct, just as many of his opponents have rejected the same by instinct. He holds that Macpherson is merely editor and translator; and that he has used no liberties with his text beyond what an editor and translator is entitled to use. He, however, labours under the disadvantage of not knowing the Gaelic language, although this difficulty is much minimised by the help of Dr Clerk's literal translation and notes. Part of his arguments is certainly new and original; and the book deserves perusal on the part of the student of the Ossianic controversy.

14. *Dr August Ebrard.*—This distinguished German divine and writer, whom Professor Blackie describes as an "impartial spectator" and a "well-trained German scholar," has written an article on this question in which, after giving a historical sketch, he indicates his arguments in favour of the authenticity of Macpherson's Ossian. He says, "in Ossian's poems there is presented to us the subject-matter of Observations and thoughts, just such as would have occurred to the remembrance of one who had taken part in these battles. And whoever may have cast this material into its present form it is certain that he has left the substance thus unaltered. And why should this not actually have proceeded from this Ossian—prince, warrior, and poet? We know that in old times it was the common custom of the Celtic tribes that the bards should accompany the army to battle, and that every warlike and heroic deed should straightway be celebrated in more or less detailed song. Undoubtedly this would happen with the numerous warlike deeds of King Finnghal. How intelligible it must, then, appear, that after the death of Finnghal and the ruin of his kingdom, the king's son, Ossian, who had fled to the Hebrides, and who was now a blind old man, should have collected into such conflex epics as "Carthonn," "Finnghal," and "Timora," the songs which had been sung, partly by himself and partly by friendly bards (as Carul and Ulin). How intelligible that these poems,

noble in themselves, as well as being reminiscences of former magnificance, should have been preserved with a fond tenacity, and transmitted from generation to generation in the usual manner, by learning by heart, in the centuries (300-900) when the Caledonian nation was so heavily oppressed by the Nordmen, Picts, Britons, and Anglo-Saxons." He further says :—" And thus all the linguistic phenomena are forthwith explained." Dr Ebrard is well known as the author of a work on the early Celtic Church, and by his Gaelic grammar.

15. *Professor John Stuart Blackie.*—In presenting the views of those entitled to be heard on this question it only remains now to give the conclusions arrived at by Professor Blackie, who is acquainted with Gaelic and thoroughly familiar with all the facts. He holds that the question has never yet been examined in a strictly philological fashion. After going through the whole of the originals recently he holds, in opposition to Mr Campbell, that the Gaelic is unquestionably the original. He brings forward five tests by which a translator's hand is clearly discoverable :—

(1.) In the English version, awkward, forced, and unidiomatic expressions frequently occur, which can be clearly traced to the influence of a Gaelic original.

(2.) In all poems of any antiquity handed down in manuscripts difficulties will occur, arising from obsolete words, errors in transcription, confused connection, and other causes. In such cases it is a common practice with translators to skip the difficulty, gloss over the matter with some decent common place, and sometimes to make positive blunders, which it is not difficult for a philologer to expose. All these signs of a translator's hand are frequent in Macpherson's English, and would be more so had he not indulged in such a habit of skipping generally, that it is difficult to say in certain cases decidedly that the skip was made because the writer of the English wished to shirk a difficulty.

(3.) It is a common practice with translators, when they find a passage a little obscure, to remove the obscurity by some manifest alteration of the phrase, or even by interpolating a line or interlarding a commentary. This also occurs in Macpherson.

(4.) It is not always that a translator writes under the same vivid vision, or the same fervid inspiration as the original poet. The instance of failure to seize the most striking features of the original, and the substitution of generic for specific epithets are frequent in Macpherson.

(5.) Most translators yield—sometimes, no doubt, wisely—to

the temptation of improving on their originals, and Macpherson, from what we know of him, was the last man in the world to think of resisting such a temptation. How much of the Gaelic as we now have it—that is, his clean copy of his own originals—was sub-jected to this process of beautification no one can tell, but de-partures from the simplicity of the original can be traced in several instances.

He thinks that the English, as a whole, is a translation from the Gaelic, and not a translation of the best quality in many respects, and that this may be accepted as one of the best ascertained facts in the range of philological investigation. Philological induction, combined with the amount of external evidence to be found in the Highland Society's report, produce a cumulative proof which he is most anxious to see how Mr Campbell can rebut. Principal Shairp thinks that Professor Blackie has hit upon the true solution of this controversy.

16. *Mr Archibald MacNeill, W.S.*, with his brothers Lord Colonsay and Sir John MacNeill, who were all familiar with the Gaelic language, firmly believed that the Gaelic text of Macpher-son belonged to the early centuries of the Christian era. Mr MacNeill published his views in a small volume in which legal acumen is brought to bear on the question, and which concludes as follows: "At what date Ossian lived we do not pretend to determine ; but this, at least, is sufficiently clear, that the Gaelic Ossian was not the production of Macpherson or any author of modern times, but must be referred to a period of remote antiquity. It further appears from the internal evidence of these poems, that they refer to a period prior to the diffusion of Christianity and the era of clanship." Of course Macpherson was clever enough, granting he elected to do so, to give a complexion of antiquity to his compositions.

17. My own opinion of the question I embody in the following propositions. I began the study of Macpherson's Ossian some twelve years ago, and exercised myself then in translating many portions of it, so I am fairly familiar with it.

I believe—

(1.) That the English is a translation from Gaelic, probably from a ruder version than that published in 1807.

(2.) That Macpherson is neither absolutely the author, nor merely the translator, of the poems connected with his name.

(3.) That he formed his original Gaelic by joining and re-casting old ballads, that he connected these ballads by paragraphs of his own composition, and that the newly-written recast matter constitutes the chief parts of the epics which he had thus formed, but in which, however, the spirit of the old productions still survives.

(4.) That the Gaelic is far more elaborate than the English, is subtler in conception, less concrete in expression, and has been likely, before the text was finally published, the subject of many alterations and improvements.

(5.) That on the whole the language of the text of 1807 is not, as some allege, essentially different from that of the ballads that are known to be genuine.

(6.) That the metre of the Gaelic text is not more irregular than that of these same ballads, the chief difference being that while the latter are mostly made up of either trochees or iambs the former frequently mixes anapaests with trochees or iambs.

The Highland Society's report, in a general way points to simi. lar conclusions. The process adopted by Macpherson was early described by Dr. Smith (1780) who is supposed to have dealt with ballads in Macphersonic fashion :—" Mr Macpherson compiled his publication from those parts of the Highland songs which he most approved, combining them into such forms as, according to his ideas, were most excellent, retaining the old names and leading events." This is what Dr Smith himself honestly did in his *Sean Dana* ; and it is rather surprising, after Dr Smith's description of the process adopted by himself, and probably also by Macpher-son, that any intelligent persons, whether Highland or otherwise, should insist on the absolute originality of every line in the texts of both Smith and Macpherson. I believe no conscientious dis-honesty was intended by either, especially by Smith. They were both influenced by the loose views of editorial functions prevalent in their day. The question of what was Macpherson's ideal of editorial functions lay ignored all along at the root of the Ossianic controversy. A seriously mistaken and uncritical view it was ; but he thought he was doing what would be for the credit of his native country.

When the writer arrived at the conclusions just indicated, ten years ago, he was not so clear as to the process by which Mac-pherson wrought the Gaelic and English Ossians into their present forms. Since then, in 1883, he entered more minutely into the question in a paper read before the Gaelic Soeiety of London and the conclusion forced upon his mind, as the result chiefly of comparisons between the various versions of the Gaelic fragments

which were found in mysterious circulation in Macpherson's life-
time, was that the Gaelic Ossian, like the English equivalent, was
a production of the last century, and that James Macpherson was
the author as well as translator of these celebrated compositions]of
the Gaelic muse. Dr Macdonald, M.P., President of the Gaelic
Society, and other expert Gaelic scholars present, while reluctant
to accept the conclusions of the paper, did not seriously attempt
to dispute them ; while Mr Macdonald Cameron, M.P., regarded
the arguments brought forward as clearly decisive on the question.
Since then Mr Macbain of Inverness ably discussed the poems
from other standpoints, and has informed the writer that the
late Dr. Cameron of Brodick adopted similar views. The great
Ossianic question may now be regarded as settled. What was
needed all along to settle it was sufficient knowledge, culture,
judgment, and honesty on the part of men familiar with the Gaelic
language. Such men have appeared since the publication of Dr
Clerk's Ossian, the first note being sounded by Mr J. F. Campbell
in his celebrated review of Clerk's work in *The Times*. Mr. H.
Maclean adopted the same views ; and the writer, in 1883, on
independent and other grounds was forced to take up the same
position. Dr Cameron and Mr Macbain, representing the mid-
land and northern Highlands, having now concurred, the students
of the Gaelic language north and south unite thus in regarding
Macpherson's Gaelic Ossian as compositions of the last century.
These compositions are great original works, and ought to be thus
described. Their spirit is ancient and Celtic, though their form
is modern. They, James Macpherson their author, and Gaelic
literature stand in the same relation to one another that we find
illustrated in the case of the " Idyls of the King," Alfred Tennyson, and Cymric literature. The only difference is that Tennyson
has not given us the " Idyls " in Welsh as well as in English, and
that Macpherson's English version is in prose instead of being in
blank verse. As long as Gaelic scholars of undoubted respectabi-
lity believed otherwise, it was difficult for outsiders like the Blackies,
Ebrards, and Waddells, who discussed the question, to be certain
of their conclusions ; but henceforth it will be inexcusable in any
man of letters to argue for the old views, as Mr George Eyre-Todd
does in an introduction to the " Poems of Ossian," published in
the *Canterbury Poets* series (1888) without taking any cognisance
of the latest deliverances of those most entitled to express an
opinion.

For a long time the controversy regarding the poems of Ossian

had only the English version for its critical basis ; so it was unreasonable then to expect a satisfactory solution of the vexed
question of authorship. Those who knew the language could only
guess at the originals ; and those who did not know it had to be
satisfied with all they could make of the English. Both parties
occupied a position critically absurd. The one side ignorant of
the language could not presume to pronounce whether the poems
were or were not a translation ; and the other had not yet the
materials for judgment before them. But now in the year 1807
appeared the long looked-for and much discussed Gaelic originals
of the Ossianic translations published some forty years previously.
The following is the title-page in full :—" The Poems of Ossian, in
the Original Gaelic, with a literal translation into Latin, by the
late Robert Macfarlane, A.M., together with a Dissertation on the
Authenticity of the Poems by Sir John Sinclair, Bart., and a translation from the Italian of the Abbe Cessarotti's Dissertation on
the Controversy respecting the Authenticity of Ossian, with Notes
and a Supplementary Essay, by John McArthur, LL.D., published
under the sanction of the Highland Society of London. *Magna
est veritas et praevalebit.* Vol. I. *London.* [Printers and Publishers' names], 1807, pp. ccxxxii., 278.

" ———————Vol. II.," pp. 390.

" ———————Vol. III.," pp. 576.

" Dana Oisen Mhic Fhinn, air an cur amach air son maith
coitcheanta muinntir na Gaeltachd. Duneidin ; clo-bhuailte le
Tearlach Stiubhart. 1818." 8vo., pp. 344.

This last is a copy of the Gaelic text contained in Sir John
Sinclair's magnficent edition of Ossian. It was printed at the
expense of Sir J. Macgregor Murray and other gentlemen that it
might be distributed among the Highlanders to cultivate and to
preserve their old chivalrous spirit. There was a copy sent for
the use of every parish school in the Highlands. These copies
were addressed to the care of the parish ministers, in whose hands
they generally remained. One thing is certain, they never reached
nor became known amongst the people in the manner in which
other books circulated amongst them.

Here were the Gaelic originals of Ossian at last ; and certainly
there was no great reason to regret the delay in their appearance,
when they were now presented in so splendid a dress. Surely now
all controversy about them should cease for ever. All Gaelic-
speaking Highlanders thought so then ; and there are many who
think similarly still.

This text was not exactly as it came from Macpherson's hands, who died while preparing it for the press. A standard of Celtic orthography was then in course of formation ; and John Mackenzie, Esq., of London, one of Macpherson's executors, engaged the Rev. Dr Thomas Ross to write out with him the text of Ossian in the style adopted by the excellent translators of the Gaelic Bible. Dr Ross, although well acquainted with the language, was not the most accurate scholar of his day. So until Clerk's " Ossian " appeared in 1870 there was no fairly correct and scholarly text of these poems. Had the text come from Macpherson's own hands, the orthography would probably have been very different. Macpherson enjoyed neither the time nor the practice in writing the language to enable him to write either consistently with himself or with any system of orthography. What he wrote, or took down, or copied at an earlier period, of which we have a fair specimen in the 7th Book of " Temora," published with the translations, is like what many educated Highlanders of the present day would write. When conducting Highland periodicals, the writer frequently received articles from gentlemen with some reputation for Gaelic scholarship which were much in the style of Macpherson's orthography. Yet these same gentlemen might be, as some of them were, profoundly acquainted with the vocabulary and idioms of the language, although they were unable to write consistently with their own or any other mode of spelling ; and were they poets of first-class genius, they could produce, as far as acquaintance with the language was concerned, poetry like that of Ossian, Macdonald, or Macintyre, the last of whom could not write at all ; whilst it will not be seriously contended that Ossian was so familiar with the pen as he was ever with the sword. The state of the text at any time since it was first moulded in Macpherson's hands could not be of the slightest value in deciding the age of the poems. Neither could it be of more service philologically than any other Gaelic books printed during the last hundred years. It could have no value like *The Book of Deer*, and *The Book of the Dean of Lismore*.

Though a very inviting field, it is not here intended to enter into examination of the words of the text. When this question has been competently investigated some of our views which at present waver will be thoroughly confirmed.

Let the question of the authenticity be in the meantime laid aside, and let the poems as they are be considered. One thing is certain—they are the clever productions of a Gaelic genius—

of a master whose works have influenced the literature of modern Europe. The healthy and grand old figure of Ossian appeared on the scene of the artificial literary world of the eighteenth century, and his tenderness, his naturalness, and his keen sympathies with the external world of form, of colour, and of movement carried before him the conventionalities of a hollow generation. Ossian, along with Cowper, was the first influence at work in bringing back the rising poets of the day to the study and contemplation of nature. The poems were translated into all the languages of Europe. This "most magnificent mystification of modern times, as a German writer has described Ossian, acted like a spell on poets in this country and on the Continent. Goethe and Lamartine felt the force of this spell ; the former acknowledged it in the "Songs of Selma" in "Werther," and the latter in "Memoirs of my Youth." The illustrious French poet has vividly described in the following passage the enthusiastic admiration of Ossian that prevailed in France in his younger days.

"It was now the period when Ossian, that poet of the genius of ruins and battles, reigned paramount in the imagination of France. Baour-Lormian had translated him into sonorous verse for the camp of the emperor. Women sung him in plaintive romances, or in triumphal strains, at the departure, above the tomb, or on the return of their lovers. Small editions in portable volumes had found their way into all the libraries. One of them fell into my hands. I plunged into this ocean of shadow, of blood, of tears, of phantoms, of foam, of snow, of fogs, of hoar frosts, and of images, the immensity, the dimness. and the melancholy of which harmonise so well with the lofty sadness of a heart of sixteen which expands to the first rays of the Infinite. Ossian, his localities, and his images harmonised wonderfully also with the nature of the mountain district, almost Scottish in its character, with the season of the year, and with the melancholy aspect of the places where I read him. It was during the biting blasts of November and December. The earth was covered with a mantle of snow, pierced here and there by the black trunks of scattered pines, or overhung by the naked and branching arms of the oaks, upon which flights of crows assembled, filling the air with their coarse cawings. Icy fogs clothed the branches with hoar frost, clouds swept in eddying wreaths around the buried peaks of the mountains. A few streams of sunshine streamed for a moment through their openings, and discovered distant perspective of unfathomable valleys, which the eye might fancy gulfs of the sea. It was the natural and sublime exposition of the poems of Ossian which I held in my hand. I carried him in my hunting pouch over the mountains. and while the dogs made the deep gorges of the hills echo with their barking, I read his pages, s itting beneath the shelter of some overhanging rock, only raising my eyes from its pages to find again, floating along the horizon or outstretched at my feet, the same mists, the same clouds, the same plains of ice or snow which I had just beheld in imagination. How often have I felt my tears congealing on the borders of my eyelids ! I had become one of the sons of the bard, one of the heroic, amorous, or plaintive shades who fought, who loved, who wept, or who swept the fingers across the harp in the gloomy domains of Fingal."

In Italy the influence of Ossian was supreme. Cesarotti tells us that he became the founder of a school of poetry there. Throughout the literary world the power of Ossian's muse was felt. The artificiality, hollowness, and conventionality of the last quarter of the eighteenth century rendered the natural echoes of the grand old voice of Cona a fresh music and a welcome relief.

There are two complete translations of these Gaelic poems before the world besides Macpherson's—Macgregor's and Clerk's. The last is absolutely literal, while Macgregor's is also pretty faithful to the Gaelic. Both versions are neither blank verse, nor rhyme, nor prose, but are couched in a species of rhythmic verse in lines of various lengths. Neither the one nor the other is ever likely to become popular, so that a literal popular version is still required for those whom Macpherson's own cannot satisfy. I have thrown into a very literal blank verse the whole of *Carrick,* from which I take the following description of Finn's encounter with the Ghost of Lodin. It is a fair specimen of the poems as a whole, and gives us an inkling of their mythology, which here and elsewhere is vague and shadowy :—

LODIN'S GHOST.

A fire descended in the dark beyond ;
The moon was red and languid in the east ;
A blast came down in sadness from the plain ;
And on its wings the semblance of a man ;—
Cru-Lodin standing pale upon the plain—
He nigh approached unto his own abode,
Holding his dark spear useless in his haud ;
His red eye like the blazing of the skies ;
His speaking like the thunder on the hill
In shadowy darkness distant far away ;

Finn lifted up his spear amid the night ;
And on the meadow was his shouting heard.

FINN.

"Son of the Night, begone thou from my side.
Betake thee to thy wind and be away !
Why camest thou to my presence, shadowy one ?
Thy semblance is unreal as thine arms.
Can thy brown form be terrible to me,
Thou Phantom of the Circles Lodin owns ?
Frail is thy shield, and weak thy vapoury cloud ;
Thy bare sword like a flame across the surge ;
Which shall be cleft asunder by the blast,
And scattered thou thyself without delay,
Begone thou Dismal Offspring of the skies !
Recall thy blast to take thee and begone."

THE GHOST.

" Would'st thou from my own circle me coerce ? "
Spake the deep voice of hollowest refrain.
"It is to me that hosts of heroes yield ;
I glance but on the people from the height,
They are dispersed like ashes 'neath my gaze.
Out of my breath proceeds the blast of death.
I journey loftily upon the wind ;
And tempests hurry forth themselves on high
Around my brow, cold, melancholy, pale ;
But calm is my abode beyond the clouds,
And pleasant the broad fields of my repose."

FINN.

"Go, and abide then on thy pleasant plains,"
Replied the mighty king with hand on hilt,
" Else, Cuhal's Son, forget not in the field.
Weak is thy spectre—and my strength is great.
Did I direct my footsteps from the hill
Toward thy hall, high on the peaceful plain ?
Or did my pow'rful spear e'er clash amid
The garments of the skies against the voice
Of the Black Ghost Cru-Lodin's circle keeps ?
Why hast thou lifted with a scowl thy brow ?
Or wherefore shakest thou aloft thy spear ?
Little I dread thy words, thou Shadowy One !
I fled not from an army in the field,
Why flee before the Offspring of the Winds ?
The Valiant Brave, the King of Lofty Bens,
He shall not flee ! He knows, though he has not
Been there, the frailty of thine arm in war."

THE GHOST.

" Begone ! flee to thy land," replied the Form,
' Flee on the dismal tempet, flee, begone !
The blast is in the the hollow of my hand.

Mine are the conflict and the speed of storms ;
The King of Sora is a Son of mine ;
He kneels down in the mountain to my form ;
At Rock of Hundreds he upholds the strife,
And scathless he shall gain the victory,
Begone to thine own land, thou Cuhal's son,
Or to thy grief experience my wrath."

THE COMBAT.

He lifted up his threatening spear on high,
And fiercely forward bent his lofty head.
Then Finn advanced, opposing him in wrath,
Wielding his blue transparent sword in hand,—
The sword—the Son of Luinn of duskiest cheek,
The steely lustre pierced the Phantom through.
The Evil wraith of death assumed a frown ;
He fell devoid of shape, far, far beyond,
Riding the wings of the dark cairns, like smoke
A sapling raises with a stick in hand,
About a hearth of discord and of gloom.

The Wraith of Lodin's form shrieked on the Ben,
Collecting his essentials in the wind ;
The Innis of the boars the tumult heard :
The trembling waves stopped action in their course.
The heroes of great Cuhal's son arose.
And in each hand a spear was held aloft ;
" Where is he ? "—and their fury gathering gloom,
And every mail loud clanking round its chief.

As formerly remarked, the " Old Lays " of Dr Smith are fully as interesting and poetical as Macpherson's Ossian ; and all who wish to read and enjoy good Gaelic poetry—fresh and idiomatic — should go to these lays. Smith's own translation is exceedingly loose and turgid as compared with his Gaelic. As already observed, Smith also comes under the suspicion of being the author of the Gaelic, as well as translator. His own account of the translation has been already given ; and there seems no good reason why its honesty and correctness should be doubted. His Gaelic originals appear to stand in the same relation to pre-existent ballad and taleologic literature that Burns' new versions of Scottish songs and ballads sustain to the older and original productions. Like Macpherson, Dr Smith cannot be said to be wholly the author nor merely the translator of these grand poetical " lays." Illustrative specimens of them are given in the next chapter. To furnish a contrast to Macpherson's Ossian and manner, I give the following lines on *Bas Airt*, or the Death of Artho :—

In battle-field he fell in fame ;
Terrible to many as he came
Like thunder through the woods, or lightning

That hid itself midst ruin frightning !
The enemies trembled, fell, and fled ;
From Artho's hand destruction sped,
Like Melmor's rocks dashed through the woods
To sink beiow in sullen floods ;
Such seemed the low-laid hero's form
Ere came death's arrow in the storm.

Dan an Deirg, one of the finest poems in Smith's volume, has been recently translated, edited, and annotated by an accomplished English scholar and graduate of Cambridge, Mr. C. S-Jerram, who has been at the pains of studying the language. To this interesting little volume is prefixed a very intelligent and fair account of the state of the Ossianic question.

Dr Smith's " Old Lays," translated by himself in too free and turgid a fashion, are as interesting as Macpherson's. " Ossian," and not inferior in any respect to that famed production. In the opening of one of these " lays," called " Finan and Lorma," we find a very pretty set of verses in which the young people around him, looking upon the heavens, are represented as addressing the aged Ossian in the following manner :—

While on the plains shines the moon, O bard !
And the shadow of Cona holds ;
Like a ghost breathes the wind from the mountain,
With its spirit voice in its folds.

There are two cloudy forms before us,
Where its host the dim night shows ;
The sigh of the moor curls their tresses,
As they tread over Alva of roes.

Dusky his dogs came with one,
And he bends his dark-brow of yew ;
There's a stream from the side of the sad-faced maid,
Dyes her robe with a blood-red hue.

Hold thou back, O thou wind ! from the mountain,
Let their image a moment stay ;
Nor sweep with thy skirts from our eyesight,
Nor scatter their beauty away.

O'er the glen of the rushes, the hill of the hinds
With the vague wandering vapour they go ;
O, Bard of the times that have left us !
Aught of their life cans't thou show ?

OSSIAN'S REPLY.

The years that have been they come back as ye speak,
To my soul in their music they glide ;
Like the murmur of waves in the far inland calm,
Is their soft and smooth step by my side.

The translation is from " The Gaelic Bards." Let us now

glance at a particular class of popular pieces that have become
mixed up with the suspected works of Macpherson and Smith.
The original of the specimens which follow was well known before
Macpherson's Gaelic Ossian appeared. The famous " Address to
the Sun " is found in English in Macpherson's *Carthon.* In the
published Gaelic of 1807 its place is marked by asterisks. The
Gaelic is inserted to correspond with the English in Clerk's edition. A new literal translation is here attempted :—

> O, thou that glidest in the sky,
> Round as the hero's full hard shield,
> Thy frownless lustre, whence on high?
> Sun, whence thy ceaseless light revealed ?
> Thou comest in thy lovely might ;
> The stars conceal from us their motion ;
> The moon pale hies from heaven's height,
> And shrouds her in the western ocean.
> Thou in thy distance art alone ;
> Who bold may dare approach thy might ;
> With age, cairn, cliff, are overthrown ;
> With age the oak falls from the height.
> The ocean shakes with ebb and flow ;
> The moon is lost in depth of night ;
> But, Victor, thou alone dost glow
> In endless joy of thine own light.
> When tempests darken round the earth
> Wih lightning, and with hoarse-voiced thunder,
> Fair through the storm thou look'st in mirth
> Upon the troubled heavens under.
> But vain to me are thy bright rays,
> Since I must see no more thy glance ·
> Gold-tressed that turns on eastern gaze
> Of heaven's cloudy countenance,
> When thou art trembling in the west,
> Through ocean's dusky doors to rest.
> But like myself thou art perchance—
> Once robed with weakness, once with strength ;
> In circling sky our years advance
> Together to one end at length ;
> Rejoice, O Sun, while thou art young ;
> Be glad, thou Prince ! while thou art strong !
> Old age is dark and void of mirth,
> Like faint moon ere her horn she fills ;
> While looking from the clouds on earth
> Where hoary mist skirts cairny hills.
> The biting blast with breath of cold
> Beats on the traveller weak and old.

It is said that this address, the original of which was supplied to the Highland Society in the year 1801, was well known in the central Highlands early in the eighteenth century. The Rev. Mr Macdiarmid wrote it down from the dictation of an old man in Glenlyon about 1770. It is said that this old man learned it in his youth from people in the same glen before Macpherson was born.

The "Address to the Setting Sun " is given at the beginning of Macpherson's *Carricthura*. It consists of eleven lines, and has been a great favourite among the people. The following is a literal translation :—

> Leav'st the blue distance of the skies,
> Unsullied Sun, with tress of gold ?
> Where west thy tent of slumber lies
> The portals of the night unfold.
> The cautious billows cower nigher
> Thy shining temples to behold ;
> Awe-struck, their heads they lift up higher
> To view thee grand in thy repose !
> Pale from thy side they back retire !
> May in thy cave sleep o'er thee close,
> O, Sun ! till thou the dawn inspire.

The above lines were written down by Mr Macdiarmid at the same time as the " Address to the Sun." In the two pieces we find abstract conceptions that we never come across in the old ballads. This gives real ground to the argument of recent writers that the poems are of modern date. Whether ancient or modern, they are poetry of a high order, superior to that of the Irish and Scottish ballads. The new theory seems to some inconsistent with the honour and veracity of more than one clergyman and gentleman of repute, who could have no personal interest in helping to palm on the public the alleged forgeries of Macpherson. There is another " Address to the Sun "—to the rising sun—in Dr Smith's Old Lays, which appeared many years before the publication of Macpherson's Gaelic. It is admirably translated by Mr Pattison, and I avail myself of his translation :—

> Son of the young morn ! that glancest
> O'er the hills of the east with thy gold-yellow hair
> How gay on the wild thou advancest
> Where the streams laugh as onward they fare ;
> And the trees yet bedewed by the shower,
> Elastic their light bright branches raise,
> Whilst the melodsts sweet they embower
> Hail thee at once with their lays.

But where is the dim light duskily gliding,
On her eagle wings from thy face?
Where now is darkness abiding?
In what cave do bright stars end their race—
When fast, on their faded steps bending,
Like a hunter you rush through the sky,
Up those lone lofty mountains ascending,
While down yon far summits they fly?

Pleasant thy path is, Great Luttre, wide-gleaming,
Dispelling the storm with thy rays;
And graceful thy gold ringlets streaming,
As wont in the westering blaze.
Thee the blind mist of night ne'er deceiveth,
Nor sends from the right course astray!
The strong tempest, all ocean that grieveth,
Can ne'er make thee bend from thy way.

At the call of the mild morn appearing,
Thy festal face wakens up bright;
Thy shade from all dark places clearing,
But the bard's eye that ne'er sees thy light."

In an Irish poem from which quotations have been made the
the bard is represented as blind. In two of these pieces we have
touching allusion to the same melancholy infliction. " Vain to
me are thy bright rays" occurs in the Address to the Sun, and
" the bard's eye that ne'er sees thy light" in the Address to the
Rising Sun. The soul of the old poet seemed to take delight in
contrasting his own sightless condition with the brilliant sun in his
course through the heavens. This tone of melancholy pleasure—
of deep and lonely nurtured feeling—so characteristic of the
Ossianic poems, is also chatacteristic of the Celtic race, especially
of the Scottish Gael, whose spirit seems to have been enswathed
in the majestic gloom of his own native glens and mountains.
The curtains of mist hanging over the silent and weird-looking
lochs, the ghost-like clouds that glided across the glens or in-
wrapped the crests of the hills, the moan of the sounding seashore mingling with the roar of a hundred streams forcing their
ways to join the boundless ocean, are sights and sounds which
naturally exerted a powerful influence on the souls of those who
lived daily in their midst. When the tempests darkened round
the earth, and lightnings flashed, and the hoarse-voiced thunder
shook the hills, how pleasant it must have been for the depressed
spirit of man to gaze on the face of the sun, looking " fair through
the storm " " upon the troubled heavens under " of a Hebridean
sky!

These are specimens of a great deal of poetry which Highlanders of the present day unhesitatingly ascribe to Ossian. Indeed, the Ossian of these pieces appears to be a poet of quite a
different calibre from that of the old ballads. One thing is clear
that whoever was the author or authors of these much discussed
productions, he or they were poets of the highest order, and must
have been Gaels born and bred in the Highlands.

CHAPTER X.

"Lean gu dlù ri cliù do shinnsear ;
'S na dich'nich a bhi mar iadsan."—SEANN DAN.

ENGLISH :
Follow thou thy fathers' fame ;
Ne'er forget thy country's claim.

AFTER the Celtic poems and translations of the Bard of Badenoch had begun to realise fame and fortune for their author, other
writers of varying gifts sought to enter into similar labours. For
literary students the Gaelic realm of letters hitherto had been
obscure and untrodden fields ; but now all at once the old Celtic
world of the Scottish past became alive with heroes of magnificent
deeds and bards of illustrious renown. The refinement, the culture, the heroic courage of grand old Scots, in the environment of
the purest chivalry, kindled everywhere admiration throughout
Europe. People wearied of the artificialities and platitudes of the
eighteenth century, allowed themselves to get into raptures over
the healthy pictures of ancient life which these Celtic compositions unfolded. The blind old Ossian was then more popular
than the blind old Homer, and all "Old Lays" connected with
the Highlands and Islands acquired a value which they never had
before. There was a general rage for Gaelic old lays and ballads,
and a search was instituted throughout the land for such productions. Bards, senachies, reciters, and singers of every description
and every rank in life were requisitioned for the supply of ancient
Ossianic ballads.

One good result of this was to make the Highlands better
known, and to help in the removal of old race-prejudices which
had all along existed in some quarters, but which had become
gre atly intensified through the recent Jacobite rebellions for which
the Highlanders as a people were not primarily responsible. John

Knox may be said to have made the Scotland of his time reforming, radical, and religious, and Sir Walter Scott the Scotland of
the nineteenth century romantic in verse and story; and James
Macpherson may be said with equal force to have made the
Highlands in the eighteenth century.   It has been said that old
Celtic lays and ballads became then the fashion.   The pioneer in
the field, it ought to be remembered, however, was not the Badenoch tutor.   Three or four years before Macpherson was heard of
there died, in June 1756, in the 30th year of his age,

JEROME STONE,

who was the first to direct public attention to Ossianic ballads.
He was born at Scoonie, Fifeshire, in 1727.   His father was a
seafaring man.   As a mere lad, Jerome became a packman; but
dealing in buckles, garters, and such small articles not suiting his
"superior genius," he sold his stock, bought books, and finally
struggled into St Andrews University, where he graduated in 1750.
He soon received the appointment of assistant in Dunkeld
Grammar School, of which he became Rector two or three years
afterwards.   In this position, acquiring knowledge of the Gaelic
language and of the people, along with his other duties, he
remained until struck down of fever, as already stated, in 1756.
At that time Dunkeld, an ancient home of Celtic activity, learning, and enterprise, was more of a Gaelic district than it is now
and Stone found himself in social and intellectual surroundings
which were new to him.   He had probably more racial kinship,
with the people than he himself knew or acknowledged, or than
even Professor Mackinnon, who has edited his collection, has
thought of.   For centuries Gaidel and Brython lived and fought
in his native Fifeshire, and their fervid life-blood has never ceased
to run in the veins of Fife men.   Probably the eloquent Thomas
Chalmers received much of the inspiration of his genius from this
Celtic source.   Stone left a collection of Gaelic ballads which was
for some time regarded as lost.   The MS., after passing through
various hands, passed two years ago into the possession of Edinburgh University on the death of Dr. Clerk, to whom it was given
when preparing his edition of Ossian, by David Laing.   Professor
Mackinnon has published the collection of ballads in the Transactions of the Gaelic Society of Inverness, 1887-88, occupying
fifty pages of the volume, and accompanied with an interesting
biographical note, to which the writer is indebted for some of the

particulars given above. These ballads are of exactly the same
character as those of the Feinne already considered. They are
merely other versions of the same poems dealing with the same
themes of the Finnic environment of the old Gaelic national life.
The first translator of Gaelic poetry deserves a memorial cairn
in any book devoted to the interests of our Anglo-Gaelic literature. Jerome Stone gave the first translation of the old Gaelic
Lays to the world in 1756 four years before the appearance of
Macpherson's *Fragments*. It appears that a St Andrews Professor was the first to interest young Stone in Gaelic poetry, and the
best of his efforts at translation was his free rendering of " Fraoch's
Death," or as he entitles it, " Albin and the Daughter of
Mey ":—

A thousand graces did the maid adorn :
Her looks were charming, and her heart was kind ;
Her eyes were like the windows of the morn,
And Wisdom's habitation was her mind.
A hundred heroes try'd her love to gain ;
She pity'd them, yet did their suits deny ;
Young Albyn only courted not in vain,
Albyn alone was lovely in her eye :
Love filled their bosoms with a mutual flame ;
Their birth was equal, and their age the same.

Her mother Mey, a woman void of truth,
In practice of deceit and guile grown old,
Conceived a guilty passion for the youth,
And in his ear the shameful story told ;
But o'er his mind she never could prevail,
For in his life no wickedness was found ;
With shame and rage he heard the horrid tale,
And shook with indignation at the sound ;
He fled to shun her ; while with burning wrath
The monster, in revenge, decreed her death.

Amidst Lochmey, a distance from the shore,
On a green island, grew a stately tree,
With precious fruit each season cover'd o'er,
Delightful to the taste and fair to see.
This fruit more sweet than virgin honey found.
Serv'd both alike for physic and for food :
It cured diseases, heal'd the bleeding wound,
And hunger's rage for three long days withstood
And precious things are purchas'd still with pain,
And thousands try'd to pluck it, but in vain.

For at the root of this delightful tree,
A venomous and awful dragon lay,

14

With watchful eyes, all horrible to see.
Who drove th' affrighted passengers away ;
Worse than the viper's sting its teeth did wound
The wretch who felt it soon behov'd to die ;
Nor could physicians ever yet be found
Who might a certain antidote apply :
Even they whose skill had sav'd a mighty host,
Against its bite no remedy could boast.

Revengeful Mey, her fury to appease,
And him destroy who durst her passion slight,
Feign'd to be stricken with a dire disease,
And call'd the hopeless Albin to her sight :
" Arise, young hero ! skill'd in feats of war,
On yonder lake your dauntless courage prove,
To pull me of the fruit, now bravely dare,
And save the mother of the maid you love ;
I die without its influence divine,
Nor will I taste it from a hand but thine."

With downcast look the lovely youth reply'd,
" Though yet my feats of valour have been few,
My might in this adveuture shall be try'd ;
I go to pull the healing fruit for you."
With stately steps approaching to the deep
The hardy hero swims the liquid tide :
With joy he finds the dragon fast asleep,
Then pulls the fruit, and comes in safety back ;
Then with a cheerful countenance, and gay,
He gives the present to the hands of Mey.

" Well have you done to bring me of this fruit ;
But greater signs of prowess must you give :
Go pull the tree entirely by the root,
And bring it hither, or I cease to live."
Though hard the task, like lightning fast he flew,
And nimbly glided o'er the yielding tide ;
Then to the tree with manly steps he drew,
And pull'd it hard from side to side :
Its bursting roots his strength could not withstand ;
He tears it up, and bears it in his hand.

But long, alas ! ere he could reach the shore,
Or fix his footsteps on the solid sand,
The monster follow'd with a hideous roar,
And like a fury grasped him by the hand.
Then, gracious God ! what dreadful struggling rose :
He grasps the dragon by th' invenom'd jaws,
In vain ; for round the bloody current flows,
While his fierce teeth his tender body gnaws.
He groans through anguish of the grievous wound,
And cries for help ; but, ah ! no help was found !

The hero's death is a tragic one; and the life of the "helpless maid!" vanishes in the usual tender regrets of bards. Our great interest in the production, apart from the early death of the gifted and sympathetic Stone, lies in the fact that he was the was the first English-speaking man of letters who attempted to deal fairly with the products of the Gaelic muse. To students of Macpherson's Ossian and Ossianic ballads it will be apparent that the Badenoch tutor merely imitated Stone in the English productions; he gave the spirit, not the letter of Gaelic poetry. Macpherson's trouble lay in the originally unexpected necessity of providing Gaelic originals which would be fair equivalents for his published English versions. The bitter assaults made on his works naturally led to his manner of self-defence. As an illustration of how *poetical* translators deal with the original materials placed in their hands, nothing better could be found than this Gaelic ballad which Stone published in English dress in the "Scots Magazine." In "Mackenzie's Report," the original Gaelic, Stone's rendering, and a literal version are supplied. The second is described as a "Translation of the foregoing," as published by Stone in the "Scots Magazine" for 1756. In order to show how a "translation" was regarded in the age of Macpherson, it may be well to give the last three verses of "Fraoch's Death" in the original, then the "Report's" literal version, and lastly Stone's poetic translation. Here are the last three verses of the Gaelic ballad:—

> Thogamar anois an cluin Fhraoich,
> Corp an laoich an Caiseal Chro.
> On Bhas ud a fhuair am fear,
> Mairg is mairion na dheigh beo.
>
> Gu mhi sud an tuabhar Mna,
> Is mo chonairceas air mo dha Roisg,
> Fraoch a chur a bhuain a Chrainn,
> An deis an Caoran a bhi bhos.
>
> Air a cluain thughte an t'ainm,
> Loch meidhe raite ris an Loch,
> Am biodh a Bheist anns gach uair,
> Is a Craos a suas an Dos.

This is the "Report's," literal translation of these verses:

> We bore to the grove of Fraoch,
> The body of the hero to its circular pale;
> After the worthy has died,
> To be alive is our regret

Cruelest of woman was she,
That ever was seen by eyes,
Who sent Fraoch to tear the branch,
After the fruit had been torn away.

The grove bears his name,
Loch Meyo is the name of the lake,
Where the monster kept watch,
And its open jaw to the tree.

This is the original material out of which Jerome Stone wrought his translation as follows :—

But now he's gone and nought remains but woe
For wretched me ; with him my joys are fled ;
Around his tomb my tears shall ever flow,
The rock my dwelling, and the clay my bed !
Ye maids and matrons, from your hills descend,
To join my moan and answer tear for tear ;
With me the hero to the grave attend,
And sing the songs of mourning round his bier,
Through his own grove his praise we will proclaim,
And bid the place forever bear his name.

The idea may come to many readers as a surprise that if Jerome Stone had been spared to perform the part of translaror of the Gaelic ballads and small epics of the Finnic mythus, he would probably furnish the world with " translations " which would not be nearer the " originals " than Macpherson's have been. The reference here is not to Macpherson's Gaelic published subsequently, but to the Ossianic compositions which became such a source of general Celtic inspiration during the latter half of the eighteenth century.

JOHN SMITH, D.D.

This writer was among the most cultured and distinguished of those who about a hundred years ago devoted time, means, and talent to the study of Gaelic literature. The labours of the Rev. Dr John Smith of Campbeltown, as an author and translator of prose and poetry, were varied and abundant. He produced a Life of Columba the Apostle of the Highlands ; a work on The Functions of the Sacred Office, which received the high commendation of Dr. Bickersteth ; and a work on Gaelic Antiquities and the History of the Druids, which is still sought after, and which exhibits considerable research and good literary powers. These works, in English, enable us to judge of the qualities of the man in general ; but it is with his Gaelic works that we have chiefly to deal. He was one of those who helped to translate the Old Testament into Gaelic, edited a version of the Gaelic Psalter, another of the Shorter Catechism ; and was the translator of some religious works, such as *Alleine's Alarm*. When engaged on the last-mentioned production, which he undertook to translate at the request of a lady, he took portions of the "Appeals to the Unconverted" with him into the pulpit, being too busy to prepare sermons of his own, with the result that a spiritual revival took place in the congregation, and anxious hearers flocked to the pastor for spiritual comfort which he felt himself totally unable to supply. It is said that this experience led to an emphatic spiritual change in himself.

How Smith was moved to interest himself in Gaelic poetry is well described in his own language in a letter to the Highland Society Committee : "(31st January 1798), I can only say that from my earliest years I was accustomed to hear many of the poems of Ossian and many tales respecting Fingal and his heroes. In the parish of Glenurchay, in which I was born, and lived till the age of 17, there were many at that time who could repeat a number of Ossian's poems ; and there was particularly an old man called Doncha (rioch) Macnicol, who was noted for reciting the greatest store of them. That any of them had been translated, I did not know till I became a student in philosophy, when, in the year 1766 or 1767, I read Mr Macpherson's translation, with which, beautiful as it is, I was by no means so much charmed as I had been with the oral recitation of such as I heard of the poems in the original language. The elegance of the modern dress did not, therefore, in my opinion, compensate for the loss of the venerable and ancient garb." When it became doubtful whether Macpherson would publish the Gaelic originals, Smith formed the design of publishing as many as he could of the originals, which "at that time would not be a few." "But," he proceeds, "finding there was no encouragement to be expected for such a work, and that those which I had already collected would not defray their own expence, nor have been ever published had it not been for the liberal support and patronage of the Highland Society of London, I gave up the pursuit of Gaelic poetry ; about which I became so careless that I never took the trouble of transcribing or preserving several pieces that had fallen into my possession." Smith is not the only one to whom the "pursuit of Gaelic poetry" and Celtic studies became a painful and barren enterprise.

It appears that Duncan Kennedy, a schoolmaster at Lochgilp-head, busied himself in collecting, transcribing, and editing in his own peculiar manner all the old Highland lays he could find in Argyllshire, and that some of his materials found their way into Smith's possession. It is understood that the latter refers to Kennedy in the following sentences : " (1802), I remember well," — Kennedy was still alive,—" that a man who had given me the use of a parcel of poems, without any restriction, had long threatened a prosecution for publishing what he called translations of his collection of poems, and alleged he had a claim to a share of the profits. I believe, however, upon enquiry, that he understood the profits were only a serious loss, as I had been persuaded to run shares with a bookseller in the publication, which to me turned out so bad a concern (when my income was but thirty pounds a-year), that I could never since think of Gaelic poetry with pleasure or with patience, except to wish it had been dead before I was born." In this same letter Smith declares that a little while before he had used the last copy he had of his Translations " in papering a dark closet that had not been lathed, in order to derive some small benefit from what had cost " him so much. Macpherson reaped the first crop of the ancient lays of the Celtic world of romance ; piled a fortune out of it ; became a member of Parliament ; bought a Highland estate on which he erected a monument for himself ; and arranged for the burial of his body in Westminster Abbey. Some of his imitators found the path of Celtic studies and poetry one of thorns, poverty and misfortune, and obscure graves, without a cairn to mark their resting-place.

Smith's Collection of Ancient Poems appeared in 1780, subjoined to the Dissertations on Gaelic Antiquities. These poems were translations, it was declared, " from the Gaelic of Ossian, Ullin, Orran, and others ; " and in 1787 he published the originals of these poems, the number being fourteen. Their titles are : *The Lay of the Red; The Death of Gaul ; The Lay of Duhona; Diarmid ; Clan-Morni*, or *Finan and Lorma*, from which following lines are taken to show the character of the verse and mode of thought :—

CAOIDH MHUIRNE AIRSON A CHLAINNE.

Och ! 's truaigh mi féin a chlann,
'N 'ur déigh gu fann aosmhor ;
Mar dharaig sheargte mi air aonach,
Ris nach pill gu bràth a caoinchruth.

Tha'n dùlach dorcha anns a' ghleann,
'S gach crann air raoin gun duilleach ;
Ach pillidh 'sa' cheitein am maise,
Ged nach faicear mo sgèimh-sa tuille.
Dh' fhàilnich siol Albha nam feachd,
Mar smùid á teach fuaraidh dorcha ;
Cha'n iognadh mise bhi trom an nochd !
'S tusa Fhionain 'san t-slochd, 's a Lorma !

Translation.

MORNI'S LAMENT FOR HIS CHILDREN.

O children 1 am weak and old !
Bereft of you I feel forlorn ;
Like oak-tree withered on the height,
Whose leaves shall never more return.

The winter darkens in the vale :
The branches bloom with leaves no more ;
The spring their beauty will bring back,
But ah ! my strength nought can restore.

The host of Alva has decayed
Like smoke from a cold house of gloom ;
This night I grieve for there are left
Finan and Lorma in the tomb.

The above Albha, Alva, is Allen in Ireland, and has no connection with Alban, with which, however, it has been often con.
founded in the old ballads. Ultra patriotic Scotchmen have frequently, likely in ignorance, rendered the Irish Almhuin into
Albin. This mistake occurs in Mr Pattison's *Gaelic Bards.*
"Once, when the kingly feast was spread on Albin's golden
slope," p. 148.

The titles of the others in order are : *The War of Linne ;
Cathula ; The War of Manus.* which includes the highly popular
Lay of the Great Fool ; Trahul, at the beginning of which there
appears the beautiful address to the Rising Sun—

A Mhic na h-òg mhaidne, ag éiridh,
Son of the young morn that risest ;

Dargo ; Conn, in which a version of a passage occurs whose equivalent is given in a translation thus :—

See Loda's gloomy form advance,
On high he lifts his shadowy lance,
Within his hand the tempests lour,
The blast of death his nostrils pour :
Like flames his baleful eyes
Appal the valiant—from the fight

They turn before the blasting light ;
His hollow voice like thunder shakes the skies,
Slowly he moves along, exulting in his might.
Vain are thy terrors, dreadful shade !
Lo ! Morven's king defies aloud
Thy utmost force.—His glaring blade
Winds through the murky cloud.
The form falls shapeless into air :
His direful shrieks the billows hear,
And stop their rapid course with fear.
The hundred rocks of Inistore reply,
As roll'd into himself he mounts the darkened sky.

The above is a specimen of Smith's verse translations. From the same poem is taken the following to show the manner of his prose translation, in which the *Old Lays* made their first appearance :—

Translation.

But Ossian alone does not experience distress ; aged Lugar, thine was part of the trouble. In thy halls were seen the feast, wax candles, and wine ; though they be now desolate, they were once the residence of kings ! But similar to the revolving year, Lugar and his beloved wife were seen houseless.

Travelling through the vales of beautiful Moialuin, the habitation of Lugar was found desolate, the kid broused on its green surface, stretching itself in sleep in the once joyous dwelling. In its window was the bird of night, and green ivy shaded its desolate walls, the greyhound and dun roe surrounded them, and his hospitable door lies sorrowful under the falling rains.

Sons of the hill, have you seen Lugar ? Probably you rejoice that he is no more. But you shall decline like him, and your relations will one day inquire for you. Your children will shake their heads with sorrow, they know not the place of your abode !

The vicissitudes of life are similar to those of the year. I lived void of trouble in the summer of youth, like firs on the green Mor-uth, careless of the storms of winter. I thought my verdant leaves would remain, and that age would not injure my branches. But now 1 am forlorn like thyself, and my aged locks are on the wings of the wind ; our joyful days are both gone on the wings of the blast to the desert.

The passage just given explains Smith's failure to impress the public with his prose versions of Old Lays. It affords quite a contrast to the style of Macpherson, which was sententious and clarified by a Saxon as simple as that of the English Bible. In his Life of Columba, Smith gave translated specimens of the Saints' Latin Hymns, of which an extract has been already given (p. 69). He rendered this passage of the *Altus prosatur* in blank verse—the beginning of the same in rhymed metre by the writer being else where supplied (p. 81). The following lines by Smith, accom* panying the Gaelic of *Tuura*, show that he appeared to better advantage in verse than in prose translations :—

OSSIAN.

Malvina, say what now renews thy woe ?
Say why thy tears, like rills, incessant flow ?
Why heaves thy bosom with the moanful cry,
Like Lego's reeds when ghosts among them fly ?

MALVINA.

And dost thou ask the cause of all my woe,
When yonder Selma's mossy tow'rs lie low ?
When bats and thistles dwell in Fingal's hall,
And roes bound fearless o'er its mould'ring wall :
—Besides, I heard upon the distant wind
A sound that rous'd my sadly-musing mind ;
It is, 1 fondly said, Cuchullin's car !
The Chief returning from the roar of war !
—A light had likewise gleam'd on Lena's heath ;
My love, my Oscar ! 'tis thy spear of death !
I said : but Oscar's spear is in the tomb ;
His shield, O Selma, in thy empty womb.
I saw its bosses cover'd o'er with rust,
And all its thongs fast-mould'ring into dust.

OSSIAN.

Ev'n so, Malvina, my brave Oscar's love !
Like those we mourn for, we must soon remove ;
No trace of us on Selma shall be found,
Save the green mound that marks our sleep profound.
Soft are the slumbers of that bed of peace :
Let then Malvina's flowing sorrow cease ;
Nor weep for friends whose actions were so bright,
Whose steps were mark'd with beams of heavenly light.

MALVINA.

Now night descends with all her dusky clouds,
And ocean in her sable mantle shrouds ;
Yet night will soon resign her place to day,
But my protracted woe must last for aye.

The Gaelic of the last four lines runs thus :—

Dh'aom an òiche le neoil,
Thuit an ceo air an lear ;
Siàblaidh an òiche 's an ceo,
Ach tha mise ri m' bheo gun ghean.

The remaining poems are : *The Burning of Taura ; Calava ;*
and *The Death of Art.* A very much quoted and admired passage
which occurs in the lay of *Taura* is here given :—

AISLING AIR DHREACH MNA.

Innseam pàirt do dreach nan reul :
Bu gheal a deud gu h-ùr dlù :
Mar channach an t-sléibh
Bha cneas fa h-eideadh ùr.
  Bha a bràighe cearclach bàn
Mar shneachda tlà nam beann ;
Bha a dà chich ag eiridh làn :
B'e'n dreach sud miann nan sonn..
  Bu shoitheamh binn a gloir ;
S' bu deirge na'n ròs a beul :
Mar chobhar a sios r'a taobh
Sinte gu caol bha gach meur.
  Bha a dà chaol mhala mhine
Dùdhonn air liomh an loin .
A dà ghruaidh dhreachd nan caoran ;
'Si gu iomlan saor o chron.
  Bha a gnùis mar bharra-gheuga
Anns a cheud-fhás ùr :
A falt buidhe mar òradh shleibhtean;
'S mar dheàrsadh gréine bha sùil.

Translation.

VISION OF A FAIR WOMAN.

  Tell us some of the charms of the stars :
Close and well set were her ivory teeth ;
White as the cannach upon the moor
Was her bosom the tartan bright beneath.
  Her well-rounded forehead shone
Soft and fair as the mountain-snow :
Her two breasts were heaving full ;
To them did the hearts of the heroes flow.
  Her lips were ruddier than the rose ;
Tender and tunefully sweet her tongue ;
White as the foam adown her side
Her delicate fingers extended hung.
  Smooth as the dusky down of the elk
Appeared her two narrow brows to me ;
Lovely her cheeks were like berries red ;
From every guile she was wholly free.
  Her countenance looked like the gentle buds
Unfolding their beauties in early spring ;
Her yellow locks like the gold-browed hills ;
And her eyes like the radiance the sunbeams bring.

This *Aisling* in the original is, like the teeth of its subject so "close and well-set," that a good translation is not easily executed. This "Vision of a Fair Woman" has nothing in common with that of the "Fair Women" of Chaucer and Tennyson ; but no one reading it can fail to remember the poetry of Moore, and recognise the Celtic source of the bright peculiarity of his melodious muse.

JOHN CLARK,

a land-surveyor in Badenoch, the county of James Macpherson, published in 1780 a small volume of translations of ancient Gaelic poetry under the title of "Caledonian Bards." Among other pieces is a poem entitled *Mordubh*, whose history is even more mysterious than that of the work of "Ossian." The translations in this volume are the most unreadable stuff that one could imagine. Clark, and even Smith, failed to catch the secret that enabled Macpherson to pour forth his inimitable prose epics. Clark's prose is frequently turgid nonsense, and it is rendered ridiculous by his coining of proper names out of unnatural collocations of adjectives. The "ingenious Mrs Grant of Laggan" put some of the surveyor's poetry into verse, and thought she was handling ancient poetic material instead of eighteenth-century stuff, which might be creditable enough were it not presented to the public under a false garb. She knew the "gentleman's character," and "the circumstance of his father and grandfather being great Gaelic scholars and collectors, who most probably had an opportunity of obtaining such poems which were not within her reach." The pious and honest Mrs Grant never fancied that this family of Clarks and others at that time might spin out such stuff as they palmed on the public, with or without ancient lays to help them. It is the volume of this Badenoch surveyor that finally and fully opened the eyes of the writer to the truth respecting the Ossianic productions of the last century. Clark and Kennedy were men of considerable gifts ;—if they had used them with greater honesty the cause of Gaelic literature would not have been so involved in suspicion a hundred years ago. Their labours, however, have not been lost. Kennedy's manuscript collections of poetry, safely deposited in Edinburgh, have great value, and Clark may be said to have produced a

Gaelic composition of some ability. Special efforts seem to have been made to get this conglomerate of *Mordubh* into appreciative circulation. It imposed on Mrs Grant, as we have seen. In a stray number of the "General Chronicle" for February 1811, which the writer found in London a few years ago, part of *Morduth*, with a literal translation, is published; and the clever editor of " The Beauties of Gaelic Poetry " commenced his splen-did volume with this poem of *The Great-Black*, with a foot-note which says : " The author of this poem, whose name is Douthal, was both a chief and a bard of great repute. The accounts which tradition gives of him are various, but the most probable makes him the Poet of Mordubh, King of the Caledonians." This was a more ancient and illustrious ancestry for the author of the poem than the genuine producer, John Clark of Badenoch, could boast of.

The Gaelic fragment, as given in the "General Chronicle," begins thus in Gaelic :—

> A' bheil thûs' air sgiathan do luathas,
> A ghaoth, gu triall le d'uile neart ?
> Thig le cairdeas a dh'ionsuidh m'aois,
> Thoir scriòb eatrom thar mo chraig !

Englished in the same as follows :—

> Art thou on the wings of thy swiftness,
> O wind, travelling with all thy strength ?
> Come to my age with kindness ;   ♦ ♦
> Brush lightly over my rock !

John Clark was a third-rate imitator, whose imitations were almost parodies. He had neither the learning nor the genius of either Smith or Macpherson, who must henceforth be regarded as great Highland bards. These two, no doubt, caused much con-fusion among our heroic lays. James Macpherson and Dr John Smith helped to give fresh currency to many of the false etymo-logies and Druidical ideas that have afflicted the Gaelic world for the last century. They have mystified our Ossianic poems and ballads, as well as the pre-Christian religion of the Caledonians. They turned upside down our early history, and placed our relations to the Irish on a false basis, creating unnecessary antago-nism between the Celts of the two countries. But honour to whom honour is due. If no James Macpherson had ever appeared, our Highland Ossian would have been as obscure, perhaps, as the extant Oisins of Ireland. In some respects he was the greatest genius that the Highlands ever produced, and ought not to be regarded with so much contemptuous indifference. He had a most peculiar gift for executing prose translation, notwithstanding the failure of his Homer. In this one respect he was much superior to Dr Smith, who, however, had the advantage of Macpherson in greater power of sweet Gaelic versification. Smith was a born poet ; all his works are evidences. The two did their best to show forth the historic, linguistic, and poetic glories of the Gael and his country ; so let us drop a tear on their cairns and pass on.

CHAPTER XI.

" It is easy to disparage the study of these scanty remains of a literary language which, though it be not dead, is more of an unknown tongue to our modern men of letters than almost any other."—DR JOSEPH ANDERSON.

THE intellectual activity created in the sixteenth century led to the formation of a new literature for the diffusion of the new learning. This literature belongs to that period in our national history when religious ferment, political and ecclesiastical change, began to operate effectually on the mind of modern Europe. The first Gaelic effort in this direction was by John Carsuel, superintendent of the diocese of Argyll, who translated and published (1567) John Knox's Prayer-Book. The English original was printed at Edinburgh in 1565, and the Gaelic version appeared within two years after that date. It is the first Gaelic book that ever was printed either in Scotland or Ireland. Only three copies were known to exist previous to 1872 ; one perfect copy in possession of the Duke of Argyll, and two imperfect copies, one in the Edinburgh University Library and the other in the British Museum. In 1872 the Rev. Dr. Maclauchlan made a complete transcript of the book, and a new edition was published page for page and line for line with the original. Philologists regard it as very valuable. Bishop Carsuel was a native of Kilmartin, well versed in the Gaelic language, and thoroughly acquainted with the people of the wide district of whose spiritual interests he had charge. In an address prefixed to his book he alludes to the manuscript literature then extant, " written in manuscript books in the compositions of poets and ollaves, and in the remains of learned men." The bishop seems to have imbibed something of the , earnest, critical spirit of nineteenth-century Christianity, and deserves our respect for giving us the first printed book in Gaelic.

Still it is unfortunate for Gaelic literature, though perhaps not for the Protestant religion, that he and others determined on the ruth-

less extinction of the popular ballads among the people. The
Ursgeuls, or prose tales, were condemned even with greater emphasis. The following verses from a ballad from which an extract
has been taken already will show the character of the popular
literature which Carsuel did not consider edifying :—

URNUIGH OISEIN.

Oisein.

'S gann a chreideas mi do sgeul,
    A chlérich leir d' leabhar bàn,
Gu'm biodh Fionn, no cho fial,
    Aig duine no aig Dia an làimh.

Pàdruig.

Ann ifrinn tha e'n laimh,
    Fear le'n sath bhi bronnadh òir,
Air son a dhìmeas air Dia,
    Chuir iad e'n tigh pian fo leòn.

Oisein.

Nan robh Clann-Morni a steach,
    Is Clanna-Baoitgne, na fir threun,
Bheireamiad-ne Fionn a mach,
    No bhiodh an teach againn féin.⁷

Pàdruig.

Còig còigeanna na h-Eirinn ma seach,
    'Sair leat-sa gu mòr am feum,
Gha tugadh sin Fionn a mach,
    Ged bhiodh an teach agaibh féin,

Oisein.

Nach math an t-aite ifrin féin,
    A chléirich dh'an lèir an sgoil !
Nach go math is flaitheas Dé
    Ma gheibhear innt' féidh is coin ?

Translation.

OSSIAN'S PRAYER.

Ossian.—O clerk of the white book thy tale
    From me no faith can win ;
That God or man could keep in pain
    The brave and generous Finn.

Patrick.—Ay, captive, he is now in hell
    Who used to scatter gold ;
Because he scorned to worship God
    They thrust him in that hold.

O. Clan-Morni and Clan Baoisgne brave,
    If they would there resort,
    Soon would we have great Finn released,
    And make our own the fort.

P. Though Erin's Clans should all unite,
    A mighty host, believe,
    Possessing all that place yourselves.
    You could not Finn relieve.

O. But hell is not so bad a place,
    Clerk, to whom school is clear?
    As good as is the high heaven of God,
    If *there* be dogs and deer?

Earnest Reformers could not regard this sort of literature as a powerful auxiliary in the recasting of a nation's faith ; so Carsuel thought the Gaelic population would benefit spiritually by the substitution of his own Gaelic liturgy for the popular songs and tales.

Ossian's " Prayer " appears to have been treated with disparagement by the Highlanders of last century as well, especially by the " clerics," who were such a source of annoyance to poor Ossian himself while he lived. One feels inclined to ask, after reading some of the old ballads, whether the Patrick who described all the ancient Finians as in hell, was a species of the modern Protestant, so well represented by the late valiant Dr Begg and the late Dr Cumming. Whether or not it is evident that he was a persistent Protestant against the heathenism of the Féinne, indeed quite a thorn in the side of the poor old bard. The Irish monks of later days, however, appear to have taken very kindly to the laureate of the Fingalians, and to have lopped off many of the excrescences of the faithful Patrick. Scottish ecclesiastics appropriated the new Irish versions, but pruned off the excrescences with which the Basque, or Spano-Iberian imagination of the south-west of Ireland, had clothed the simple originals. Carsuel, in the sixteenth century, under the pressure of Reformation doctrines, was the first to touch unkindly the hoary locks of the ancient bard. The Féinne and their singer, however, survived in the affections and traditions of the population, until the Gospel according to the English Puritans and our own Scottish Covenanters began to outroot entirely the semi-heathen and Finian ideals of the people. So now in many districts of the Highlands, and throughout the Islands, much to the disgust of students of folk-lore, like Campbell of Islay, the only singing you hear is, not the rehearsal of the old heroic lays or the Ossianic duans, but the Psalms of David or the hymns of Sankey. As already remarked, the "clerics" of last century treated the Ossianic compositions with as little respect as Patrick, Carsuel, or Spurgeon would. At the end of a copy of Ossian's Prayer there is a stanza by Duncan Rioch Macnicol, who was then styled the "Modern Ossian," very much in the fashion of our present day Gaelic bards, who dub themselves as of this or that ilk. Duncan, whose feelings towards the old bards must have been *rioch* enough, describes poor Ossian in the following terms, given already in the original (p. 87), in sending the copy to the Rev. Donald Macnicol, Lismore :—

> To Master Donald take this story ;
> There he dwells beside the billow ;
> The prayer said by Ossian hoary,
> Who was aye a worthless fellow.

The last line is a condensation—though Duncan Rioch was probably in a fit of humour, supposed to be a rare state of soul for a Highland Celt—of the Protestant or Evangelic disposition of Patrick, Carsuel, and Peter Grant. These remarks have been suggested by the specimen of Gaelic which follows. Specimens have already been given of the style of writing ancient Gaelic from the earliest period down to the beginning of the sixteenth century. To those who may have paid a little attention to them it may have been interesting to discern the gradual change which Gaelic has undergone, until we find it about 1600 beginning to take the Scottish form out of which our present standard of the Gaelic Bible has been developed : —

Gaelic Prose, 1567.

Agas is mor an doile agas an dorchadas peacaidh, agas aineolais agas indtleachda do lucht deachtaidh agas scriobhtha agas chumdaigh na gaoidheilge, gurab mó is mian leo agas gurab mó ghnathuidheas siad eachdradha dimhaoineacha buaidheartha bregacha saoghalta do cumadh ar thuathaibh dédhanond agas air mhacaibh mileadh agas arna curadhaibh agas fhind mhac cumhaill gona fhianaibh agas ar mhoran eile noch airbhim.

TRANSLATION :

And great is the blindness and sinful darkness, and ignorance, and evil design, of such as teach and write, and cultivate the Gaelic language, that, with the view of obtaining for themselves the vain rewards of this world, they are more desirous, and more accustomed, to compose vain, tempting, lying. worldly histories, concerning the *Tuath de.dannan*, and concerning

15

warriors and champions, and *Fingal* the son of *Cumhal*, with his heroes, and concerning many others which I will not at present enumerate.

The Highland love of Paganism was destined to flourish down to our own time, a Stornoway woman having been seen worshipping the moon as recently as the beginning of the present century, the parish minister of Uig at the time being the witness. In his Hibbert Lectures (1888) Professor Rhys says—" It is worthy of note that this kind of Paganism died hard in the islands on the Armoric coast ; in fact it lasted, in spite of Church and State, down to the time of the Norsemen's ravages." Fifteen centuries of vigorous Christianity have not yet extirpated the serpent of superstition in the British Islands.

After the publication of Carsuel's Book of Prayers, which led the way, the only species of literature that the press helped to diffuse for more than a century was of an ecclesiastical or religious character. In the seventeenth century appeared a translation of Calvin's Catechism, " *Faoseid Eoin Stiubhairt*," the Synod of Argyll's translation of the Psalter, the Confession of Faith in the eighteenth century, followed by catechisms and summaries of Christian doctrine. Endeavours were made to awaken the people out of the spiritual lethargy induced by the age of inaction which preceded the Reformation era. The only successful way to reach the heart of the people was felt to be through the medium of their native tongue. Towards the close of the last century, for this end, translations of all sorts of religious works became numerous, even Roman Catholic Highlanders having a bulky volume of a summary of Christian doctrine translated for their use.

During this time the Highlanders had no version of the Scriptures in their own tongue, Welshmen and Irishmen being favoured earlier than they in this respect. The first portion translated was the Psalter by the Synod of Argyll in 1659. The Bible was not much known in the north-west at this period. A few individuals possessed the Irish version, but this was never much in practical use. Preachers used the English Bible, of which they gave their own extemporaneous translation as they went along. A good specimen of written Gaelic towards the end of the seventeenth century will be found in the Rev. Robert Kirk's preface to his metrical version of the Book of Psalms. To the ordinary reader it is hardly distinguishable from the Irish of the same period. The Highlander will be glad to have an opportunity of reading in his own language such an eloquent encomium on the Psalms which he prizes so so dearly.

Gaelic Prose, 1684.

Ataid na Psalma taitneamhach, tarbhach : beag nach mion-fhlaitheas làn dainglibh, Cill fhonn-mhar, le ceol naomhtha. Mur abholghort Eden, lionta do chrannaibh brioghmhoire-na beatha, agus do luibhennibh iocshlainteamhail, amhluidh an leabhar Psalmso Dhaibhioth, a ta na liaghais air uile anshocair na nanma. Ata an saoghail agus gach beò chreatair da bfuil an, na chlarsigh ; an duine se is Chlairseoir agus duanaire, chum moladh an mor. Dhia mirbhuileach do chein ; agus ata Daibhidh do gnà mar fhear don chuideachd bhias marso ag caoin-chaint gu ceolmhar ma nard-Rí.

ENGLISH :

The Psalms are pleasant and profitable. A church resounding with sacred melody is almost a little Heaven full of angels. As the Garden of Eden, replenished with trees of life of potent efficacy and with medicinal plants, so is this Book of Psalms of David, which contains a remedy of all the diseases of the soul. The world and every living creature it contains are the Harp; Man is the Harper and Poet, who sings the praise of the great wonder-working God ; and David is ever one of the company who are thus employed in sweetly and tunefully discoursing about the Almighty King.

The Highland clergy at this time were, as a class, fairly well-educated. This will be seen in the accounts of English travellers who now began to take tours to the Celtic north-west. In earlier times the intercourse between the Highlands and the great world beyond was greater than in the seventeenth century. Before the seats of government were all removed from the districts of the Gael further south, the communication with Ireland and the Continent of Europe in the north and in France was considerable. Till the days of Queen Elizabeth relations were fitfully sustained between the insular court of the Princedom of the Isles and the English Court. It was during the seventeenth century that the Gaelic regions became a very *terra incognita* to South Britain. Now a learned and sympathetic visitor arrived, from whose pages we get glimpses of the state of learning and culture among the Gaels.

It is a Welshman, Professor Rhys of Oxford, that has given us the best work on Celtic philology and Celtic paganism, in the present day ; and it was a Welshman that wrote the best book on the same subjects upwards of 200 years ago. Edward Lhuyd's great work on Celtic scholarship appeared in 1707. The title runs thus :—"*Archæologica Britannica,* giving some account, additional to what has been hitherto published, of the Languages, Histories, and Customs of the Original Inhabitants of Great Britain, from collections and observations in travels through Wales, Cornwall, Bas-Bretagne, Ireland, and Scotland. By Edward Lhuyd, M.A. of Jesus College, keeper of the Ashmolean Museum in Oxford. Oxford : Printed at the Theater for the author, MDCCVII." Were the matter within the bounds of the 460 folio pages of this handsome volume printed in the style in which books are now generally published it would make three or four very considerable volumes. At the beginning of an appendix the following note occurs : "Having since the printing this Irish dictionary sent copies to Ireland and Scotland in order to have it improved, the following supplement consists chiefly of some notes returned thence by two gentlemen well known to be able scholars and masters of that language." It is in connection with these "copies," I suppose, that the poetical complimentary verses inserted at the beginning of the volume were sent to the author. These verses were written in Latin, Gaelic, and Welsh. Two or three Latin ones and four in Gaelic are sent from the Highlands. The character of this great work may be gathered from the titles of the several departments : Comparative Etymology, 40 pp. ; A Comparative Vocabulary of of the Original Languages of Britain and Ireland, 130 pp. ; An Armoric Grammar and Vocabulary, 33 pp. ; Some Welsh Words, A Cornish Grammar, British MSS., and a British Etymologican, 86 pp. ; A Brief Introduction to the Irish or Ancient Scottish Language, and *Foclair Gaoidheilge-Shasonach no Bearladoir Scot-Sagsamhuil;* An Irish-English Dictionary,'136 pp. ; two pp. describing Gaelic MSS., and An Index. In the preface he proceeds to explain what induced him "to an undertaking so laborious, so little diverting, and so much out of the common road."

It is interesting to note how this laborious Oxford student met the prejudices of the day. The undertaking "proceeded not from any conceited opinion, as some might be apt to imagine, of the plausibleness of these languages. Most of us commonly hear or read too much to be ignorant that the generality of people are rather disposed to a ridiculing than a favourable reception of anything in that kind. This did not, I own, in the least discourage me, as well knowing that the same prejudice in the like case prevails in all other great governments, and that in any uncommon undertaking the judgment of men of distinction (or at least particular experience in the subject proposed), is to be only regarded. The inducement I had was no other than a seeming probability that such an essay might in this curious age contribute not a little towards a clearer notion of the first planters of the three kingdoms, and a better understanding of our ancient names of persons and places." No grammar of the Scottish Gaelic appeared up to the time of Lhuyd ; but he speaks of "a Scotish gentleman who had some thoughts of publishing " one. It would be interesting to know who this gentleman was ; perhaps he was one of those who sent the poetical addresses to Lhuyd.

In connection with this great work Lhuyd experienced the same discouragements which often beset similar works of learning. He was told by some considerate critic that his volume would meet with but a cold reception ; for it consisted "only of etymology and Welsh and Irish vocabularies." The critic exclaims, "Now there are not half a dozen or half a score in the kingdom that are curious in that way. The world expected, according to his promise and undertaking, a natural history, which is a study of established request, and that a great many are curious in." But Lhuyd has in the published list the names of two hundred lords, knights, and gentlemen of learning and distinction belonging to England alone. This was something to begin with for such a work, and must have been rather a disconcerting refutation of the critic's remark about "half a dozen " readers. It is quite possible that this complaining critic looked forward to an interesting dissertation on the strange human animals that inhabited in those days Lorn, Mull, and Islay, and other Celtic parts. He and others could scarcely realise to themselves that the Celtic barbarians who dwelt in those distant regions could write and talk good English ; and in their leisure hours exercised themselves in the composition of Latin verse or Gaelic poetry.

Lhuyd was accompanied everywhere on his travels by David Parry, A.B. of Jesus College, Oxford, who wrote a small section of the work. It is a very interesting picture that the travels of these learned Oxonians in the Highlands suggest seventy or eighty years before the mighty Johnson visited the Western Isles, which in earlier ages were so well known throughout the ecclesiastical world. Here is a specimen of Latin verse from the pen of a Highland minister two hundred years ago : —

IN EDV. LUIDI GLOSSOGRAPHIAM.

Quid si reversus spiritus afforet
Jam Buchanani, nobile callidi
   Tentare plectrum, pristinumque
    Officium renovare chordis ?

Antiqua tellus, dic, age, Scotia,

Quem destinares Tu, facili Virum
Ornare versu ; quem parares
Non humili celebrare cantu ?

Luidus priorum qui Britonum decus,
Poscit Camœnas ; pulvere sen diu
Fœdata purgator reponat,
In superam referatque lucem.

Sive Ille morsu temporis improbo
Exesa fida restituat manu,
Atque acer Interpus recudat
In veniens renovata sæclum.

Sive Ille vocum exquirere origines
Longo recursu gestiat, et suo
A fonte deducat, redire
Ad veterem faciatque ritum.

Quamvis dolendo pressa silentio
Jam Buchanani conticeat lyra,
Stat fama Luido, vendicantque
Perpetuam sibi scripta laudem.

ANDREAS FRAZIER, *Eccl. Scot. Presb.*

Another poetical address is sent from the romantic district of
North Argyll, where many of the deeds recorded in the ancient
ballads took place, and where, no doubt, the distinguished Cymric
scholar received hearty Highland hospitality from Colin Campbell,
pastor of Ardchattan. The conclusion runs as follows :—

Restituit Scotis sublapsa ; caduca Britannis ;
Celtis et Pictis deperdita. Cornubiensis
Cantaber, et Scotus quam linquam agnoscit uterque,
Comparat : Affinis sensus hacarte resolvens,
Et renovat surdis aures et lumina cæcis.
Linguas prisca loqui, cogit dum vera fateri,
Literulis larvas fucos dum vocibus aufert,
Hispanum Scotum de divisâ stirpe, Britannum
Historiæ ut taceant, statuit ; sermonis amussi
Albanii metas Bretonis Cambrique resignans.
Primus enim Cephilos Scotus, Pephilosque Britannos,
Nosque notas Britonum sib'lasse ostendit anhelas.
 Mille alia invenit doctis celebranda Camœnis :
Cedite Banniades : Non vestra cupressus erica.
 Amicitiœ et gratitudinis ergô

COLLINUS CAMPBELL, *Ardchattanus Pastor*, Lornensis.

The Gaelic addresses are highly interesting to the philologist, as
showing Scottish Gaelic in a transition state. At the period of
Lhuyd's visit to the Highlands and Isles, and down to the middle

of last century, the Highland clergyman wrote either in Latin or Gaelic. It was at that time, also, that the Scottish Gael began to depart from the old style of Gaelic writing and orthography. This departure might have been dictated to some extent by a Protestant feeling, but was mainly caused by the desire to make the orthography exactly expressive of the popular speech. The difference between the Irish and Scottish dialects was rendered greater by the change. Highland clergymen of that period being of the better families throughout the country, were generally well-educated gentlemen. Even generations after, we find more literary talent than can be found in many places to-day.

A glimpse of the state of the country after the gory struggle which ended on Culloden Moor shows a far higher state of literary culture than an outsider would readily believe possible in the circumstances. The Ossianic controversy which subsequently arose brought forward the names of many clergymen who during the last half of the eighteenth century were a credit to their country. Such men were the Rev. James Calder and the Rev. Dr Alexander Fraser, in the north-east ; the Rev. Thomas Ross of Lochbroom, the Rev. Mr Macqueen of Kilmuir, in Skye, and the Rev. Dr. Macpherson of Sleat, in the north-west ; the Rev. Dr John Macarthur of Mull, the Rev. Dr Macnicol of Lismore, Johnson's formidable opponent, the Rev. Mr. Woodrow of Islay, and the Rev. Dr John Smith of Campbeltown, with his accomplished brother, Dr Donald Smith, in the south-west ; the MacLaurins of Cowal, the distinguished divine and the professor of mathematics, the Stewarts, translators of the Bible, Professor Adam Ferguson of Edinburgh, and Professor Macleod of Glasgow, the Rev. Dr Macintyre of Glenorchay, Dr Grahame of Aberfoyle, and the Rev. Messrs Macdiarmid, Gallie, and Maclagan, in the central Highlands. The atmosphere in which such men breathed—and they were scattered throughout all parts of the Highlands—could not be altogether one of ignorance ; and the large mass of the people were, no doubt, largely benefited by the culture of and intercourse with their clerical superiors.

Dr Samuel Johnson, notwithstanding many surly prepossessions, besought, with that good broad honesty of his nature, such educated Highlanders and Irishmen to furnish the world with correct information regarding their language and literature. All English readers know of his tour to the Hebrides, whither he journeyed more than a century ago, in those days of difficult travelling, to judge for himself concerning the people among whom appeared so remarkable a poet as Ossian. He did not visit Ireland, but early in life he corresponded with an accomplished Irish gentleman, Mr Charles O'Connor of Ballinegare, Roscommon, in relation to Irish literature. In his first letter, April 9, 1737, he says :—" Sir William Temple complains that Ireland is less known than any other country as to its ancient state. The natives have had little leisure and little encouragement for inquiry, and strangers, not knowing the language, have had no ability. I have long wished that Irish literature were cultivated. Ireland is known by tradi-tion to have been once the seat of piety and learning, and surely it would be very acceptable to all those who are curious, either in the original of nations, or the affinities of languages, to be further in-formed of the revolutions of a people so ancient, and once so illus-trious." He hopes O'Connor will continue his Irish studies, and speaks of the great pleasure he has in hearing of the progress of his undertaking. Twenty-two years afterwards Johnson renews the correspondence, and complains of O'Connor disappointing him :— " I expected great discoveries in Irish antiquities, and large publi-cations in the Irish language, but the world still remains as it was —doubtful and ignorant. What the Irish language is in itself, and to what languages it has affinity, are very interesting questions, which every man wishes to see resolved that has any philological or historical curiosity. Dr Leland begins his history too late ; the ages that deserve an exact inquiry are those times (for such they were) when Ireland was the school of the west, the quiet habita-tion of sanctity and literature. If you could give a history, though imperfect, of the Irish nation from its conversion to Christianity to the invasion from England, you would amplify knowledge with new views and new objects. Set about it, therefore, if you can ; do what you can easily do without anxious exactness. Lay the foun-dation, and leave the superstructure to posterity." This is a very interesting and remarkable letter, and exhibits Johnson as entirely free from the vulgar anti-Celtic prejudices which long obtained in many quarters after his day. It pointed to the lines of study which the Celtic student should follow. But both Irish and Highland scholars failed to comply with the lexicographer's wishes. Philo-logy did not then exist, and accurate philosophical histories had not then made much progress. Celtic scholars travelled to Spain and Egypt and other places in the East for the cradle in which the first pure Gaelic baby was rocked ; linguistic affinities were sought in Hebrew and Arabic ; while Gaelic or Celtic was sometimes de-clared to be the mother of all languages. This race of Gaelic Orientals continued to exist till recently, if indeed it is even now wholly extinct. The Irish, however, at last have abundantly shown the great extent of literature, manuscript and printed, which is enshrined in their language. The recent works of learned Irishmen are evidence that the interest is not abating in Irish literature. While it is admitted that the Irish Gael is in possession of some literature, it is yet denied that the Scottish Gael has any literary remains to show. And indeed, looking at the barrenness of the Highland hills, and the bareness of the Highland glens, the stranger from the sunnier South is apt to think that no literature could flourish on so sterile a soil. The lakes and straths, swept by the fresh breezes. he feels too coldly uncongenial—too frigid a home for the cultivation of letters—too dreary a land for the muses to dwell in. Men of stout arms and lion hearts have issued from these regions. That fact is recognised. But it is not well known that also there, far from what have hitherto been regarded as the great civilising centres, letters and knowledge have had for ages their sacred precincts and earnest votaries. Unpromising though the Highlands look to the literary eye, yet we find that even Dr Samuel Johnson, no lover of either Celts or Scotsmen, touches with pathetic beauty in two or three sentences written upwards of a century ago, on the conditions under which, even in the heart of the Highlands and Isles, in times of old, the production of Gaelic literature was possible : " We are now treading that illustrious island which was once the luminary of the Caledonian regions, whence savage clans and roving barbarians derived the benefits of knowledge and the blessings of religion. Far from me and from my friends be such a frigid philosophy as may conduct us indifferent and unmoved over any ground which has been dignified by wisdom, bravery, or virtue. That man is not to be envied whose patriotism would not gain force upon the plain of Marathon, or whose piety would not grow warmer among the ruins of Iona." Dr Macculloch, again, speaks of our country as owing a " deep debt of civilisation, of letters, and of religion " to the same place. From that little isle, lying grandly with its white brows of sand on the bosom of the mighty Atlantic, learned men went forth twelve and thirteen hundred years ago to Ireland, to England, and to many places on the Continent of Europe, to found colleges and establish churches. Adamnan and Bede testify that at that period Gaelic and Latin learning was cultivated in "the Celtic colleges of Iona, Oransay, Ardchattan, Uist, Rowdill, and Melrose," and then and subsequently also in a score of other academic centres of Gaelic learning and activity.

Towards the close of the eighteenth century, when translations of Gaelic poetry brought the genius of the Celtic spirit in contact with the intellectual forces of modern Europe, many who hitherto despised our Gaelic literature, began to look into this neglected field. Lord Bute, a Scot, with Gaelic sympathies, was Prime Minister then. The extract to be immediately given from a letter by the distinguished Lord Bannatyne, who, as Sheriff of Bute, and subsequently as Judge on Circuit at Inveraray, became interested in Gaelic manuscripts, will show the attention bestowed on the subject by men of position. Lord Bannatyne used his influence to get the valuable Gaelic manuscripts of Major Maclachlan of Kilbride in Argyllshire transferred to the Highland Society, and in writing on the subject says :—" The result, you know, was, that by means of the Rev. Francis Stuart, minister of Craignish, I obtained confirmation of the fact that his family had once possessed a very large collection, of which he had given two or three to General Sir Adolphus Oughton and the late Sir James Foulis, both of whom were Gaelic scholars, and that there still remained above twenty in his possession." Elsewhere we come across these and other titled gentlemen acquiring knowledge of Gaelic over a hundred years ago. It was the Earl of Eglintoun, with the approbation of Boswell and Johnson, that inspired the publication of the *Gaelic Analysis* by Shaw, who describes the acquisition of the language late in life by Sir James Foulis in the following terms :—" who, late in advanced years, has learned to read and write it, and now drinks of the Pierian spring untainted by reading fragments of poetry in Fingal's own language." Shaw was delighted with the patronage which his aristocratic friends bestowed on Gaelic. The following verses, translated by Sir James, found a place in his Grammar :—

CLAIDHEAMH GUTH-ULLIN, OR *The SWORD of*
GUCHULLIN.

Chuir e an claidheamh, fada, fiorchruaidh,
Fulanach, tean, tainic, geur,
'So chean air a chuir ann gu secair,
Mar chuis mholta gan dochair lein,
'Se gu dirach, diasadach, dubh-ghorm,
'Se cultuidh, cumtadh, conolach,
Go leathan, liobhadh, liobharadh,
Go socair, sasdadh, so-bhuailte,
Air laimh-chli a' ghaisgaich ;
Gur aisaiche do naimhdan a sheachnadh,
No tachairt ris 'san am sin ;
Cho bu lughe no cnoc sleibh,
Gach ceum a dheanadh an gaisgach.

TRANSLATION BY SIR JAMES FOULIS, BARONET.

He seized his sword, thick, broad, and long,
Well-forged, well-hammered, tempered strong,
Polished, of purest metal made,
Like lightning blazed the shining blade ; .
Jagged like a saw, it tore and hewed,
Inured to slaughter, blood-embrued;
Dire horror, and destructive fate,
On the full age attentive wait;
'Twas certain death its stroke to feel ;
Strength-withering, life-devouring steel,
Even valiant foes, struck at the sight,
Durst hope no safety but by flight ;
Their ranks wide-scattering all abroad
From hill to hill the hero strode.

CHAPTER XII.

" Land where Religion paves her heavenward road !
Land of the temple of the living God !
Yet, dear to feeling, Scotland, as thou art,
Shouldst thou that temple e'er desert,
I would disclaim thee, seek the distant shore
Of Christian isle, and thence return no more."

THE subject of the ancient hymns and religious poetry of the ancient Gaels was discussed in earlier chapters, as also the religious compositions of mediæval times. After the stormy era of the Reformation and the Jacobite period, the sacred muse of the Highlands began to make her voice heard once more. The sacred bards of the Early and Mediæval times have thus received attention ; it now remains to treat of those of Modern days. The light of the Reformation movement failed for some generations to reach the masses of the people in many districts of the Highlands. The hindrances were many : the want of suitable earnest pastors, and the large extent of the districts assigned to each. It ought also to be remembered that the complete translation of the Bible into Gaelic is not yet a century old ; and even although there had been a translation earlier there were not many who were able to read it. The Highlanders then were also in the first stages of a transition state. They felt the system of clanship crumbling under their feet. Quarrels were easily fomented. The strong and sagacious took advantage of the times, and took care to adjust themselves to the developing circumstances of the future. Jacobitism found a stronghold in the Highlands, not because the people were Papists or religiously indifferent or fervent lovers of the Stuarts, but because they had a strong sense of justice and loyalty, sore as they had frequently suffered for their fidelity. Jacobite adventurers regarded the Highlands and Islands as a suitable field for their treasonable operations—isolated from the mighty stirring current of the kindling spirit of the times—a spirit that began to question the right divine of kings to govern wrong. The conflict between the enlightened Protestant mind and the enslaving spirit of Jacobitism came to an end on Culloden Moor. Many of the Highlanders forsook the Stuart cause earlier. Argyllshire in the west, and almost whole counties in the north and north-east, did not either stir for Prince Charles or espoused the opposite side. Evangelical religion had turned the current of the people's thoughts in those districts. Especially was this the case in the north, where able and godly ministers—some of them Lowland ministers, who found asylum there from persecution—brought back the clans to the knowledge of the true religion.

Yet even in the north there were many inaccessible glens and corners where many—often desperate men—made for themselves a home, and where they lived in a state of heathenism. And in this state they continued almost down to our own time. Uncomplimentary as they were in many respects to the religious character of his countrymen, there is no doubt the following lines were very applicable last century. The author—Dr Macgregor, the Gaelic apostle of Nova Scotia—laments that the Highlanders were ignorant and blind, and that learning was rare among them :—

> " Bha na Gaidhil ro aineolach dhall,
> Bha ionnsachadh gann nam measg :
> Bha 'n eòlas co tana 's co mall,
> 'S nach b'aithne dhaibh 'n call a mheas.
> 'Se b'annsa leo 'n arigiod 's an òr
> A chaitheadh go gòrach truagh,
> Ri amaideachd, òranaibh, 's òl,
> Ri bannsaibh, 's ri ceòl da'n cluais."

This description of Macgregor was perfectly true, and applicable to the Highlanders at the close of the great Jacobite struggle—so absorbed were Highland energies with the social and political enterprises of that disastrous period that the education and religious training of the people were quite neglected. At the same time there were many quiet corners north and south in which the Gospel muse found an asylum, and one of these we find in Glendaruel, Argyllshire, a spot closely associated with the early Celtic romances and our ancient Gaelic manuscripts.

DAVID MACKELLAR.

The date of this author's birth is unknown, but he appears to have flourished in Glendaruel early in the eighteenth century. Among the traditions preserved of him is the account that he was blind, and that after the celebrated Hymn or Holy Lay associated with his name was composed, his sight was restored.

Laoidh Mhic-Ealair, or Mackellar's Hymn, was greatly prized among religious people, and became very popular before Buchanan began to tune his sacred lyre in Rannoch. His fame rests chiefly on this one production, although it is declared that in his youth he indulged in the composition of profane pieces. According to Reid, his hymn was first published in Glasgow about the year 1750. It had, however, an earlier publication among the people through many persons that learned it by heart and loved to repeat it on account of its helpful statements of Gospel truths. It consists of thirty-three stanzas or quatrains, and furnishes a Scriptural exposition of the theme he took up. The date of his death is as uncertain as that of his birth, but one authority tells us that a granddaughter of his lived in Glasgow in the second quarter of this century. The following verses remind us of the manner of Buchanan, in whom we detect traces of Mackellar's muse :—

> 'N uair chàidh Criosd gu péin a bhàis
> 'Sa dh'uiling e air son an t-sluaigh,
> Sgoilt brat an teampuil sios gu làr,
> 'S dhùisg na mairbh an aird o'n uaigh.

> Chreathnaich an talamh trom le crith,
> Air a' ghréin gu'n tainig smal ;
> Le feirg Dhé do chrath e 'n sin ;
> Dh'fhuiling Criosd an bàs re seal.

ENGLISH :

> When Christ endured the pain of death,
> For men Himself a Victim gave,
> The temple's veil was rent in twain
> As forth the dead came from the grave.

> With heavy thunder shook the earth,
> The sun endured a darkening cloud ;
> Beneath God's wrath he trembled then
> Awhile Christ lay within the shroud.

JOHN MACKAY,

This sacred bard is supposed to have been born about 1690, and has been described as " a poet, a scholar, and a gentleman," and as of Mudale, parish of Farr, Sutherlandshire. He belonged to the Clan-Abrach Mackays. A son of his, William, married and resided at Knockfin, in the parish of Kildonan, and is said to have been a contemporary of Rob Donr. Mackay. He was a man of deep religious spirit ; and attained considerable local distinction among the people of his district on account of the saintliness of his character. In his " Metrical Reliques " John Rose describes Mackay as " an eminently pious man," and gives the following account of the conditions under which one of the poems was composed : " The first of these poems was composed by him on a fine moonlight night in harvest while he happened to be out in the fields, lying on his back, contemplating the glory and majesty of the heavenly luminaries."

Some men of the Sutherlandshire Militia stationed in 1746 at Dunkeld, immediately after the Rebellion, are represented as pious soldiers, who, having sought out Dugald Buchanan of Rannoch, used to sing to him the religious poems of Mackay of Mudale. The Sutherlandshire men used to relate that Buchanan sang Mackay's hymns "with great glee," and that it was the latter's compositions that moved the former to sing in sacred strains himself. There is probably little or no foundation for this last statement. Mackellar had far more influence on Buchanan's mind than Mackay ; but at the same time the story of the " Men " of the far north is very instructive as indicating how readily men of Evangelical sympathies and genuine Christian life understood one another.

Five of Mackay's compositions are preserved in Rose's collec · tion. They are fair expositions of the pulpit themes with which the " Men " of the north in those days were familiar, and appear to have been well appreciated by the author's religious contempo-poraries, by whom they were orally preserved. The last, from which the following two verses are taken, is composed in a simple easy measure, and is entitled " *The Complaint*," in which we have early indications of that Christian experience,-- of the painful self-analysis and introspection,—for which the " Men " subsequently became so remarkable :—

> 'S moch a thréig mi do shlighe,
>   'S gu bheil m' fhiachan gun àireamh ;
> Gabh ri toillteannas Chriosda,
>   'S na iarr aig mo làmh-s' iad.

> Dean mi réidh ris na phearsa,
>   Thoir gu comunn a ghraidh mi ;
> Cuir an àireamh na treud me,
>   'S mise chaora bha caillte.

ENGLISH :

> I early wandered from thy path,
> My debts I ne'er can reckon o'er ;
> The worth of Christ accept for me
> And at my hand seek them no more.
>
> In Him atonement let me find,
> Me in his love's communion keep ;
> Give me a place among the flock,
> Though I have been so lost a sheep.

DONALD MATHESON.

Matheson, a sacred bard of considerable originality and spiritual insight, was born in the parish of Kildonan, Sutherlandshire,
in 1719. At that time there was much religious fervour and feeling in that part of the country as well as throughout the north in
general. So the "Sacred Poetry of the North" towards the end
of last century makes a pretty large volume. While Buchanan
was tuning his sacred harp in the central Highlands, Matheson
began his religious strains in the far north. Matheson cultivated
a small farm, and lived to the age of sixty-three, his death taking
place in 1782. He exercised great religious influence in his own
parish—his power of satire contributing much towards this influence. A single poem of his was declared by the parish minister
to have done more good than all his own preaching for a series of
years. As a poet he stands as high as his countryman Rob Donn,
with whom he has many points in common, although Matheson's
poetry is decidely sacred, which Rob Donn's is as decidedly not.
His Gaelic is frequently unintelligible to the western and southern
Gael, which is one reason why his poems have not been in greater
request among them. The following verse shows his manner in
Gaelic :—

> Ar sinnsear o thùs,
> 'Nuair chaill iad an lùth's,
> Gùn mhill iad an cùis
> Air sùsdanan àill ;
> Tha'n truailleadh so lionmhor,
> Dh'fhag mis 'anns an fhionan,
> Mar chraobh a th' air crionadh
> Gun fhiogais gun bhlath.

ENGLISH :

> Our ancestors marred
> At the very beginning,
> Their strength and their case
> In old ways of sinning ;

> The corruption widespread
> In the vineyard has left me,
> Like a poor withered tree—
> Of all bloom it bereft me.

When Matheson's Poems were first published early in this century, they were accompanied with a preface from the hands of the Rev. Dr Macdonald of Ferintosh and the Rev. John Kennedy of Killearnan, in which the natural gifts of the poet, and his great Christian graces are referred to in very high terms : "Though destitute of the advantages of education," say the writers of the joint preface, "he was one of the most celebrated Christians in that or perhaps any other country. He possessed a clear and comprehensive view of Divine truth, and discovered a deep and practical experience of its power on the heart and life." In the imperfect sketches of Matheson's life which have been preserved there are strong indications of the religious and ecclesiastical discontent which prevailed among the laity in those northern districts at the time, and of the latent dissent which subsequently developed. It is interesting to read that "at one time the parish church being vacant, Matheson headed a deputation from the people to their Presbytery in quest of a minister. Finding the Presbytery stiff to move, 'I could sooner accomplish my errand with the great Hearer of prayer,' he said, 'than with the Presbytery.' One member, a clergyman of the unmitigated old Moderate school, or as our Anglican friends would express it, of the extreme High Church party, ridiculed him as not possessed of education or influence entitling him to be heard. 'You may mock,' he replied, but I can tell you the word of Scripture by which the Lord first wounded my conscience. I can also tell the word by which Christ was made precious to my soul ;—I suspect that is more than *you*, sir, can say.'" If poor Burns had been fortunate enough to have a little of this spirit his contact with the graceless members of the Presbytery of Ayr might have had a happier issue for himself.

There were clergymen of considerable culture in Caithness and Sutherland in the days of Matheson. Interesting sketches of some of them will be found in local religious histories such as Auld's "Ministers and Men in the Far North." Kennedy's "Days of the Fathers in Ross shire" is another pleasant, gossipy work, in which the struggle of light with darkness is vividly pourtrayed. At the same time there were many spots in the central and western Highlands where the truths of Christianity were scarcely known. Among

these places was Abriachan, on the north-west bank of the
romantic Lochness, some ten miles west of Inverness. To this
day it is difficult of access, notwithstanding the recently well-
made winding road from the level of the loch to the villages. It
is a wild and barren like gorge, surrounded east and west by hills
of a similar character. To the north lies a dreary moor, which
declines in the direction of Beauly.

The character and habits of the people at the beginning of the
eighteenth century harmonised well with the nature of the place
where they fixed their habitations. From this rather inaccessible
nest they carried on for years with impunity a regular system of
smuggling. They had every natural advantage on their side; they
were reluctant to give up a profitable though nefarious traffic, with
the lawfulness of which their consciences were not much concerned; and so hitherto they had refused to submit themselves to
the more civilised conditions under which the people around them
began to settle. This was the sphere of labour assigned by the
Society in Scotland for Promoting Christian Knowledge to the
poet-evangelist MacLauchlan, who was virtually the first to preach
the Gospel to the people of Abriachan.

LAUCHLAN MACLAUCHLAN.

This bard-evangelist was born about the year 1729. He came
of a family who occupied for generations a portion of the farm of
Kinmylies, called Balmaclauchlan, near the town of Inverness.
He was about sixteen years of age when the Rebellion of 1745
broke out, and remembered well seeing the wretched fugitives
from that disastrous field of battle being cut down in their flight by
the English soldiery. While quite a young man he was selected
by the society already mentioned to be one of their evangelist-
teachers at Culduthel, some three miles from Inverness. After a
few years of successful labour there he was sent to Abriachan,
where by the weight and general excellence of his character and
the judicious exercise of his talents, the people soon became
quite transformed. It is said that the godly people of the district
used to travel ten and even twenty miles to hear the bard Mac-
Lauchlan exhort. He was twice married, but had no family by
his first wife. In his second wife he found a truly congenial companion. While he was an admirer of the famous Hector Macphail,
minister of Resolis, she was equally devoted to the no less famous
James Calder, minister of Croy, the two being, along with Mr

Alexander Fraser of Kirkhill, the most eminent ministers in the
north at that time. The poet died in the year 1801, and his
remains lie interred in the churchyard of Kirkhill. MacLauchlan
was evidently a remarkable man in his day, and appears to have
possessed very fair culture. An English letter of his addressed to
his son, a divinity student, afterwards the Rev. James Mac-
Lauchlan of Moy, shows how well he could write English, and
how well versed he had been in evangelical theology—" I say
when two things are awanting, to go along with either the
doctrines of law or gospel has little or no effect ; *i.e.,,* when
either wants a homely or particular application. It may be sound
morality or sound gospel (even when both differ), yet so general
that attentive hearers may hear, and never be made to cry out,
What shall we do to be saved? Secondly, when law or gospel is
not attended with the operation of the Spirit of Christ, what can
be expected to be the consequence ?   . There is no wind so
proper to winnow Christ's corn as that of the gospel. . . . I
might say a great deal on this subject, but one thing I find is,
when some would maintain that never man spake like this Man,
yet when Christ would address Himself with particular homeliness
the very same lips would cry out, *Crucify Him! Crucify Him !*
And this is come on the Church of Scotland, that she is now filled
with a silly general strain of preaching when and where soundest
fearing if truth is told so homely as to say like Nathan to David
' Thou art the man,' the speaker would become a prey ; and if
such is the case with such as can preach orthodox law and gospel,
what can be said of such as can but lecture out harangues that are
neither true morality nor gospel ? . . . I think some, and no
small part, of the distinction between a picture and the real being
of grace is first in the begetting, next in the birth, then in the feeding, next in the growth, &c." This letter, like his poetry, shows
what a keen insight into human nature the bard possessed, and
how well he understood the causes of the religious deadness of his
day throughout the Church of Scotland. The poet makes here
the "silly general strain of preaching " the cause of this deadness ;
elsewhere, in one of his poems he attributes the sad state of
things in the Church to patronage. He was right in both cases.
It was the patron that forced on the people preachers of the " silly
general strain " stamp. The revival of religion in the first quarter
of this century owes much to the good seed sowed by such earnest,
faithful men, as MacLauchlan ; and not a few of our ablest ministers of the present day have descended from such worthy ancestry

The late Rev. Dr Thomas MacLauchlan of Edinburgh, the eminent Celtic scholar and eloquent preacher, was a grandson of the
poet-evangelist of Abriachan ; and one of the doctor's sons, Hugh,
is possessed of poetical endowments and literary talents worthy
of his great-grandfather.

It is very difficult to give satisfactory translations of any poetry,
but Gaelic measures and turns of expression present peculiar difficulties. I have endeavoured in what follows to give renderings of
some verses of all the poems of MacLauchlan that have come
down to us. The longest is the " Elegy " on Macphail of
Resolis ; but much of his poetry is said to have been lost. After
committing several of his poems to writing, the author, forming
but a low estimate of his own abilities, committed the MS. to the
flames.

We first give a few verses of the " Elegy " above referred to,
although it cannot be said to be the best specimen of the poet's
productions—

MACPHAIL'S "ELEGY."

Well may Resolis deeply mourn ;
We share her sorrow o'er his urn ;
Our holy feasts shall ne'er henceforth
Enjoy the great Light of the North.

No more we see that guiding Light ;
Oft did he tell in words of might
The danger great to Albin nigh
In clouds of gloom athwart our sky.

Well in our slumber may we start :
He warned, ere hence he did depart,
That from the ominous day to come
He would be taken to his home.

As Lot was saved from Sodom's fate
Ere God poured out His fury great,
So judgment from the Lord we dread
Since good Macphail, our guide, is dead !

In the " Elegy " we find several good verses bearing on the subject
of patronage in the Church of Scotland. They show us how gall-
ing that yoke of Parliament was always felt to be ; and how clearly
Bible-cultured people, of no pretence to a knowledge of the mysteries of statecraft, discern the radical ills by which communities
and individuals are fatally afflicted. It was only in 1874 that
statesmen legislatively acknowledged the evils which were so

patent to the poetic eye of MacLauchlan of Abriachan a century
before :—

PATRONAGE.

Our Mother, by State's wiles untaught,
A thoughtless slumber low has brought ;
Dark perils grew before her face,
In watchless and unfaithful days.

Her true-soul'd witnesses are rare ;
The gospel now so few declare ;
Our secret griefs we cease to hide
Since conscience everywhere has died.

Though Patronage had her interred,
Like Lazarus unsepulchered,—
Forsaken in the bonds of death,
All stinking with corruption's breath ;

Yet when her Head the word has spoken
The stone is raised ; Death's power is broken ;
The Patron's power disappears,
And we'll have praise instead of tears.

The " State of the World," or the worldly, is another poem of
considerable merit.   It not unlikely represents much of the style
of thinking and manner of the bard in his preaching addresses.
Indeed our religious bards in general give us a good deal of general preaching and exhortation in their productions.   Buchanan
has done so ; so has Macgregor ; while Grant's hymns, as well as
those of Dr Macdonald, are very much evangelical sermons in
verse   The following translation is as literal as the exigencies of
rhyme and metre can admit :—

THE WORLDLY.

When proudly they stand
    On the heights of the world
The storm then descends
    And below they are hurled !
When they are least anxious
    They're hurried away,
For iron misfortune
    Will brook no delay.

When life's breath is going,
    At grim Death's command,
Think not thine own power
    Had helped thee to stand,
Think not those weak hands
    Had preserved thee thy strength ;

Thy frail members yield
To Death's summons at length.
Of better blood boast not,
Vain child of the sod ;
We are all from that Adam
First fashioned by God.
We are all from that Adam,
In him our life lay ;
And all have to carry
These bodies of clay.

In this clay, soul-fashioned,
We march to the tomb,
Leaving loved ones behind us
When entering its gloom.
How much, then, thou takest
Of all this world's good ?
Some few yards of linen,
Some few deals of wood.

There are eight lines of a little poem called " An Samhla," or
The Comparison. which reminds us of the generally subjective
state of mind which the Highland men were wont to cultivate so
assiduously. In Morrison of Harris and in Macrae of Petty we
see the extreme spiritual self-analysis which they carried on. I
also give a rendering of a few verses of a fair poem on those given
to riches. It has the same preaching ring that we find in the one
on the state of the world :—

THE COMPARISON.

I'm like a barrel sealed,
Whose stores the others cannot see ;
The gazer scans in vain ;
Good wine or poison it may be :
But strike thou in some spot
Where all the staves are not so sound,
Soon thou shalt see the stuff
Outpouring on the ground.

THE TRUE RICHES.

I mourn for you that follow ill,
Ye who misspend the days of youth ;
The cup of sin you daily fill,
And grieve afar the God of Truth :
He keeps you while you fast advance
In fleshly pleasures' passing train ;
But yours will be inheritance
With heirs of everlasting pain.

If thou wouldst follow Him each day,
Be meek and mild—extinguish pride ;

To sinful lusts do not give way,
And all dark habits cast aside.
Though great thy faith be and thy pray'r,
They cannot ease thy grievous load,
Unless thine be a covenant share
In the soul-sealing work of God.

Behold her of Samaria :
Deep in her soul the poison flowed ;
But when the face of Christ she saw
Her heart turned from the guilty road.
A drink before that spring supernal
She sought with lips all parched and sore ;
He gave her of the life eternal,
Which slaked her thirst for evermore.

Though MacLauchlan has not left much to prove that he possessed the gift of satire, yet it seems that some of his poems helped
his preaching considerably in extirpating the habit of card-playing
once so universal in the Highlands—it used to be carried on at
baptisms, weddings, and even late wakes. Highlanders have had
a terrible dread of being satirised by the bards. To have come
under the satiric tongue of the poet acted like a social excommunication ; and bards frequently availed themselves of this power to
accomplish ends different from that to which MacLauchlan had
set himself in the following verses :—

CARD-PLAYING.

Oft I gazed with saddened feeling
On the weak that went astray ;
Men of outward name and promise
Whom I sought to teach the way.

When I entered they were sitting
The enjoyment to begin,
At the table where the Christian
Cannot shun committing sin.

They would rather have my absence
For they felt a glow of shame :
Stopping then they promised never
To take up the godless game.

With a pack of Satan's leaflets
There the husband's hands between,
They lost time and vainly wasted
Light at wicked work, I ween.

MacLauchlan's poems have been considered at greater length
than the mere quality of his poetry might warrant because they

shed light on the life and manners of the Highlanders during a particular time in a circumscribed district, and because hitherto they, in common with those of several other religious bards, have received no attention whatever. On the other hand, the great bards of the secular life have been very abundantly written upon and their merits exhibited.

DUGALD BUCHANAN.

The Highlands produced several religious poets of considerable merit during the eighteenth century, although the areas of living religious activities were undoubtedly very limited. Chief among them was Dugald Buchanan, whose hymns have taken a very high place. He has been compared to Cowper, but he reminds us more of the celebrated Welsh bard Goronwy Owen, who has much in common with Buchanan. It is curiously sug·gestive that the sacred bard of Anglesea and the sacred bard of Rannoch, the religious representative poets of their respective countries, should be found composing highly spiritual poems, and at the same period writing elaborate ones on the awful theme of the " Day of Judgment," while the polished Addison and ethical Johnson were delivering their well-finished articles on mere moral platitudes to a highly conventional generation. Perhaps the Highlanders have received, apart from the Bible, no greater gift than the holy and sublime strains of the muse of Buchanan, who impressed his personality and character on all the Gaelic-speaking portion of his countrymen who in his days were in the throes of painful political changes, and about to enter on a new era of severe trial and uncertainty. Much of what the world has admired in the Highland character since is due to the formative and healthy influence of Dugald Buchanan's hymns.

Dugald Buchanan was born in 1716 on the farm of Ardoch, Perthshire, where his father rented a farm and was the owner of a small meal mill the remains of which are still standing. His people were deeply religious people, of whom he speaks with much affection and respect in the autobiographical sketch which he left written in English. It is remarkable to find such people in Balquidder at that period—in the country of Rob Roy, who the year before the poet was born had marshalled his men on the field of Sheriffmuir under the banner of the Pretender.

Young Buchanan was educated in one of the schools belonging to the Society for Promoting Christian Knowledge, which was formed in 1701. There he received a good education, which was afterwards supplemented by attendance on some classes in Edinburgh University, while he was superintending the printing of the Gaelic New Testament. And this last fact reminds me that I have recently counted more than twenty well-known Gaelic bards who received University education; so the general cry of illiteracy is not applicable to the majority of them who at least were trained in the rudiments of learning.

Buchanan was afterwards appointed by the Presbytery of the bounds to be catechist and evangelist in the district of Rannoch, where he laboured with much acceptance and success. He died of virulent fever in June 1768, when he was fifty-two years of age. His death was profoundly mourned by every family in the district. His widow survived till 1824, and one of his daughters died as recently as 1854.

It is said that Buchanan composed a good deal of poetry that has never been published. He published his religious poems or hymns in 1767. They are eight in number, the longest, "The Day of Judgment," is 408 lines in length. This poem is also his best. It is dramatically vivid and very sublime. Indeed, Buchanan is the only Gaelic bard that exhibits much sublimity. He was a man of culture, of even judgment, and of true insight into human nature. There are many evidences of his acquaintance with the literature of his own and other times. While he knew something of Shakespeare and other masters of English literature, he became especially a student of the living religious thought of the England of his day. The writings of such men as Philip Doddridge and Isaac Watts helped to feed his spiritual needs and to colour the products of his own genius. ⨉

The works of Buchanan have maintained their popularity to the present day. In 1875 the twenty-first edition of his poetry appeared, accompanied by a new sketch of his life by the Rev. Allan Sinclair, late Free Church minister of Kenmore. In November of the same year, a monument, in the form of an obelisk of Peterhead granite, was erected to commemorate his name and genius at Kinloch-Rannoch.

The poems of Buchanan, in whole or in portions, have been frequently brought before the English-speaking world. Macgregor, Maclachlan of Canada, Pattison, Sinclair, Blackie, and Macbean have attempted translations with varying successes. As in the case of the finest lyrics on less sacred themes, the translation of these hymns presents peculiar difficulties which can only

be fairly overcome by translators whose own spirits are in holy
unison with the language and sentiments of the author.   It is
quite evident that such a master-translator as Professor Blackie
cannot feel at home among religious truths and experiences, with
which his sympathies are not very warm.   What Buchanan calls
" conversion " Blackie would describe as a new point of " ethical
departure,"—a cold and philosophical conception of an all-im-
portant event which could scarcely charm the hearts of religious
folks of the poet's type.   Only the pens of a Mason Neale and
like-minded men can glide along sympathetically on these sacred
heights of holy thought and life.

The first of the hymns is called *The Majesty of God*, which
begins in octosyllabic verse as follows :—

> O what is God ! or what His name !
> Angels in glory cannot know ;
> Where he is veiled in dazzling light
> No thought or eye can ever go.

This is one of the less popular of his hymns, the theme being of
a more abstract nature than that on which he dwells generally.

The hymn which stands second in the order of publication is
called *The Sufferings of Christ.*   This beautful production has
greatly impressed Highland religious thought, and that before the
Gaelic Scriptures were yet entirely translated or in the hands of
the people.   The form of verse chosen is very happy, and one
into which the Gaelic language flows with liquid ease and beauty.
Its spirit and manner may be imperfectly gathered from the following lines :—

> It is my Saviour's sufferings
> My song will now proclaim,
> That High King's life of humbleness
> In birth and death of shame ;
> The miracle most wonderful
> That e'er to men was told :
> God who was from eternity—
> An infant born behold !

The poet then rehearses in tender and mellifluous strains the
more suggestive events of the Lord's earthly life, and ends in a
few verses of extreme beauty, pathos, and simplicity, detailing
the agonizing circumstances of His death and crucifixion.   The
air to which the hymn is usually sung is very pretty and plaintive,
and is a great favourite in the Highlands.   At a time when living

Gospel preaching was far from general, the rehearsal of this and other similar productions on Sunday in many humble Highland homes, helped to keep alive the flame of spiritual life.

The next is the greatest of his poems or hymns—*The Day of Judgment*. The poet begins in his usual Scriptural simple style, but as he proceeds the treatment and the language become elevated and majestic. We seem to see the *dramatis personæ* acting their gorgeous parts on the canvass of the poet's grand conceptions. The verses beginning with " 'N sin fàsaidh rudhadh anns an speur," are regarded as very sublime. But there is no translation of this poem that will convey anything like a fair impression of the original. The following verses may give some idea of the manner of the poem :—

Then, like the morn enkindling red,
A glowing spreads throughout the skies ;
Where Jesus comes a glare is shed
By heaven's burning tapestries.

The clouds all suddenly unfold
To make for the High King a door ;
And we the Mighty Judge behold,
Whose glory streams forth evermore.

The rainbow glows around his form,
His voice resounds like mountain-floods ;
Outflashing o'er the sullen storm,
His lightning eye pours from the clouds.

The sun, great lustre of the skies,
Before His glorious Person pales ;
At length her failing brightness dies
Before the light His face unveils.

Her robes of gloom she will uptake,
The blood-red moon drops down in space ;
The mighty heavenly powers shall shake,
Outcasting planets from their place.

Like tempest-shaken fruit on trees,
So shall they tremble in the skies ;
Like heavy rain-drops on the breeze,
Their glory like a dead man's eyes.

The poetical conceptions of Buchanan on this subject have woven themselves into the theological ideas of the Highlander, like those of Milton into the religious thought of England.

The Skull is well-rendered by Professor Blackie, whose version begins thus :—

I sat all alone
By a cold grey stone,
And behold a skull lay on the ground !
I took in my hand,
And pitiful scanned
Its ruin, all round and round.

Without colour or ken,
Or notice of men,
When a footstep may trample the ground ;
A jaw without tooth,
And no tongue in the mouth,
And a throat with no function of sound.

In thy cheek is no red,
Smooth and cold is thy head,
Deaf thine ear when sweet music is nigh ;
In thy nostrils no breath,
And the savour of death
In dark hollow where beamed the bright eye.

No virtue now flashes
'Neath eyelids and lashes,
No message of brightness is sped ;
But worms to and fro
Do busily go
Where pictures of beauty were spread.

And the brain that was there
Into ashes or air
Is vanished, and now hath no mind
To finish the plan
It so boldly began
And left—a proud folly—behind.

From that blank look of thine
I gather no sign
Of thy life-tale, its shame or its glory ;
Proud Philip's great son
And his slave are as one
When a skull is the sum of their story.

The poem called *Winter* begins in this manner :—

The summer has ended,
The winter is nigh us ;
The foe of all living
Comes to spoil and to try us ;
Mars all that is lovely,
And tramples it under—
Full ruthless to all things,
He rages for plunder.

His wings he spreads o'er us,
  The sun behind pushing ;
While fiercely to scourge us
  His brood is forth rushing ;
The white-pinioned snow from
  The sky is forth flying,
The hailstones like shot
  From the stormy north hieing.

When he breathes upon it,
  Its soul leaves the flow'r ;
His lips the proud bloom
  Of the garden devour ;
The robes of the uplands
  And forests he tears them ;
His ice-flags of azure—
  The choked streamlet wears them.

His breast's frozen whistle
  Wakes loud the commotion
Of the waves as they surge
  O'er the barm-swollen ocean !
The sleet he congeals
  O'er the moors in their whiteness,
Clean scouring the stars
  Till they dazzle with brightness.

The poet, after this introduction, goes on to moralise at great length, drawing his lessons from the seasons and their changes. His poems are eight in number, and altogether constitute but a very small volume.

The titles of the other poems not referred to above are—*The Dream, The Hero,* and *Prayer.* An excellent sketch of his life and conversion written by the author himself in good English, has been translated into Gaelic, and is found frequently prefixed to the Hymns. This acount the author solemnly signs, and prays that this transaction of his signing himself as the Lord's consecrated servant on earth may be ratified in heaven. Buchanan tells us that he was an anxious hearer at one of the sermons which the distinguished evangelist George Whitefield preached at Cambuslang on the occasion of the latter's visit to Scotland.

Buchanan, in conception and utterance, shows more than the other Gaelic bards the effects of his acquaintance with English literature. The religious subjects which were the theme of his poetry partially account for this. When in Edinburgh Buchanan became acquainted with several distinguished men in the Scottish capital—among others, the celebrated David Hume, who was much impressed by the culture and character of the Sacred Bard of Rannoch.

CHAPTER XIII.

" Here one thing springs not till another die,
Only the matter lives immortally."
                              —SYLVESTER'S DU BARTAS.

THE authors whose works come under notice in this chapter
may be described as belonging to the Anglo-Gaelic era of Highland history, when the influence of English thought, movements,
and manners began to penetrate into the most sequestered corners
of the north west. This influence came in through the two channels of the religious literature of English Puritanism and Imperial
politics. When the Highlander came under the spell of the
former in such works as those of Bunyan, he no longer cherished
alien feelings towards Bunyan's fellow-countrymen, many of whose
struggles and sufferings were akin to his own ; nor did he want
any longer to nurse a spirit of mere Gaelic separatism that might
conflict with the national purposes of the latter. We, therefore,
find traces of English reading and culture in all the Gaelic poetry
that has been produced since the commencement of this era.
Even very early last century there is evidence that English
thought began to exercise some influence on the compositions of
the Highland poets. As already pointed out, English literature
contributed not a little to the development of Dugald Buchanan's
sacred muse. The chief Gaelic poets of this period were fairly
well educated, and knew the English language well. Several of
them were clergymen who had gone through a course of training in Scottish Universities.

There are three elements of sadness that enter into the poetry
of this period—first, the sorrowful cry of baffled Jacobitism ;
second, the vain cry of enthusiasts over the disappearance of
Gaelic habits and customs ; and again, the intense wail of a
fatherland spirit over the depopulation of the Highlands. Along
with greater devotion to the cultivation of erotic poetry these are

the themes of the bards of this era, who feel painfully conscious that the ground of this transition period is fast slipping away from under their feet.

ROBERT MACKAY.

This famous Sutherlandshire Bard, better known as Rob Donn, or Robert the Brown, was born in the parish of Durness in 1714. He is said to have composed verses between his third and sixth years, like some other poets, early lisping in numbers. For a long time before his death he filled the humble office of principal herd for his chief's (Lord Reay) cattle. He died in 1778, when he was sixty-four years of age. Although most of his pieces cannot be said to be religious—some much the reverse—we are told that he was an elder in the national Presbyterian Church. His death was deeply regretted over the whole country, where his memory is still most warmly cherished.

His poetical works were collected and edited early in this century by the late Rev. Mackintosh Mackay, Ll.D., who wrote a memoir of the bard. Sir Walter Scott directed Lockhart to review Mackay's Poems eulogistically in *The Quarterly Review*, giving him a place among the real sons of the muse. The monument to his memory has inscriptions on it in Gaelic, Greek, and Latin, so that Rob Donn has had fair justice done him.

Mackay wants imagination and the overpowering feeling we find in two or three others of the Gaelic bards. But although he does not stand among the very first of the Gaelic poets, he is yet a powerful, refreshing, and influential singer, with a good deal of wit, point, and satire. He is a shrewd and sensible man, with a Wordsworthian tendency to exalt the commonplace into fit themes for poetry.

His *Elegy on Ewen* is one of his best-known pieces. The morning he composed it he heard of the death of Pelham, then Prime Minister to King George the Second ; and he contrasted his death with the dying state of poor Ewen, in whose house he had stayed the previous night. Ewen could not converse with the bard, who, after kindling the fire in the morning for the dying man, composed the poem from which the following stanzas translated by a clansman of the bard—Mr Angus M. Mackay— are taken :—

'Tis thus thou dost instruct us, Death,
That we should turn ere yet too late !
The longest lives are but a breath,
Thou callest hence both small and great !

But these thy latest actions ought
To ope at once our slumberous eyes—
Thy sudden leap from Britain's court
To this low nook where Ewen lies !
 Long time, O Ewen, yes, long time,
 Has dread disease foretold thy fate ;
 Now nigh Death's door dost thou repine,
 With no one to compassionate !
 If unimproved the time has passed,
 And many a crime been done therein,
 Yet hope remains while life shall last,
 O yet repent thee of thy sin !

If we believe thy word, O Death,
These lessons we shall ne'er let slip !
There is no mortal drawing breath
Too vile for thy companionship !
The solemn truth when will we learn,—
Death's vision is both high and low—
From Ewen's sores thou didst not turn,
Great Pelham felt thy mortal blow.

Thou makest grief in court and hall
When at thy touch earth's glories fade,
The ragged poor man thou dost call
For whom no mourning will be made !
All men, O Death, thy face shall see,
And all be forced with thee to go !
Watchful and ready we should be
'Twixt Pelham high and Ewen low !

And all around thy victims fall,
Unseen thy sudden bullets fly ;
The noises round us loudly call
That we should be prepared to die.
Thou that art lowest in the throng,
Hast thou not heard that Ewen dies ?
And thou whom riches render strong,
That low in death great Pelham lies ?

Friend of my heart, and shall not this
Make all our thoughts to heaven tend ?
Society a candle is
That flames away at either end !
Where shall we find a humbler man
In Scotland than thy father's son ?
And in all Britain greater than
This Pelham, save the king, was none !
 Long time, O Ewen, &c.

This old beggar did not yet lose his power of hearing, and feeling insulted by the manner in which his name was introduced into the moralising verses he snatched up a club towards the close of the song, and creeping behind the bard aimed a blow at him with all the strength of his withered arm. Rob barely escaped, and tried to southe the enraged old man.

Mackay shows great detestation of greed in his poems. One is a dialogue between the world and the greedy man. The wants of the bard in his humble station were few and easily supplied, so he could contemplate with sorrow the growing spirit of selfishness that began to creep in along with advancing civilisation and change of habit. This spirit he rebukes in the following verse from an address to Lord Reay :—

> Hadst thou by nature been a man of greed,
> How soon had grown the tempting glittering hoard ;
> If thou to pity's tears hadst deigned no heed,
> And hard-wrung rents with human curses stored !
>
> But no, for when the yearly rents were paid,
> It was more joy to thee a thousand-fold
> To see a glad face in God's image made,
> Than the king's image on the yellow gold !

Like many of the bards, Rob appears to have suffered from a sore affair of the heart. A yellow-haired Annie deceived him, and ran away with a fair carpenter from the south, and he sang *Is trom leam an àiridh*. It seems the courting was carried on at a shieling, a favourite place of resort for fond swains and tender maidens :

> Oh, sad is the shieling,
>   And gone are its joys !
> All harsh and unfeeling
>   To me now its noise,
> Since Anna—who warbled
>   As sweet as the merle—
> Forsook me—my honey-mouthed,
>   Merry-lipped girl !
>
> .   .   .   .   .   .
>
> Ach, ach, now I'm trying
>   My loss to forget—
> With sorrow and sighing,
>   With anger and fret.
> But still that sweet image
>   Steals over my heart ;
> And still I deem fondly
>   Hope need not depart.
>
> So fancy beguiles me,
>   And fills me with glee,

17

> But the carpenter wiles thee,
> False speaker ! from me.
> Yet from Love's first affection
> I never get free ;
> But the dear known direction
> My thoughts ever flee.

The above verses are Pattison's translation. It is said that the deceitful " Anna " led an unhappy life afterwards, and never recovered her old spirits after the memorable parting at the " shieling," of which the bard sings so pathetically.

While Rob Donn is not equal to Macdonald or Macintyre in the highest qualifications of the poet, he is their superior in power of satire. His two rival bards have confounded vituperative language with satire, but Mackay never. He is a great favourite with his countrymen, who are very proud of him, and have laudably done all they could to make known his poetry and perpetuate his fame.

In many respects Mackay is a typical representative of the northern counties, where the intense Celtic spirit and feelings of nationality which characterise Argyllshire Celts do not prevail so extensively. The Teutonic element brought in by the Norse is stronger in the North, and may partly account for this apparent lack of Celtic enthusiasm and of the usual Celtic grace of style. In his own way, though exercising his sportive muse in a more confined and humbler sphere, Rob Donn might be described as a sort of Highland Praed or Calverley.

The bard was in the service of two of his clan on whom he has composed well-known elegies. These two were Lord Reay and John Mackay. The elegy on the latter has been translated as follows by the clansman already referred to in a good sketch which appeared some years ago in a London periodical :—

> Some keep the verbal law of man,
> And yet hard creditors are they ;
> They store what legally they can,
> What the law *makes* them, that they pay !
> Though want and misery they see,
> Not less through pity grows their sum ;
> Shut eyes and purse alike will be
> Against the poor and needy one !
>
> This bastard honour grows apace—
> The creed of numbers beyond ken,
> Who, greatly to their own disgrace,
> Would rather owe to God than men !

Theirs will be loss beyond recall
When God shall sum up all their debt—
"Thou heededst not the poor man's call,
I also will thy prayers forget!"

.   (.   .

If thou another's want didst know
Thou couldst not in thy goods rejoice;
Towards the poor thy heart would glow
Although his wants ne'er found a voice.
Ah, sooner lose a pound of gold
Than take to thee an ounce of sin,—
The waters shall bring manifold
For all thy treasures cast therein!

I saw the gentle who was poor,
And he was full of gloom and grief,
He passed the once wide-opened door
Where now no more he finds relief!
I saw the widow in her tears,
I saw the beggar hungering;
The orphan now unclothed appears
Unnoticed by the unpitying!

Who needs advice must want it now,
And see the prosperous times depart;
All clouded is the poet's brow,
With none to reverence his art.
None seek to make the poor rejoice;
And when I ask why joys are fled,
They answer me with tearful voice—
"Alas! is not MacEachainn dead?"

I see the gathering of the poor—
Now poor indeed since thou art dead,
And closed for aye the open door
Where Love consoled and Bounty fed!
And strangers now are praised to me
As lib'ral—I knew only *one*—
But ah! the wandering stars we see
After the setting of the sun!

DUNCAN MACINTYRE.

This bard, Mac-an-t-Saoir—the Irish MacTear—meaning the son of the joiner or carpenter, a recent intruder among the names of the Gaelic clans, is one of the great Highland poets to whom the Gaelic patriot refers with a pardonable measure of pride. Ossian, Macdonald, and he are the chief names on the roll of our bardic annals.

This famous hunter bard, frequently called Duncan *Ban*, or *fair-haired*, was born on the 20th of March 1724, at Druim-

liaghart, in Glenorchay, Argyllshire. His parents lived in an
out-of-the way spot, far from the parish school, so Duncan never
learned to read or write. Yet, rising from a humble sphere of
life, with only the education that the traditions, the popular
poetry and scenery of his native hills could afford, he has left us
compositions which we would not willingly allow to perish.
Highly cultivated some of his mental powers must have been.
His memory was something wonderful ; and yet there have been
at all times in the Highlands men equally trained like Macintyre
to remember and rehearse thousands of lines of poetry. Upwards
of six thousand lines of poetry composed by himself have been
published. All this he carried about with him for years, along
with the poetry of others, an immense mass of which he knew
and was able to repeat, until the Rev. Dr Stewart of Luss, one of
the translators of the Bible, was at the trouble of taking them
down to the poet's own dictation some time before 1768, when
they were first published in one 12mo volume of 162 pages. A
second edition appeared in 1799 and a third in 1804. These
were all the editions before his death took place in the year 1812.
But thousands knew them who never read them ; while many of
his more popular pieces found their way into other Gaelic collections. There have been several other editions since Macintyre
died.

The first song of Duncan Bàn was composed on a sword with
which he was armed at the Battle of Falkirk, where he served on
the Royalist side as a substitute for Mr Fletcher of Glenorchay.
The sword was lost or thrown away in the retreat, and his em-
ployer refused to pay the sum for which he had engaged the bard.
But Duncan's song became popular and incensed Fletcher so
much that, meeting the poor poet one day, he suddenly struck him
on the back with his walking-stick, and bade him "go and make
a song about that." Macintyre appealed to his patron the Earl
of Breadalbane, who compelled Fletcher to pay the bard the
stipulated sum, 300 merks Scots (£16 17s 6d).

Soon after the noble Earl—always kind to the bard--appointed
him forester and gamekeeper in Coire Cheathaich and Ben-Dorain,
the subjects of his two chief and finest poems. He was afterwards in the same capacity with the Duke of Argyll at Buachaill-
Eite. Then he joined the Fencible Regiment raised in 1793 by
the Earl of Breadalbane, where he served as a sergeant until
1799, when it was disbanded. He afterwards served in the City
Guard of Edinburgh till 1806, when he was enabled to live com-

fortably on his own savings and on the profits of the third edition
of his poems. He died in Edinburgh in May 1812, in the 89th
year of his age, and was buried in the Greyfriars Churchyard,
where a monument has been raised for him.

Duncan Bàn, in some respects, is the first of the Gaelic bards ;
Professor Blackie seems inclined to rank him above Ossian. He
is certainly less artificial than the Gaelic Ossian of 1807—more in
harmony with the life and sentiments of the Highlanders. He is
the natural outcome as well as the true exponent of the spirit and
manners of the period of Highland history which was then drawing to a close. His powers as a poet are of the highest order.
But the sphere of his life being so circumscribed, and the themes
on which his muse was exercised were so temporary and local in
their character, that Duncan Bàn can never receive from the
the world that homage to which his wonderful and lofty genius
entitles him. He has been called the Burns of the Highlands ;
and, perhaps, his genius is equal to that of Burns, taking into
consideration the difference in their education. Burns, however,
shows more intensity of conception and stormy passion ; while
Macintyre dwells with more luscious delight on the beauties and
glories of the external world.

Professor Blackie is a great admirer of Duncan Bàn, and
has given us what will always remain a delightful translation
of Macintyre's unique poem, *Ben-Dorain.* The translator of
Goethe's " Faust "—whose new edition of his translation of the
great German bard's work must ever be regarded as the best—
possesses the poetical ingenuity and subtilty, as well as deftness in
rhyme, necessary in a translator of *Ben-Dorain.* *Coire-Cheathaich*
is a poem equally celebrated with *Ben-Dorain,* translated into
English by Pattison, whose version has been utilized by Mr
Robert Buchanan, the distinguished dramatist and poet, with
slight alterations, in one of his works. Through these translators
the English reader is put in possession of some fair knowledge of
the muse of the Hunter-Bard of Glenorchay.

Here is the first verse of *Coire Cheathaich,* or The Braes of the
Mist :—

My misty Coire ! where hinds are roving ;
My lovely Coire ! my charming dell !
So grand, so grassy, so richly scented,
And gemm'd with flowers of sweetest smell.
Thy knolls and hillocks in dark-green clothing,
Rise o'er the green sward with gentle swell,

Where waves the cannach, and grows the darnel,
And troop the wild deer I love so well.

Duncan's chief love-song is characteristic. It is composed for
his " spouse newly wedded," and not for an unmarried maiden.
This is how the bard describes the manner in which he made
choice of "Fair Young Mary " :—

My net I cast in the waters clear,
    And strained hard to draw it to land,
And lo ! I had caught a bright sea-trout,
    That lay like a swan on the strand.
Pleased was my soul with the fortune
    That came with such joy to my hand ;
My spouse ! thou art the star of the morning !
    Blest be thy slumbers and bland !

" Aged and grey ". he visited the hills for the last time, and
composed his " Last Farewell to the Hills," one of the most
pathetic of his poems. Taking a retrospect of the past, he sor-
rowfully sings :—

And yesterday I trode yon moor—
    How many a thought it moved !
The friends I walked with there of yore,
    Where were those friends I loved !
I looked and looked, *and sheep, sheep still,*
    Were all that I could see :
A change had struck the very hill—
    O world ! deceiving me.

Few descriptive poets excel Macintyre in his representations of
external things, whether animate or inanimate. Everything he
touches he invests with the glow and the beauty of poetry. The
hills with their mist and deer, the streams and lochs with their
teeming inhabitants, and all the natural inhabitants of his native
glens and mountains, were congenial themes of his muse. " His
Address to his wife—Mairi Bhan Og—may be read beside the
sweetest and most expressive of the Lowland lyrics, while it certainly breathes a refined courtesy and a purity of sentiment which
these do not always possess, and which is not in any way insigni-
ficant in such a man, whether taken as an index of his moral
nature, of his intellectual endowments, or of the kindliness of
nature in gifting him with such unaffected manliness and good
taste." Macdonald could be sweet and tender when he chose;

it was far from being his nature. Macintyre is generally genial and tender, for it is the habitual attitude of his mind and heart. We are told " he was like the rest of the poets, vety fond of company and a social glass, and was not only very pleasant over his bottle, but very circumspect."

I give here a specimen of his poem, *Ben-Dorain*, of which we have a translation from the pen of Professor Blackie :—

My delight it was to rise
With the early morning skies,
　　All aglow,
And to brush the dewy height,
Where the deer in airy state
　　Wont to go ;
At least a hundred brace
Of the lofty antlered race,
When they left their sleeping-place
　　Light and gay ;
When they stood in trim array,
And with low deep-breasted cry,
Flung their breath into the sky,
　　From the brae :
When the hind, the pretty fool,
Would be rolling in the pool
　　At her will,
Or the stag in gallant pride,
Would be strutting at the side
Of his haughty-headed bride,
　　On the hill.
And sweeter to my ear
Is the concert of the deer
　　In their roaring ;
Than when Erin from her lyre
Warmest strains of Celtic fire
　　May be pouring ;
And no organ sends a roll
So delightsome to my soul
As the bravely-creste l race
When they quicken their proud pace
And bellow in the face
　　Of Ben Dorain.

Nor will they stint the measure
Of their frolic and their pleasure
　　And their play,
When with airy-footed amble
At their freakish will they ramble
　　O'er the brae.
With their prancing and their dancing,
And their ramping and their stamping,

And their plashing and their washing
      In the pools,
Like lovers newly wedded,
Light-hearted, giddy-headed
      Little fools.
No thirst have they beside
The mill-brook's flowing tide
And the pure well's lucid pride
      Honey-sweet ;
A spring of lively cheer,
Sparkling, cool, and clear,
And filtered through the sand
      At their feet ;
'Tis a life-restoring flood
To repair the wasted blood,
The cheapest and the best in all the land ;
And vainly gold will try
For the Queen's own lips to buy
      Such a treat.
From the rim it trickles down
Of the mountain's granite crown
      Clear and cool ;
Keen and eager though it go
Through your veins with lively flow,
Yet it knoweth not to reign
In the chambers of the brain
      With misrule ;
Where dark water-cresses grow
You will trace its quiet flow,
      With mossy border yellow,
So mild, and soft, and mellow,
      In its pouring.
With no slimy dregs to trouble
The brightness of its bubble
As it threads its silver way
From the granite shoulders grey
      Of Ben-Dorain.

Then down the sloping side
It will slip with glassy slide,
      Gently welling,
Till it gather strength to leap,
With a light and foamy sweep,
To the corrie broad and deep,
      Proudly swelling ;
Then bends amid the boulders,
'Neath the shadow of the shoulders
      Of the Ben,
Through a country rough and shaggy,
So jaggy and so knaggy,
Full of hummocks and of hunches,
Full of stumps and tufts and bunches,

Full of bushes and of rushes,
    In the glen.
Through rich green solitudes,
And wildly hanging woods,
With blossom and with bell,
In rich redundant swell,
    And the pride
Of the mountain-daisy there
And the forest everywhere,
With the dress and with the air
    Of a bride.

The number and variety of Macintyre's compositions is very large, all sorts of themes being regarded as fit for the exercise of his poetic fancy. Like those of the Highland bards, however, his subjects are generally more of local and personal than of the larger human interests—a fact which is not at all surprising when his education, calling, circumstances, and surroundings are considered.

Personal satires and eulogies, as well as the ordinary events of Highland humble life and occupations, form the circle of themes with which his muse is occupied. But wherever he gets the opportunity of seizing upon new subjects he straightway rushes at them, and turns them over in the rural though rich alembic of his intellectual and ethical processes, with results which show shrewdness, sagacity, and poetic powers of observation of a high order. In the corrie, on the hillside, or after the chase, Duncan Bàn is at home, and his poetry then rises to the highest pitch of the true pastoral. Elsewhere his muse necessarily travels on lower planes. But, like all his countrymen, inspired by visions of the great bens and far-reaching valleys, he is ever eager to extend his sphere of observation as well as his horizon of knowledge.

In his suggestive poem in *Praise of Dunedin*, or of Edinburgh, where the patriarchal poet died at the good age of eighty-nine, there is a current of pleasant and pawky observation which reminds us of the great changes that have come over the Scottish capital as over *Ben-Dorain* of the poet's "Farewell." The following verses of a very literal rendering describes the author's impressions of what usually attracted his gaze in "Bonnie Dunedin ":—

There's many a noble lady
    A poor man here may meet
In gown of silk or satin
    That sweeps along the street;

And every pretty thing wears stays,
  To keep her straight and spare ;
And beauty-spots on her fair face
  To make her still more rare.

Each one, as well becomes her,
  Polite among the rest ;
And proud, and rich, and ribbony,
  And round and gaily dressed :
The clothes on the young maidens
  Just showing to your eye
A strong and pointed well-made shoe—
  I thought the heels too high.

When I went into the Abbey,
  It was a noble sight
To see the kings in order,
  From King Fergus, as was right ;
But now since they are gone from us,
  Our Alba wants the Crown—
No wonder that her once gay court
  Is like a desert grown.

There is a lantern made of glass,
  With a candle in each place,
That yields a light to every eye
  Around a little space.
Nor less a cause of pleasure
  Are the instruments they play,
That give a sweeter music
  Than the cuckoo does in May.

It is difficult to say how far the recovery of the regalia, her
Majesty's frequent residence in the Highlands, ths crowds of
tourists northward every year, and, above all, the Home Rule
movement, might affect the sentiment of the line—
        "Our Alba wants the Crown "—
but undoubtedly in these days of gas illuminations and electric-
light glories, the " lantern made of glass with a candle " would be
no "cause of pleasure " to the most unsophisticated son of the
mountains.

Macintyre composed an Elegy for himself, from which the following expressions of a feeble faith are taken :—

Loudly shall the trumpet peal
  With echoes in all quarters heard ;
From the fields shall wake the dead
  Left by others there interred ;
All that perished in distress
  In the storm or in the flood ;

To Mount Zion go the host
To triumph through the Saviour's blood.
To the world I say farewell,
To all there on pilgrimage ;
Light and gay I lived my season
Until I am weak through age :
Changèd now my powers be
While death stares me in the face,
As I pray for welfare yonder
Savèd through my Saviour's grace.

Contemporary with and immmediately after the great singers
Macdonald, Mackay, and Macintyre were many other bards
whose inspiration is clearly traceable to their era. Some of them
composed very largely, although in many cases not more than
one or two of their compositions are remembered. Many of the
composers were well educated, and had they written in a language
better understood in the world in general, their names would have
been better known. The present Highlanders, while frequently
singing their songs, do not know so much as the names of the
the authors. The same may be said also of Lowlanders with regard to many of their own songs.

RONALD MACDONALD.—The merits of this bard were over-
shadowed by the great fame of his father, *Mac Mhaighstir Alasdair*. He was a man of considerable attainments and of undoubted poetic gifts, and published a selection of his own and
his father's poems in 1775. He was to publish more, but did not
meet with suitable encouragement.

LACHLAN MACPHERSON.—This writer, probably better known
as "Strathmasie," his territorial designation, and described as
a gentleman and a scholar, was born about the year 1723, and
died in 1767. He gave able assistance to James Macpherson of
Ossianic fame in his translations. The relation of Strathmasie to
the work has been a subject of very acrid discussion. His own
acknowledged poems are in good idiomatic Gaelic, and in style
and metre are quite different from the Gaelic poems of James
Macpherson's Ossian, but quite like the poetry of the other
Gaelic bards. In all his published poems there is not a stanza or
even a line *a la* Ossian. In poetic power and originality he is
much behind Duncan Bàn and *Mac Mhaighstir Alasdair*, but he
has shown that he is quite able to write tolerable poetry. The
titles of his poems are--*An Elegy on Cluny; The Fellowship of*

Usquebay ; A Marriage ; The Dun Breeks ; A Hunting Song ; The Advice ; An Amorous Piece ; Satire on Mice.

JOHN ROY STUART.—Colonel Stuart was a native of Kincardine in Badenoch. He first served in the French army against the British Government. He was afterwards with Prince Charles on the fatal moor of Culloden. After lurking for some time in this country he managed to escape to France, where he died. His signal bravery at Culloden was observed by the Duke of Cumberland, who asked who he was : "Ah, that is John Roy Stuart." "Good God !" exclaimed the Duke, "the man I left in Flanders doing the butcheries of ten heroes! Is it possible that he could have dogged me here !" Stuart's Poems—the principal of them is on *Culloden Day*—are impetuous, racy, and vigorous. An English bit of humorous verses, called *Roy Stuart's Psalm*, extemporised where he was hiding on one occasion, runs thus :—

> The Lord's my targe, I will be stout,
> With dirk and trusty blade,
> Though Campbells come in flocks about,
> I will not be afraid.
> The Lord's the same as heretofore,
> He's always good to me,
> Though red-coats come a thousand more
> Afraid I will not be.

KENNETH MACKENZIE.—This bard was born in 1758 at *Caisteal Leahuir*, near Inverness. When quite a young man he went to sea, but returned in 1789, when he began to collect subscribers' names for his proposed volume of poetry. Some time after the publication of his poems he was procured the rank of an officer in the 78th Highlanders, through the joint influence of Lords Seaforth and Buchan. After leaving the army he got the situation of postmaster in an Irish provincial town. He was living in 1837. His poems are of an high order, polished, smooth, and well-finished. One of his songs has become a universal favourite— *Am Feile Preasach.*

ALLAN MACDOUGALL.—This highly popular bard, better known as *Ailein Dall*, or Blind Allan, was born in Glencoe in 1750. His parents were poor, so Allan, incapacitated by his infirmity of blindness for the usual spheres of industry, turned his attention to music as a means of livelihood. He soon became well known as a fiddler in the district, and by engagements at country weddings and raffles earned a little to support himself. The poems also he composed helped to make him popular; and with the assistance of Mr E. MacLachlan, latterly of Aberdeen, who was then a tutor in the neighbourhood, a volume was prepared and published. Soon after this Colonel Ronaldson Macdonald of Glengarry took the poet under his patronage. In 1828 he travelled the counties of Argyll, Ross, and Inverness for subscribers for a new edition of his poems, but after procuring 1000 names, and going to press in 1829, the poor poet died. He was buried in the churchyard of Kilfinan. He has been regarded as the last of the family bards. He was a man of true poetic gifts; many of of his songs are still highly popular, such as—

"Nam faighainn gille r'a cheannach."

JAMES SHAW.—Poor James Shaw, otherwise called *Bard Loch-uan-Eala*, was born about 1758. He subsequently lived at Ardchattan, where he received some kindness from General Campbell and his lady. He died in 1828 suddenly on board a steamboat when returning from Glasgow, where he was trying to get his poems printed. He has been described as idle and dissipated. *Bidh Fonn Oirre Daonnan*, one of his songs, is still very popular.

DONALD MACDONALD.—Like the Bard of Lochnell this composer too fell a victim to his own infirmities of character. Macdonald, also called *Am Bard Conanach*, was born in 1780 in Strathconon, Ross-shire. He was a sawyer by trade, which he pursued after he removed to Inverness, where he did not fail to give scope to his convivial disposition. His moral conceptions of things do not seem to have been of a very high order, judging by his well-known song *Fhuair me Sgeula mioch an dè*.

ALEXANDER MACKINNON.—This composer, whose father was a farmer in Morar, Arisaig, was born in 1770. Early in life he enlisted in the 92nd Regiment, and was present at the Battle of Alexandria in 1801, where he was wounded. He was discharged, and enjoyed his pension for some time; but disliking the quietness of civilian life, he again joined the army, where he remained till he died at Fort-William in 1814. His principal poems are on *Landing in Egypt*, *The Battle of Egypt*, and *The Battle of Holland*. These are characterised by much poetic fire and warlike enthusiasm.

ANGUS FLETCHER.—This gentle and cultured bard, the author

of the highly popular production *Clachan ghlinn Daruadhail*, was born on the west bank of Loch Eck, in Cowal, 1776. He was educated at the parish school of Kilmodan. Afterwards he lived for some time in Bute, till he become. in 1804, parochial schoolmaster of Dunoon. He is also the author of some other songs that have become popular, especially *The Lassie of the Glen*, which, in an English dress from Fletcher's own pen, is well-known. This song was first published in the " Edinburgh Weekly Journal."

ALLAN MACINTYRE.—Very few Highlanders have ever heard of this author. Macintyre, known as *Ailein nan Sionach*, or foxhunting Allan, was a native of Kintyre. He published early in the century a small volume of his own, and other poems, but few of his productions are now sung, and his book is rather scarce.

DONALD MACLEOD.—This author published while he was still young a volume of original and other poems in 1811. Young of Inverness was the publisher, and probably he and others influenced the young author in his selection of such pieces of questionable taste and authorship as those of the *Ceisteir Crubach* and *Mordubh*. MacLeod's productions are rated very highly by his countrymen who delight in designating him, *Am Bard Sgiathanach*, or The Skye Bard. While Macleod is undoubtedly a man of good poetic parts, he ranks much below his far more distinguished and gifted son, Neil Macleod, whose songs have deservedly taken a high place in popular esteem.

Other bards of various gifts, and authors of published volumes of poetry during this period, are—

Duncan Campbell, who describes himself as a native of Kilmun, Cowal, published a " Gaelic Song Book" at Cork, 1798.

John Macgregor, published a volume of 227 pages in 1801, at Edinburgh. There is none of decided merit.

Angus Kennedy, a native of Ardgour, Argyllshire, published a volume at Glasgow in 1808. One or two of his songs have become very popular.

William Gordon, a native of Creich, Sutherlandshire, published a volume of 156 pages in 1802. He was a soldier, and in his latter days composed religious hymns.

Margaret Macgregor's poems appear in Mackintosh's Collection in 1831.

There were many other composers of one or a few songs or poems which may be found in various collections of whom we know little or nothing more than their mere names. To this class belong Donald Macintyre of North Argyll, George Morison of the far North, William MacMurchie of Kintyre, Alexander Macinnes of Glencoe, Maclachlan of Kilbride, and some female composers who are only known as the wives or daughters of men described as of certain localities. There does not appear to have been a parish or clachan in the Highlands and Isles that has not brought forth its own singer.

WILLIAM ROSS.

This sensitive and delightful poet was born at Broadford, Isle of Skye, in 1762. He received good education at the parish school of Forres, where he highly distinguished himself. He made a particular study of his native language, and was also well acquainted with Latin and Greek. He sang sweetly, and played on the violin, flute, and other instruments with considerable skill. He became parish schoolmaster of Gairloch, Ross-shire, where he was a very successful teacher. He did not fill this situation. however, very long. He died of consumption in 1790, in the twenty-eighth year of his age. His early death is said to have been hastened by a love disappointment. In *Cuachag nan Craobh*, one of his best known songs, he indulges in melancholy and painful reflections. It is addressed to a cuckoo that settled on the branch of a tree beside him. He remembers his false love and sings :—

> Nought to me but a sting all her bright beauties bring—
> I droop with decay, and I languish ;
> There's a pain at my heart like a pitiless dart,
>   And I waste all away with anguish.
>
> She has stolen the hue on my young cheeks that grew,
>   And much she has caused my sorrow ;
> Unless now she renew with her kindness that hue
>   Death will soon bid me " Good morrow."

Death did soon bid poor Ross " good morrow ; " and in this song, like Michael Bruce, he sang his own elegy. How pathetically the poet cries in the prospect of death !—

> If she were thus low, with what haste should I go
>   To ask how the maiden was faring :
> Now short the delay till a mournful array
>   The brink of my grave will be bearing !

Ross is a poet of a high order, and one of the sweetest minstrels the Highlands have produced. Many of his songs are highly popular. The exquisite sweetness and finish of Ross appear in his praise of the " Highland Maid," the first two stanzas of which are rendered as follows by Mr Angus Macphail, whose early death has been a loss to Gaelic literature :—-

> My pretty Highland maiden,
> With tresses golden bright,
> And blue eyes softly shading.
> And soft hands snowy white ;
> O'er Scotland's hills and plains
> With thee I fain would go,
> Wrapped in our native tartan plaids
> That in the breezes flow.
>
> Give me my Highland dress,
> "'Tis grand beyond compare';
> Give me my Highland maid,
> Sweet, smiling, young, and fair ;
> Then banish sleep and care,
> From eve to rosy morn,
> In happy love beneath our plaid,
> The proudest dress that's worn.

Ross is one of the best known and best loved of all the Gaelic bards. His career, so similar to that of Keats, ends so prematurely and pathetically that his memory has become engraven on the hearts of all who hear his story and love to sing his songs.

EWEN MACLACHLAN.

Ewen MacLachlan, a poet of real culture, sweetness, and light, was born in 1775, in Torracaltin, Coiruanan, where his ancestors, who originally came from Morven, were for several generations. His great grandfather was a bard of note. He was educated first in the parish school of Fort-William, and afterwards in King's College, Aberdeen. While carrying on his studies he was tutor successively in the family of Cameron of Camishy, in that of Cameron of Clunes, and in that of Macmillan of Glenpean. He distinguished himself highly at school and at the University, especially in classics. He intended to enter the Church, but on the eve of taking license some friends dissuaded him from taking the step, recommending him to wait, and aim at a professorial chair. Among these was the gentle author of " The Minstrel," Professor Beattie, who thought much of MacLachlan,

and became his fast friend.   In 1798 MacLachlan published some
of his own productions in Allan Dall's volume, which he himself
committed to writing for the Blind Bard.   These were the
" Songs of the Seasons," etc., and several books of Homer's
Iliad translated into Gaelic heroic verse.   In 1818 he published
his " Metrical Effusions," where Greek, Latin, English, and Gaelic
poems appear.   He was engaged by the Highland Society of Scotland to compile a Gaelic dictionary.   For this work he was eminently qualified, being intimately acquainted with old Gaelic, as
well as with Eastern and classical languages.   He died before the
work was finished, in 1822, in the 47th year of his age.   When
he died he was head master of the Grammar School of Old Aberdeen, a post for which his classical attainments peculiarly fitted
him.   A love-song by MacLachlan—*Gur gile mo Leannan*—is
still among the most popular in the language.   He himself has
furnished us with an English equivalent, which will give a fair
idea of the more tender qualities of his genius.   These simple
and pretty verses, usually sung to a plaintive air, come to us laden
with the purity and freshness of the mountain breeze :—

> Not the swan on the lake, or the foam on the shore,
> Can compare with the charms of the maid I adore ;
> Not so white is the new milk that flows o'er the pail,
> Or the snow that is show'r'd from the boughs of the vale.
>
> As the cloud's yellow wreath on the mountain's high brow,
> The locks of my fair one redundantly flow ;
> Her cheeks have the tint that the roses display.
> When they glitter with dew on the morning of May.
>
> As the planet of Venus that gleams o'er the grove,
> Her blue rolling eyes are the symbols of love ;
> Her pearl-circled bosom diffuses bright rays,
> Like the moon, when the stars are bedimm'd with her blaze.
>
> The mavis and lark, when they welcome the dawn,
> Make a chorus of joy to resound through the lawn ;
> But the mavis is tuneless—the lark strives in vain,
> When my beautiful charmer renews her sweet strain.
>
> When summer bespangles the landscape with flow'rs,
> While the thrush and the cuckoo sing soft from the bowr's,
> Through the wood-shaded windings with Bella I'll rove,
> And feast unrestrain'd on the smiles of my love.

MacLachlan counted a number of distinguished men among
his friends—among others, Alexander, Duke of Gordon ; the late
Glengarry, Sir John Sinclair, Dr Gregory, and Lord Bannatyne
Macleod.   His funeral was attended by the Professors of the

University and Magistrates of the city to show their respect. His remains were removed to his native Lochaber for burial. On the way to the burial place at Killievaodain in Ardgour the hearse was met and accompanied to the last resting-place by Glengarry and a number of his clansmen dressed in their native garb. Few of MacI achlan's talents and culture in modern times have devoted their energies to the cultivation of Gaelic literature. There is a reason : the practical spirit of the nineteenth century has, perhaps desirably, cooled even the enthusiasm of bardic natures.

JOHN MACLEAN.

Among the bards of some note who flourished in the first quarter of this century is John MacLean, usually styled the Laird of Coll's Bard. He is one of the last of the order of family bards, or seanachies. But the office in his case does not appear to have been of much advantage to himself—it was more honourable and and ornamental than remunerative. MacLean was born in the Island of Tiree in 1787. As an instance of the tenacity with which Highlanders cleave to the traditional pedigrees of their families, it may be mentioned that he traced himself back through the MacLeans of Treisinnis, of Ardgour, and of Duart to the great *Hector Roy of the Battles,* who was killed at Harlaw in 1411. But this is a small claim as compared with that advanced by a Dublin schoolmaster, John O'Hart, who, in a pamphlet dedicated to her Majesty Queen Victoria, whom he regards somewhat as a fellow-sovereign, pretends to trace his pedigree to the mighty monarchs of Eire who once reigned in " Tara's Hall ! " Mac-Lean published a collection of poetry, most of the pieces being his own composition, in 1818 ; another volume of his own poems appeared at Antigonish in 1836. His works complete have since been issued in excellent style under the title of " Clàrsach na Coille " (Harp of the Wood), edited with intelligence and care by the Rev. A. M. Sinclair of Nova Scotia, whose Gaelic scholarship and enthusiasm are well known on this side of the Atlantic. It is said that " in the poet's younger days the people of Tiree led merry lives; they did not trouble themselves with hard work ; they had, however, plenty to eat and drink. The island was full of distilleries, and whisky-drinking was carried on to a very great extent. There were capital dancers in the place, and certainly these men did not allow their legs to become stiff through want of exercise upon the floor." This picture of island-life suggests the material which was frequently the source of inspiration to bardic lucubrations. After learning the trade of shoemaking, MacLean started for Glasgow, where he married. In 1810 he was drafted into the militia, but was discharged next year. In 1819 he emigrated to Nova Scotia, where he lived till the year 1848, much respected and appreciated by all his countrymen who knew him. It appears that Maclean has composed religious poetry, though little known—some of his hymns being printed in Glasgow in 1835. Here is an account of this side of his nature : " It was not till he had been several years in Barney's River that he turned his attention to this species of composition. His hard lot in this world no doubt tended to direct his attention to a better world. He had always led a good moral life—a more truthful or a more honest could not be found. He had always observed the worship of God regularly in his family." MacLean is a bard of considerable powers, but cannot be compared with the bards whose names are known wherever the Gaelic language is spoken. One song of his has been highly popular, mainly because of the sweet air that is attached to it. The following verses will show the manner of the song, *Och a rùin gur tu air m'aire :*—

> Each day I sigh here a lonely stranger,
> I cannot sing with my heart love-laden ;
> I was right foolish to give my promise
> To her of Canna, the youthful maiden.
>
> It was with gladness I left the island,
> Home of my childhood and my devotion,
> To seek the gold here that may be found not
> In those bare islands amid the ocean.
>
> How proud and happy I was with Allan
> Beginning work in the gray of morning ;
> 'Twere better far to be there than labour
> A lonely stranger 'neath Lowland scorning.
>
> I would not stay in my native island,
> To my ambition the land was narrow ;
> When Lowland lasses inquire in English,
> I say in Gaelic, "I came from Barra."

This song is so painfully simple and commonplace, notwithstanding its popularity, that it can scarcely bear translation at all, unless the translator is permitted to introduce some of the stock sentiment and phraseology of the muse. One of MacLean's best pieces is on the *Laird of Coll's Boat.* Another of more than average merit was written shortly after his arrival in Nova Scotia

It shows the bard ill at ease in his new surroundings in the *Coille Ghruamach*, or Gloomy Wood.   It opens thus :—

> I stray alone in these woods of shadows,
> My thoughts are restless, I feel in pain ;
> This place conflicts with the laws of nature,
> My strength forsakes me in heart and brain.
> I cannot sing the old songs of Albin,
> My bosom saddens to hear their strain ;
> My Gaelic dies since I speak no longer
> That tongue still cherished beyond the main.
>
> Alas ! small wonder although I sorrow
> Behind the hills in this gloomy wood,
> In this lone desert by Barney's River,
> *With bare potatoes alone for food.*
> Ere cultivation is seen rejoicing
> O'er all the land and the trees are cleared,
> My strength will fail in an arm exhausted
> While yet the children are left unreared.

MacLean is one of the last of the old order of bards.   His poetry shows little or no trace of English reading ; and the theme of the majority of his poems is the praise of the Laird of Coll or some kindred chieftain.   Very appropriately might the happy couplet of Sir Walter Scott describing the old and infirm minstrels of other days be applied to MacLean—

> "A simple race ! they waste their toil,
> For the vain tribute of a smile."

It ought to be mentioned, however, that the Laird of Coll showed on more than one occasion that he did not forget his enthusiastic senachie.

CHAPTER XIV.

POPULAR SONGS.

" Ho gur toigh leam I he gur toigh leam !
Ho gur toigh leam féin a' Ghàilig !
'S toigh leam i 'sgàch àit am bi mi ;
Bheir i ann am chuimhn' a' Ghàidlh'ltachd."
—Chorus of Popular Song.

ENGLISH :

Ho, I love the sweet old Gaelic !
It reminds me of the Highlands,
Hay, I love that tongue of heroes,
Everywhere in far or nigh lands.

CONSIDERABLE activity was shown in the beginning of this century in collecting the floating mass of poetry then extant in the Highlands. Celtic patriots who dreaded the immediate decease of the ancient language of Albin set themselves in praiseworthy fashion to the task of rescuing this popular literature from the devouring jaws of time and change. A brief survey of the various publications which were the practical outcome of this happy determination will exhibit no unworthy results. These results, in many cases achieved at great self-sacrifice, are more deserving of notice when it is remembered how expensive it was then to publish bulky volumes, especially in the Gaelic language, and how limited was the constituency to whose support the persistent patriots appealed. Their devotion to their venerable mother-tongue, supposed to be on her death-bed, deserves our gratitude ; and if their ghosts occasionally revisit in the glimpses of the moon, the scenes of their self-denying labours, they must be gratified to hear still the echoes of their much-loved tongue resounding as of yore through the glens and by the seashore as well as in crowded halls in our large centres of population. Peace be to their manes ! and long may the torch of Gaelic enthusiasm, which they kept lighted, and handed down to us, be preserved a burning power in the bosoms of our Highland countrymen.

It is not proposed to do here much more than the mere enumeration of some of these collections of poetry. This itself will be sufficient, along with the array of Gaelic bards that have already passed in review before us, to show further how unfounded is the general dictum that there is no Gaelic literature—no books in the language of the Highlander.

Some popular songs of this period are—" Mairi Dhonn " and " Mairi Ghreannar," by Kenneth Mackenzie of Lochbroom ; " 'Scanail m'Aigne," and " Soraidh Slàn do'n Ailleagan," by the the brothers William and Alexander Mackenzie, of Lochcarron ; " An Làr Dhonn," by Murdoch Mackenzie, of Achilty, Ross-shire ; " Thug mi'n Oidhche ruoir san Airidh," by John Macgilli-vray ; " Gaor nam Ban Muileach," by Margaret Maclean of Mull ; " O'n tha mi fo Mhuladh air m'Aineol," by the Rev. Charles Stewart, D.D., of Strachur ; " Nighean Donn na Buaile," by the Rev. Duncan Macfarlane, latterly of Perth ; " Gu ma slàn a chì Mi," by Hector Mackenzie, an Ullapool sailor ; " A Nighean Bhui Bhan," by Donald Macinnes ; " Mo run geal Og," by Chris-tina Ferguson, of Contin ; " Thainig an Gille Dubh," by Lady Malcolm Raasay : " A Mhairi Bhòidheach," by a North Uist scholmaster ; " Moladh Caber-Féidh," by Norman Macleod of Assynt, whose two sons, Professor Macleod of Glasgow and the Rev. Augus Macleod of Rogart, were well known last century.

Anonymous pieces are many : " An Gille Dubh ciar Dubh," " Mo Nighean Chruinn Donn ; " " Fear a' Bhàta ; " " Cuir a Chinn Dìleas ; " " An Nochd gur faoin mo Chadal domh ; " " Och mar tha Mi ; " " Ho-ro Eileinich, Ho-gu " (the three last being evidently composed by Islaymen) ; " Tha Tigh'n Fodham " (MacDhughail, 'ic Lachuin ?), a verse of which Boswell boasted of being able to sing when he was with Johnson on his tour in the Hebrides. The popular collections of songs will supply many more.

Since 1812 the following collections of miscellaneous pieces of poetry have appeared :—P. Macfarlane's (1813) ; in this volume was first published a part of MacLachlan's translation of Homer (the 3rd Book). P. Turner's (1813), mostly culled from the works of the well-known heroic bards. H. and J. MacCallum's (1816), principally Ossianic or heroic ballads. J. MacLean's (1818), containing much original matter. Inverness collection (1821, Fraser) ; James Munro's *Ailleagan* (1830), which has maintained its popularity all along. Other small things appeared early in the century—*Eoin Bheag nan Creagaibh Aosda* (1819) ; *Ceilleirean Binn nan Creagan Aosda* (1819), and a choice collection of Scotch

Songs with Gaelic translations (Inverness, 1829). " The Harp of Caledonia," " An t-Aosdana," " The Mountain Songster," " An Duanaire," have been published more recently, and are still in circulation. The most valuable of all the collections is '· The Beauties of Gaelic Poetry "—a magnificent volume, on which much labour was spent, by John Mackenzie. The productions of many of the Gaelic bards are given in this work, along with bio- graphical notices, and much critical and explanatory matter. Mackenzie, who was a native of Wester Ross, was a man of great talent and industry ; but his æsthetic and moral tastes not being of a high order, he allowed many pieces of an immoral ten- tendency to appear, which somewhat marred the work. It is the *magnum opus* of Gaelic literature. The '· Oranaiche," by Archi- bald Sinclair (1879) is another large and excellent work, which does great credit to the compiler and publisher. With the ex- ception of the " Beauties," which is of a different sort, there is no collection in Gaelic like Sinclair's, whether we regard the variety, the extent, and the quality of the contents.

While the " Beauties" contain the best productions of the princi- pal bards during the last three hundred years. the " Oranaiche," gives us the better known songs of the present century, many of the lyrics being the compositions of living writers, from whom Mr Sinclair, olten at very considerable trouble to himself, obtained the manuscripts, and took down the words at the author's or others' dictation. There are two hundred and ninety songs in this handsome volume, many of them very long—a gene- ral characteristic of Gaelic songs—and not a few, it must be admitted, more of the nature of poems than of lyrics. The songs in this collection are of all sorts—humorous, patriotic, satiric, and sentimental. The latter class predominates ; indeed, it constitutes three-fifths of the whole. In considering the range of poetic culture discernible in this volume, it is remarkable to note the almost total absence of martial songs. The bards of this century would appear to have been baptised in the perennial stream of the tender passion of which they sing with such evidently luscious delight. This is the one great theme which they take up with the devotion of their whole being. Another subject which here and there gives a tinge of sadness to the book is the depopulation of the Highlands, which is so fitted, like the troubles of a jilted and suffering lover, to elicit, in all its intensity, the melancholic element in the Celtic nature. *Mac-na-bracha* (Son of Malt) also comes in for requent and hearty praise, drinking *Deoch-slainte* being capable at all times of invoking in many Highland bosoms the purest and most generous feelings and sympathies. It ought to be observed, however, as Sheriff Nicolson suggests in his excel-lent volume of Gaelic proverbs, that although *usqueba* is so much identified with the failings of the modern Highlander, this exhila-rating beverage was almost unknown to the Gael until last century, the drink known till then being mostly " fion dearg na Frainv," *the red wine of France.* It has been remarked above, that this volume does not present us with many martial lyrics. This fact reminds us of the great change that has come over the Highlands. The obvious explanation is that the warlike ardour which was wont to flow forth in battle incitements has been toned down by the altered circumstances of the people since the day of Culloden, and runs now into the natural stream of the tender passion. On the other hand, if we go back to the days of Finian chivalry we find a martial element in all the productions of the bards ; and this continued largely to prevail as. long as the Gael habitually carried about with him his claymore, ready to fight for his person or follow his chief to the field.

One of the best, and the only genuine martial song in the " Oranaiche," is the first in the volume, *Buaidh leis na Seoid*, by Alexander Macgregor, schoolmaster at Dull. It contains six-teen stanzas of four lines of twelve syllables in length, and having a chorus takes a long time to sing it ; but the martial enthusiasm it breathes, along with many suggestive historical references, are such that audiences sit frequently spellbound till the whole piece is rehearsed. Of the humorous pieces in the volume mention may be made of *The Dun Horse, The Minister and the Bailie*, and *The Advent of an Escaped Irish Balloon on the shore of one of the Hebrides.* The author of the last-mentioned represents the whole island as in commotion when the monster approached the shore —old men and old women taking for granted that this could be no less a personage than the devil himself, who came at last to claim his own.

There are upwards of fifty names of composers in the " Oran aiche," many of whom are still living, and who are not known on the pages of another book. With this fact before us surely it cannot be affirmed that the race of bards is gone. I was once present at a meeting of a Highland Association in Glasgow, where I was informed there were no less than six bards, authors of published, well-known songs. It is difficult to conceive how so many of the irritable genius could work in harmony or dwell together

in unity and in poetic brotherhood. Among the fifty above-men-
tioned occur the following less known Celtic names :—Lady
D'Olyly D. Orr, MacMurchie, MacPhail, Macroy, MacLugas,
MacAffer, Wilkinson, etc. etc. Let us now glance at some of
the best-known songs.

Gu ma Slan a chi Mi, the composition of an Ullapool sailor,
the air of which is very pretty, is a highly popular song. I have
tried to render some verses of it thus :—

Full happy may I see thee,
 My faithful auburn maid !
Sweet girl with flowing tresses
 In pretty smiles arrayed.
My soul was oft-uplifted
 By words thy lips have said ;
And oft by strains of gladness
 My fluttering heart allayed.

This night to me how dreary
 Upon the ocean tide !
My slumber is full cheerless—
 To thee my fancies glide.
Without thee here I sorrow,
 My thoughts are at thy side ;
I pine away in anguish
 Till thou become my bride.

Warm eyes are thine like berries,
 With lashes sweetly lined ;
Fresh cheeks are thine like rowans,
 In loveliness enshrined.
My heart is filled with fondness
 For one so true and kind ;
And ever since I left thee,
 The days like years I find.

'Twas said I shunn'd thee, dearest,
 Ere hither I was borne ;
My kiss that I denied thee
 While leaving thee forlorn.
Let no such tale, dear, grieve thee,
 Reject their speech with scorn ;
Thy breath to me smells sweeter
 Than dewy grass in morn.

Some of the most popular songs are anonymous. *Ho-ro Eileinich* belongs to this class, and is a great favourite at large Highland
gatherings on account of the swinging character of the air and
metre. Here are a few verses :—

O, green island of the sea !
Native home, I love but thee :
Fairest fields of earth that be,—
    The bonnie braes of Landai.

There afar I see Ardmore,
Home of game that I adore ;
There my heart is evermore
    Among the hills of Landai.

Thy dark brow though rocky be,
Early shines the sun on thee ;
Heights of deer ! I long to see
    Beyond the shore of Landai.

Oft there fell beneath my hand,
Spotted seal upon the sand ;
Snowy swans upon the strand,
    And heathcocks in fair Landai.

O ! I love thee, Islay green,
Of my youthful days the scene ;
Where the best of men have been
    Who loved the songs of Landai.

One of the finest songs in the language is *Muile nam Mor
Bheann*, or Mull of the High Hills.   On account of its peculiarity
of metre, it does not lend itself readily to easy translation.   Some
of its verses run thus :—

In Mull of the woods there lives the maiden
For whom my poor heart is now love-laden :
Though dead be that love like joys of Eden
I woo no lasses in Cowal.

CHORUS.

All cheerless and lonely here I sorrow ;
No fond ray of hope is seen each morrow,
My heart has refused fresh love to borrow ;
It turns to the wood-crowned island.

Like beautiful sheen of rosy morning
The glow of thy cheek is sweetly burning ;
The troth of my love if thou art spurning
Soon linen and sods will shroud me.

For thine is thecharm that wins devotion
The graces of form that wake emotion,
As bright as the sea-gull on the ocean,
Or cannach on brows of Morven.

Were mine thy fond kiss I'd cease repining,
Thy love would restore my health declining,
O ! let me behold the beauties shining
Around the maiden of Morven.

A glance into the *Oranaiche* and other collections of Gaelic songs will reveal to the casual student of Gaelic literature what vast treasures of lyrics the language contains. These songs admirably exhibit the emotional lyrical spirit of the Gael, and leads us to much of the source of the genius of song which has rendered Scotland so deservedly renowned.

The Rev. Angus Macintyre, late of Kinlochspelvie, composed several poems of great merit. His love song, "O's runach leam an ribhinn donn," is very pretty. A translation by Mr H. Whyte will be found in an interesting little volume recently published, "The Celtic Garland." Here are some verses :—

> I dearly love my auburn maid
> That dwells behind the mountain,
> At eve I'll meet her in the glade,
> To roam by dell and fountain.
>
> Though here with hounds I chase the deer,
> Where streamlets bright meander,
> To yonder glen, where dwells my dear,
> My thoughts will ever wander.
>
> The birds that round about me fly,
> Pour forth their notes of gladness ;
> While here alone I sit and sigh
> In sorrow and in sadness.
>
> Her hair around her shoulders flows
> With graceful waving motion,
> Her snow-white bosom heaving goes
> Like sea-gull on the ocean.

One of the popular songs and airs among Highlanders is that of "Finary." The verses that have become so well-known in connection with this song are not those to which the air was attached originally. The original song was "Irinn àrinn u horo," by Allan Macdougall, a lyric of fair merit, but which has never attained to anything like the popularity of "Finary." The author of "Finary" appropriated an air already popular, like the author of "Màiri Laghach." The reputed author of "Finary" is the elder Dr Norman Macleod, and certainly the theme of the song is founded on an event in his personal history. It is a farewell to Finary, where the manse of his father was situated, in Morven, on the occasion of Norman leaving home to attend the first session at Glasgow University. The sentiment is very pathetic and natural, and very readily lays hold of the tenderest chords of the heart of the home-loving Highlander. There is something about

it, the antiquarian reference to the past. and its touches descrip-
tive of natural scenery, which remind us of the genius of Macleod.
Yet it has been doubted whether he was the author of the original
English version—the English one being regarded as the original.
Mr Neil Campbell, of County Down, now of Glasgow, a man
who knows a good deal of generally unknown facts relating to the
Gaelic literature of this century, once told the writer that the Rev.
Mr Kelly, of Campbeltown, once Dr Macleod's friend and col-
league in that town, was the author of the English version, which,
apart from the home-loving sentiment and air, is rather poor
poetry. The following is the first verse, which shows reason but
the veriest imperfection of rhyme :—

> The wind is fair, the day is *fine ;*
> Swiftly, swiftly runs the *time ;*
> The boat is floating on the *tide.*
> That wafts me off from Finary.

But apart from the artistic execution of the verses, the sweet,
high-souled, and patriotic sentiments conveyed in them would
always recommend them to the warm-hearted and emotional Gael.
The history of " Fionnairidh " has always seemed to me something like that of " God Save the Queen," or " The Address to the
Cuckoo." The names of Bruce and Lowe are connected with the
last just as those of Macleod and Kelly are with the first. One of
the few who could authoritatively decide the precise authorship of
" Fionnairidh "—was that true and highly-gifted Highlander the
late Dr John Macleod of Morven ; and also his learned relative Dr
Clerk of Kilmailie, who could write with accuracy of the different
versions, English and Gaelic, of *Eirich agus tiugainn, O.*

The following Gaelic version—eight stanzas, there are four
more—are given as they came through the hands of the late
Archibald Sinclair, who had probably something to do with it.
It was first printed on a leaflet, was then copied into the "¡Gael "
in 1872, and has been several times published in whole or in part
since :—

> Tha 'n latha maith, 's an soirbheas ciùin ;
> Tha 'n uine ruith, 's an t-àm dhuinn-dlùth ;
> Tha 'm bat' 'g am fheitheamh fo a siùil,
> Gu 'm thoirt a null o Fhionn-Airidh.

> Tha ioma mile ceangal blath
> Mar shaighdean ann am féin an sas ;
> Mo chridhe 'n impis a bhi sgaint'
> A chionn bhi fagail Fionn-Airidh.

Bu tric a ghabh me scriob leam fhéin,
Mu 'n cuairt air lùchairt Fhinn an tréin ;
'S a dh'éisd mi sgeulachdan na Fèinn
'G an cur an céill am Fionn-Airidh.

'S bu tric a sheall mi feasgair Mairt
Far am biodh Oiscin sinn a dhan ;
A' comhead gréin' aig ioma tra
Dol seach gach la 's mi 'm Fionn-Airidh.

Beannachd le athair mo ghraidh,
Bidh mi cuimhneah ort gu brath ,
Ghuidhinn gach sonas is agh
Do 'n t-seann fhear bhan am Fionn-Airidh.

Mo mhathair !—'s ionmhuin t' ainm r 'a luaidh—
Am feum mi tearbadh uait cho luath ?
Is falbh a'm' allabanach truagh
An cian uait féin 's o Fhionn-Airidh !

Soraidh leatsa, brathair chaoin,
Is fòs le peathraichibh mo ghaoil ;
Cuiribh bròn is deòir a thaobh
'S biodh aoibh oirbh ann am Fionn-Airidh.

Beannachd le beanntaibh mo ghaoil !
Far am faigh mi fiadh le lagh :
Gu ma fad' an coileach-fraoich
A' glaodhaich ann am Fionn-Airidh.

The chorus consists of *Eirich agus tiugainn, O,* " Let us rise
and come away," repeated tree times, with a fourth line, " Farewell, farewell to Finary." The following rendering is an adapta-
tion by the writer. The form " Finorie " is used to preserve a
sort of sympathetic sympathy with and likeness to terms with
similar endings in Lowland ballads, such as " Glenorie," etc.
This form has also more sympathy with the music :—

TRANSLATION :

The day is good, the wind is fair ;
The sands of time the hour declare ;
There rides the boat that hence will bear
    Me far away from Finorie.

A thousand ties my soul enchain ;
Like arrows they awaken pain ;
My heart is nearly broke in twain
    Since I must leave thee, Finorie.

Often alone I sought the hold
Where mighty Fingal lived of old ;
Often I heard long legends told
    Of Finian deeds in Finorie.

Often I viewed at Eve the spring
Where Ossian tuned his harp to sing ;
Where sheen of gold the sun did bring
    Upon the heights of Finorie.

Farewell, dear father, best of men,
Far from me in the Highland glen !
Heav'n smile on thee till back again
    I come to see dear Finorie.

Mother ! a name to me most dear ;
To lose thy tender care I fear ;
But in my snareful journey here
    I think of thee and Finorie.

O brother of my love, adieu !
Dear sisters, hide your grief from view ;
Your tears suppress, your joys renew ;
    Be happy while at Finorie.

Farewell, ye mountains capp'd with snow ;
Ye wild resorts of deer and roe ;
Long may the heath-cock live to crow
    Among the braes of Finorie.

But matters are still further complicated in connection with this
favourite song. A gentleman from North Argyll assured the
writer that another Gaelic version was in general circulation long
ago in Mull and Morven. This might have been the original
one by Dr Macleod himself, from which Kelly translated ; and
the fact that the original chorus, " *Eirich agus tiugainn O,*" has
been known only in Gaelic favours this supposition. Surely old
folks in Morven must still be able to repeat this supposed original
version if it ever had existence. If so, it is to be hoped that
some one will take the trouble of giving it to the world. But
whoever the author was, the song has obtained unquestionable
hold of the Highland heart, no doubt largely because it refers to
an early event in the history of the " Highlander's friend," the
good, genial, and large hearted Norman Macleod.

Poetry like that of A. Mackay, of Moyhall (1821), of Archibald Grant, of Glenmoriston (1863), of John Macinnes (1875),
Callum Macphail (1879), and of John Macfadyen (1890), shows
excellent ease in verse-making, and no small amount of humour
at times ; but it does not demand serious examination. That
so many volumes should be published indicates much activity
and energy on the part of an obscure Gaelic muse.

Another bard of the name of Grant may be mentioned as belonging to this class. Many of the popular lyrics have been com-

posed by authors who have not given us more than one or two
songs. *Mo Nighean Dubh* was written by the Rev. Mr Morrison
of Petty ; *Mairi Laghach*, by John Macdonald of Lochbroom ;
Bonneid is it, by A. Macalister of Islay ; *Eilein an Fhraoich*, by
M. MacLeod of Lewis. The mass of lyrics of this class is something enormous. When translated into English they are felt to be
simple—sometimes painfully simple—metrical inartistic utterances
of love-enkindled hearts. Attached to tender and often very
pretty airs they have lived on the lips of thousands, and have
cheered weary workers in the field and at the fireside. Of the
nameless class of plaintive lilts is the following :—*Mo Run Geal
Dileas*, well known throughout the Highlands. There are many
versions of it, and the number of verses is scarcely ever the same.
The chorus rather unintelligible, and may have belonged to an
earlier set of verses. The verses translated give a very fair conception of the merits and the spirit of the original. Like the
Laureate's *Mariana*, many of these Highland singers show much
of the " a-weary, a-weary " condition of soul, and people of pretended lofty moral culture condemn the poor lyrists for manifest-
ing such excess of feeling.

> My faithful fair one, my own, my loved one,
>   My faithful fair one, return again ;
> O, I return not ! my love, I may not ;
>   For my own dear one is weak with pain.
>
> O, that I were in the form of sea-gull,
>   That swims so lightly upon the sea ;
> Soon would I leave for the isle of Islay,
>   Where lives the maiden that grieved me.
>
> O, that I were with the best of maidens !
>   In pleasant glades of the mountain side ;
> With none to hear us but woodland songsters,
>   I'd kiss my own one with loving pride.
>
> I was a season in foreign regions—
>   In sunny climes that are far away ;
> None with thy beauty my eye could find there ;
>   And with the fairest I would not stay.
>
> I will not strive with the tree that bends not,
>   Though on its branch-tops sweet apples grow ;
> Farewell be with thee, if thou hast left me,
>   Ne'er came an ebb-tide without a flow.

Mairi Laghach has become a great favourite, and has been
translated more than once. The author was John Macdonald,

latterly of Crobeg, in Lewis. He adopted the chorus of an inferior song which a *Muracha nam Bo* composed for his own daughter, who did not seem to elicit much admiration from the ungallant bachelors in the neighbourhood. Macdonald took up the
air and composed the set of verses that are now so popular. It
is worthy of remark that in his case also the subject of his song
was a baby, and not a grown-up girl or woman. Steering his
barque across the Minch his thoughts reverted to the friendly
home he left behind him in Stornoway, and anxious to examine
his poetic gifts he composed his song to *Wee Mary*, as it might
be rendered, who then could not walk. Eventually she became
his wife. Once on a visit to Ireland, the author was surprised to
hear, while he himself was still a young man, his own song sung in
an adjoining room, which shows how readily a song that catches
the popular ear and taste will travel.

An endeavour is made to be as literal aspossible in the following translation, which must necessarily want much of the aroma
of the original :—

Early roved my Mary
  With me through Glen-Smeoil,
When young love's keen arrow
  Pierced me to the soul.
With such living fervour
  We together drew,
That none under heaven
  Ever loved so true.

Oftentimes with Mary
  To the hill I strayed,
Innocent and happy
  Through the grassy glade :
Cupid ever busy
  Teaching us to love,
As we rested foudly
  In the sun-lit grove.

Though the wealth of Albin
  Were assigned to me,
How could I be happy,
  Dear one, without thee ?
I would rather kiss thee,
  As my own true bride,
Than possess the treasures
  Found in Europe wide.

Thine the snowy bosom,
  Filled with love for me,

Breast of beauty fairer
Than the swan on sea :
With the lovely tresses
Round thy ears that stray,
Golden curly wavelets
In their fond array.

All the pomp of princes
Did our pride surpass,
With our bed of grandeur
On the leaves and grass :
Flowers of the desert
Heart and soul to feed ;
Streamlets from the mountains
Nourishing each seed.

Nought that men invented—
Pipe nor harp—could play
Music with the sweetness
Of our love-born lay :
With the larks above us,
Thrushes on the spray,
Cuckoos in the greenwood
Warbling to the May.

It is of course impossible to preserve the music of the original in any translation ; the renderings given above are intended merely to indicate something of the spirit of the lyric treasures en-shrined in Gaelic. Any one turning to our collections of poetry, especially to Sinclair's " Oranaiche," will at once see that the Highlands are as rich as the Lowlands in song literature, and that the poetry produced, is of an equally high order. There are hundreds of pieces nameless and claimless on the lips of thousands which will continue to be sung as long as there will be a tongue to speak the Gaelic language. Such has been the poetic litera-ture which for ages the Gael has chiefly loved and cherished, and the better recognition of which would enable the Highlander and Lowlander alike to show to the world a body of song such as no country of the size of Scotland has ever yet produced. Many suppose that the ancient language of Caledonia is dead or dying ; —it was never read nor written so extensively as now. And it ought to be further remembered that the lyric genius of the High-land Celt is not confined to what we have in Gaelic. Many men of Gaelic extraction have exhibited their gift of song and music in other spheres. Not to speak of the poets Ferguson and Burns, in whose veins Celtic blood largely flowed, Thomas Campbell, was one of these. Hector Macneill, the hope of Scotland after the the death of Burns, was another. The connection of Lord Macaulay with the lyric genius of the Gael has been already pointed out. The songs of Dr Charles Mackay are known to all the readers of English poetry ; and those of Peter Macneill of Tra nent are on the full tide of popular esteem. The names of George Macdonald and Robert Buchanan are familiar to all the students of contemporary literature. In the kindred spheres of music and the drama we come across the names of Mr Hamish M accunn, Dr A. C. Mackenzie, President of the Royal Academy of Music, and the prima donna Miss Macintyre. Scores of others might be mentioned whose genius is traceable to their Gaelic extraction, there being scarcely a Highland clan name that has not its representative among the crowned sons of song. In the ecclesiastical world the stars of Celtic or Gaelic names are a legion. The position of Archbishop in the great see of York has been attained successively by two men of Gaelic extraction —the eloquent Magee being a descendant of the Mackays of Islay, and his successor MacLagan being a member of a distinguished Highland family which has given us the Gaelic bard Mac-Lagan, a profound Professor of Theology, late of Aberdeen— and now the Archbishop himself.

The survey which we have just taken of our popular poetry clearly indicates that the Gaelic is still the language in which many compose and write. Many would heartily sing thus with Professor Blackie : —

> Is there a Gael that dare despise
> His mither tongue and a' that,
> And clips his words in Saxon wise ?
> He's but a cuif for a' that,
> For a' that, and a' that,
> Their hums and ha's and a' that,
> We'll still be true to speech we drew
> Frae mither's lips for a' that.
>
> The deep, full-breasted Highland tongue,
> Wi' *gairm* and *glaodh* and a' that,
> Ere Roman fought or Greeklings sung,
> Was sounded loud for a' that.
> For a' that, and a' that,
> Their classic lore and a' that,
> On Highland braes the Celtic phrase
> Comes banging out for a' that.

At the same time we have no wish to preserve Gaelic, as Professor Blackie has said, in any artificial or galvanised existence. We merely ask fair-play for it on the scene of linguistic competition.

And this fair-play it is now more than ever likely to receive, the Highlanders having their own representatives now in Parliament and in the county and parochial councils. As long as bards continue to arise—and there is no sign that the supply will be readily exhausted—and the people love to rehearse their strains, so long will the Gaelic remain a living factor in the land. In these pages it is attempted to show the extent and nature of this sort of literature of the people ; but as Highlanders we do not wish, in attempting to bring the literature of our language before the world, to challenge comparison with other bodies of literature. Our main purpose is served if we succeed in showing to our fellow-countrymen, Highland and Lowland, that there are national literary treasures which have been hitherto comparatively overlooked, and which ought in an important degree to add to the already high fame of bonnie Scotland as a land whose glens and bens, whose rivers and lakes are everywhere vocal with songs of love and patriotism.

CHAPTER XV.

"That poet turned him first to pray
In silence ; and God heard the rest,
'Twixt the sun's footsteps down the west."
—E. B. BROWNING.

BEFORE the plough of cruel eviction from their homes cut deep furrows into the Highland heart, the bards, such as Duncan Bàn, loved to sing of the pleasures of the chase ; but the second quarter of the nineteenth century witnessed a change in this respect. A new, if not a revolutionary spirit—at least one of discontent—got abroad throughout the land. This "divine discontent" seized upon the Highland bards, and the burning strains of Maclachlan of Morven and William Livingston, no longer ran in the older moulds of Macintyre and others. The extension of the franchise, the study of history and the science of language, the growing sympathy with oppressed nationalities, the revival of Christian forces, and the increasing value attached to human life, —these and many other "cries of the human," helped forward a movement which may be fitly described as a *Celtic Rennaissance.* This Highland movement was reinforced by kindred and sympathetic influences from Ireland, Wales, and circles of social and linguistic learning on the Continent, until it eventually bore statutory fruit in the Highland Land Act of 1886, which constitutes an Imperial Charter of hereditary right to their native land for the Gaelic-speaking communities of Scotland. This was an achievement which even bards with millennial visions and hopes could scarcely look forward to a generation ago.

The wails of the bards over Highland depopulation, however, nursed the people's discontent as well as their resolution to assert themselves. A good proportion of the authors whose compositions come under notice in this chapter come under the spell of the Celtic Renaissance. Indeed this spirit of national resurrection is the vital force pervading their productions which would be poor and barren without it.

EVAN MACCOLL.

At the head of the Bards of the Victorian era stands Evan MacColl, who was born in 1808 at Kenmore, Lochfyneside, Argyleshire, where his father was a small farmer. Young Mac-Coll eagerly seized on all the sources of culture within his reach, and at an early age became familiar with some of the chief works of English literature. He was born and educated in the midst of strongly Celtic influences and associations which continued to mould his mind and heart throughout his whole career.

In 1836 he published " *The Mountain Minstrel; or, Clarsach nam Beann,*" a series of English and Gaelic poems and songs He is one of the best known of our living Gaelic bards. Fletcher of Dunans and Campbell of Islay, to whom the English and Gaelic parts of his volume are respectively dedicated, befriended the young bard, who had proved himself highly deserving of the patronage they extended to him. The genius of MacColl is entirely lyrical, very few poems of any length having come from his pen. His English songs are generally playful and pleasant, but do not show much depth of passion. His Gaelic poems have the same ring as his English pieces, but are more natural, and show the bard at his ease in the use of language. MacColl is a sweet and intelligent singer, but in real power of thought and expression he is not Livingston's equal. The following verses show MacColl in his more vigorous style :—

" Ho ! landed upon Moidart's coast is Scotland's rightful King ! "
Such was the news to which the Gael once gave warm welcoming ;
And soon, glad-buckling on their arms, stout chiefs and clansmen true
Have sworn in his good cause to try what good broadswords can do.
No cravens they to count the cost of failure ; man alive !
We'll never see their like again—the Clans of 'Forty-five.

Brief time hath passed till Finnan's vale is all alive with men
From east and west in loyal haste proud gathering to their ken
The royal standard is unfurled—their prince himself is there,
Their loving homage to receive, their dangers all to share ;
Grey chiefs, who for his fathers fought, the fire of youth revive,
To stirring pibrochs marshalling the Clans of 'Forty-five.

Let no man say that to restore a deed proscribed they arm—
They think but of *his* loving trust, his Highland heart so warm,
His royal rights usurped—and they upon his princely brow

Would place his father's crown or die. Too well they kept their vow.
Let men who prate of loyalty in this *our* day derive
Instruction in that virtue from the Clans of 'Forty-five.

Ay ! let them think of brave Lochiel and Borrodale the bold—
Of Keppoch and Glengarry, too, those chiefs of iron mould—
The Chisholm, Cluny, Brahan's lord, the Mackintosh so keen,
The Appin Stuarts and MacColls, the ~~mighty~~ Maclean, *dauntless*
With many a Chief and Clan besides, who quickly did contrive
To make theirnames immortal in the famous 'Forty-five !

The poet, who entered the Liverpool Custom-House in 1839 through W. F. Campbell of Islay, M.P. then for Argyleshire, removed to Canada in 1850, where in a similar position at Kingston he remained until he was superannuated in 1880. The venerable poet, now in the eighty-third year of his age, resides in Canada, where a son of his is an able Congregational minister, and a daughter known as a poetess of much merit.

None of the Gaelic bards had a wider acquaintance, nor a larger outlook of life than MacColl. But in the midst of all new associations and attractions, he remained at heart frankly and even sternly Highland. The following verse of an address (1878), to a well-known Highland patriot, Mr John Murdoch, illustrates this phase of his character :—

> I think I see thy manly form,
> Firm and unyielding as Cairngorm,
> The poor man's cause maintaining warm,
>   Just like a true-souled Highlander ;
> I see the scorn within thine eye
> *As some evicting Chief goes by*—
> One whose forbears would sooner die
>   Than dispossess a Highlander.

Before Celtic things were held in such esteem as they are now, or rather, perhaps, before their value was appreciated as recently, men of Celtic extraction like Macaulay and Charles Mackay wrote of the Highlanders and Highlands, not only without discrimination and sympathy, but without knowledge, and even in a spirit of savage contempt. The latter lived to express regret for his earlier conduct ; the former had not the same opportunity of modifying his earlier impressions, and his Highland fellow-countrymen were not slow to declare their minds on the subject. Among those who sought to pay back the illustrious historian in his own coin was Evan MacColl. On the occasion of Macaulay's death some one had written " Macaulay now is registered among Eng-

land's mighty dead!" On this MacColl wrote verses the first
and last of which are as follows :—

> Hech, sirs! "Macaulay's registered
> 'Mong England's mighty dead!"
> Let us hope that he lies buried near
> Her first mean-mighty Ned.
> Scotland can never well forget
> The zeal of those two men,—
> The one to stab her with the sword—
> The other with the pen.
>
> .   .   .   .
>
> But let that pass,—he's there—John Bull
> Is not so much to blame ;
> He lived to magnify John's rule,—
> John magnifies *his* name.
> The wonder, after all, is how
> John could be fooled so far
> As a mere meteoric light
> To worship as a star.

The warm and generous heart of the bard is revealed in much of
his poetry. His little poem, *Let us do the best we can*, shows his
sympathy with the struggling poor :—

> Mark yon worldling lost in self,
>   Dead to every social glow ;
> Wouldst thou, to own all his pelf,
>   All life's purer joys forego ?
> Truest wealth is doing good—
>   Doctrine strange to him, poor man !
> ·If we can't do all we would,
>   Let us do the best we can.

One of the best criticisms on MacColl's poetry comes from the
pen of Hugh Miller : " There is more of fancy than of imagination in the poetry of MacColl, and more of thought and imagery
than of feeling. In point, glitter, polish, he is the Moore of
Highland song. Comparison and ideality are the leading features
of his mind. Some of the pieces in this volume are sparkling
tissues of comparison from beginning to end."

JAMES MUNRO.

A little volume, *Am Filldh*, mostly written by James Munro
(1840), author of the "Gaelic Grammar," contains a great deal of
first-class poetry. In the composition of small pieces of the sentimental kind, Munro is scarcely inferior to Livingston in fresh

ness and condensation, and is MacColl's equal. We have in the "Filidh" several pieces by other hands, as well as excellent translations from the English. Munro was a man of thorough culture, and profoundly acquainted with the extent and idioms of the Gaelic language. Of all this there is undoubted evidence in his poetry. Here is a rendering of one of Munro's songs, which is attached to a very fine air:—

Dark winter is going;
Kind breezes are blowing;
The mountains are glowing
    With colours more fair.

The face of the flowers
Grows fresh 'neath the showers;
And warmer the bowers
    Appear in the glare.

The summer advances
With heat-shedding glances;
His sunny beam dances
    With joy on the cold.

The little birds singing,
The woodlands are ringing;
The primrose is springing
    To deck the green wold.

The sun in fresh power
Calls forth bird and bower
In robes of fair flower
    Enchanting to see

But, honey-lipt lover,
Thy charms I look over;
In them I discover
    Sweet beauties more rare.

Come with me, then, dearest,
To woodlands the nearest,
To plight troth sincerest
    Of love evermore.

JOHN MACLACHLAN.

The late Dr Maclachlan of Rahoy, in Morven, stands high as a poet. A little volume of his poems was published in 1868. Like all the singers whose works have become popular in the Highlands, all that he wrote was intended to be sung. He looks at nature as a man of culture and tender sympathies, and with an independent eye; and what he sings comes with all the freshness of the evening breeze as it sweeps o'er the Highland loch. One theme he especially dwells on—the depopulation of the High-lands. His heart is saddened as he sees the Lowland shepherd, who has no sympathy with the place, the people, or their language, treading with his dogs the glens and hillsides where many expatri-ated Gaels had once their happy homes. He has also written several love lyrics which are admirable in conception and expres-sion. A song on "Drink," *Cha'n òl mi deur tuille*, is the best of that sort in the language. Dr Maclachlan lived all his days in Morven, beside his accomplished neighbour, the Rev. Dr John MacLeod, himself a man of no mean poetic powers. Although a skilful practitioner, and possessing considerable talents, he never sought for a more ambitious sphere. He loved the people around —he was widely known—and they loved him in return. He never married, and he lived till he was an old man, not perhaps less liked by his neighbours for his weakness for a dram, which he and they thought a necessary beverage in chill and misty Morven. Here is a translation, well executed by Mr H. Whyte, of one of Maclachlan's poems :—

O lovely glen ! as through a haze
    Of tears that dim mine eye,
Upon thy futile fields I gaze,
    Fair as in days gone by.

Thy stately pines their tall heads rear
    O'er fairy knolls and braes ;
Thy purling streamlets now I hear,
    Like music's sweetest lays.

Thy herds are feeding as of yore
    With sheep upon the lea ;
The heron fishes in the shore,
    The white-gull on the sea.

The cuckoo's voice is heard at dawn,
    The dove coos in the tree ;
The lark, above thy grassy lawn,
    Now carols loud with glee.

Repose supremely reigns o'er all,
    Low crowns the mountains hoar ;
And vividly they now recall
    The days that are no more.

Thy gurgling brooks, and winds that fleet
    Through groves of stately pine,
Awaken with their converse sweet
    Sad thoughts of auld lang syne.

Thy peaceful dwellings, once so bright,
    In dreary ruins lie ;

The traveller sees not from the height
The smoke ascending high.

To yonder garden once thy pride,
No one attention shows,
And weeds grow thickly side by side,
Where bloomed the blushing rose.

Where are the friends of worthy fame,
Their hearts on kindness bent ;
Whose welcome cheered me when I came,
Who blessed me as I went ?

Full many in the churchyard sleep,
The rest are far away,
And I forlorn in silence weep,
With neither friend nor stay.

Death in my breast has fixed his dart,
My heart is growing cold,
And from this world I'll soon depart,
To rest beneath the mould.

A new edition of his poems, with a sketch of his life from the pen
of Dr Cameron Gillies, was published some twelve years ago
under the auspices of the Glasgow Morven Association, whose
members had also in hand the erection of a monument to the
bard's memory.

ANGUS MACDONALD.

The compositions of Angus Macdonald, the Glen-Urquhart
Bard, show poetic genius of a high order in the few poems of
his which have yet seen the light. He has left some poems in
manuscript which it is hoped, will some day be published. The
poems in the *Gael* and in the *Inverness Transactions* remind us
of the productions of very kindred spirits. Livingston and R.
Macdougall. He and Livingston seem to have diligently cultivated the style and manner of Ossian, particularly of the Gaelic
of 1807. . He was a master of rich idiomatic Gaelic, and having
also the "accomplishment of verse," he could make himself terrible or tender, just as his muse was stirred. He had a particularly true eye for the beauties of nature ; and was always accurate
and graphic in his descriptions. He possessed a keen and cultivated ear—was a teacher of music for some time ; so his verse is
full of melody and harmonious cadences. He excelled in poetry
of the Ossianic type ; but, like all masters of the art, he shows
also much tenderness in his love lyrics. He was appointed the
first bard of the Inverness Gaelic Society, an office filled by Mrs

Mackellar afterwards.   He received in 1869 a medal for a prize poem from "The Club of True Highlanders," London.   His daughter, Mrs A. Mackenzie of Inverness, has inherited some of her father's genius, and is herself the author of compositions of considerable excellence.

MARY MACKELLAR.

A volume of goodly size, *Poems and Songs : Gaelic and English*, by this poetess, was published in 1881.   Mary Mackellar has for many years been well-known as a woman of bright poetic powers ; and her talents in this respect were sometime ago recognised by the Gaelic Society of Inverness, when she was appointed Bard. Her poems are characterised by much vigour and freshness, and evince a subtlety of conception which is quite beyond the ability of the ordinary Gaelic versifiers.   It is premature yet to judge what position she may take among the Gaelic bards.   Her songs, superior as some of them are, have not yet been accorded much popularity.   There is a sort of straining—an occasional abstruse Browning element in her Gaelic pieces—which is probably the cause of this, and which has evidently resulted from too close a following of the abstract conceptions of modern English poets, the natural utterance of which Gaelic is somewhat unfitted for. She possesses keen and nervous sensibilities, and looks at nature with a warm, sympathetic, and observant eye.   Like the brook from the gully she bursts forth with rich thought and melody ; but her poems frequently want breadth of basis.   She has generally the true inspiration, but she does not manage sufficiently to lose her self-consciousness—to fall into that state of *abandon* which is needed for the production of the highest forms of poetry.   At the same time she has proved herself one of the best Gaelic poetesses the Highlands has produced.   Her English pieces are vigorous and readable.   They are not inferior to her Gaelic poems, although occasionally exhibiting want of Wordsworth's "accomplishment of verse" so keenly felt by Hugh Miller in his own case. All Highlanders welcomed Mary Mackellar's excellent contribution to their native literature.   She died in 1890 in Edinburgh, and members of the Cameron Clan—her maiden name being Cameron—accompanied her remains to their final resting-place in her native Lochaber.

DUGALD MACPHAIL.

This cultivated poet, a native of Mull, author of *An t-Eilein Muileach*, one of the popular songs in the language, was a man of strong and well-cultivated intellect, who did not at all give us what might be expected from one of his rich poetic endowments. But what he has done is first-class. The most of it will be found in the "Oranaiche." Macphail was also known as a most effective Gaelic speaker, as well as a clever writer of Gaelic stories. He has done good work in translating religious productions, his translation of MacLaurin's magnificent sermon on "Glorying in the Cross of Christ" being one of the best little books in the Gaelic language.

There are several minor bards whose names have for a long time been known in different parts of the Highlands—

ROBERT MACDOUGALL, author of "A Gaelic Guide" to Canada, where he resided for some time, published an interesting volume of poems in 1840. Along with original pieces of great merit he gives a translation of *Tam o' Shanter*, and of some poems of Byron, whom he somewhat imitated. He was the first, along with James Munro, of the new school of poetry to which Livingston, Angus Macdonald, and others of the present day belong.

ARCHIBALD CAMPBELL, of Kinloch-Earn, brought out a neat volume of songs and poems in 1831. One or two of them have become very popular. His style is unaffected, and the sentiment natural. The whole volume is fully of average merit.

JOHN CAMERON, of Ballachulish, author of "Dan Spioradail" (1862), has written several poems and songs of considerable merit. The best-known is *Duil ri Baile-ehaolais fhaicinn*. Like Mary Mackellar, Cameron did not continue a worshipper at the shrine of the sacred Muse, to which he seems to have been devoted in his early days.

JOHN CAMPBELL, of Leadaig, is well-known as the author of several excellent poems, one of which has been translated by Professor Blackie. There is much taste as well as evidence of fair culture in all that Campbell has written. His poetry is distinguished by the pastoral sweetness and light of a simple Highland life.

JOHN MACKORKINDALE, a native of Islay, afterwards in Canada, possesses true poetic insight, and had he continued to cultivate Gaelic poetry he could produce excellent work. Parts of a poetic dialogue on "Dun Bhrusgraidh" by him were reprinted in the first volume of *The Gael.*

GEORGE CAMPBELL, late of Kinabus, in the same island, composed a great deal of poetry of more than average merit, but his compositions were never collected and published. *Fuirich a Ribhinn phriseal* is to be found in the " Oranaiche." The maiden addressed is Jean Wodrow, daughter of the Kildalton minister, who published in 1771 a mellifluous rhyming version of *Fingal*, founded on Macpherson's English.

THE REV. DONALD MACRAE, a native of Plockton, late of Ness, Lewis, was a true poet, although he did not produce much. A sweet, pathetic poem,˙by him, *The Emigrant's Lament*, written on the occasion of many of his congregation in Lewis leaving for Canada, has been much admired, and has been translated into English by a daughter of late Rev. Dr Gibson of Glasgow :—

THE EMIGRANT'S LAMENT.

We've gone to the shore,
With those who no more
Shall see their own isle
    For ever.

Th' iron ship's now their home,
Through white, curling foam
They speed, some in joy,
    Some weeping.

See childhood's glad eye ;
But list woman's sigh !
Even manhood's stout heart
    Is breaking !

Hot streaming tears flow,
Now silent in woe,
They're looking behind
    In sorrow.

Still sailing on west,
From the land they love best,
They gaze upon nought
    But Muirneag !

See Muirneag depart !
Dear hill of their heart
Now lost to their view
    For ever !

'Tis sunk in the sea,
Each cheek becomes pale !
Oh ! list yon wild wail
    For Muirneag !

Dear friends, loved so well,
Are left far behind,

Fond bleeding hearts swell
With anguish !

The bereaved pastor continues the wail further in a more religious
strain, hoping—

,   When time shall have passed
            May all meet at last,
            Safe at yon fair haven,
                In glory !

WILLIAM LIVINGSTON.

The Bard of Lochfyne is probably the best-known hitherto of
the Gaelic *singers* of this century ; but his place is disputed by
the sweet lyrist of Rahoy.   Though not so popular as these two,
as a mere singer, because he has produced so few songs suitable
for singing, William Livingston must be regarded as the most
powerful poetic personality among the Celtic bards of this century.
Like Browning among the English poets, Livingston is less known
than minor claimants for bardic recognition, because the general
reader of Gaelic poetry is not always capable of appreciating anything higher in the poetic scale than smooth flowing verse and
mellifluous rhymes that make no demand on the severer exercise
of thought.   But his position as a bard among his contemporaries
has been more than once recognised by a few of the most distinguished Celtic scholars and critics of his time.   In competition
for prizes offered by the Glasgow Celtic Society, on three occasions Livingston obtained the first prize, some of the adjudica-
tors being the late Rev. Dr Smith of Inverary ; the late Rev.
Duncan MacNab of Renfield Free Church, Glasgow ; and the late
Rev. Duncan MacLean of Glenorchy ;—the last being himself a
sacred poet of very considerable genius.   Many of his competitors
on these occasions are authors of very popular songs, but their
productions must be credited with more rhyme than poetic
power.

William Livingston was born in Gartmain, in Islay, in the year
1808.   There are not many of his kith and kin in that island now,
nor is there any evidence that his humble progenitors were anything else than some of those nomadic individuals or families, of a
Celto-Germanic character, unconnected particularly with any of
the well-known clans, but who, in the political economy of the
Highlands were ranged under the name of " siol Dhomhnuill," or
some other, and in latter days became more unreasonably Celtic

in their race antipathies than the purer Celts themselves. The late notorious Mitchell and the present leaders of the Irish Home Rulers are Irish instances of what has been stated. The bard Livingston is a Scottish instance ; and the proximity of his native place to Ireland's northern coasts may have some suggestive value, especially when his training, or rather no training, and the sources of his historical and social knowledge are taken into consideration. There is another Livingstone of Highland extraction— his family were originally from Mull—who has had some connection with Glasgow like his namesake the bard ; but Dr David Livingstone, the devoted and distinguished African traveller, turned his attention and directed his labours to the amelioration of the condition of Africa's benighted and dusky children. Livingstone, the traveller, regarded all the sons of humanity, whether they were black or white, of whatever race, as the sons of the one great Father, equally good and precious in his sight, and all of one blood ; but Livingston the bard devoted all his energies to the patriotic rehearsal, in prose and verse, of the doughty deeds and ancient prowess of our Scottish ancestors ; with him the Scotsman alone ought to occupy the position of lord of creation, especially if it could be proved he was a Celt,—and the Englishman especially, on account of his continual oppression of the smaller kingdom of Scotland, he, like Irishmen of a certain order, regarded with intense dislike, as the universal tyrant throughout the civilised world. The bones of the distinguished traveller Dr Livingstone were deposited in their final resting-place in Westminster Abbey amid the sympathetic tears of all civilised nations. He was a cosmopolitan patriot, one of the few extraordinary men whom God vouchsafes in the progress of the ages for the enlightenment of the dark places of the earth and the promotion of the highest interests of universal humanity. Livingston, the bard, whose pursuit after knowledge under unusually unfavourable conditions, and whose indomitable perseverance and fervour of heart were not unlike those of David Livingstone had but a very limited vision of the functions of his mission into the world. The duties which he assigned to himself were the magnifying of Scotland's fame and glory, the lashing in Wallace and Bruce fashion of the Teutonic intruder from the south of the Tweed, and the special vindication of the Celtic character from the continual aspersions of the uncircumcised Saxon. He did his work with a will, but there was no need for it. It was as uncalled for as Thomson's work on *Liberty*, which, undertaken in an unwise moment, notwithstanding its fine poetry, the public, not without reason, condemned to "gather spiders and to harbour dust." When highly needed work goes without its reward it cannot be a matter of surprise that unnecessary ebullitions of patriotism do not always pay ; so poor Livingston, like not a few of the order of Bards, died somewhat neglected in an obscure street of the philanthropic city of Glasgow. But he did not die unknown to a few sympathising friends. The members of the Islay Association and others were always anxious to relieve the necessities of the poet when his temper and ways made it possible to be of some service to him. In some respects his own independence was like that proud independence of his native country, of which he was so fervent a singer. He died in 1870, his wife predeceasing him a few weeks.

Much of the character of Livingston is traceable to his up-bringing. In youth he received no education, and his earliest training when a boy was herding cattle. Was not Rob Donn, the Sutherlandshire Bard, also a herd ? But it was thought fit to set the embryo herd-poet to learn a trade, and he served his time at tailoring, which he carried on in a desultory fashion all his days, and in which he was intelligently and sympathetically assisted by his frugal wife. He was thus a grown-up man before he got any education, and all he ever got was self-taught ; and had his pride permitted him to tell the story of his struggles after knowledge, English, Latin, French, Greek, and a little Hebrew, it would fur-nish an interesting chapter in the annals of the pursuit of learning under difficulties. The manuscripts of his in possession of the writer show the extraordinary pains he took with his work—his endeavours after a purer English style, even when well-advanced in years—and what a long time he was a wooer of the muses be-fore he arrived at the intensity of poetical conception which dis-tinguished his later poetry. His earlier efforts do not seem to have been very successful, and they are of a somewhat humorous character. He almost stands alone among the prominent Gaelic bards in having given us no love songs. The reason is that he was probably a married man before the dormant powers of his poetic nature awakened. While there is much tenderness in all his descriptions of nature, the reader of his poetry must feel that he is always surrounded by an atmosphere of martial enthusiasm and intense patriotic sentiment. He was too wise to attempt the singing of a passion the power of which did not evidently per-meate his nature ; but the love of fatherland, the story of the gory struggle of Scottish independence were to him all-absorbing sources of inspiration ; and to these he always turns, and finds in them the congenial themes on which he enthusiastically lavishes the rich poetic gifts with which he was endowed.

Livingston published his first volume of poetry in 1858. A smaller volume followed a few years afterwards, in 1865 ; and in 1868 a few poems in pamphlet form, one of them being a prize production—being the third piece for which he received a prize from the Glasgow Celtic Society. The year before his death he began to arrange his poems with a view to publishing them all in one volume, but before he transcribed more than half a dozen of them his pen was arrested by an invisible Power.

> ".Death's subtle seed within,
> Sly treacherous miner ! working in the dark
> Smiled at the well-concerted scheme."

I well remember how the old bard, with his magnificent beard, which he often stroked with evident admiration, and which seemed to be growing up to his very eyes—small piercing eyes that scanned the neighbours suspiciously—emphasised the hope that when the proposed volume would appear, it would contain fully as much first-class poetry as the works of either of the three Gaelic modern bards, Mackay, Macintyre, or Macdonald. It is pleasant to know that the work which the bard had so much at heart has been accomplished under the auspices of the Islay Association, mainly at the suggestion and with the assistance of a patriotic countryman—Mr Colin Hay—who is a great admirer of Livingston's poetry.

The longest of Livingston's poems is a dramatic piece entitled *The Danes in Islay.* It is the only proper dramatic poem in the language. The subject is one that the poet could take up with much enthusiasm, as he pictured to himself the Norse army in a fleet of sixty-three sail entering the spacious Lochindaul, and dropping anchor there with no friendly intent. The bard's historical and antiquarian knowledge stood him here in good stead. The great Macdonald, Prince of the Isles, is the central figure, and next to him the aged but faithful Mackay of Rhinns, both of whom are immediately informed by their watchful scouts of the advent of those hereditary foes, the Norse invaders, on the green shores of Islay, which was once in their own possession. The fiery cross is sent all over the island to call together the brave subjects of the Macdonald to defend their homes and hearths. A battle takes place ; and in the final struggle there are many heroes

20

who do great and incredible deeds, chief among whom are—
Nuagan Mor, a Norse prince; Raosbun, Gilleathain Thora, and
Donncha Mor Laorain. Though this is one of the most ambitious
of Livingston's productions, yet it is not equal as a whole, and not
so finished, nor of so high an order as, for example. his prize
poems ; but the lyrical portions of it are very fine, the marching
song of Mackay of Rhinns, to the tune of *Mnathan a' Ghlinne so*,
being quite a gem. Here are some verses of a war chant which
occurs in the poem. The Norse invaders are supposed to rehearse
the following wild and fierce lyric as they drop anchor in the harbour of Lochindaul :—

> Here we come, but we thus will not leave you—
>   The axe, axe ;   •
> To-morrow will startle and grieve you
>   With the axe, the axe.
> A red blazing torch in each dwelling—
>   The axe, the axe ;
> Your goods plundered, your captured wives yelling—
>   The axe, the axe.
> Fleeing, and cursing, and wailing—
>   The knife, knife ;
> The girth of your knees shall be failing
>   For the knife, knife,
> They who meet us shall leave that place never—
>   The knife, knife ;
> Morn or eve shall they see them for ever—
> ·   The knife, knife ;
> None shall live to tell of the Reaver
>   With the axe, axe ;
> But the raven above shall be croaking—
>   The axe, axe ;
> And then feast on their limbs till he's choking—
>   The axe, axe.
> You now live who in blood then shall welter—
>   The knife, knife ;
> Cave or hole cannot hide you or shelter
>   From the knife, knife.
> Through your throats the hoarse chorus ascending—
>   The knife, knife ;
> In that cry screams and groans shall keep blending—
>   The knife, knife.
> All these ills shall your great men entangle—
>   The axe, axe—
> Ere their heads on our green withs shall dangle—
>   The axe, axe;
> The nerves of their necks we will rend them—
>   With the axe, axe ;
> To the anvil to roast then we'll send them—
>   The axe, axe—

> The head of Mackay shall we shinty—
> The axe, axe—
> Down the Rhinns, where his kin shall grow scanty,
> With the axe, axe.

The *Danes in Islay* is not the only *cath* or battle that the bard has sought to immortalise in tough classical Celtic. We have also several vigorous poems on the battles of Scotland's earlier struggles for independence. Livingston's muse is nearly wholly of a martial order, which, while it explains his want of popularity among what he would regard as a somewhat effeminate generation, is the more remarkable when it is remembered how purely sentimental the most of his contemporary bards have been. The titles of three other poems are—*The Battle of Mona Phraca*, *The Battle of Dail-righ*—regarded as his best—and that of *Tra-Ghruinard*, where the great Sir Lachlan MacLean of Duart fell, pierced by the fatal shaft of the dwarf *Dubh-Shee*, who offered services the Knight of Duart despised. The dwarf is described by the bard in pretty expressive terms—" *Treoich a ghuir an Diabhul 'san Lag an Diura !* " The best of all his poems is the 100 lines (the number was limited) prize poem on the achievements of the Highland regiments in the Crimean war. There is nothing better, and not many poems equal to it in the whole range of Celtic poetry. The best-known of his poems is *Fios thun a' Bhaird*, or Word to the Bard, supposed to have been sent to him in Glasgow from a farmer's wife in Islay, the late Mrs Blair, of Lonban, who showed much kindness to the bard when on a visit to his native island, and whose son is the popular minister, the Rev. Robert Blair, who was a constant friend of Livingston, and who edited the complete edition of his works (1881). In this delightful poem he describes in stanzas of great beauty and tenderness the changes that have taken place, the ruins of the depopulated districts, and the natural scenery of the island. The following are the opening stanzas of the *Message to the Bard :—*

> The morn is bright with sunshine,
>   And soft the west wind sighs ;
> The loch is calm and quiet,
>   Since peace reigns in the skies.
> Bedecked with canvas gaily,
>   Barks glide unwearily ;
> To the Bard rehearse the story
>   Of these things I hear and see.
> This is the month of blossom,
>   When the herds of cattle go

To the glens of lonely corries,
　Where they neither reap nor sow.
But in these green-clad inches
　My kine now never be :
To the Bard rehearse the story
　Of these things I hear and see.

On heathy heights in thousands
　Stray flocks of kine and sheep ;
And deer rush o'er the wild steeps
　Where freshening breezes sweep—
The noble antlered race
　Bedewed that tread the hills with glee,
To the Bard rehearse the story
　Of these things I hear and see.

One of the most admired of Livingston's poems is that on the
achievements of the Highland regiments under Sir Colin Campbell in the Crimean War. As much of its beauty consists in a
sort of proverbial form of expression, of which the bard was a
consummate master, and in a rhythm of consonantal rhymes,
much of what is powerful in the original becomes quite prosaic
when rendered literally into English. Here is the first half of the
poem, which may indicate something of its manner :—

ALMA.

Tidings of awe came to my ear—
An ominous threat that war was near ;
I sought out Albin's central height,
To view the distant scene of fight.
I saw beneath one standard there—
The figure of the Northern Bear.
There thousands in their armèd might
Panted for battle's fierce delight.
O'er Alma's heights the Russians rolled,
Defiant, warlike, keen, and bold ;
In war-array the hostile force
Stood there in ranks of foot and horse ;
Then came the order for the Gael
Those scarpy brows of death to scale.
Down from that hoary rocky crest
Poured showers of fire into their breast ;
Forward the fearless heroes leapt ;
Mid clouds of slaughter on they swept ;
" For Victory " the Lion roared ;
The Finian clans unsheathed the sword,
Like rapid swollen floods in Clyde ;
Grand, swift as Es-linn's silver tide ;
So rushed the heroes in their might
Of ardour to the field of fight,

Beneath that proud, unconquered shred
Of ancient fame the Gaels were led ;—
With those broad brands ye did unsheathe
Ye left destruction, groans, and death ;—
Ye from the land of hill and flood
Heroic thus the foe withstood ;
And from those rocky heights of woe,
Ye swept disgraced that host of snow.
They trembled as they saw with dread
The lion, rousing, raging, red,
To scatter with resistless force
And ire their columns, man and horse ;
Deeds sure to kindle our emotion
While earth remaineth wed to ocean.

BALACLAVA.

'Mid thund'ring guns and clash of arms
I saw amass the Russian swarms
   On Balaclava's dusky plain ;
There waved the eagle fierce and fell
   To widen more its ravenous reign,
Like a foul bird of restless hell.
Thousands responding bent on prey,
And gorging blood her power obey ;
The hoarse-voiced horn began to bray ;
The steeds of war began to neigh, &c.

Notwithstanding his exceeding patriotism it cannot be said that
Livingston was either very generous or magnanimous.   While,
haunted with painful suspicions he allowed the canker of vin-
dictiveness to mar the finer elements of his nature.   His envy
also rendered him almost intolerable to all his Highland literary
friends in Glasgow.   But these, as one of them once remarked,
could afford to prize all that was good in the bard and overlook
his shortcomings.   When this friend was dying William came to
ask his forgiveness, which he was assured he had, with the remark, " William, my ghost will not trouble you." This gentleman knew the bard's selfish motive in asking pardon, and the
superstitious reason for his so doing.   Notwithstanding all this,
the man was not many days in his grave when the bard began to
attack him in a scurrilous letter in the newspapers, which, however, was not inserted.   He might be described as a Celtic
brother of Walter Savage Landor, whom he resembled in several
respects.   But the sphere of life in which Livingston was born,
and his want of early education, ought to make us charitable in
our judgments of the savage element of his character.   It must be

acknowledged, at the same time, that beneath the barbarian patriotism of his nature there lay a depth of tenderness and warmth of a grateful heart, which we discern in several of his pieces on individual persons.   There can be no doubt, also, that many of his eccentricities arose from finding himself out of joint in the social world, where mere patriotism or poetic talent cannot frequently obtain the means or influence which self-conscious spirits so hopelessly look for.

Blar Shunadail, a piece of considerable length and merit, was published in *The Gael* after his death.   The only other piece of importance is *Driod-fhortan Imhir an Racain*, a poem of five or six hundred lines long.

It ought to be mentioned that two gentlemen, one belonging to Kintyre and the other to Cowal, were constant friends to Living-ston—the late Mr Gilchrist, printer, Glasgow, and also Mr Duncan Whyte, of the same city.   Livingston was intensely Celtic in all his ideas and habits.   He has written a good deal of prose in English ; but in that language he is like a lion in chains.   He published "A Vindication of the Celtic Character," a goodly volume of strong Celtic feeling and prejudice, such as we would now expect from an Irish Celt ; also, several parts of a history of Scotland, which he did not finish, he and the publishers having disagreed on account of the strong anti-English feeling dis-played by the writer.   He swallowed the old Scottish chroniclers, especially their anti-English prejudices, and accepted as pure truth all that they have recorded.   The Scotsman of the days of Bruce and Wallace scarcely cherished so much of the spirit of nationality and animosity against England as Livingston did.   At the same time there was an element of hollowness in his assumed patriot ism, into which, however, he sought to thoroughly work himself, like some others of his countrymen of the present day.   It can scarcely be denied that an element of unhealthiness prevailed in the moral basis of his nature ; but unlike many others of the Highland poets, the smallest trace cannot be found in his works A few years ago a monument was erected to his memory in Jane. field Cemetery, Glasgow.   Well has he described his own spirit in the following quatrain of Scotch :—

> We see the buckles glancin'
> On his *fraochan* shoon,
> *He'll mak' the Lawlands Hielan'*
> Ere he'll lea' the toun.

NEIL MACLEOD.

This author, the son of the well known *Bard Sgiathanach*, Donald Macleod, is undoubtedly chief among the living singers of the Gael. Several of his songs have become very popular, such as *An Gleann 'san robh mi Og*. All his productions are characterised by purity of style and idiom, freshness of conception and gentleness of spirit, and liquid sweetness of versification. His "Clarsach an Doire" contains as much variety of good popular songs as any volume of a single author in the language. The Gaelic Society of Inverness has just appointed him to the position of Bard to the Society in succession to Mary Mackellar. May he long live to wear his laurels, and continue to delight his countrymen with new songs of his native land and people.

REV. DONALD MACCALLUM.

The Rev. Donald Maccallum, a native of central Argyleshire, now a parish minister in Lewis, is the author of a small volume of songs and poems entitled *Sop as gach Seid*. His works evince a genuine poetic spirit,—a quiet meditative mood and thoughtful observation that so many parts of the Highlands are so well fitted to produce and nurse. Mr Maccallum has perfect command over the language and the "mechanic exercise" of verse ; but he will probably be more remembered in Highland history as almost the only minister of the State Church in Scotland who had the moral courage to stand up for the people in the struggle of the crofter agitation in the years 1883-86.

DR JOHN MACGREGOR.

This writer, Surgeon-Major Macgregor, M.D., of the Bombay Army, a native of Lewis, has kept alive the Gaelic muse for many years in the far-off fields of Hindostan. In that land of many languages and many races Dr Macgregor composed many excellent lyrics in his native tongue of the Gael, and got them printed there as well. In the midst of his honourable and successful career, the poet's fancies continually turn to home scenes and dear ones left in the old country. Memories of *Mairi na h-Airidh*, " Mary of the Shieling," or some others, find pleasant embalmment in smooth-flowing verse. In 1890 appeared a long English poem from his pen, *The Girdle of the Globe*, which has been very well received by many who are well-entitled to judge, some of the lyrics scattered throughout the cantos showing the spirit and power of utterance of the true poet. We look foɪ much more some of these days from his pen, especially when, as he may do before long, he retires from the honourable service of his country to cultivate the favours of the muse at home.

MARY MACPHERSON.

Mrs Macpherson (née Macdonald), a native of Skye, had some bitter experiences of life some twenty years ago or more, when she was about fifty years of age, and then her latent powers of verse-making began to assert themselves. In recent years she has composed largely on themes of local interest,—on the land question, her favourites among those by whom this question has been kept alive, and on her own personal grievances. Like Rob Donn she has been very fortunate in having some *patroni* who have patriotically espoused the cause of her muse and borne the expense of publishing in excellent style her compositions. The highly competent pens of Mr John Whyte and Mr Alexander MacBain have helped in the production of the volume (Inverness, 1891). The one took down the poems in correct writing from the composer's dictation, while the other has supplied an introductory biographical sketch. The portraits of the poetess in various attitudes representative of Highland home industry are a good feature of the volume.

——o——

If we follow the Highlander across the ocean we find him there as fond of poetry and song as he was in his original home. The Rev. D. B. Blair, of Canada, has contributed a good deal to Gaelic literature. He is the author of many original poems of much merit, one on the Falls of Niagara being particularly excellent. He has translated parts of Virgil's Æneid from the Latin. It was said some time ago that he had ready for the press a Gaelic grammar and a new Gaelic version of the Psalms.

The Rev. A. M. Sinclair, of Nova Scotia, is also a worshipper of the muse. He, indeed, belongs to a family of bards. The Gaels on this side are particularly indebted to Maclean Sinclair for his valuable contributions to their literature, his last two volumes (1890) being a handsome addition to the catalogue of good Highland books

But it is not in America alone that we find the cultivation of the Gaelic muse. If we go to New Zealand we find there Farquhar Macdonnell, once of Plockton, a composer of considerable genius, and one of whose songs has become a popular favourite.

It is not only in Canada and New Zealand but also in Australia that the Gaelic muse is kept alive.   Here are verses of a pretty poem in Gaelic and English by the Rev. A. Cameron, a native of Lochaber, from that broad continent in the Antipodes.   The author holds communion with the Ree waterfall, Nether-Lochaber, in a dream :—

> I gaze on thee thou wondrous fall !
> As I had done long years ago ;
> I travelled far on duty's call
>   Since last I saw thy currents flow.
>
> In days gone by, when joy was young,
>   'Twas my delight to sit me here ;
> When thy grave voice, so full and strong.
>   A pleasant song was to mine ear.
>
> Methinks I hear thy waters say,
>   In greeting accents bathed in tears,
> " Where did thy wandering footsteps stray
>   These many long and weary years ?
>
> " I missed thee on the rocky brink,
>   Thy youthful shadow on the pool,
> When thou would'st say as thou would'st think
>   Thy daily lesson for the school :
>
> " When none but I was to thee near
>   Save He who guides our weary ways,
> To whom creation all is dear,
>   As joining in His glory's praise."

We have thus seen that throughout India, America, and Aus- tralasia we can find singers and composers of Gaelic songs, repre- senting leal-hearted sons of the Highlands, who have nobly served their country, their people, and their God.

CHAPTER XVI.

" O happy saints ! rejoice and sing !
He quickly comes, your Lord and King ! "
—W. D. MACLAGAN, D.D., *Abp. of York.*

THE religious Highlander of the present day is known to be
stubbornly opposed to the use of hymns of human authorship in
public worship. His prejudice was deepened and played upon
recently in connection with a Union controversy between two
well-known ecclesiastical bodies. One result has been that many
of the southern Highlanders who were in the habit of using the
translated Scripture Paraphrases have discontinued the practice.
But notwithstanding the prejudices of many Highlanders against
hymns, all the writers of sacred poetry have been very popular
among them. There were many authors of religious poetry
whose compositions did not become much known until the beginning of this century. To this class belonged *John Ban Maor* and
Bean a' Bharra, under whose names a good deal of verse appears
in a collection by Duncan Kennedy of Melfort, who plays a rather
unenviable part in the Ossianic controversy. The names of other
two authors also occur in the volume—Macindeor and Mackeich.
Macfadyen, a Glasgow student, published a volume of hymns in
1770, but nothing more is known of him or his work.

WILLIAM MACKENZIE.

This poet was born at Balvicphadrick, on the estate of Culduthel, near Inverness. His father, who was a farmer at Burlum,
bestowed some pains on the education of William, who, after his
marriage, rented successively the farms of Bailedubh, in Tordar-
roch, and that of Cnocbui, in the parish of Daviot. He afterwards
gave up farming, and was appointed by the Society for Propagating Christian Knowledge to teach one of their schools at Leys, in
the parish of Croy, some three miles from Inverness. He laboured
there as teacher and evangelist for forty years. He died in 1838

at the advanced age of ninety, and was buried in the churchyard of Dunlichity. Mackenzie appears to have been a man of fair culture and was well read. His poetry, although not first first-class, has a masculine, sensible ring about it. A good deal of it consists of excellent sermon matter, expressed in clear natural language and smooth and flowing verse. Scripture history and the usual evangelical doctrines of Christianity with an underlying practical application, constitute his general theme. He has also composed several elegies and addresses to persons. The poet deals thus with a certain class of religious professors :—

> Bheir iad cuireadh dhuitse dh'òl
> Le daimh is mòran carthannas ;
> 'S bidh iad cho cràbhach an àm,
> 'S gu'm feum thu'n dràm a bheannachadh.

ENGLISH :

> They will invite thee to the drink
> As friends each hour grow thicker ;
> And then each one seems so devout
> That thou must bless the liquor.

DONALD MACRAE.

If not the most powerful, this bard is certainly the keenest and subtlest that the Highlands have produced. His father was a native of Glenalchaig, in Kintail ; but Donald was born in the parish of Petty, Inverness-shire, the date of his birth being 11th November 1756. His parents were poor people in humble life, and their son got no education whatever. But Christian teaching and Biblical knowledge became a deeply cultivating power in his case. He earned his livelihood by labouring at his loom, when he lived as a cottager on the estate of the Earl of Moray in his native parish of Petty. He lived to the good age of eighty-one, his death taking place in 1837. He was buried in the churchyard of Petty, where a small tombstone points out his grave. He got his poems published in Inverness some time before he died, under the title of *Spiritual Songs*. He has composed a considerable quantity of poetry, the most of which is first-class when the bard's theme is of more than local interest. He combines the spiritual insight and holy sympathies of George Herbert with the subtlety of Shelley. He is the only bard that distinctly illustrates the tendency to mysticism in Highland religion manifested in some quarters. His profound self-analysis may be seen the poem *Luireach :*—

Bha 'n inntinn dhiomhain riamh mar tha,
Aig spionadh tràth na h-ùmhlachd,
Mar eun aig itealaich gu h-àrd,
'Snach gabhadh tàmh 'san dùthaichs'.

Is coslach mi ri madadh tàir',
Le lotaibh grannd a' bùraich,
Ach le a theangaidh a rinn slàn
Na leòin a ta 'ga chiurradh.

ENGLISH :

The mind of vanity e'er so
  Obedience true o'er-riding,
Like birds on flight in highest heaven
  And ne'er on earth abiding.
I am so like that dog despised
  That with sore wounds is moaning,
But with his tongue has healed his hurts
  That caused his painful groaning.

MARY CLARK.

This poetess—*Bean Torra dhamh*—who was the daughter of Ewen Macpherson, schoolmaster in Laggan, Badenoch, appears to have been a woman of great piety. She began first to compose in English, but her husband, whose name was Clark, persuaded her to compose in Gaelic. At the beginning of this century she went to Inverness to get her poems, some thirty in number, written, she herself being at that time blind, and also to publish them. Her works appeared some time ago, anew edited and very well translated by the Rev. John Kennedy. Mrs Clark is a natural and intelligent singer, but without much freshness or originality. The warmth of her religious feelings renders her pieces more readable than they would otherwise be. She died at Perth at an advanced age.

MARGARET CAMPBELL.

Margaret Campbell was born at the farm of Clashgour in Glenorchay. Her father's name was Peter Campbell. She was married a second time to a Cameron at Fort-William, when she became much reduced in circumstances. She published a little volume of songs in 1785 ; a second edition, which relieved her embarrassments a little, in 1805. Her *Laoidh- ean Spioradail* appeared in Edinburgh in 1810, a volume which seems to have escaped Reid's notice. The hymns are thirty-four in number. An English appendix gives an abstract of the themes with which the hymns are occupied. The metre is not always very regular, but a few of the pieces show some poetic vigour.

REV. PETER GRANT.

Next to Dugald Buchanan, the author whose hymns are best and most widely known, is the late Peter Grant, a Baptist minister in Strathspey, who published the first edition of his hymns as early as 1813. As he tells us in one of his poems, he was deeply impressed with the extent of practical heathenism among the Highlanders. He complains, as Bishop Carsuel in the sixteenth century did before him, that the Highlanders loved the tales of Fingal and Ossian more than the Gospel, and that they spent all their spare time in the recital of these vain heathen stories. Carsuel gave his own generation a liturgy, and Grant to his a series of Gospel hymns; and it need scarcely be asked which of them was the more successful. The hymns became immediately widely popular, and edition after edition was called forth, and they have maintained their popularity to the present day. Grant is not a powerful poet, but he is a very sweet singer. His hymns and poems have a holy fragrance about them that is quite captivating. The simplicity of the conception and the naturalness of the style at once affect and enchain the heart. Grant succeeds where a hymnist of more ambition and power would fail. The warmth of his earnest nature is felt in every stanza he has written. He died full of years and honours, beloved by all who knew him. A sweet poem of his begins with the experience of a child emerging in heaven :—

> 'S leanabh solasach mi
> Gle og chaidh á tim ;
> Chaidh mo threorach o'n chich do'n uaigh ;
> 'S ged bu ghoirid mo thim
> Gabhail fradharc do'n tir,
> 'S mor th'agam ri innse do'n t-sluagh.

ENGLISH :

> A child joyful, beloved,
> Early from time removed,
> From the breast to the grave they bore me ;
> Though brief was that state
> I have much to relate
> To the many I see before me.

REV. JAMES MACGREGOR, D.D.

Macgregor (1759-1830), sent by the General Associate Synod to Nova Scotia in 1786, has written hymns (1819) which have been highly valued by sections of Highlanders at home and abroad. He was a native of St Fillans, in Perthshire, and wrote and spoke Gaelic with greater purity and elegance than the natives of that county· in the present day are able to do. The University of Glasgow conferred on him the degree of D.D. in recognition of his arduous and successful labours in the Colonies among his countrymen. His poetry, although not of the first order, is yet sweet and natural—metrical effusions in which the simple truths of the Gospel are rehearsed with earnestness and freshness. The following verses are translated from his poem on *The Resurrection :—*

> Great must be that might,
> Keen must be that sight,
> That so wisely all parts exhume ;
> All the craven and brave,
> The master and slave,
> He shall call from the dust of the tomb.
>
> Widely scattered though be
> Heads and bodies, yet He
> Reunites them in one again ;
> Then forth shall be hurled
> From the graves of the world
> All the ashes of slaughtered men.
>
> The bones that are placed
> On the hill or wild waste,
> In the desert, or pit, or shore ;
> In the ocean deep,
> 'Neath the river's sweep—
> To life he shall then restore.
>
> When the earth shall be shaken
> All classes shall waken—
> The poor, and the king, and the brave ;
> Then forth shall be rolled
> The young and the old,
> The maiden, and lover, and slave.
>
> Some will rise in great fear
> When the Lamb shall appear,
> The just from the evil to sever ;
> Some will wake with delight,
> In garments all bright,
> As the heirs of the kingdom for ever.

Macgregor's grandson, the Rev. George Patterson, D.D., has written his life, much of which is founded on an autobiographical sketch.

REV. JOHN MACDONALD, D.D.

Dr Macdonald, of Ferintosh, as "The Apostle of the North," is a household word in the Highlands. As an orator, preacher, and evangelist, no man of his day was the instrument of greater good to his countrymen, by whom his memory will be warmly cherished for generations. In *The Gaelic Messenger* (1829-30) appeared the first and the best of his poems, which have been the delight of more than one generation of Highlanders. This was a poem of three parts—*The Christian on his Journey to, at, and beyond Jordan.* Some of his other poems are biographical. His poetical works were published in a neat volume in 1846. Here are a few verses translated from the "Christian's Journey:"—

ON THE WAY TO JORDAN.

He often sought for special grace
  At mercy's fountain free,
To keep up aye a cheerful face
  Hard though the heart might be ;
And by that smile of happiness—
  That fragrance sweet he found—
He helped a holy cheerfulness
  In all the saints around.

He hated all hypocrisies,
  The silent face of gloom,
The moaning and the plaintive sighs
  That savour of the tomb.
But the sweet breath of life he knew
  Amidst the tainted air ;
Heart-brokenness that came to view
  Would have his tender care.

ON THE BANKS OF JORDAN.

I hear the floods of Jordan roll,
  My flesh is seized with dread ;
But shame shall ne'er approach my soul,
  By hope of heaven led.
That hope the Rock of Ages showed
  To those who went before,
Who safely trod the sacred road
  That leads to Canaan's shore.

My spirit trembles with affright
  As down to death I go ;
Around me glide the shades of night,
  And weary doubtings grow.
Before is an eternity
  Unreckoned by our years ;

The shoreless and the boundless sea
That wakens shrinking fears.
But on the Christ my eye doth rest,
I trust his gracious power ;
He succoured me when sore distressed,
And He will save that hour.
Yea, He a help will yet provide,
While I am on this shore ;
The waters great He will divide,
Till Jordan I am o'er.

BEYOND JORDAN:

That Christian who once fearful stood
Where high the waters swell'd
Lamenting there before the flood,
Corruption still unquell'd,
Has entered now into that rest
Whose light aye filled his eye ;
His spirit now in glory drest
Surrounds the throne on high.

The popular and living character of Macdonald's preaching genius is everywhere apparent in his hymns. Sweetness, elegance, and genial, broad spiritual-mindedness, have rendered his compositions universally pleasing. He will probably ever remain the chief type of the Highland preacher.

REV. DUNCAN MACDOUGALL.

The name of this sacred bard was once very popular in the South-West Highlands and Isles, and his memory is still green with many aged Christians particularly in the island of Tiree, where he laboured with success as a Nonconformist minister. His hymns—*Laoidhean Spioradail*—appeared in 1841, and for many years continued to be great favourites in certain circles. Macdougall and Peter Grant belong to the same order of simple bard-evangelists who have always been a spiritually elevating force in humble quarters where more ambitious labours have been failures. Their productions have been sermons in verse which the common people have received with greater gladness than has been accorded to the more elaborate and ambitious utterances of the regular pulpit.

JOHN MORRISON.

Morrison, originally a blacksmith to trade, and latterly a Free Church catechist in Harris, is one of the most powerful and ingenious of the bards. I do not know in any language a poem like his *Duin og is seann Duin' agam* in its subtlety of conception, its felicity of expression, and its cunning weavings and turnings of verses. Its theme is the " holy war " in the Christian soul, which he treats not at all in the style of Bunyan, but in quite an original fashion. It was published in 1835, again in America along with many of his other poems. His poetry shows that he was profoundly exercised and interested in the spiritual problems and difficulties of the Christian life. Few men ever obtained a deeper insight into the human heart, and fewer still possessed equally great poetic gifts for uttering what has been seen and felt. A good edition of his whole works is much required; and it was once hoped that his son, Dr Morrison of Edinburgh, would satisfy the wishes of his father's admirers. The bard died in 1852, sixty-two years of age, before any of his works in book-form appeared.

Usquba has been the theme of frequent laudations by the secular bards; the following verses are from a preaching poem of a very different strain :—

> Ye friends whom I cherish, nurse not in your mind
> That I sing in this song from a motive unkind ;
> My theme is the drink-plague—that ill-unconfined,
>   That feeds on our ravage and ruin.
>
> Ye cannot dislike though the satire be keen ;
> For disgrace, woe, and want are where'er it has been ;
> And spirits immortal enslaved may be seen
>   Its road to the devil pursuing.
>
> Degraded is he who delights in its breath,
> For its trade has been plann'd in the regions beneath ;
> Its curse has been wed to consumption and death
>   In bodies' and souls' undoing.

REV. DUNCAN MACCALLUM.

This was an able minister of the Church of Scotland, who was for some time settled at Arisaig. *Collath* is a poem of the heroic kind, which Mackenzie had inserted in " The Beauties" as a specimen of ancient poetry ! Mr MacCallum published it first anonymously, as he did another booklet in which he acknowledged himself to be the author of *Collath*. His poetry shows fair poetic gifts. We meet with MacCallum again as the author of a Church History.

REV. DUNCAN MACLEAN.

The late Free Church minister of Glenorchy, Mr MacLean, was a religious poet of great power and originality. Buchanan,

Morrison, and he are poets of the first order. The " Gaelic
Hymns " of MacLean appeared in 1868 in a small closely-printed
volume. The pieces in this volume are rather religious poems
than hymns. A keenly æsthetical spirit pervades all that Mac-
Lean has written ; and he has written more than any of the first-
class religious bards. He is exceedingly rich in poetic illustration,
and very profound in thought. He was a man of wide general
culture, and he brought the power and fruits of it with him into
the sphere of Gaelic religious poetry. But though his countrymen
highly appreciated his able ministrations in that language in the
pulpit, they do not appear to be ready to understand that they
have such a deep mine of fresh and original thought in his poetry.
The thoughtful reader, however, will at once feel that MacLean is
a man of great culture and a poet of a high order, in full sympathy
with man and the works of creation. Like Morrison of Harris,
he is too profound for the present popular taste   Here are some
translated verses of one of his best poems, on the scenery of his
native place :—

> As I sit on the knoll, on the steep scarpy height,
> And lonely survey all that falls 'neath my sight,
> My crowding thoughts, stirred in their slumber, fast roll
> In currents resistless all over my soul.

> Loch Tay there I see with a beautiful shade
> On its bosom that's pure as the breast of a maid ;
> Like a child in sweet rest, in its fairy bed laid,
> Touch gently its locks ere its glory will fade.

> Oh fair is the vision before me outspread !
> Kind nature's bright face that awakens no dread,
> The green woods where songsters attune on each tree
> Their throats for sweet warbling—beloved of me.

> The Dochart is rushing to Lochy's domain
> To meet her, good woman, so gentle and plain ;
> When they have embraced and are wed into twain
> His fierceness forsakes him, he yields to her strain.

> Glen Dochart, Glen Lochy, are bright to the view,
> With their corries of green when their dress they renew ;
> With the shadowy nooks where the streamlet fast rushes,
> Where you hear the gay chorus of robins and thrushes.

> All changeless I see them, hill, river, and road,
> But where are the people that once there abode ?
> Some rest in their graves 'neath the slumberous sod,
> But the many are scattered o'er ocean abroad.

> The smoke rises high from our house as before,
> In volumes encircling the same as of yore ;

But where is that father so kindly nursed me,
And, gentlest of mothers—O, where now is she ?

The schoolhouse, unaltered, stands there all alone,
But where the young friends of my bosom are gone?
The schoolhouse is there still, but where are the boys
With whom I oft tasted of innocent joys?

The church there I see on the desolate street,
But where are the crowds that I there used to meet ?
The minister, too, who had won my regard ?
The answer of echo is, " Under the sward."

MacLean was a scholarly man and possessed rich gifts for preaching to his fellow-countrymen. His style was concise and suggestive, his matter well-arranged and weighty, while the inspiring spirit invested all with a heavenly force and meaning which greatly delighted all the more thoughtful Highlanders.

MINOR RELIGIOUS POETS.

The Hymns of John Morrison of Skye (1828), are now scarcely read. Others also published religious poems and hymns ; but there is none of them of any particular merit. They are just sermons and Christian experiences put in respectable verse. They, however, helped no doubt to propagate, especially in some parts of the west, the earnest evangelical teaching of the authors. *The Gaelic Elegies*, published in 1850 by the Rev. W. Findlater of Durness, do not show much poetic freshness either ; but owe much of their interest to their religious character and Christian senti-ments. Two of the elegies are on Dr Macdonald of Ferintosh, and on the Rev. A. Stewart of Cromarty. MacEachern of Eis-dale (1866) scarcely reaches mediocrity. The Rev. A. Farquhar-son, a native of Perthshire, who spent the most of his life in Tiree, also published a good deal of religious poetry, scarcely equal in merit to Macdougall's. He died a few years ago. The Rev. Malcolm MacRitchie, a native of Lewis, wrote a good many poems and hymns, which were published upwards of 30 years ago. They are superior to those already mentioned in poetic vigour and freshness of expression. A small volume by Cameron of Uist is just published (1891). Hendry of Arran and D. Macdougall have both composed a quantity of religious poetry ; as also Alexander Cook, a native of Arran, who was a lay preacher of great ability. The writer published a poem of considerable merit by Cook in *Bratach na Firinn* in 1873. Macquarrie and Macintyre, both of

Ross and Mull, the former a Baptist preacher and the latter a farmer, have both composed religious poems and hymns. It would be needless to catalogue the names of others whose names have never taken the smallest hold of public attention. It is very remarkable that men of powerful genius in all countries have often sunk to mediocrity whenever the theme was purely religious. There are not, it appears, many hymns in any language, with the exception of the Psalms, that can be described as first-class poetry.

COLLECTIONS OF RELIGIOUS POETRY.

Many laudable attempts have been made to bring the power of the sacred muse to bear on Highland life. Principal Daniel Dewar, D.D., published a considerable collection of hymns in 1806 for public worship. It was translated wholly from English, and consisted of paraphrases and hymns then current in the English language. Another collection by John Munro appeared in 1819, printed by D. Mackenzie, Glasgow. This is made up chiefly of translations from Watts's hymns, and many of them are well rendered. Another appeared in 1832, published by John Reid. This tiny volume is neatly printed, and consists mainly of translations from the Olney hymns. Some of the compositions in Kennedy's collection have been referred to already. The " Sacred Poetry of the North," edited by John Rose, and published in 1851, is the most valuable collection of sacred poems yet given to the Highlanders. The authors whose works are contained in this volume have been already brought before the reader in chro-nological order. In more recent times many of the hymns of our own day, translated by Archibald Macfadyen, Rev. Dr John Mac-Leod, and others, were published by Duncan Campbell in 1874. A new edition of the same is just published, the collection being in request among Baptists who have always encouraged more hymn-singing in public worship than their Presbyterian neigh-bours. The latter, however, are beginning to cultivate more liberty in this respect. A few of the hymns sung in Scotland by Mr Sankey in 1874, were translated by the Rev. Alexander Mac-Rae of Clachan, and were received with much appreciation. The first part of " The Highland Hymnal," by the writer, was published in 1886. In connection with Highland hymnology, ancient and modern, Mr Lachlan MacBean, Mr Stewart of Killin, and Mr Alexander Carmichael have done good work in exhibiting some of the treasures of the Gaelic sacred muse. Still a good volume of Church Praise with music has never yet been given to the Highland Gael.

SCRIPTURE PARAPHRASES.

These were first translated by the Rev. Alexander Macfarlane of Kilmelfort and Kilninver. Forty-five of them were published in 1753. They were afterwards revised and remodelled, and published in complete form by the Rev. John Smith, D.D., to whom also we are indebted for the best version of the Psalter. During the second and third generations of this century, the Paraphrases, through no lack of life or poetic merit, fell into disrepute in some Highland districts, particularly in the north-west, through theological controversies in whose train rather mechanical theories of inspiration began to be introduced. These views, hitherto unknown among the Gaels, now followed out to their logical issues, led to the rejection of all hymns of mere human authorship in public worship. This result, however, is only temporary ; and in its operations confined to certain circum-scribed districts.

THE PSALTER.

The first fifty Psalms were published in 1684 by the Rev Robert Kirk of Balquidder. A version by the Synod of Argyle appeared in 1694.

Several other attempts were made in the eighteenth century to produce a good translation of the Psalms in metre, chiefly under the auspices of the Synod of Argyle. At last there appeared in 1783 a version which has been generally received by all good judges of Gaelic idioms and poetry as the best. The author of this version of the Psalter was the elegant Dr John Smith, who received the unanimous thanks of the Synod of Argyle for " executing it in so faithful and beautiful a manner."

An effort was made to force upon the Churches another trans-lation of the Psalter by the Rev. Dr Ross of Lochbroom, a man of considerable ability and distinguished for his knowledge of Gaelic. This version, however, is marred by obsolete phrases and idioms, and has never obtained universal circulation in the High-lands.

CHAPTER XVII.

THE GAELIC REVIVAL.

" Dùisg a leoghain euchdaich, 's dean éirich gu faramach,
Air brat ball-dearg, breid-gheal, 's fraoch sleibhe mar bharan air ;
Tog suas do cheann gu h-eutrom, 's na speuraibh gu caithreasach,
'S theid mi-fhìn cho géire 's a dh'fheudas mi d'arabhaig :
Togam suas do mholadh prìseal, 's do cheann rìoghail farasda,
Cha'n'eil ceann no corp 's an rìoghachd an cruaidh-ghniomh thug barrachd
    ort,—
An ceann cruadalach àrd sgiamhach, maisach, fìor-dheas, arranta,
'Stric sgairt ri uchd an fhuathais, ri âm luchd t'fhuatha tarruinn riut.
                                                    —MACDONALD.

ENGLISH :

Awake thou furious lion ! awake with lusty roar,
On thy bright blood-stained standard, heath-circled as of yore ;
Thy head lift up full lightly in heaven with raging might,
And I will rush with fervour to mingle in thy fight :
I raise thy praises precious round thy calm regal head ;
None e'er throughout the kingdom excelled thy deeds of dread ;—
That head of strength and valour where fearless beauty glows,
Oft roared it out its terrors when onward pressed the foes.

THIS was the spirit and manner in which the great poet Alex.
Macdonald went about rousing his countrymen to lofty deeds of
valour in the second quarter of the eighteenth century. He
lavished all his poetic enthusiasm on the " praises " of the national
lion, and the inspiration of his muse and of that of a hundred
others bore fruit a century afterwards. Such poems as Macdonald's
have had a profoundly formative influence on the minds of the
young Highlanders of our own times,—especially the more sus-
ceptible and less sordid spirits, who would not deny their country,
race, or language for all the golden success that self-effacement as
Gaels could secure. These enduring sons of the Highlands and
Islands succeeded at last, although in the midst of much
obloquy and secular loss, in accomplishing a Gaelic revolution ;
—in creating a Gaelic revival, and ultimately a powerful agitation that bore a fruit that has justified the more sanguine expec-
tations and claims of bards and patriots. This has been the

fruit of a century of Gaelic effort devoted to the study of the lang uage, history, and interests of the people. While the foes of such an endeavour have been numerous and supercilious, even in selfish Highland quarters, let it not be forgotten that a great deal of sympathy and practical help came from many kindly hearts and hands among our Lowland fellow-countrymen.

It is interesting to trace the influences that have brought about this bloodless revolution in the Highlands, some of whose people a little over a century ago were engaged in rebellion against the present dynasty. A healthy form of Christianity and common sense have done it all. The meaning of the one came to them through the translation of good religious writings and the Gaelic Bible : and the exercise of the other became possible through the instructed good qualities of the Highlanders themselves. I therefore in this last chapter devote some paragraphs to the results that the chief forms of Gaelic endeavour have produced.

THE GAELIC BIBLE.

The first portion of the Bible translated was the New Testament, in 1767, by the Rev. James Stewart of Killin. Dugald Buchanan, the poet, accompanied Mr Stewart to Edinburgh to superintend the work through the press. The title-page bears that the translation was undertaken at the request and at the expense of the Society in Scotland for Propagating Christian Knowledge. The translator adopted an orthographical system, which has been perfected into a standard of Gaelic by succeeding scholars. The first edition of the translation of the Old Testament was published in the following order :—

Part I., 1783, translated by John Stuart, D.D., of Luss.
Part IV., 1786, translated by John Smith, D.D., of Campbelton.
Part II., 1787, translated by Dr Stuart.
Part III., 1801, translated by Dr Stuart.

The fourth part, assigned to Dr Smith, contained the Prophets, which had afterwards to be revised, Smith's version being more poetical than literal. Dr Stuart was a son of the translator of the New Testament, and received in 1819 for his labours in connec tion with the first and other editions of the Gaelic Scriptures the sum of £1000 from the Lords of the Treasury, a Government favour which has not been always recognised. A new and revised edition on which Dr Alexander Stewart, of Dingwall, was engaged with Dr Stuart, of Luss, under the instructions of a large committee of Gaelic scholars appointed by the General Assembly in 1816, was published in quarto in 1826, It is acknowledged by all competent judges that this Gaelic version of the Scriptures is beyond all praise; that in many instances it adheres more closely to the original than the English Bible, whose beauty and excellence have won universal admiration. The translation of the Old Testament was also undertaken at the expense of the Society for Propagating Christian Knowledge, and through its liberality the Scriptures were sold at half the cost price. On the publication of the Revised Version of the English Bible, a committee of Gaelic scholars undertook the revision of the Gaelic Bible ; but on account of some difficulties with the Society for Propagating Christian Knowledge the fruit of their labours has not yet appeared.

TRANSLATIONS INTO GAELIC.

It is mostly religious works of the Evangelical and Puritan type that have been translated into Gaelic. The masterpieces of Bunyan, Brooks, Baxter, Burder, Owen, Howe, Doddridge, Alleine, etc. etc., have been rendered into good, popular Gaelic, and have had immense circulation. Hundreds of religious works have been translated, some as old as *The Imitation*, and as recent as Newman Hall's *Come to Jesus*. The principal translators have been the Macfarlanes, Dr Smith, MacLaurin, Rose, Dr Macgillivray, Dr Mackintosh Mackay, the Rev. Allan Sinclair, and the Rev. A. Macgregor, translator of the Apocrypha. It was Mac Eachen, a Roman Catholic priest, that translated *The Imitation.* Several books of Homer's *Iliad* were translated by the accomplised Ewen MacLachlan of Aberdeen; Virgil's *Æneid* by Blair ; and *Tam O'Shanter* and other poems by Robert Mac-Dougall, the bard. As is well known, the Queen's Book has been translated into excellent Gaelic by Mary Mackellar. The Good Templar and Masonic rituals were, with the help of the present writer, translated by Duncan Macpherson and Angus Nicholson respectively. Not the least important of recent efforts of this kind is the admirable translation of that great Highland charter of Gaelic emancipation, the Crofters' Act, from the able and accurate pen of Mr Henry Whyte.

TRANSLATIONS INTO ENGLISH.

A good deal of Gaelic literature has been translated into English, whilst the " Ossian " of Macpherson has been rendered into

Latin and into most of the European languages. Following is a list of the names of those who have published anything of importance : —

Jerome Stone . . .	1756	Patrick Macgregor .	1840
James Macpherson .	1760	Robert Munro . . .	1843
Rev. J. Wodrow . .	1771	Rev. Dr MacLauchlan	1862
Ewen Cameron . .	1777	J. F. Campbell, Esq.	1866
John Clark	1778	Rev. Thomas Pattison	1866
Rev. Dr Smith . .	1780	Rev. Dr Clerk . . .	1870
Rev. Dr Ross . . .	—	Robert Buchanan .	1872
The MacCallums . .	1816	C. S. Jerram, Esq. .	1873
Mrs Grant	—	Professor J. S. Blackie	1876

The names of some others, such as Sinclair, the Whytes, MacBean, etc., will occur to the Gaelic reader. The works translated by these writers would fill many volumes. The works of Macpherson, Dr Smith, Dr MacLauchlan, J. F. Campbell, Thomas Pattison, Dr Clerk, and Professor Blackie have received much attention, and are well-known. Macpherson and Smith translate, on the supposition of translation, very much in the style of Pope in his Homer with this difference, that their paraphrastic renderings are only in prose. MacLauchlan, Campbell, and Clerk have adopted a rigid literality of rendering which the Ossianic controversy, among other reasons, compelled them to follow. These writers give the original Gaelic along wth the English version. So does Jerram. whose *Dan an Deirg* is scholarly and accurate, very much in the style of Clerk's *Ossian*. In the *Gaelic Bards* of Pattison the original is not given, the work being intended for popular use among English readers. Pattison's translations are metrical and rhyming ; and so are Blackie's in his admirable and interesting work, *The Language and Literature of the Scottish Highlands.* Those to whom the Gaelic is a sealed language have kindled the flame of patriotic enthusiasm by the healthy mountain breezes which the perusal of these translations has brought down.

GRAMMARS AND DICTIONARIES.

Several good grammars and dictionaries have been published. Shaw, towards the end of last century, published a grammar and dictionary which are not of much value. Stewart's Grammar in

1812 is still the best, and any new grammar must take Stewart's as a basis. Currie, MacAlpine, Forbes, and Munro have also pub- lished grammars. Munro's is a work of real scholarship and value, but badly arranged. Dr Macgillivray and L. MacBean have also written grammars, but the best of all recent attempts is that published by the late D. C. Macpherson, Edinburgh. Good grammars have also been written by Irishmen, and even Germans, from which much help may be obtained. The vocabularies of Macdonald and Macfarlane paved the way for the High- land Society's Dictionary, published in 1828, a noble monu- ment of Gaelic talent and industry. It appeared in two large volumes. Its departments are—Gaelic, English, and Latin ; Anglo- Gaelic, Latino-Gaelic. There are 837 pages in the first volume, and 1016 in the second. The general conduct of the work was entrusted to the Rev. Dr John MacLeod of Dundonald. He was assisted by the Rev. Drs Irvine, Macdonald, and Ewan Mac- Lachlan. In its progress through the press the work was carefully superintended and corrected by the Rev. Dr Mackintosh Mackay. None of the Celtic languages can boast of so extensive and learned a lexicon, although it is defective in etymology, the science of language being then only in its infancy. Armstrong and Mac- Alpine have also produced excellent and useful dictionaries. That of the former is not much inferior to that of the Highland Society's, while MacAlpine's has perhaps been the most successful of all. The indefatigable labours of the Macfarlanes, father and son, have been placed to the credit of Drs MacLeod and Dewar, whose names were thought a necessary guarantee by the publisher that their dictionary was of standard value. Theirs and MacAlpine's are in general circulation. That of the latter is a pronouncing dictionary, and has been highly appreciated by those anxious to acquire the language. The translations of phrases and idiomatic expressions under the principal words are acknowledged to be a chief excellence of the work. The English-Gaelic part of Mac- Alpine's dictionary was compiled by John Mackenzie, editor of "The Beauties of Gaelic Poetry," who had some peculiar ideas of reform in Gaelic orthography. He was heartily execrated by the irascible MacAlpine for his labour, which was no doubt a hack business undertaken for publishers whom Mackenzie could not control. A good deal of material for an etymological dictionary was left by the late Dr Alexander Cameron of Brodick, the publi- cation of which is looked for under the editorial care of Mr Alex. MacBain, M.A.

PROSE WRITERS.

The number of Gaelic prose writers is very limited. This fact is the result of various causes on the surface of things. Till the beginning of this century the vast masses of the Highland people were utterly unable to read, and even those who were able to make use of books turned to English productions sooner than to Gaelic ones, a tendency that is not invisible even in our own day. All that the plain Highlander has been able to consume in the way of literature he has found in the Book of Books—the Bible —and in the many translations of religious literature placed within his reach. Families and individuals destitute of the spiritual instinct have found all the literary sustenance needed in the old popular tales and poetry which circulated from mouth to mouth rather than in written forms. To the Finian tales and similar stuff the Highlanders of the nineteenth century were till recently as partial as those of the sixteenth century were to the oral literature of the same pagan character against which Superintendent Carsuel raised his ineffectual protest at the time of the Reformation. This oral form of literature required neither money nor ability to read for its enjoyment ; while the manner of its culture helped to relieve the weariness and monotony of Highland life. Literature in books, which meant money, was therefore at a discount.

But to the great credit of sagacious patriots of the Presbyterian Church of Scotland, efforts were continually made to teach the people to read and to circulate healthy literature. The Society for Promoting Christian Knowledge rendered splendid services in both respects, as did also in later times the circulating Gaelic-School teachers, whose labours early in this century converted many a dreary moral wilderness into fair fields of spiritual life. Similar excellent work has been accomplished by the Ladies' Associations of Edinburgh and Glasgow during the last forty years. And now at last well-trained teachers are to be found in Board Schools established by the national system of education introduced by the Act of 1872, under which the good old parish schools have vanished. But with all these revolutionary changes there is no adequate encouragement yet afforded to the teaching of Gaelic, which a prejudiced Government Department in London feels reluctant at heart to acknowledge. This state of matters is a sufficient explanation of the fact that our Gaelic prose literature is so scanty, and that the writers of it have received so little reward for their patriotic labours.

In the following paragraphs will be found the names of the most of those who are the authors of volumes of Gaelic prose, or who are otherwise recognised as having contributed considerably to our prose literature : —

REV. HUGH MACDIARMID.—This well known minister of Callander is the author of a goodly volume of sermons which have had a fair circulation in the South Highlands. They exhibit no special ability in the author, but are plain common-sense productions which would not rouse much holy enthusiasm in the reader, nor make serious demands on his intellect. At the same time they were often in request in pious homes, where, on the poor man's great Day of Rest, they might be brought forth to be read.

PRINCIPAL DANIEL DEWAR, D.D.—Though the Principal of a Scottish University, Dr Dewar did not allow himself to get contemptuous towards the language of his forefathers like many much smaller men when they get into posts of honour. As pointed out elsewhere, Dewar published early in the century a fair collection of Gaelic hymns, the preface to which shows him to be a man of culture and devout spirit. We find his name also associated with a popular dictionary, and with all enterprises of his time for the uplifting of Gaelic life. "The Gaelic Preacher," a booklet by Dr Dewar, is well-known to the present generation of Gaelic readers.

REV. JOHN MACMILLAN.—This Arran preacher was one of the ablest men who occupied Gaelic pulpits in the early part of this century. The unction and power of his sermons are still remembered by old folks in his native island, where his labours have been highly esteemed and loved. "Macmillan's Sermons" is a posthumous volume issued under the editorial care of his relative, the Rev. Mr Stewart, who in their publication has conferred a boon on his Highland fellow-countrymen. The founders of the great publishing house of Macmillan were not unrelated to the distinguished preacher of these sermons.

REV. MACKINTOSH MACKAY, LL.D.—This Sutherlandshire divine was the most distinguished and thorough Gaelic scholar of his time. He collected and edited Rob Donn's poems, no small achievement in itself ; had a prodigious share in the production of the Highland Society's Dictionary, and published the *Fianuis* at the time of the Disruption of the Scottish Establishment—a monument of good Gaelic prose and powerful exposition of great principles in the language of the Gael. The pages of the *Fianuis*,

however, being largely controversial, they are now very much forgotten like the many pamphlets which the Union controversy
subsequently brought forth. For many years Dr Mackay was one
of the best known ministers of the Scottish Churches at home and
abroad. In Australia he helped divided Presbyterians to unite,
but on his return home in his old age he opposed a similar union
in Scotland. He kept up his interest in Gaelic studies to the very
last, and his love of accuracy continued to the end. Mr William
Mackenzie, publisher, of Glasgow, engaged him to write a Gaelic
Church History (1872), which in his last years he accomplished
with all the care and scholarship which distinguished his work
for the great Gaelic dictionary in his younger years.

REV. ALEXANDER BEITH, D.D.—This remarkable divine has
only recently passed away over ninety years of age. As early as
1824 he published a little book on "Baptism" when he was
minister at Oban. It is interesting as being one of our earliest
original prose works.

REV. NORMAN MACLEOD, D.D.—Well has Dr Macleod been
styled "The Highlander's Friend," for no Gaelic man of eminence has ever identified himself with his countrymen more
thoroughly than he. The favourite of Royalty, the personal
friend of Sir Robert Peel, few men of his cloth have ever received more public honour and respect ; and his no less famous
son found a people, when he came forward publicly, affectionately
ready to welcome him. It is as a powerful writer of Gaelic prose,
however, that the elder Norman will be remembered. His writings are full of wit, wisdom, and humour, and will be read by
Highlanders as long as Gaelic continues to be spoken. No other
man has fashioned by his literary efforts the mental habits of his
countrymen so much as he. He has been the Dickens (*plus*
powerful religious feelings) of the Highlands. No Highlander ever
knew better than he how to touch the heart-chords of his country
men. In many of his labours he had a worthy and scarcely less
able coadjutor in his brother, the Rev. Dr John Macleod of
Morven. His works were collected, edited, and republished by
his accomplished relative, the Rev. Dr Clerk of Kilmallie.

Macleod's *Leabhar nan Cnoc* became their first introduction to
Gaelic literature to thousands of Highlanders who never lost the
first impressions it left on their minds in youth. The first volume
of the *Gaelic Messenger* for 1830 was condemned by some as
too light and racy ; the second and last for 1831 received so little

support that the magazine was stopped. The late Mr W. R. MacPhun, the publisher, informed the writer, in 1873, that the parcels of " Messengers " sent to the Highlands and Islands came back at the end of the year, *after they had been read*, without any accompanying payment, of course. Dr Macleod and his enterprising publisher saw then that it was time to give up the business. Some who have lost time and money in recent times over Gaelic affairs may find some cold comfort in this incident in the experience of our greatest of prose writers.

JOHN MACKENZIE.—The compiler of " The Beauties of Gaelic Poetry " wrote largely in prose, for which he had great natural gifts. He was the author of an admirable " History of Prince Charles," in which much easy and idiomatic Gaelic will be found. His other works of " The Beauties," " The English-Gaelic Dictionary," " The Gaelic Melodist," etc., are so well-known that no further description of them is necessary. The late Gaelic publishers, Maclachlan & Stewart of Edinburgh, employed Mackenzie on various works for years.

REV. DUNCAN MACCALLUM.—This Arisaig minister has come before us already as the author of *Collath*, once sent forth as an ancient heroic poem. He is better known as the author of a Gaelic Church-History, which is written with fair ability. This has at least the distiction of being the first of the kind in the language.

REV. JOHN FORBES.—The author of the " Double Grammar " (Gaelic and English in parallel columns), second edition (1848), was a very clever and a very learned Highlander. He translated much into Gaelic, in which he wrote with purity and ease. He was very ingenious in coining new terms for conceptions hitherto alien to Gaelic. He and Munro having no access to the works of the ancient writers of the Celtic Missions Churches described by Zeuss became thus needlessly neologists. Forbes's *Lochran*, *Long Gheal*, etc., are well-known to the readers of Gaelic religious literature.

REV. ARCHIBALD CLERK, LL.D.—Dr Clerk's greatest work is the elaborate edition of Macpherson's Ossian (1870), with new translations and notes, and Macpherson's original prose version running at the foot of the pages. All that Celtic culture and accurate knowledge of Gaelic could do for the Gaelic of 1807 Clerk has done ; and the splendid work, in two volumes, was published at the expense of the generous Marquis of Bute. But all to no avail; for I find, just as I write, that even Professor Mackinnon at last has given up the old faith in Ossian. Dr Clerk's prose writings were numerous as editor and contributor in connection with periodical literature. He, in conjunction with Dr MacLauchlan, undertook the revision of the Gaelic Bible, but with results rather unsatisfactory.

REV. THOMAS MACLAUCHLAN, LL.D.—A very difficult task was taken in hand by MacLauchlan when he undertook the transcription and modernisation of the MS. and Gaelic of the Dean of Lismore's Book. This work he also translated literally into English. He, too, edited Macpherson's Gaelic Ossian, the small edition in circulation having been issued under his care. Like Dr Clerk he had a hand in and helped various Gaelic enterprises of his time. Among others he had charge of the new edition of Carsuel's Liturgy. His "Celtic Gleanings" (1857), and "Review of Gaelic Literature" (1872) in Fullarton's work on the Highlands and Highland Clans, were the first attempts to give us an account of the literature of the Gael. His "Early Scottish Church" was a creditable production, considering the limited materials which were then available for the general historian's purposes.

REV. ANGUS MACKENZIE.—Mr Mackenzie, a native of Lewis, has the honour of being the only man who has ever attempted to write a complete history of Scotland in Albin's ancient tongue. His *Eachdraidh na h-Alba* (1867) is written with much ability and in good idiomatic Gaelic. It covers the whole period of Scottish story, and ought to have an extensive circulation among Highlanders. But it is feared that although sold very cheaply it had not the sale it so well deserved.

REV. ALEXANDER MACGREGOR.—This excellent and patriotic "Sgiathanach" was among the best story-tellers of his age, ranking probably, as far as that gift is concerned, next to Norman Macleod. Tales and sketches on almost everything Highland were continually pouring from his facile pen for many years. His translation of the Apocrypha, undertaken at Lucien Bonaparte's request, will remain a fine monument of his knowledge of his native tongue. The Gaelic Society of Inverness and *The Celtic Magazine* were much indebted to him during the first years of their existence. When he died he was minister of the West (Established) Church of Inverness.

REV. ALEXANDER CAMERON, LL.D.—No one in this generation has contributed so much towards accurate Gaelic scholarship as the late Free Church minister of Brodick. He taught Gaelic with great success for years at Glasgow University to scores of Highland students who, but for his enthusiasm and self-denying labours, would be settling in Highland pastorates with more than enough of Latin and Greek and Hebrew but quite ignorant of Gaelic grammar. The more learned products of Dr Cameron's pen were published in the *Scottish Celtic Review* begun in 1880. This periodical was chiefly written by himself and largely filled with philology. Mr MacBain of Inverness is understood to be preparing for the press the materials left behind by Dr Cameron.

REV. JOHN GEORGE MACNEILL.—The Free Church minister of Cawdor began writing Gaelic articles while still a student in 1873. He contributed a large proportion of the general contents of two volumes of *Bratach na Firinn* in which also a telling short story, *Tighnacloiche* appeared from his pen. *An Soisgeul ann an India* (1888) is a living, natural and idiomatic translation of Miss Rainy's admirable volume on the Gospel in India. This is one of the most interesting, books in the language the reader finding here the life and customs of Aryans in the East described in the ancient tongue of Aryans in the extreme West of Europe, the children of Sanscrit and of Celtic being once more brought there into close contact. Mr MacNeill has edited the Free Church Gaelic Quarterly with much spirit and success for some years. The Gaelic preface to the *Oranaiche* and a biographical sketch and notes to the second edition of " Pattison's Gaelic Bards " are from his pen.

PROFESSOR DONALD MACKINNON, M.A.—After ages of unreasonable neglect of the Gaelic language, it is satisfactory to Gaels at last to be able to point to the Celtic Chair in Edinburgh University as an academic recognition of its claims; and it is not less satisfactory to know that the first occupant of the Chair is a scholar well fitted to adorn the position. Professor Mackinnon's first contributions to the literature of his native language appeared in *The Gael*, and showed that the native ability and culture which secured him recognition in other spheres of study might be of exceptional service to Gaelic literature. Mr Mackinnon has published a text-book for the use of his class ; and has contributed more than one series of fresh and delightful articles to the columns of *The Scotsman*, which will no doubt appear some day in a more permanent form.

REV. WILLIAM ROSS.—Coming early under the influence of Dr MacLauchlan, Mr Ross, in the midst of much public work and various activities, has carried on his Gaelic studies and Celtic researches, which have been of a careful and extensive character. He has taught with success a Gaelic class, and lectured on Gaelic literature for many years at the Free Church College, Glasgow. He has also rendered a good deal of public service in connection with Highland education.

REV. ROBERT BLAIR, D.D.—This able and popular minister of the Church of Scotland has contributed very largely to our Celtic periodicals, delivered many delightful Gaelic lectures, and has in various ways heartily promoted the cultivation of the Gaelic language. He has edited an edition of the poetical works of Livingston, and supplied a good biographical sketch of the bard.

HENRY WHYTE.—"Fionn " is well-known to the Gaelic-reading public at home and abroad as a clever and industrious Anglo-Gaelic journalist. A volume of Gaelic-English and English-Gaelic metrical translations, "The Celtic Garland " (1881), has has had a very good circulation. In prose and verse, in English and Gaelic, Mr Whyte shows great versatility and considerable culture ; while his knowledge of the music, manners, and life of the Highlanders is extensive.

JOHN WHYTE. —Although his name is attached to no special volume, Mr Whyte has for many years been recognised as one of our ablest Gaelic scholars. He writes with elegance and accuracy in both languages, and, like his brother Henry, is well able to express himself in verse as well as in prose. He wrote largely for *The Gael, The Highlander*, etc. ; while recently he transcribed for the press the poems and songs of Mrs Macpherson.

LACHLAN MACBEAN —MacBean's *Lessons in Gaelic* has been perhaps the most popular of all the helps provided for the student anxious to acquire the language. The author has for many years been a successful journalist, but in the midst of his professional duties he has found time to produce some remarkable works, particularly translations from such standard authors as Dugald Buchanan, etc. Mr MacBean is equally at home in the use of the Gaelic and English languages, and it ought to be said that his translations have the desirable quality of being readable in their English dress. Perhaps the fact ought not to be omitted

22

that his works have been published by a gentleman who has shown considerable enterprise for many years in connection with Gaelic publications—Mr John Noble of Inverness.

The list of those known as fair writers of Gaelic prose is now well-nigh exhausted. Mackellar, Dugald Macphail, and others whose names appear in other chapters might also be described as prose writers. Among others the following also may be mentioned as having used a Gaelic pen with varying successes :—

Rev. Neil Dewar of Kingussie is an able and accurate Gaelic scholar, who helped in the publication of an edition of the Gaelic Bible with references.

The *Rev. D. M. Connell* is the author of a little treatise on astronomy published more than forty years ago.

Dr D. Black of Poolewe published a booklet on medicine and nursing in 1877 which is well written and full of valuable knowledge and guidance.

Dr Morrison of Edinburgh, son of the sacred bard of Harris, wrote for some time a good deal for the columns of *The Gael.*

The *Rev. John MacRury* has supplied in excellent style much of the Gaelic Supplement to *Life and Work*, the organ of the Established Church. He has also written well versions of some ancient Gaelic tales.

Dr John Clerk has exercised his able and ingenious pen in verse and prose products of various kinds.

Dr Hugh Cameron Gillies, another gentleman of the same profession, author of a small Grammar and Text-book. is at home in the use of the Gaelic language, and has edited some poetry and music.

Malcolm Macfarlan, the author of a little interesting work of Gaelic Phonetics, has written a good deal in Gaelic with care and fair accuracy.

The *Rev. James Dewar*, late of Oa, Islay, produced quite a unique little work. and one of some ability—a Gaelic reply to the celebrated " Claim and Protest " of the Free Church of Scotland.

There may be some small productions of merit, such as a Sermon by the *Rev Archibald Cook*, and similar publications, which are unnoticed here ; but I do not think that many works of any importance have escaped reference. As already mentioned in another chapter, the Gaelic is cultivated in Canada as at home. We are all familiar with the name of the Rev. D. B. Blair, but there have been many others in the Dominion who have laboured to keep the flame of Gaelic literature alive. Patrick Macgregor the well-known barrister, was one of them ; and the name of Dr Neil MacNish reminds us that there are not a few even now—men of ability and patriotic spirit—who strenuously uphold the interests of Albin's ancient tongue.

PERIODICALS.

Strenuous efforts were put forth early in this century to supply the Highlanders with useful literature in their own tongue, but the necessary sustained support has not hitherto been accorded to such efforts. Popular poetry and religious writings have therefore been the main channels through which literature has reached the Gaelic mind. The following list embraces the chief publications of this kind :--

In 1803 the *Ros-Roine*, a magazine, commenced, but the publication ceased with the fourth number.

In 1829-31 *An Teachdaire Gaidhealach*, a monthly, was sent forth by W. R. MacPhun, publisher, Glasgow, with the elder Dr Norman Macleod as editor.

In 1835-36 *An Teachdaire Ur Gaidhealach* was published.

In 1840-43 *Cuiartear nan Gleann* appeared, with Dr Macleod once more as chief support and editor.

In 1848 *Fear-tathaich nam Beann* made its appearance only to succumb, like its predecessors, after a brief existence.

Some of the writers associated with these efforts were Lachlan Maclean, Archibald Sinclair, Campbell (the Glasgow publisher), and the late Rev. Dr Archibald Clerk of Kilmallie.

The Disruption of the Church of Scotland in 1843 became the chief theme of an ably conducted periodical, *An Fhianuis*, edited by the Rev. Dr Mackintosh Mackay.

Even in Canada attempts were made to keep the Gaelic alive by means of magazine literature. Between 1840 and 1841 Urquhart published in Canada *Cuairtear nan Coiltean* ; and about 1851 John Boyd published *An Cuairtear Og* in Antigonish, N.S.

For many years afterwards no efforts were made to publish magazines till 1871, when Mr Angus Nicholson, a native of Lewis, published in Canada the first three numbers of *An Gaidheal* (THE GAEL). On the advice of some Celtic friends the spirited projector of this venture transplanted his young sapling into Scottish soil in 1872, where it continued to appear for about six

years.   In 1872-4 *Bratach na Firinn*, chiefly a religious magazine, appeared, published by the writer in his undergraduate days.
At present the Church of Scotland's own organ of " Life and
Work " has a *Gaelic Supplement*.   The Free Church issues *The
Gaelic Record*.   Gaelic articles have also appeared in the newspapers of Inverness and Oban, editors having discovered
of late years that the insertion of Gaelic articles is not inimical to
the circulation of their journals.   *The Celtic Magazine*, ably
carried on for some years by Mr Alexander Mackenzie, and the
Highland Monthly at present, though not written in Gaelic, have
helped forward Gaelic scholarship.   Nor must I omit to mention
the earlier patriotic efforts of Mr John Murdoch in *The Highlander*,
in writing the language and advocating its claims—efforts which
ought to find a special place in the pages of the historian of the
Gaelic Renaissance of this quarter of the nineteenth century.

HIGHLAND SOCIETIES.

The Highland Societies of London and Scotland have contributed materially towards the cultivation of Celtic literature, although the latter for more than half a century has developed into
a merely agricultural association.   The Scottish one has given us
the learned " REPORT " on the Ossianic literature, which Henry
Mackenzie, author of " The Man of Feeling," edited as well as
the magnificent Dictionary already described.   The London
Society helped to give Smith's *Seann Dana* to the world more
than a century ago, and Patrick Macgregor's *Genuine Remains* of
Ossian in 1840.   This Society still flourishes under royal and
aristocratic smiles in London, and in recent years, under the guidance of Dr Farquhar Matheson, Dr Roderick Macdonald, M.P.,
and others, has helped many Highland youths with bursaries to
enable them to obtain University training.   The Gaelic Society
of London was formed in the year 1777, and is still rejoicing in a
vigorous manhood.   In those days there were many Gaelic
patriots about the metropolis who had made considerable fortunes
abroad and in the south ; and they felt it a sacred duty to encourage organisations which might nurse the apparently decaying
spirit of the threatened Scottish nationality.   Some twenty years
ago the Gaelic Society of Inverness was formed, and to it the Celtic
world is indebted for a series of annual volumes of Transactions
in which we have materials for a rich museum of folk-lore, poetry,
tradition, history, philology, etc.   These volumes will be of the

utmost value for the future student. Two names deserve special mention in connection with these volumes—that of Mr William Mackenzie, Principal Clerk of the Highland Land Court, a gentleman who wields a facile pen in both Gaelic and English; and that of Mr William Mackay, solicitor, Inverness, who is among the most distinguished archæological lawyers in the country, and who has furnished contributions of the highest value to these volumes. The Gaels of Glasgow more recently formed a Gaelic Society, of which Mr Magnus Maclean, M.A. of Glasgow University, is the admirable secretary. This Society has made a good beginning with the publication of the first volume of its Transactions lately published. Perth and other large towns have also their Gaelic Societies in this country, and if we look across the Atlantic we find quite a large number of them in Canada. The Gaelic Society of Toronto, of which a distinguished native of Islay—Mr David Spence—has been a moving spirit, is in a very flourishing condition.

In the great political change which has just come over the dreams of Highlanders the Gaelic language has been of the most undoubted service. Indeed it is through its judicious use as a political weapon that this change was brought to a successful pass in 1886. It was the thousands of the Gaelic Land-Law Reform manifestoes sent forth from London in 1883-4, that organised the Highlands and Islands for the brilliant Parliamentary triumph of 1885, by which the first practical fruits of the Gaelic revival were reaped. And here it may be interesting to preserve a copy of one of these manifestoes, which played so prominent a part in bringing about the Imperial recognition of Highland rights. The following prose paragraphs may be referred to as a specimen of the Gaelic of the period as well as a monument of the services rendered by the use of Gaelic in an important national crisis : —

A GAELIC LAND-LAW REFORM MANIFESTO.

" *Comunn Gaidhealach Lunnuinn airson Lagh an Fhearainn Athleasachadh.*

"Chuireadh an Comunn so air chois an toiseach air son gu'm biodh Teachdairean Rioghail air an cur feadh Gàidhealtachd agus Eileana na h-Alba a rannsachadh mu chor agus mu ghearan na Tuadh Bhig anns na ceàrnaibh sin ; mar an ceudna air son atharrachaidhean a dheanamh air Laghan an Fhearainn, a shocruicheadh gu dainghean Màil Chothromach,

Greim Seasmhach airan Fhearann, agus Pàidheadh air son Athleasachaidh-
ean maille ri leithid d o Ath-shuidheachadh air an Fhearann 'sa bhiodh
feumail air son math an t-Sluaigh.

" Air an dara là do Sheptember 1884, choinnich Fir-ionaid o na Comuinn
Ghàidhealach a tha air son Lagh an Fhearainn Ath-leasachadh ann an Co-
Labhairt ann an Inbher-feothrain ; agus dh'aontaich iad air a bhonn a
leanas mar Chlar-innsidh air son a' Chomuinn Ghàidhealaich a tha air
son Lagh an Fhearainn Ath-leasachadh :

" Gu'm biodh Cuirt Fearainn le comasan breith agus riaghlaidh air a
stéidheachadh air son Gàidhealtachd agus Eileana na h-Alba air son gach
ceist a dh'éireas eadar na h-uachdarain agus an Tuath a shocrachadh ; agus
an coitcheannas a dh'òrdachadh gu'm biodh am fearann air a roinn agus
air a chur am feum air son math an t-sluaigh.

"Làn ughdarras gu bhi aig a' Chùirt—

' 1mh.—A shuidheachadh nam màl a bhios air am pàidheadh, agus nan
cumhnantan air am bi am fearann air a ghabhail.

' 2mh.—A mheudachadh nam bailtean anns am bheil Croitearan a nis,
agus a dheanamh bailtean ùra agus tuathanachais air fearann 'sam
bith a chi a' Chùirt freagarrach ; pàidheadh iomchuidh a bhi air a
thoirt airson call 'sam bith a thig air an fheadhainn aig am bheil am
fearann an dràsd.

' 3mh.—A dh'òrdachadh gu'm biodh tighean freagarrach, le roinnean do'n
fhearrann, air an ullachadh, air cùmhnantan ceart, air son seirbheis-
ich agus luchd-òbair an fhearainn.

' 4mh.—A shochrachadh gach riaghailt a bhuineas do Shealg ; gun fearann
'sam bith ri bhi air a ghabhail air son seilg ás eugmhais aonta na Cùirt.

"Gu'm bi comas aig Luchd-riaghlaidh nan Sgìrean, fo sheoladh na Cùirt,
air aigiod rioghachdail fhaotainn an iasad air urras nan cìsean, gu bhi air a'
thoirt an coingheall do'n Tuath Bhig, Croiteirean, is Coitèirein, a dh'ullachadh thighean is stoc ; na h-iasaid so ri fuireach fo bhoinn ath-phàidhidh
air urras nan tuathanachais, nam bailtean, nau croitean, 's an stuic gus am
faigh Luch-raighlaidh nan Sgìrean an cuid féin air ais.

"Gur h-ann aig a' mhuintir a tha ag àiteachadh a' ghruinnd a bhios còir
air toradh gach ath-leasachadh no seilbh a bhios air a chruthachadh ann no
air an fhearann leosan a tha 'ga oibreachadh ; agus bidh e comasach doibh
an còirchean 'nan gabhaltais a reic no air dòigh eile dealachadh riu ; a' mhuinn-
tir a thig 'nan déigh gu bhi fo na h-aon chùmhnantan, 's an seilbh air na
h-uile chòiricheau agus shochairean, a bha aig an fheadhainn a bha rompa.

"Gu'm bi gabhaltais cinnteach no seasmhach aig uile luchd-aiteachaidh
an fhearainn ; se sin ri ràdh nach bi iad air an gluasad cho fhad 's a bhios
na màil a shuidicheas a' Chùirt air am pàidheadh, agus cùmhnantan a
ghabhaltais air an coimhlionadh."

HISTORY AND ARCHAEOLOGY.

The earlier labours of many Highlanders in these fields are not

now of so much value, but a similar remark is equally applicable
to those whose names are associated with other peoples and their
history. The results of such efforts as these are certainly not
Gaelic literature, but they are referred to here as kindred and in-
dispensable in understanding it. Such books as Grant " On the
Descent of the Gael " and Logan's " Scottish Gael " remind us of
the earlier periods, while we are able to point to Skene's monu-
mental work " Celtic Scotland " as embodying the fruits of the
Gaelic learning of our generation. The " Antiquarian Notes "
and other excellent productions from the pen of Mr'Fraser-
Mackintosh, M.P., show that some of our legislators in these
times take a living and hearty interest in the annals of their ancestors. That splendid series of publications, " The Historians
of Scotland," the Celtic student will find a much-prized possession ; and the series of volumes the Rhind Lecturers have given
us will be felt to be equally valuable. Gregory, Browne (supplemented by Keltie), and others have written on general Highland
history and the achievements of the Highland regiments. And a
large number of writers have published important works on county
and clan histories.

Among those who have published clan histories the name that
undoubtedly stands highest is that of the indefatigable Mr
Alexander Mackenzie of Inverness, whose labours in this field are
quite gigantic. He has produced many large and interesting volumes
on some of the chief clans, and the fulness and accuracy of them
are acknowledged by those most competent to judge. In this
field Mr Mackenzie stands head and shoulders above all his
fellows. As projector and editor of the *Celtic Magazine* first, and
subsequently of the *Scottish Highlander*, he has supplied his
countrymen with an immense mass of Highland lore of every description.

Very interesting volumes of Celtic waifs and strays, Gaelic tales,
and folk-lore have been published by Mr Nutt, London ; and to
these have been contributed exceedingly valuable notes by Mr
Alfred Nutt. The material for these volumes has been supplied
by able ministers of the Church of Scotland – the Rev. Mr Mac-
Innes, Rev. J. G. Campbell of Tiree, and the Rev. Mr Macdougall of Duror. The name that stands highest in this sphere of
folk-lore is undoubtedly that of the Rev. Alexander Stewart, LL.D.,
the well-known and accomplished " Nether Lochaber," whose gifted
pen has shed the lustre of literary beauty on all it has touched.
Dr Stewart's powers are as versatile as they are original and full of

the patriotic spirit. For more than a generation he has poured forth rich contributions in poetic prose and in verse, in English and in Gaelic, on natural history, literature, and folk-lore.

In the preceding chapters an attempt has been made to point out the value of the literary treasures which lie enshrined in the Gaelic language, as well as the fact that no previous age has witnessed more Celtic activity than the present, and that the tongue of Ossian is still a subject of fond use and devotion with many. As an interesting proof of this the following verses may be appropriately introduced as a Gaelic close to the volume ; and in relation to them it may be stated that they were first sung in a London church at a Gaelic service, with organ accompaniment, by a congregation of Gaels, Scots, Welsh, and Angles !—

THE GAELIC NATIONAL ANTHEM.

A NEW VERSION.

I.

Dhia, gléidh an sluagh le d' ghràs !
An rìoghachd ás gach càs !
    Dhia, gléidh an Crùn !
Biodhmaid a ghnàth fo d' làimh
Le buaidh os ceann gach nàimh,
'Nad ghràdhsa faotainn sàimh !
    Dhia, gléidh an Crùn !

II.

A Thighearna, Dhia na glòir,
Dean air gach diblidh fòir
    Is gléidh an Crùn !
Cum suas Victoria chaomh :
Roinn ceartas air gach taobh :
Dìon oighreachd bhochd do naomh !
    Dhia, gléidh an Crùn !

III.

Ar sùil tha Riutsa suas :
Seall air ar cor le truas ;
    Is gléidh an Crùn !
Cuir cuibhreach uile mu sgaoil !
Tog sinn á slochd an t-saogh'il !
A steach do thìr a' ghaoil !
    Dhia, gléidh an Crùn !

INDEX.

www.ingramcontent.com/pod-product-compliance
Lightning Source LLC
Chambersburg PA
CBHW021108270326
41929CB00009B/780